LAW AND HISTORY IN CERVANTES' *DON QUIXOTE*

Law and History in Cervantes' 'Don Quixote' is a deep consideration of the intellectual environment that gave rise to Cervantes' seminal work. Susan Byrne demonstrates how Cervantes synthesized the debates surrounding the two most authoritative discourses of his era – those of law and history – into a new aesthetic product, the modern novel.

Byrne uncovers the empirical underpinnings of *Don Quixote* through a close philological study of Cervantes' sly questioning of and commentary on these fields. As she skilfully demonstrates, while sixteenth-century historiographers and jurists across southern Europe sought the philosophical nexus of their fields, Cervantes created one through the adventures of a protagonist whose history is all about justice. As such, *Law and History in Cervantes' 'Don Quixote'* illustrates how Cervantes' art highlighted the inconsistencies of juridical-historical texts and practice, as well as anticipated the ultimate resolution of their paradoxes.

(Toronto Iberic)

SUSAN BYRNE is an assistant professor in the Department of Spanish and Portuguese at Yale University.

TORONTO IBERIC

1 Anthony J. Cascardi, *Cervantes, Literature, and the Discourse of Politics*
2 Jessica A. Boon, *The Mystical Science of the Soul: Medieval Cognition in Bernardino de Laredo's Recollection Method*
3 Susan Byrne, *Law and History in Cervantes'* Don Quixote
4 Mary E. Barnard and Frederick A. de Armas (eds), *Objects of Culture in the Literature of Imperial Spain*
5 Nil Santiáñez, *Topographies of Fascism: Habitus, Space, and Writing in Twentieth-Century Spain*

SUSAN BYRNE

Law and History in Cervantes' *Don Quixote*

UNIVERSITY OF TORONTO PRESS
Toronto Buffalo London

Toronto Buffalo London
www.utppublishing.com
Printed and bound by CPI Group (UK) Ltd, Croydon, CR0 4YY

Reprinted in paperback 2013

ISBN 978-1-4426-4527-1 (cloth)
ISBN 978-1-4426-2640-9 (paper

Library and Archives Canada Cataloguing in Publication

Byrne, Susan
Law and history in Cervantes' Don Quixote / Susan Byrne.

Includes bibliographical references and index.
ISBN 978-1-4426-4527-1 (cloth). – ISBN 978-1-4426-2640-9 (pbk.)

1. Cervantes Saavedra, Miguel de, 1547–1616. Don Quixote.
2. Cervantes Saavedra, Miguel de, 1547–1616 – Knowledge – Law.
3. Cervantes Saavedra, Miguel de, 1547–1616 – Friends and associates.
4. Baeza, Gaspar de, b. 1540. 5. Giovo, Paolo, 1483–1552. 6. Law in literature. 7. History in literature. I. Title.

PQ6353.B97 2012 863'.3 C2012-901839-2

University of Toronto Press acknowledges the financial assistance to its publishing program of the Canada Council for the Arts and the Ontario Arts Council.

University of Toronto Press acknowledges the financial support of the Government of Canada through the Canada Book Fund for its publishing activities.

for Bill

Contents

Acknowledgments

My profound thanks to Isaías Lerner of the CUNY Graduate Center for having asked the question that led to this study, and for his unstinting help, support, and friendship as it progressed. I am also gratefully indebted to Yale colleague, mentor, and friend Roberto González Echevarría, whose own *Love and the Law in Cervantes* clearly demonstrated the interplay of that legal-literary thematic in the author's works, who questioned the place of 'non-literary forms' in literary history in his *Myth and Archive,* and whose remarkably enthusiastic encouragement and trust has been crucial to me. My fortune in supportive surroundings is unmatched, and I thank each and every one of my wonderful colleagues at Yale: Rolena Adorno, Noël Valis, María Rosa Menocal, Aníbal González, David Jackson, Paulo da-Luz-Moreira, and Kevin Poole. Particular thanks to Paulo for having read and commented on an early version of my first chapter, to Rolena for pestering me on the title from the start and then helping with its concrete form at the end, and to Kevin for sharing my angst.

I began work on this project while at SUNY, Oneonta, and I also thank Beth Small and all my colleagues there, most especially Gustavo Arango, whose passion for all things literary warmed up the cold winter days up north. Early on, Michael Armstrong-Roche invited me to share my research with the Renaissance Seminar Group at Wesleyan University. I thank the group for their liberal camaraderie and comments, and Michael for his questions and inspiration on the idea of a *mos hispanicus.* The suggestions of the anonymous readers for the University of Toronto Press led to many improvements in the manuscript, and their thoughtfulness is very much appreciated. I most gratefully acknowledge the patience and persistence of University of Toronto Senior Humanities Editor Suzanne Rancourt, the skill and kindness of Associate Managing Editor Barb Porter and the diligence of copy editor Miriam Skey. My thanks also to two historians who have been particularly helpful: I.A.A.

Thompson of the University of Keele, for filling out specific detail from one of his own books with information from his notes, and Richard L. Kagan of Johns Hopkins University, whose generous and judicious counsel led to a number of improvements in the manuscript. I am also greatly indebted to Ottavio di Camillo who started me down the road to legal-literary connections with the *Cantar de mío Cid*, and to Tom Lathrop of the University of Delaware for his supportive advice and bibliographical information.

I thank the many tireless librarians of the Beinecke Rare Books and Manuscript Library at Yale University, Mike Widener of the Paskus-Danziger Rare Books Room of the Lillian Goldman Law Library at Yale Law School, Vanessa Pintado and John O'Neill at the Hispanic Society of America in New York, Fabián Cerezal and Father Modesto González Velasco at El Escorial in San Lorenzo, Madrid, Rosario Jiménez Vela, Gracia Fernández Maldonado, Práxedes Morillas Pérez, and José Francisco Olivencia Duesto at the Archives of the University of Granada, David Torres Ibañez and his staff at the Archives of the Real Chancillería in Granada, photographer Christián Erquicia, Teresa Díez de los Ríos and her staff at the Archivo Histórico de Protocolos in Madrid, the gestión fotográfica team of Patrimonio Nacional in Madrid, as well as all the librarians and staff at the Fondo Histórico of the University of Salamanca, and the Public Library of Toledo.

My husband Bill Connors deserves special thanks for innumerable reasons, among them his big generous heart which is my ballast, many thoughtful conversations in which he has shared his own intimate knowledge on art and artists, and for being the model I watch, listen to, and learn from as he practises his own art with unmatched dedication and integrity.

I am further indebted to all those who heard and commented on brief talks presented during meetings of the Modern Language Association (Philadelphia 2006 organized by Fred de Armas, and Los Angeles 2008 organized by Ana Laguna), the Asociación Internacional de Hispanistas (Paris 2007 and Rome 2010), the Asociación Internacional Siglo de Oro (Santiago de Compostela 2008), the Asociación Internacional de Cervantistas (Münster 2009), and the Yale Whitney Center for the Humanities Fellows Group (February 2010). A few sub-sections of this book are revised versions of earlier articles: 'Cervantes' *Don Quijote* as Legal Commentary,' 2007, *Cervantes* 27.2: 81–104; 'Cervantes and the *Histories* of Paolo Giovio: Translators and Truths,' 2009, *Cervantes* 29.2: 185–201; 'Miguel de Cervantes y Paolo Jovio: los caballeros antiguos y modernos y el de la Mancha,' 2010, in *Nuevos caminos del hispanismo* ... edited by Pierre Civil and Françoise Cremoux, 72–82, Madrid: Iberoamericana; and 'Aspectos histórico-jurídicos en las obras de Miguel de Cervantes,' 2011, in *Compostella Aurea: Actas del VIII Congreso de la AISO*, edited by Antonio Azaustre Galiana and Santiago Fernández Mosquera, 501–8, Santiago: Servizo de Publicacións. I thank the editors of the *Cervantes* journal and the conference Actas for having published my work, and for allowing me to use the material in this book.

My research for this project was aided by two generous grants, one from the Griswold Research Fund of the Whitney Humanities Center, and another, a Faculty Research Grant from the MacMillan Center for International and Area Studies, both at Yale. That support was a major factor in the completion of the book, and I am extremely grateful to both committees and their sponsors/underwriters. The book was published with the assistance of the Frederick W. Hilles Publication Fund of Yale University.

Finally, thanks to Mike, Janet, Steve, Pat, Tom, Mary, and Sally, each of whom either has my back or is at my back at any given moment.

Note on Texts

All quotations from *Don Quixote* in Spanish are from the Sabor de Cortazar and Lerner edition: Miguel de Cervantes Saavedra, *El ingenioso hidalgo Don Quijote de la Mancha,* 2 vols, ed. Celina Sabor de Cortazar and Isaías Lerner, prologue by Marcos Morínigo, Buenos Aires: Eudeba, 2005 [1965]. The abbreviation DQ is used for this text, with or without a specific quote. References to other editions of the *Quixote* are indicated by Cervantes, followed by the date of the edition. Throughout, I use the English-language spelling Quixote for both the book title (in italic) and the protagonist's name, and leave the spelling Quijote in Spanish quotes. Citations of the *Novelas ejemplares* are to the Sieber edition: Miguel de Cervantes Saavedra, *Novelas ejemplares* I and II, ed. Harry Sieber, Madrid: Cátedra, 1995.

All quotations from Paolo Giovio's *Elogios* in Spanish are from the 1568 edition as translated by Gaspar de Baeza. Worldcat indicates that the volume is available in six libraries worldwide. The website of the Junta de Andalucía offers an online version, although with certain lapsus. I modernize the Spanish orthography only in adding accents to facilitate the readings. The frontispiece reads: *Elogios o vidas breues, de los Caualleros antiguos y modernos, Illustres en valor de guerra, que están al biuo pintados en el Museo de Paulo Iouio.* Es autor el mismo Pavlo Iovio. Y tradúxolo de Latín en Castellano, el Licenciado Gaspar de Baeça, Granada, Hugo de Mena, 1568.

Quotations from Giovio's *Histories* in Spanish are to the microfilmed edition. There is also an edition available on the website of the Junta de Andalucía: http://www.juntadeandalucia.es/cultura/bibliotecavirtualandalucia. Baeza's translation of the *Histories* was published in 1566, in two volumes, both in Granada, by two different publishers. I use *Histories* for this work, as internal dating and chapters are continuous. The first volume, published by Hugo de Mena, ends with chapter 24 in the year 1527; the second volume, published by

Antonio de Librixa, picks up with chapter 25, still in the year 1527, and then continues to end with chapter 45 in the year 1544.

Citations from the prologues and dedications of Gaspar de Baeza to Giovio's volumes are indicated as, for example, (Baeza 1568, Al lector) and are so noted in the bibliography, for ease of reference. Unless otherwise indicated, all legal volumes are cited by Book.Title.Law as, for example, Fuero Juzgo VII.2.7, referring to Book VII, Title 2, Law number 7.

Unless otherwise indicated, all translations from the Spanish, Italian, and Latin are my own. All quotes are given in English translation in the text, with the original in Spanish, Latin, or Italian, when longer than two or three words, included in the notes. While this makes the number of notes seem overburdensome, it allows a reader to follow my text and arguments without internal duplication of information and the concomitant need to skip over, or read twice, the same extended citation. In most cases, I have not translated for aesthetic purposes but, rather, with an eye to analysis of the original language. Certain subtleties are masked in translation as, for instance, the 'desaforadas locuras' considered by Don Quixote in the Sierra Morena (DQ I.26). Literally 'mad acts contrary to the *fueros,* or law books,' this phrase is translated by Grossman, for example, as 'excessive madness.' Grossman's fine translation renders the sense of the passage, but loses the literal juridical reference, which is my focus. Another example: Grossman's translation of 'conjeturas verosímiles' (DQ I.1) as 'reliable conjecture' captures the idea, but loses the literary reference with its very particular word choice, which relates, in my reading of the text, to a passage in Baeza's translation of Giovio's *Elogios.* A philological analysis necessitates a more literal than literary rendering of the original and since that is my aim, I have chosen the former and provided my own, more literal translations.

Illustrations

LAW AND HISTORY IN CERVANTES'
DON QUIXOTE

Introduction: Cervantes' Quixotic *mos hispanicus*

The field of jurisprudence recognizes *mos italicus* (Italian practice) and *mos gallicus* (French practice) as two approaches to historical legal codes, their acceptance and incorporation (*mos italicus*) or their rejection as outdated (*mos gallicus*). That simple description will be further explained in what follows. There has never been a named Spanish juridical practice specifically called *mos hispanicus.* Here, I propose the idea as a possible reading of Miguel de Cervantes' *Don Quixote* and as the novelist's creative resolution of a sixteenth-century polemic debated in the contemporary disciplines of law and history. Legal historians describe this sixteenth-century conundrum as 'possibly one of the most violent polemics of all western juridical history' (Guzmán Brito 1978, 11).[1] To exemplify, Guzmán Brito quotes from a 1582 publication by Alberico Gentili, a believer in the *mos italicus* approach, who summarizes the attacks that had been levied against him and his colleagues: 'the old-style interpretors [those of the *mos italicus* approach] are plebian, mournful, inept, sophists, barbarians, pig slop, ignorant of good arts, deaf and servile writers in our disciplines, disposed to quarrel over any triviality, sycophants, pettifoggers, a plague on the talented, pompous, repugnant dross, tormentors, a scourge on the studious, shysters, imposters, born to the hoe, not very well composed mentally' (Guzmán Brito 1978, 12, citing Alberico Gentili).[2] The quote from Gentili confirms the virulence of the debates.

As these juridical battles between the partisans of *mos italicus* and *mos gallicus* were being waged, jurists studying under Juan de Orozco at the University of Salamanca were seeking a middle ground (Salustiano de Dios 2001). That effort did not bear fruit in a named legal tradition, but we can read a subsequent creation – *Don Quixote* – as a literary realization of their aim, and as an encapsulation of the lived reality behind those discussions.

We know that in *Don Quixote*, Cervantes privileges contentious deliberation on history and true histories. We also have good reason to link Cervantes to legal matters, although we do not have any indication that the author ever formally studied the law. For the purposes of this study, Cervantes' connections with the world of jurists and jurisprudence are important, and so it bears mentioning from the start that his grandfather, Juan de Cervantes, was an attorney who held various government posts, including 'legal counsel' for the city of Córdoba (Sliwa and Eisenberg 1997, 106). Documents attest to many legal episodes in the life of Miguel de Cervantes: his father Rodrigo de Cervantes, jailed for debt when Miguel was five years old, was also a named party in various legal cases. A warrant for the arrest of a Miguel de Cervantes was issued in 1569 for having wounded one Antonio de Sigura in a duel; whether or not this is the author Miguel de Cervantes is still debated by scholars. However, that same year, author Miguel de Cervantes goes to Italy, which leads to the inference that he was fleeing the arrest warrant and, while he stays in Italy, there is a legal filing in Spain for proof of his nobility, apparently an attempt to justify his actions in the duel.

In 1575, while returning from Italy after having fought and been wounded in battle, Cervantes was taken captive by Barbary pirates, and then spent five years imprisoned by the Turks in Algiers. Those years would be the first but not the last time that he personally experienced life in prison. After his return to Spain in 1580, one of Cervantes' official commissions was to provision the troops. In 1587 the author was excommunicated for appropriating wheat from church property and in 1592 he was imprisoned for three months following another charge of having appropriated wheat from churchmen (canónigos). In 1597, after having entrusted government funds to a merchant who then went bankrupt, Cervantes was once again imprisoned for three months, following the 'abuse of power' by an attorney (Canavaggio 1998). In 1605 another incident involved the Cervantes household in legal proceedings when a wounded man found at the door to their home was helped by the author's sisters and daughter. In 1610 there were more legal proceedings over the ownership of a house in Madrid.

These various episodes reveal that, notwithstanding any lack of documentary notice of formal legal training, Miguel de Cervantes did have extended experience with the law. Among those identified by scholars as Cervantes' friends and acquaintances are many with legal training and / or experience. To this group I will add Gaspar de Baeza, one of the group of scholars who studied under Orozco at the University of Salamanca. There are multiple personal connections between Cervantes and Baeza who also exemplifies, in the range and qualities of his own work, the confluence of disciplines that inform Cervantes' writings. These acquaintances, together with Cervantes' intimate experiences with law and the polemical legal situation in Spain,[3] as well as contemporary literary debates over history, poetry, laws, and truths, place *Don Quixote*'s author at the centre of this maelstrom of literary-legal-historical developments. Cervantes' creative writings are a literary groundbreaker, but also a legal-historical snapshot.

As a preemptory caveat, I do not wish to say that Cervantes wrote legal texts, nor that he himself was a lawyer. He was a novelist whose works encapsulate and communicate the vital experience of life in late sixteenth-century Spain. However, his novelistic treatment of historical and juridical materials did foreshadow changes in both disciplines. Cervantes' art (literature) acted as a fulcrum for those other fields of letters (history and jurisprudence), highlighting their inconsistencies and anticipating the resolution of their paradoxes. What also needs to be stated from the start is that I do not pretend to be either historian or legal scholar, or to break new ground in those disciplines. History and law are integral parts of this study but, for my purposes, they play a supportive role as building blocks of the literary work. My central focus is how those disciplines inform Cervantes' creation, how he wove juridical and historiographical debates into a new literary genre.

1 History, Jurisprudence, and the Creation of the Novel

for without good letters,
broken and maimed is all pretence of erudition,
much as memory without virtue

(Gaspar de Baeza)[1]

History as preceptive commentary and justice as thematic content are two key elements of Miguel de Cervantes' *Don Quixote,* as evidenced in the author's multiple references to the contentious literary debates of his day, his use of formal and thematic aspects of contemporary historiographical questions, and his protagonist's exploration of the meaning of justice. Cervantes' masterpiece created a new paradigm and, from his synthesis of empirical and fictional impulses, 'the novel emerges as a literary form' (Scholes 2006, 15). To a large extent, the literal basis of that empirical impulse was the fruit of a convergence of juridical and historical thought in the sixteenth century. Cervantes incorporated materials that have since been forgotten, in an era when intellectual synthesis was the model, and the specialized parameters of law, history, and literature were fluid and flexible.

In what follows, I will focus on the resonance in Cervantes' writings of specific juridical and historical volumes emblematic of the sixteenth century's philosophical debates in those two fields. While the breadth of the author's borrowings from those other disciplines extends beyond any one text, specific seeds of Cervantes' creative art can be found in the works of Italian historian Paolo Giovio and Spanish jurist Gaspar de Baeza. The realism of *Don Quixote* is based, in part, on its author's appropriation of elements from, and dialogue with, those legal and historical writings. As did Baeza, Cervantes glossed the laws; as did Giovio, Cervantes insisted on the truth of his history while creating character portrayals with a liberal dose of invention. Speaking more broadly, while sixteenth-century historiographers and jurists in Spain, Italy, and France sought the philosophical nexus of their fields, Miguel de Cervantes created one, with the verisimilar adventure story of a protagonist whose history is all about justice. In so doing, he established a benchmark for the modern, realist novel.

Scholars have recognized the importance of historical-social contextualization to the study of *Don Quixote* (Sabor de Cortazar, Ettinghausen),[2] noted the links between contemporary historiographical preoccupations and Cervantes' work (Wardropper, Gaylord),[3] and even called *Don Quixote* 'metahistoriography' for its author's portrayal of a 'periphrastic realism' that, in part, 'refuses to consider the real world and imaginative literature as mutually exclusive' (Friedman 2006, 17, 16). Alban Forcione has insisted that Cervantes is aware of 'the responsibility and licence of the artist to manipulate freely events and circumstances to present a higher reality' (1970a, 246), and Isaías Lerner studies the author's manipulation of stylistic concepts such as heteroglossia and polyphony, a 'slippery use of linguistic codes' to signal both historical and literary references that would have been commonplaces in Cervantes' day but no longer have the same resonance, and their use as the creative author's dialogue with other works, both imaginative (books of chivalry) and epic (Ercilla's *La Araucana*) (Lerner 1998, 210).[4] Anthony Close disputes a 'prior assumption that he [Cervantes] is different from the culture surrounding him by virtue of being endowed with an Olympian freedom to play ironically with its codes' and adds: 'one can only achieve a plausible understanding of his difference by pre-supposing that he is fully immersed in them' (2000, 5). If we take 'codes' to mean operating principles or norms of conduct, then both history and jurisprudence are key to such an understanding. Germane to a clearer analysis of those encoded messages in Cervantes' work are sixteenth-century developments in intellectual thought on those two disciplines, and on the relationship between them.

Law developed out of usage and custom, that is, the history of similar acts and decisions rendered on them. Cervantes' contemporary Baltasar de Céspedes states unequivocally: 'all of our law, on which depends the good administration of the republic, originated in history' (1965, 228),[5] and even a cursory reading of early law books elucidates this process. At times, the histories of similar acts underlying the legal codes are taken from sources that we might consider fictitious as, for example, Barcelona's customary law, the Usatges, which states that Barcelona was founded and constructed as a city prior to Rome, and that the proof of this law is found in the histories of Hercules.[6] Both historiography and lawmaking are arts based on the witnessing – or filtering – of past events, and 'deciding what one will write is, irremediably, inventing the past' (Lerner 1991, 125).[7] Law codifies one version of events and societal reaction to them, and realist fiction is artful historical writing, that is, the creative relating of imagined events true enough in a mimetic sense to make a reader accept them as such whether or not they might actually be a part of that ephemeral category we refer to as 'historical truth.' Prior to realist fiction, legal volumes told those same stories, with decisions rendered in cases that pitted the testimony and arguments of one man's true narration of a history against those of another's. Roberto González Echevarría notes that German Romantic Jacob Grimm argued for a common origin of literature and law (2005, 19). Hegel suggested an 'intimate relationship' between 'law, historicality, and narrativity' (White 1987, 13). Carmen Rabell offers that Jolles, Bragantini, and Pabst have all mentioned that the 'simple form' of the [Italian] *novella* was 'the case ... and ... that the genre probably originated in the fictional cases in vogue during the Roman empire' (2003, 33). María Carrión (2010) has studied the law in relationship to representations of marriage in Early Modern Spanish theatre.

Looking to the legal sources offers insight into, for example, the inspiration for the history of *Lazarillo de Tormes,* the first picaresque novel. The background to Lazarillo's story is found in a series of pragmatics issued by the Catholic Monarchs Ferdinand and Isabel.[8] The first pragmatic (law promulgated to sanction a perceived social excess, or abuse) of the series is dated 1487 and was issued in response to complaints by clergy that magistrates were entering their homes to search for suspected 'public women' (mancebas públicas), i.e., women of ill repute; the pragmatic forbids the searches. The second pragmatic was issued in 1491 and ordered that no woman could be charged with being a concubine unless her husband himself were to register the complaint and bring the charges. Two later pragmatics altered that earlier pair, illustrating and suggesting the developing story line for *Lazarillo.* In 1502 the Monarchs rescinded the 1487 pragmatic and re-allowed the searches on the basis of additional magistrate's proofs of the existence of women of ill repute in the clergy's abodes. Just one year later, in 1503, they amended the 1491 law (in which only a husband can bring the charge against his wife), expressing outrage that the priests were exploiting a loophole by marrying their 'public women' to other servants in their homes as a way of avoiding arrest.[9]

These pragmatics tell the history behind the genesis of *Lazarillo:* faced with illicit behaviour, the justices acted, the clergy complained, and the king and queen gave the latter the benefit of the doubt and accorded only the husband of a married pair the power to complain of the situation. Further proofs of women in the clergy's homes led to a curtailing of the loophole's exploitation. Friedman has said that the picaresque 'gives voice to the silenced' (2006, 14).

The anonymous author of *Lazarillo* gives voice to the one party in the series of pragmatics who remained puzzlingly silent, offering a plausible reason for that cuckolded husband's failure to complain that combines legal pragmatism with socio-economic historical detail. In *Lazarillo* that voice is fashioned as a deposition letter to 'Vuestra Merced' (Your Grace), and we see it as the foundational text of the picaresque novel but, clearly, the truth of *Lazarillo*'s history includes a substantial dose of legal reality.[10] Similarly, Miguel de Cervantes will take foundational material from the actual legal situations of his day, although with a broader perspective and a more imaginative use. For Friedman, Cervantes 'takes this template [the picaresque] and converts it into baroque art' (2000, 104). I agree as to the appropriation of the picaresque as part of the foundational material for the *Quixote*, although I would not call Cervantes' novel 'baroque,' given its experimentational free-wheelingness, and ironic more than satirical tone. Claudio Guillén has called the *Quixote* a 'countergenre' to the 'pseudoautobiography' of the picaresque (1971, 146, 157). These literal legal sources for *Lazarillo* make the first picaresque less 'pseudo' and I hope to make clear in what follows that Cervantes was aware of that borrowing from literal sources. He did not counter that genre so much as incorporate its principles in a more highly creative and skilled manner.

In the late nineteenth century, jurists Antonio Martín Gamero and Eduardo de Hinojosa noted the resonance of Spanish legal developments in early literary works of Castile and Aragón. In the mid-twentieth century, Juan Ossorio Morales spoke to the specific understanding to be gleaned from the intersection of legal and literary writings:

> Through the literary texts – and particularly those of a narrative and dramatic sort – in which an author purports to reflect the social activity that surrounds him and the environment in which he lives, we are able to perceive how juridical norms were understood by contemporaries and, what's more, how they were made fun of; how reality reacted against laws and how, in many cases, those laws were impotent to achieve the legislator's desired end in imposing them. The legal texts tell us what ought to have been; the literary texts tell us what really was. (1949, 18–19)[11]

Ossorio Morales also points out that in *Don Quixote,* the protagonist and his squire Sancho Panza argue opposing sides of the legal question on parents versus children deciding whom the latter will marry. Don Quixote's arguments reflect those expressed in King Alphonse X's Siete Partidas, which accorded parents the right to choose a spouse for their offspring, whereas Sancho Panza 'shows himself in favour of marriage based on love' in conformance with Spain's usage and customary laws as laid out in the Visigoth's Fuero Juzgo – until, that is, Sancho speaks of his own daughter's marriage; at that moment, he insists on his right to choose her future spouse (Ossorio Morales 1949, 36–40).[12] The struggle between the ideals and methods of those two particular legal collections (Fuero Juzgo and Siete Partidas) exemplifies, writ large, the underlying environment of Spain's legal debates from the thirteenth through the sixteenth centuries: a struggle between local use and custom and state-imposed legal compilations based on Roman statutes.[13] The same struggle was playing itself out (or would do so) in most of the recently emerging European countries.[14] In *Don Quixote* Cervantes includes wry commentary on both sides of the debate, glossing the legal codes in a fictional manner. I use the term 'gloss' for Cervantes' incorporation of aspects of legal and historical writings, as it accords with common legal, historiographical, and literary practice of his time, and also allows for the author's multiple layers – from the ironically comic to the serious, thoughtful, and highly critical – of commentary on and interpretation of those socio-historical texts and documents. Study of those underlying layers of commentary can restore elements of that contextual perspective.

Justice as an ideal ironically personified in a law-breaking protagonist has long been accepted as one of the principal thematic threads of *Don Quixote*. Various aspects of sixteenth-century Spain's legal environment as background to the author's works have been studied: Kagan (1981) details the very active courts, multiple legal cases, and litigants; González Echevarría (2005) addresses the legal repercussions of the amorous incidents; Agustín Basave Fernández del Valle (1968) and Horacio Castro Dassen (1953) highlight certain criminal acts and outcomes; Augusto Martínez Olmedilla (1905) and Carmen Vega Carney (1994) write on Cervantes' use of legal language and underworld argot. Some editions of *Don Quixote* include notes explaining the specific legal phrasings employed by its author (Cervantes 1947–9, ed. Rodríguez Marín; Cervantes 2005, ed. Sabor de Cortazar and Lerner; Cervantes 1998b, ed. Rico). Literary scholars have argued that Cervantes might have studied law (Rodríguez Marín 1920, 1947; Herrero García 1948; Astrana Marín 1948), and jurists have offered studies of, and even held conferences on,[15] the multiple legal references in the text (Aguilera Barchet 2006, Álvarez Vigaray 1987, Alcalá-Zamora y Castillo 1961, Alcalá-Zamora y Torres 2001, Galbis 1981, Prat Westerlindh 2006, Batiza 1964).[16]

The conclusions of this last group of twentieth-century jurists are that Cervantes was not a trained legal scholar with a systematic legal mind, as his more fanciful than reasonable results for specific cases and scenarios would not pass judicial muster. Like Ossorio Morales, Álvarez Vigaray recognizes that 'the literary texts tell us something about law that legal texts, incapable of expressing, leave unsaid' (1987, 16) but says of Cervantes: 'he was not a professional from whom we might expect original juridical ideas and thoughts, a precise technical approach nor refined concepts' (42–3), and adds that although there are legal ideas in the works, there is not systematic legal thinking (47).[17] Castro Dassen offers two reasons for Cervantes' non-conformance with juridical principles, both based on internal aspects of the literary work, as opposed to the legal environment of its author: 'the anachronism of the institution of knights errant, and the innocence, candor, and insanity of Don Quixote' (1953, 114).[18] Similarly, Alcalá-Zamora y Torres does not dispute that Cervantes 'shows a command of [legal] notions and technicalities throughout the work,' but then highlights 'four cardinal points in Don Quixote's judicial weakness' (2001, 86), that is, weaknesses in the protagonist's actions and decisions.[19] What the jurists fail to address is Cervantes' incisive commentary on the laws through his portrayal of those acts; the judgments of the legal scholars only underscore the creative art of Cervantes who, in Don Quixote, reflects his society's struggle with a contentious legal climate in a way that transcends the literal debates, and lays the basis for realistic fictional art.

The second principal thematic thread of Cervantes' *Don Quixote* is 'history,' specifically in its relationship with or opposition to 'fiction.' Edward Riley points out that 'one of the more original implications of Cervantes's theory is that history does in fact intervene in the novel in a way it does not in poetry' (1962, 127–8). Vicente Gaos sums it up by saying that Cervantes 'does not confuse truth and fiction; he fuses them' (Cervantes 1987, 3:121).[20] Recognizing Cervantes' 'lifelikeness akin to history,' Anthony Close studies the author's work for its literary, rather than literal, values: 'the continual analogies that he [Cervantes] makes between fiction and history would seem to suggest that the determinant of lifelikeness is an empirical, extra-literary one. Rather, it is poetic and rhetorical: the singularity of the artistic conception; the efficacy with which it is made present' (2000, 335). I agree that the author's poetic efficacy and polished creative skills make the work what it is, but I also believe that the underlying literal foundations are empirical, and that study of them as such will leave us better informed as to Cervantes' creative process and environment. Thus, we recover more of the original sense of the text.

The division between 'truth and fiction,' highlighted by Cervantes in everything from his protagonist's reading of certain 'histories,' which leads to his invention of a new imagined life for himself in imitation of those volumes, to the novel's internal debates on history, truth, and, particularly, true histories, is never called 'fiction' by Cervantes. Don Quixote's creator emphasizes true histories, the truth of histories, and the proper telling of histories, setting the stage for his protagonist to fly into a rage when puppeteer Maese Pedro [AKA Ginés de Pasamonte] alters what Don Quixote believes to be the true details of a chivalric history (DQ II.26).[21] But the concept of 'historical truth' and its relationship to 'fiction' as we understand those syntagms today, is misleading when speaking of the late sixteenth century.[22]

'Fiction,' in Cervantes' day, was a polysemic word in flux: primarily used for the negative 'deception' or 'trickery,' it was also beginning to be used for 'lies' or 'inventions' in a positive light, understood as the creative part of a written work.[23] A 1558 Italian translation of one of Paolo Giovio's texts uses the Italian *finta,* or fiction, for the historian's Latin 'lies' in its negative sense.[24] Various sixteenth-century Spanish authors use 'fiction' to gloss over certain unsavoury details of Greek fables.[25] In 1598 Spanish medical doctor Cristóbal Pérez de Herrera argues for social reform and uses 'tricks and fictions' (embelecos y ficciones) to describe the dissembling excuses offered by those citizens who shun work (fol. 11v).[26] CORDE shows such uses starting from the late fourteenth century, for example: 'fiction and lie' (ficción y mentira) and 'fiction and pretence' (ficción y simulación) in *De vestir y de calzar* de Fray Hernando de Talavera.

In his 1596 preceptive work (*Philosophía antigua poética*), Alonso López Pinciano distinguishes between 'lying histories' (historias mentirosas) and 'truthful fables' (fábulas verdaderas) but he also speaks to their permutations and congruences (1953, 2:5).[27] His characters discuss Aristotle's distinction between poetry and history, and then identify 'fable' as the 'soul and essential part' (2:7) of a poem, further specified as its plot or argument. They subsequently conflate this plot-fable with fiction, saying that 'fictions that do not have imitation and verisimilitude are not fables, but nonsense' (2:8).[28] Fiction is here invention or creative writing that can either be a well construed, verisimilar mimesis (fable) or not (nonsense). In the same work, one character distinguishes three types of 'fable': those of 'pure fiction . . . all is imagined' as in books of chivalry; those that 'build a truth upon lie and fiction . . . thereby offering a fine and truthful piece of advice' such as Aesop's fables; and those that 'build a thousand fictions on the basis of a truth . . . such as tragedy and epic' (1953, 2:12–13).[29] For this character, 'fiction' refers to the details of invention or creative writing in a positive light. López Pinciano's characters say that the same event, once written, might be considered either a fable or a history: an eyewitness account will be the latter and he who writes it, a historian; the exact same event is determined to be a 'fable' and its writer a poet, if he who writes about it is not an eyewitness (2:9–10). That is to say, the truth of the narrated events is determined by a detail completely exterior to them, the physical proximity of the writer to them as they took place. Speaking of the multiple voices in *Don Quixote* who debate the truth of events in the Cave of Montesinos (DQ II.23),

Gaylord relates the episode to peninsular Spanish reaction to conquest histories, asking: 'in the absence of corroborating stories, how is one to evaluate the testimony of a single eye-witness? The problem haunted sixteenth-century historians of the past and of the near-present in cases where its momentous events occurred far from the reader's territory' (1998, 139). Cervantes will assert a different kind of proximity, with eyewitnesses who do not even concur on events witnessed.

In the *Persiles* Cervantes says that whatever one writes in a history can come to seem like truth by virtue of the truths it accompanies, but that the same is not true in a fable, in which 'it is right to fashion the actions with much punctuality and pleasure, and much verisimilitude, so that despite its lies which will cause dissonance in one's mind, it might come to form a truthful harmonious whole' (Cervantes 2003, III.10, 527).[30] López Pinciano's 'fiction' or the detail of invention in creative writing is, for Cervantes, 'lies.' Whereas López Pinciano has the physical proximity of the writer as key to a determination of 'fable' or 'history,' Cervantes makes the physical context of the written work key to its truthfulness. So did Paolo Giovio, in retelling the history of Preste Juan de las Indias, a character we also find in *Don Quixote* (see below). Cervantes consistently, insistently, and ironically labels *Don Quixote* a history (Byrne 2010). He makes his protagonist's story true by saying that it is, by including numerous eyewitnesses to its episodes, and by basing its thousand fictions and lies on the truths of contemporary histories and laws. Cervantes makes specific reference to another form of semi-truthful history, the elogium, the title used for a series of written portrait descriptions by Italian historian Paolo Giovio, who also made his *Histories* true by saying they were, by including numerous eyewitness reports, and by using documents to attest to their veracity. History and law were both recognized as malleable and manipulable in the sixteenth century, and 'fiction,' in its various permutations, was a part of both. Rodríguez Pequeño has pointed out that Cervantes' response to these debates on history is to invent the novel (2008, 265). I would agree, but not limit the response to historiographical commentary, as I believe the two threads of history and jurisprudence converge in the work, as they did in the debates. To write 'fiction,' Cervantes joined dissonant yet pleasing lies to legal conundrums, and so made literary history.

Historians today date the earliest questioning along the combined lines of history and jurisprudence to the turn of the fourteenth-to-fifteenth centuries, with Guarino da Verona, whose questions as to rhetorics and style for historical writings became preoccupations with 'res e verba' (Cotroneo 1971, 25). Rico's description of Juan Luis Vives' focus in *De disciplinis:* 'verba, res y mores' (Rico 1993, 103) broadens and encapsulates the debate: the letter, matter, and spirit of things. Sixteenth-century jurists Françoise Baudouin and Jean Bodin both 'argued that the jurist must be a historian' and 'the historian must be a jurist' so as to properly interpret events and texts (Grafton 2007, 69). Jurists, like historians and creative writers, were concerned with meaning and how best to express it. In the sixteenth century, as history breaks out of the scholastic parameters that had restricted it to the mere relation of past events, its scope is broadened to include causality. That makes it inextricably tied to legal thinking, and both jurists and historians of the era appreciated and commented on that connection. Nineteenth-century German philosopher Dilthey called Vives 'one of the founders of modern psychology' for his sense of the philosophy of history as investigation of causality, or why man acts as he does (Montero Díaz 1948, 22).[31] Grafton notes how Baudouin 'explained that the marriage of history and jurisprudence was ancient, natural, and necessary' and 'called for a history that would not [just] narrate events, but also lay bare their causes' (2007, 70–1). Kagan points out that part of the job description of the Head Chronicler of the Indies, as specified in the Recopilación de leyes, was 'to reflect on the causes of events and the motives underlying individual actions' (2009, 151). One key difference leads to the realist novel: for jurists and historians, causality is a concern that focuses on a closed past; for novelist Cervantes, causality allows for verisimilitude in the creation of believable and timeless characters and plot.[32] It is what could be the cause, instead of what was the cause. This incorporates Aristotle's history (what was) versus poetry (what might have been) distinction. Cervantes takes the causality of poetry's 'might have been' and mixes it with legal and historical detail and debate on what actually was.

In his translation of Giovio's *Histories,* Spanish jurist Gaspar de Baeza writes a dedicatory epistle to Francisco de Erasso, addressing the substance (*res*) and style (*verba*) of the Italian historian's work:

> Of all genres of letters, there is none more agreeable nor pleasing than history, and among all the Greek, Latin, and Barbarian histories that have been written for us over these many past centuries, there is none (in my opinion) that should be preferred [to Giovio's]. Taking into account the military discipline of our time, I don't know which even deserves to be compared with the histories that this very wise man Paolo Giovio, Bishop of Nochera, has left us. Let us appreciate the seriousness, elegance, and magistral words with which the events are related; the ingenuity, diligence, and rare erudition of the author; the truth, variety, and grandeur of the cases and events included in these histories; the wisdom, wit, vices, and virtues of the princes and captains mentioned with particular diligence by this excellent man and of incomparable use to the reader. (Baeza 1566, Dedicatoria, *Histories*)[33]

Baeza then explains how he sees the relationship between the historical and juridical disciplines:

> Now some might believe that writing history is somehow foreign to my profession. Most certainly, they fool themselves: for looking beyond the idea that all sciences are histories, it is most certain that there is nothing that so improves human prudence as does history, and jurists well know that for governing the Republic and practising law, prudence is necessary. Jurisconsult Modestin wrote a condensed version of Virgil's *Aeneid.* Jurisconsult Celius Antipatrus wrote extended histories. Alciato, a very learned man in law, illustrated the histories of Cornelius Tacitus. Jurisconsult Zazius wrote about Cicero's epistles. Philosopher Plutarch wrote history divinely. The sainted Jerome wrote the histories of illustrious men. Doctor Carvajal wrote the history of King John.[34]

Baeza's view of history – it is epic (*Aeneid*), philosophy (Plutarch), saint's lives, law – is impressively inclusive, and his point, that jurisprudence demands prudence, which one learns from history, is reflected in Cervantes' views on readers and writers.

In 1606 Spanish dictionary definitions of prudence start to use discretion as a synonym;[35] Cervantes' did so one year earlier, in his prologue to the 1605 *Quixote:* 'By God, brother, only now am I beginning to see how foolish I was for deceiving myself by thinking, for all this time that I have known you, that you were discreet and prudent in all your acts' (DQ I, Prologue).[36] Toward the end of that prologue, the same friend advises the author to write his history in such a way that 'the discreet might admire the invention, while the solemn will not be unappreciative of it, nor the prudent stop praising it' (DQ I, Prologue).[37] The focus of the parallel synonymous phrases is that any history will be judged by its readers,[38] as Cervantes tells his reader again in chapter 24 of the 1615 Second Part of the novel. The same unidentified narrative voice from chapters 1–8 of the 1605 novel interrupts at the start of II.24 to tell the reader that 'he who translated this great history from the original says' (DQ II.24)[39] that in this section there were certain caveats written in the margin, in Cide Hamete's own hand. The Arab author has noted that he cannot be persuaded that the episode in the Cave of Montesinos really happened as related by Don Quixote, given that all the previous episodes were 'possible and verisimilar' (contingibles y verisímiles) (DQ II.24), but that this one just does not convince him, as it falls so far outside the boundaries of reason. Cide knows that Don Quixote cannot have lied, given who and how he is, but he also says not to blame him if the adventure 'seems apocryphal' (parece apócrifa) (DQ II.24). The interruption ends with: 'You, reader, are prudent, so judge it as you see fit' (DQ II.24).[40]

Cervantes' precepts for a 'true history': insist that it is a history, use its internal narrative voices to doubt it, flatter the reader as discrete and prudent, then tell them they must decide. Cervantes positions the reader as competent judge of conflicting testimonies. Paolo Giovio's prescription for the historian offers a parallel: 'I always knew that writing history was a serious office that called for excellent character, since it requires revealing so much that is the object of envy, with swift preparation and no little time, while conjoining exacting prudence with eloquence' (1984, 255).[41] Zimmerman points out that the Latin *prudentia,* 'to contemporaries connoted practical wisdom in conducting affairs' (1995, 267). This is the focus of Jesuit theologian and historian Juan de Mariana who, in his 1599 mirror-of-princes work (*De rege* ...) calls prudence both virtue and art (Braun 2007, 101–33). Cervantes' friend Luis Cabrera de Córdoba (1559–1623) advises that 'one of the most crucial ways to attain prudence, such a necessary trait for a prince in the art of reigning, is to know histories' (1948 [1611], Discurso I, 11), and identifies the aim of history as a public good, for the narration of the particulars of great deeds and excellent virtues can perfect prudence, allowing the living to learn from that 'mute teacher' that is experience (Discurso IX, 35).[42] For historian Giovio, prudence and judgment are necessary for writing history; for jurist Baeza and historian Cabrera de Córdoba, reading history teaches the prudence necessary for governing; for novelist Cervantes, the proof of the truth of a history is in the discretionary judgment of the prudent reader.

Following on a 1560 debate in Italy regarding Renaissance philosopher Francesco Patrizi's refutation of Aristotelian and Ciceronian historical precepts, 'Françoise Baudouin, theorizing the *coniunctio* between history and jurisprudence, will signal what is without doubt a new perspective, speaking profoundly on the inherent problem and criticism of sources, [and] pointing out the definitive links between historiography and politics' (Cotroneo 1971, 15).[43] Irena Backus offers a concise description of Baudouin, and his place in the *mos gallicus* versus *mos italicus* debates:

> François[e] Baud[o]uin (1520–73)[44] ... son of a Flemish lawyer, he studied law at Louvain at the time when the *mos gallicus* was introduced ... the *mos gallicus,* which was first adopted in France in 1520 ... consisted in interpreting Roman law as a system which was as such applicable only to the conditions and the historical context of imperial Rome. This meant that any sixteenth-century lawyer who took it upon himself to interpret it had to acquire some knowledge of Roman history, which would enable him to understand the original context and to see how it differed from the conditions and context of his own era. This entailed invariably relegating some (if not most of) Roman law to the status of an historical document.

> Until then, the commonly received system of Roman law interpretation was the *mos italicus* devised by Bartolomeo Sassoferrato, a fourteenth-century Perugian lawyer. According to the *mos italicus,* Roman law was applicable as such not just in its own time, but also in later centuries. This entailed no knowledge of history: various stratagems of logic and rhetoric were permissible to adapt it to the context in which it was interpreted. Sometimes, the two *mores* blended together. The *mos italicus* was by its very nature flexible, and could accommodate even methods that contradicted its principles. The success of the *mos gallicus* in France is well documented. Inevitably, it accentuated the national sentiment in considering Roman law as 'not ours.' However, it also influenced the study of history as a contextual discipline. Many lawyers, including Baud[o]uin and Masson, were first and foremost historians. (Backus 2008, 170–1)

Baudouin's works include gloss and commentary on various codes of the classical era, as well as his volume comparing the historical and legal disciplines. Donald Kelley calls Baudouin 'the most original' of the disciples of Alciato (1970, 115). Baudouin's philosophical and very literary opening chapter to his 1561 *De institutione historiae vniuersae, et eivs cvm ivrisprvdentia coniunctione …,* in which he describes men as spectators, actors, and judges in life's theatre, echoes Juan Luis Vives' *Fabula de homine* and prefigures Shakespeare's and Calderón's world-as-a-stage motif. Like Cervantes, Baudouin places each man in the central position of judge:

> From God we are fashioned and placed in this world as if in a grand amphitheatre, primarily as spectators, but also as actors, and even, in a certain way, as if we were judges. I say spectators not only in the manner of things presenting themselves to our eyes but, also, as to those matters understood and retained by our memory, in which our past endures and our present lives. If we have eyes, we cannot fail to see the things of nature: every day we observe the tireless rotation of the celestial orb, and earth's immobile globe, with its wondrous difference and variety but also constancy and regularly recurring changes: indeed, men say that this is surely the birth of, and the cause for, early philosophical considerations. (Baudouin 1561, chapter 1, after dedication, no page or folio numbers)[45]

Spain's libraries hold numerous copies of Baudouin's works, which is not surprising.[46] After having been Calvin's personal secretary, the French jurist then became 'one of the reformer's religious adversaries' (Backus 2008, 170). Charles V banned the works, but in 1564 Phillip II lifted that ban (Kelley 1970, 143). Baudouin's words on 'life as a theatre' invoking man as spectator, actor, and judge seem tailor-made for Cervantes's protagonist Don Quixote,[47] and

Fig. 1 Gaspar de Baeza. Handwritten gloss on last folio of Ordenamientos reales, El Escorial, ms. Z.I.10. Courtesy of Real Biblioteca del Monasterio de El Escorial, San Lorenzo, Madrid, Spain. Copyright © Patrimonio Nacional.

Baudouin also 'defined history as an interdisciplinary task that required not only artistic composition, but systematic assembly and interpretation of the evidence' as 'no witness always told the truth' (Grafton 2007, 96, 97). The same principles inform the novel, with Cervantes combining law and history, speaking on the (un)reliability of sources through multiple narrative voices, linking his history to politics, describing characters who are, and telling his reader that they must be spectators, actors, and judges, as well as having his protagonist create and define the world on the basis of matters seen and retained by his memory, to wit, the details of his reading of books of chivalry, a fine ironic detail that exchanges juridical-historical-philosophical speculation for free-wheeling ironic creation.

Sixteenth-century legal scholars split into factions to interpret Roman law as either applicable or not in their own era, that is, as adaptable or not to their historical circumstance. These arguments also solidified their interest in history, a field in which many of them had started. The Spanish voice in those movements studying history in conjunction with jurisprudence and philosophy has not been granted its own named tradition in those debates, and the *mos italicus* and *mos gallicus* have never been joined by a *mos hispanicus.* The following quote from jurist and historian Gaspar de Baeza, handwritten on the final folio of a manuscript containing all of Spain's Royal Ordinances from the fourteenth to the sixteenth centuries, illustrates the perspective of one Spanish jurist who appreciated the link between history, use and custom, ordered statutes, and social mores (see fig. 1):

> Although these legal constitutions of prior centuries might seem an unorganized assemblage, they offer useful knowledge and aquaintance with past times and ways. I do not mean to say that these constitutions in the common Spanish language, taken as a whole, offer an understanding of the presiding legal codes of any given moment, but the reader will find much here to admire, in the innate quality and letters of the ancient ways, as well as in their full history of our birth. An avid intent to combine earthly matters with Christian study does not waste good hours, for without good letters, broken and maimed is all pretence of erudition, much as memory without virtue. The most learned man of that time strove for a blessed life not through the pursuit of supercilious erudition but rather with charitable works, to prepare himself for the heavenly kingdom where Paul had reserved him a place in the great glory of that compassionate inheritance to which are summoned and received all good Christian peoples. (El Licenciado gaspar de baeca)[48]

Baeza saw the values, strengths, and worth in the old laws (*mos italicus*) instead of dismissing them out of hand as dated (*mos gallicus*). He theorized their use as a history lesson that, accepted realistically, would contribute to a greater understanding and betterment of the present, with an Augustinian focus on the eventual celestial city gained by charitable and compassionate actions in this world. In *Don Quixote* Cervantes will lay down further principles of that *mos hispanicus,* holding up the past for both admiration and ridicule, glossing legal anomalies while highlighting their solid principles, and joining the debate on historical versus contemporary law.

Cervantes' exploration of the cause and effect of reading, of truth and truthful histories, of law and justice in action is a creative but also philosophical approach to the same debates, an encapsulation of *verba, res,* and *mores* in the mind of one man, and its impact on the rest of the world around him. Don Quixote and Sancho Panza personify the debate on history and jurisprudence, and elucidate how historical law both can and cannot be applied in a contemporary context. Cervantes makes it specific to Spain's own legal codes and history while offering a humanist, inclusive, yet discriminating eye for philosophical detail as a part of the whole picture. His gloss on the actual laws, and on the unreliability of history, includes very knowledgeable commentary on the humanist scholarship of those disciplines. *Don Quixote* is a fictional creation with multiple interwoven threads of the intellectually and societally driven legal and historical debates of the author's lifetime. Similarly, Cervantes' *Novelas ejemplares* are briefer snapshots of particular situations within that same environment. The connections between the legal and historical volumes and the author's creations can be, at least in part, traced through Spanish jurist Gaspar de Baeza's own legal glosses and Italian historian Paolo Giovio's works, specifically in Baeza's translations of Giovio's *Elogios* and *Histories.*

2 Giovio, Baeza, History, and Law in Cervantes' Works

Chronologically, the lives of Paolo Giovio (c. 1486–1552), Gaspar de Baeza (1540–c. 1570?), and Miguel de Cervantes (1547–1616) span the entire sixteenth century. Biographical detail on Cervantes is scarce, most particularly for the first half of his life. Our information comes from the author's works themselves, mainly the prologues, and documents uncovered by scholars over the years (Pérez Pastor 1897, Astrana Marín 1948, Rodríguez Marín 1947–9, Sliwa 2005). There have been a number of biographies and biographical studies of Cervantes,[1] and the website of the Centro Virtual Cervantes offers a chronology of the author's life events, prepared by Jean Canavaggio, that is accompanied by notice of the documentation and literary pieces that attest to each.[2]

Paolo Giovio

T. Price Zimmerman's excellent 1995 biography on Giovio offers more details on the Italian historian than are available for either of the two Spaniards, detailing Giovio's family life and education, his work in the papal courts, his broad interests, likes, and dislikes, as well as his relationships with ambassadors, courtiers, writers, and soldiers. Some of that detail is available in Giovio's letters which, when published, also undermined his reputation as they made clear his attempts to gain favours from patrons so as to finance the publication of the *Histories*. Those requests would lead to aspersions cast on the truth of the events related in the volumes, although Zimmerman's research counters those concerns: 'the tradition of Giovio the mendacious was more often the product of hearsay than of familiarity with the substance of his work … More than many humanist historians, he honored the Ciceronian injunction to tell not only the truth but the whole truth' (1995, 266). The biographer exemplifies the truthfulness of Giovio's *Histories* by telling how, despite pressure from the emperor and his emissaries, the Italian historian refused to make changes to the reported details of Charles V's Tunis campaign (Zimmerman 1972). Zimmerman attributes much of the contemporary criticism of Giovio's works to personal animosities: 'the contemporary Florentine historians were vitriolic' (1995, 263), and further refutes their reproaches with the example of late sixteenth-century Italian writer Traiano Boccalini and his *Ragguagli di Parnaso:* Boccalini writes that 'censors ask Girolamo Muzio to substantiate his demand that Giovio's histories be burned on Parnassus for the lies they contain [but] he is only able to mumble that he has heard it said they are mendacious' (Zimmerman 1972, 49).[3] Clearly, unsubstantiated hearsay is not admissible in the court of Parnassus. Spanish writers will offer widely divergent opinions of the Italian historian.

Among Cervantes' contemporaries there are volatile debates as to which historians are telling the truth, which have the right to tell that truth, and how prejudicial 'nationalistic' attitudes might pervert the telling. Head Chronicler of the Indies Antonio Herrera y Tordesillas offers the general commentary that 'foreign historians' (historiadores forasteros) neither agree among themselves on Spanish history, nor speak the truth when they tell it (1606, 2:20). The particular polemic surrounding the works of Giovio is reflected in Cervantes' work, which also shares formal aspects with that of the Italian historian. For example, Cervantes' much-discussed and studied multiple narrative voices in *Don Quixote* have a parallel in Giovio's *Histories,* in which the Italian historian writes on the basis of first-hand knowledge as well as interviews with and reports from returning soldiers and emissaries, an approach to historical detail that gives his volumes a lively, journalistic tone and multiple narrative voices.[4] The 'I' who at times inserts himself to attest to the truth of an event most frequently seems to be Giovio although when the context is a report from someone else the reader has to wonder. In translation, the depth of the web of voices becomes even more intricate, with the additional 'I' voice of translator Gaspar de Baeza, who also inserts his own comments on particular events. Similarly, Cervantes' narrative voice is both specific to its author in its control of perspective and commentary on events and narrations, yet multiple in its attribution, by that same author, to various others who find, translate, and tell the history, while simultaneously attesting to its veracity or lack thereof. As in Giovio's works, when Cervantes' 'I' comments, the reader almost always has to wonder which 'I' is speaking.[5]

Particularly problematic for Spaniards in Cervantes' day were certain events narrated in Giovio's *Histories.* The Italian historian details atrocities committed by Spanish soldiers in Italy, tells of battles won and lost by troops under Spanish command, and relates the exploration and conquest of the New World. Gaspar de Baeza dedicates his translation of Giovio's *Histories* to King Phillip II of Spain and, in the dedication letter, speaks very positively of Giovio, whom he calls a 'most learned man (who all nations, in conformity, call the father of history)' (Baeza 1566, 'Dedicatoria,' *Histories*).[6] Spaniard Luis Zapata (1526–95) also praises Giovio, including the Italian historian in a poetic work listing 'ingenious modern men' (ingenios modernos):

> Fracastorio, Luys Vivas y Pontano,
> Dante, Petrarcha, Ariosto y Sanazaro,
> Castellón, Pietro Bembo, el Peregrino,
> Paulo Jovio, Tansilo y Aretino. (*Carlo famoso*, XLVII, fol. 255v)[7]

An earlier sixteenth-century Spanish writer is more matter-of-fact in his references to the Italian historian: 'Here I have summed up and collected what I will say on this: particularly, I follow Paolo Giovio in a specific tractate he wrote on the same matter' (Mexía 2003, 116).[8] Mexía's editor, Isaías Lerner, notes that the reference is to Giovio's *Commentario de le Cose de Turchi*, a Spanish translation of which was published in Barcelona in 1543 (Mexía 2003, 116, n. 11). This small coterie of Spanish admirers of the Italian historian would be heavily outphalanxed by Giovio's detractors on the Iberian Peninsula, a much more vocal and vitriolic group.

Even before Baeza's translation of the *Histories* was published, Juan Martín Cordero had insulted the Italian historian in his prologue to *Eutropio varón consular* (1561) (Gil Fernández 2003, 78–80). Once Baeza's Spanish translation of the *Histories* was published in 1562,[9] there was a scathing reaction from one of the Spanish soldiers who had participated in a number of the campaigns narrated, including the Sack of Rome.[10] Gonzalo Jiménez de Quesada would spend the last years of his life writing a chapter by chapter refutation of the *Histories* which he titled *AntiGiovio* (*Antijovio*). He praises Baeza's translation as one of the best he has ever seen of a Latin work translated into Spanish,[11] but vigorously denies the work's content, particularly the unfavourable reports on the behaviour of Spanish soldiers during the Sacks of Rome and Lombardy. Jiménez de Quesada lambastes Giovio as an 'Italian serpent' (1952, 298) who writes 'things dreamed up in his head, which is like that of Medusa' (193), although as the Spaniard ostensibly denies the reports, he also patently confirms them with defensive statements such as 'that is why it is called a Sack' (455).[12]

Jiménez de Quesada dedicates his work to fellow soldier and veteran of the wars in Italy, Luis Quijada. These are the same two surnames that Cervantes says other authors would give to his protagonist (DQ I.1), a detail that is particularly worthy of note given other echoes of the enraged Spaniard's text in Cervantes' *Quixote*. For example, Jiménez de Quesada denies that the Spaniards 'fled' from the Turks, insisting that, rather, they 'retreated,' a distinction Cervantes will have Sancho explain to Don Quixote: 'retreating is not fleeing, nor is waiting wise when danger surpasses expectations' (DQ I.23).[13] The *AntiGiovio*'s author uses the archaic 'péñola' (1952, 440) for his pen, as will Cervantes' historian, Cide Hamete Benengeli (DQ II.74), and Jiménez de Quesada shows himself anything but one of the 'punctual, truthful, and in no way passionate historians' (DQ I.9) recommended by Don Quixote, as he rants and raves against Paolo Giovio: 'some of his things shock me and others make me laugh, but there are yet others that particularly make me mad enough to become choleric' (1952, 101); 'O Italian word, spoken for Italian purpose!' (1952, 163).[14]

Other Spaniards seem to have agreed with Jiménez de Quesada's negative opinion of the Italian historian. Cabrera de Córdoba references Giovio's work a number of times in his own preceptive work on historiography (*Historia para entenderla y escribirla*), citing the Italian historian as an example *ex contrario* of the need for unbiased judgment: 'Paulo Giovio has a breast full of ire and melancholy when it comes to the Spaniards and the Florentines,' and then Cabrera de Córdoba responds in kind, adding, 'despite what the Florentines say, that a doctor of his, knowing his ill humour, tried to purge him with a bag of gold, a very convenient medicine for his particular illness' (Cabrera de Córdoba 1948 [1611], 92).[15] Bernal Díaz del Castillo criticizes historians who 'exaggerated the violence of the conquistadores' deeds,' naming Giovio among them (Rolena Adorno 2007, 188). Fernando de Herrera explicates Garcilaso's verse on 'the daring Spaniard' (el osado español) with a long harangue against all Italian historians, naming Giovio among others (Herrera 1972, 552, Égloga 2, vv. 1539–40 n. H-716), and Lope de Vega criticizes Giovio in verse:

> This time, Giovio is fooled,
> in his celebration of Spanish ignorance;
> A trait that, in his land, is seen as heroism.
>
> (Lope de Vega 1968–1971, letter 343, p. 428)[16]

Given the number and tenor of these commentaries, it would be impossible for Cervantes not to be aware of the works and, as will be seen in what follows, Cervantes also makes his own commentaries, both preceptive and thematic, on Giovio's works.

As a very early voice in the Renaissance's developing interest in history and historiography, Giovio's methods, style, and interests parallel those that will, in Cervantes, lead to the emergence of a literature that combines history, fable, poetry, imagination, and reality. A stickler for truth and detail in his *Histories* and *Lives* (biographies), Giovio also wrote very popular character sketches to accompany portraits hung in his personal museum at Lake Como. These *Elogia,* as Giovio titled them, are studied by art historians as a first in the use of descriptive labels directly linking portrait to person depicted (Klinger 1991, 212). In the written texts, Giovio highlights the connections with demonstrative pronouns that invoke specific physical traits such as colouring, gesture, and bearing, and then links those to both character traits and specific deeds of the portrayed's biography. Not all of the descriptions were factual, as Giovio included insolent, improbable details that are impossible to verify historically.[17] For example, the elogium of Renaissance poet Angelo Poliziano contains details about his 'enormous nose' and 'half-blind absurd eye' that come from sarcastic epigrams written by the poet's rival Michele Marullo;[18] another elogium tells what seems to be an apocryphal history with 'certain Spanish horsemen' chasing Horuchi Red Beard, who flees 'at top speed across the hot desert sands, dropping gold coins behind him so as to slow down the Spaniards' (Giovio 1568, fol. 192r);[19] yet another repeats gossip only to purportedly deny it, saying it is not true that the 'certain ascetic pallor' of Italian nobleman Egidio Viterbo's countenance is due to his habit of 'eating cumin seeds and inhaling the smoke of smouldering straw.'[20] The Italian historian's model was not the Greek *eulogia,* or praise of a deceased hero but, rather, Roman legal usage of the term 'elogium,' a use akin to today's 'criminal record' (Zimmerman 1995, 206), a sort of warts-and-all character portrayal with information from some real, and some not-so-real, sources. Giovio, who was trained as a medical doctor, also offers information on contemporary diseases: of Francisco Gonzaga, the Marquis of Mantua, Giovio says that he was 'generous and candid, never deceitful. But he was indecent, playing with women and, so, going from one to another he swelled up with pustules (that were just beginning about that time) and sad and miserable, he died an unsuccessful man burdened with great regrets' (Giovio 1568, fol. 131v).[21] Various volumes of *Elogia* were published, in groups of great men, warriors, and men of letters; within fifty years, there would be more than thirty-two editions of the works (Klinger 1991, 202), although Baeza's Spanish translation does not figure in those lists.[22] The title of the volume most clearly related to Cervantes' work reads in literal translation from Giovio's Latin, *Elogia of illustrious men, virtuous in war, found painted in the Museum;* it was first published in Florence in 1551, and it was, as far as I have been able to determine, the only volume of the *Elogia* translated into Spanish. Baeza's translation was published in Granada, Spain, in 1568.

In his Spanish title, translator Baeza adds a phrase defining an elogium and a temporal reference, identifies the museum, and translates Giovio's Latin 'men' with the Spanish *caballeros,* a word used for both gentleman and knight: *Elogios o vidas breues, de los Caualleros antiguos y modernos, Illustres en valor de guerra, que están al biuo pintados en el Museo de Paulo Iouio.*[23] An English translation of this expanded title would read: *Elogia, or brief lives, of ancient and modern knights, illustrious in war, found painted in Paolo Giovio's museum.* The index to the *Elogios* reads like an encyclopedia of adventurers, with many of the same names we hear praised by Don Quixote in Cervantes' novel: Alexander the Great, Red Beard, Hernán Cortés, Hannibal, Charlemagne, Preste Juan de las Indias;[24] there are Visigoth, Persian, and Polish kings, Pandulfo Petruchi tyrant of Siena, and Narses the eunuch, among others. Both the form and the idea became very popular in Spanish letters of the second half of the sixteenth century: see, for example, Francisco Pacheco's *Retratos,* Arias Montano's *Effigies,* and Rodrigo Caro's *Varones insignes.*[25]

In his dedication of the translated *Elogios* to Spain's King Phillip II, Baeza praises the volume as 'a work in which Fortune's fickleness and the inconstancy of human affairs are represented live, so that one can almost see them with one's own eyes, which consoles the unfortunate, and keeps the fortunate from becoming arrogant in their happiness'; then the translator adds 'the brevity and variety, and the fact that it is written in both prose and verse keep it from becoming tedious' (Baeza 1568, 'Dedicatoria,' *Elogios*).[26] This last preceptive comment reminds us of the priest's words in *Don Quixote:* 'epic can be written just as easily in prose as it can in verse' (DQ I.47),[27] and all the elogia follow this model of praise in prose then verse, both frequently written with a patently ironic tone. In Baeza's Spanish translation of the *Elogios,* there are additional poems not found in the original Latin or in the Italian translations, apparently added by Baeza. Some of that verse was penned by friends shared by Miguel de Cervantes and the jurist.

Giovio's own description for his writings seems to point the way to the development of the modern novel. The Italian historian compiles information and then writes what he calls 'a piece of chorography, or political geography, a mélange of geography, natural history, history, social customs, literature, and religion. "Chorography," Giovio contended (echoing Polybius), was the mirror necessary for whoever wishes to see and clarify the where, how, and when of events' (Zimmerman 1995, 66).[28] The novel as we conceive it today is this mixture combined with character portrayals that link person to context. Giovio's *Elogia* vividly illustrate his concept of historical chorography; they are brief narratives related with a linguistic prowess that brings events and persons to life in a free-flowing language that entertains as it exemplifies. This is also what Cervantes does in *Don Quixote.* Gianfranco Folena's description of Giovio's linguistic prowess in Italian (Toscano) as 'idiomatic words and phrases in unexpected contexts ... linguistic irony ... polyphonic plurilingualism ... paratactic rhythms that go from asindeton to polisindeton ... range of tones from serious and solemn to facetious, satirical, and then grotesque' (Folena 1985, 137, 139, 140) could just as easily be applied to Cervantes' Spanish. Gaspar de Baeza's skill in translation, as we have seen praised by his contemporary Jiménez de Quesada, was also recognized by others; in his introduction to the works of sixteenth-century poet Gregorio Silvestre, Pedro de Cáceres y Espinosa calls the jurist 'the great translator' (el gran traductor) Gaspar de Baeza (Cáceres y Espinosa 1592, fol. 13r). Baeza's translated *Elogios* swing with the same linguistic prowess we find in Cervantes, a prose that sweeps along the reader who only stops to cackle with laughter at particularly jocular passages, such as the unseemly death of Pyrrhus, king of the Epirotes, an indomitable man killed when 'a woman from Argos gave it to him with a brick to the head' (Giovio 1568, 4v), or the Visigoth king Totilo, 'beaten by a old eunuch who only stood about two feet tall' (Giovio 1568, 9v).[29]

Taking into account the chronological discrepancy of their respective life spans, there are certain connections between Giovio (c. 1486–1552) and Cervantes (1547–1616). Both writers dedicated works to members of the Colonna family, Giovio his *Dialogus de viris et foeminis aetate nostra florentibus* (*Dialogue Concerning Men and Women Flourishing in Our Times*) to Vittoria Colonna, and Cervantes his *Galatea* to Ascanio Colonna, the son of Vittoria's cousin Marcoantonio Colonna, General of the papal galleys at Lepanto (Avalle-Arce 1988, 10) during the battle in which Cervantes fought and was wounded, suffering the loss of the use of his left arm. Like many sixteenth-century readers, both Giovio and Cervantes also shared an affinity for books of chivalry.[30] Zimmerman tells the story of Giovio and his friend Ariosto observing the people in the plaza of Mantua during a 1530 visit by Spanish emperor Charles V, while comparing the passers-by to the characters of Ariosto's *Orlando furioso* (Zimmerman 1995, 112). Cervantes' own comment on Ariosto comes in chapter 6 of the First Part of the *Quixote,* when the priest and barber are examining the protagonist's library and the former calls Ariosto 'a Christian poet' and says he is better in the original Italian than in Spanish translation. In the Prologue to the 1605 *Quixote,* Cervantes' unnamed friend makes the claim that *Don Quixote* has been written as a commentary on the books of chivalry, a statement that can be read as a literary disclaimer and / or a red herring, and one that has been disputed at least since 1878, when Díaz de Benjumea pointed out that the literature of chivalry was already 'a cadaver' (un cadáver), and suggested that Cervantes' own insistence on that point begs questioning (1878, 218, 199–200).[31] Speaking of Cervantes' time in Italy, Frederick de Armas notes that the author would have seen art works censored by the Counter-Reformation as palimpsests offering glimpses of the 'hidden beauties of the past' that simultaneously taught him how to mask polemical details in his own creations, that is, to censor his work before others would do so (2006, 9, 205). I agree, and firmly believe that Cervantes used the mention of books of chivalry as a cover, necessitated by the amount and the tenor of some of the legal commentary in his own work, specifically to evade censorship.

Further incidental connections in the writings of Giovio and Cervantes include Giovio's 'aversion to gunpowder as the nemesis of knightly valor ... a gallant knight fighting for honor and glory with lance and sword could be brought low by a common foot soldier with a gun' (Zimmerman 1995, 6), matched by Don Quixote's comment on the 'diabolical invention of artillery ... which allows that a vile and cowardly arm might take the life of a valiant knight' (DQ I.38).[32] Addressing Cervantes' comparison of the ermine with feminine purity (DQ I.33), Rodríguez Marín offers Giovio's *Empresas* as one of the possible sources (Cervantes 1947–9, I.33), and Carlos Romero Muñoz notes the same in his edition of Cervantes' *Persiles* (Cervantes 2003, 634). Cervantes includes elogia for his characters in *Don Quixote* and, in the *Novelas ejemplares,* he specifically debates the precepts of such elogia while writing his own.

Although Italian historian Giovio died in 1552, he was not buried until 1574 in the Laurentian Library in Florence (Zimmerman 1995, 262). We know that Cervantes was in Italy that year, in Naples, Túnez, and Palermo, and that he left Naples on 7 September 1575 (Canavaggio 1998). Whether or not the Spaniard was in or near Florence on the date that Giovio was finally laid to rest is unknown, although Cervantes does praise the city through his character 'El licenciado Vidriera' (The Glass Licenciate) who spends four days in Florence, and to whom 'Florence was most pleasing, as much for her agreeable location as for her cleanliness, her sumptuous buildings, refreshing river, and gentle streets' (Cervantes 1995, II.49).[33]

Gaspar de Baeza

The scant biographical information available on Gaspar de Baeza tells us that he was born in 1540 and died during the last third of the sixteenth century. Nicolás Antonio reads the jurist's surname as a patronym and says that he left Baeza to study at the University of Salamanca:

> Born in the famous city of Andalucia from which he took his last name. Having realized that he was blessed with a great talent, he aspired to fame for knowledge, and so set out on the royal road that would take him there, that is, following the advice to study civil law at the University of Salamanca. There, he took classes with Juan de Orozco, a highly esteemed scholar famous for his commentaries titled *Ad duos priores Digestorum.* Having studied philosophy and theology, as well as geography and history and, so, being well-equipped with the best criteria in all

> fields of letters, Baeza dedicated himself to writing. At a very young age, having not yet turned thirty – although his prudence, love for God and ideas on divine and eternal matters were more those of a mature man – death snatched him away. But for that, he would have become a specialist in Civil Law and the other disciplines as well. (1999)[34]

Astrana Marín offers a tantalizing detail on that early death, saying that Baeza committed suicide (1948, 2:530–1, n. 5).[35] This piece of information is not included in other sources, which do lament the jurist's untimely demise but do not specify how it came about. The Biblioteca de Andalucía offers that the jurist was born in Baeza (Jaén) in 1540, that he studied at the Universities of Granada and Salamanca, and that he died in 1569.[36] The Director of the Archives of the Real Chancillería of Granada, David Torres Ibáñez, was kind enough to answer an email query by offering that consultation of the descriptive catalogues and expedients of the Archives had not turned up any information on Gaspar de Baeza, but that an on-site search of the legal documents held might show him named as a lawyer or judge on specific cases. A subsequent on-site search turned up just one case naming Gaspar de Baeza as a minor in a legal case brought in 1553, when the jurist would have been thirteen years old. The named siblings are Gonzalo, Gaspar, Francisco, Rodrigo, Costanza, and Isabel; their parents Gonzalo de Baeza and Joan de Maryena are deceased, and the case finding went against the family and for the merchant who was suing over a matter related to the children's guardianship.[37] Similarly, an on-site search of the archives of the University of Granada revealed various students and professors with the surname Baeza in the registrar's books, but none specifically identified as Gaspar.

The *Privilegio* of Gaspar de Baeza's legal tractate on debt and debtors, dated 22 October 1569, grants to the jurist's brother Rodrigo de Baeza all rights to the publication of the work written by his deceased brother: 'Rodrigo de Baeza, resident in Granada, you have informed us that your brother, licentiate Gaspar de Baeza, now deceased, wrote a book on impoverished debtors and whether they should be turned over to their creditors, titled *Declaración de la ley del fuero*' (Baeza 1570, Privilegio).[38] In his dedication of the work, Rodrigo de Baeza laments his brother's untimely death at the age of thirty-six.[39] However, another Baeza brother, Melchor, in the dedication of his brother Gaspar's *Opera omnia* (published in 1592) says that 'Charon took his brother at the age of thirty' (Baeza 1592, 'Dedicatoria'),[40] and King Phillip II grants Melchor another six years of publication rights to his brother's work, indicating that the privileges, already prorated for ten years, were set to expire on 22 October 1589. The details on Gaspar de Baeza's death would seem to be further contradicted by a document held by the Archivo Histórico de Protocolos in Madrid, which indicates that the

Fig. 2 Power of attorney, Rodrigo de Cervantes to Gaspar de Baeza, 25 Feb. 1577. Archive of Rodrigo de Vera. Signatura 496, folios 196r–197r. Courtesy of Archivo Histórico de Protocolos de Madrid. Comunidad de Madrid.

(Fig. 2 continued)

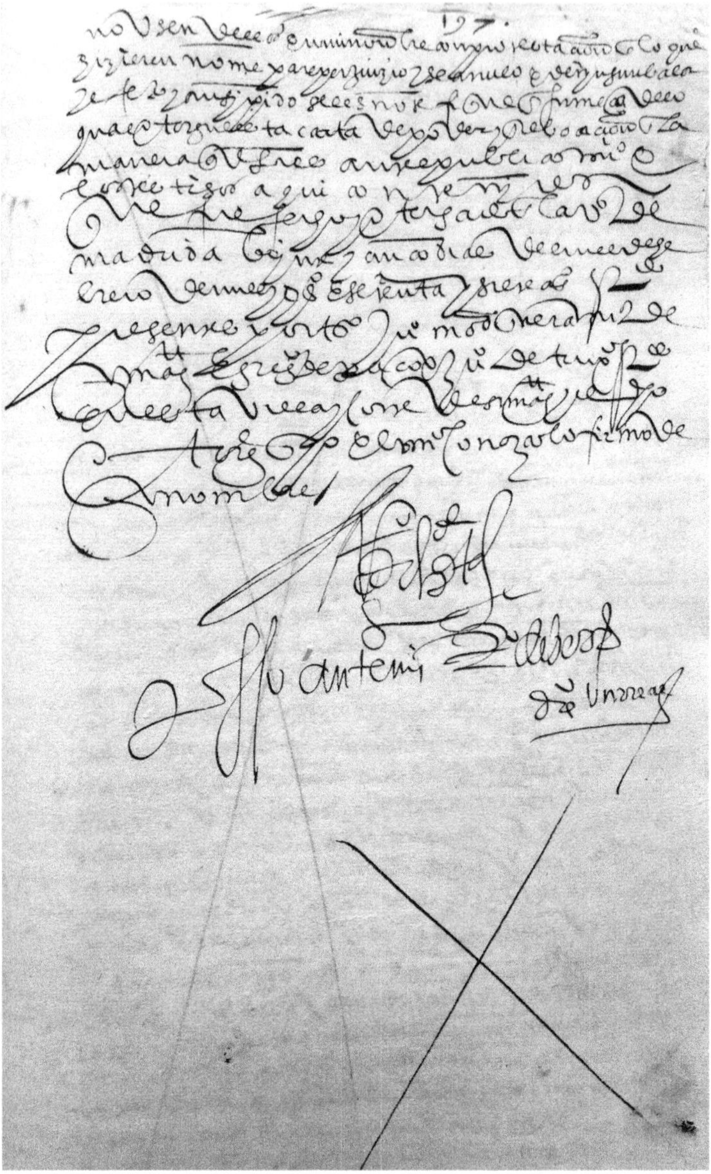

(Fig. 2 continued)

jurist, or another jurist by the same name, was alive and living in Granada on 25 February 1577, when Cervantes' father Rodrigo de Cervantes conferred on him power of attorney to recover funds (800 ducados) owed the author's father by another attorney, licenciate Pedro Sánchez de Córdoba (see fig. 2).

This document is executed by the same notary, Rodrigo de Vera, who prepared and signed the 1569 documents regarding Miguel de Cervantes' nobility (Sliwa 2005, 1569/12/22 Madrid), and the testimonial documents on the captivity of Miguel and his brother Rodrigo (Sliwa 2005, 1576/11/09 Madrid). On close examination, the document does seem to read 1577 (setenta y siete), with identical 't' in the setenta and the siete numbers (see fig. 3), although the 't' in seventy could be an 's,' which would make it 1567 (sesenta y siete) and would accord with the other facts offered by various sources, specifically on the jurist's death.

The document has been consistently dated to 1577 by Cervantes scholars, following on its first reference by Pérez Pastor in 1897,[41] although in his own mention of it, Astrana Marín goes on to say that jurist Baeza probably met Cervantes' father Rodrigo when both were in the court the previous year, which Astrana Marín identifies as 1566.[42] Astrana Marín also points out that Gaspar de Baeza was a friend of the fathers of both Miguel de Cervantes and Spanish scholar and poet Fray Luis de León, whom Cervantes praises: 'Fray Luis de León, of whom I speak, I revere, adore and follow' (Cervantes 1999, VI, Canto de Calíope, stanza 84).[43] A letter dated 1 April 1561 from the twenty-one-year-old Baeza to Lope de León, judge of the Chancillería of Granada and father of Fray Luis, is included in the latter's *Opera,* and reads in part that Baeza finds Fray Luis de León 'a bright, quick, wise and sharp genius' whose sermon on the death of Domingo de Soto had been 'an energetic, vehement, full, elegant, and pleasing oratorical torrent'; Baeza tells the poet's father: 'León, you have engendered a León [lion] whose voice (if appearances do not deceive) will also be heard by posterity' (León 1891–5, 7:285–7).[44]

Another long-lasting family connection is Gaspar de Baeza's brother Rodrigo who, for a period spanning over twenty years, was the notary signature on a large number of legal documents signed by Cervantes' uncle Andrés, mayor of the town of Cabra.[45] One Luis de Baeza married Miguel de Cervantes' aunt Doña Leonor de Torreblanca – she is the 'widow' of Luis de Baeza, the 'sister and heiress,' along with her brother Rodrigo, of Miguel's uncle Andrés, and the 'mother-in-law' of Juan Batista Álvarez.[46] Pedro de Carmona, identified as the son of a Luis de Baeza, was a witness for the defence in a court case against Miguel de Cervantes, when the latter was charged with confiscating wheat from church properties. Cervantes' lawyer brought Pedro de Carmona in to testify about the poor condition of the wheat (Sliwa 2006, 456).[47]

Fig. 3 Section of power of attorney, Rodrigo de Cervantes to Gaspar de Baeza, 25 Feb. 1577. Archive of Rodrigo de Vera. Signatura 496, folios 196r–197r. Courtesy of Archivo Histórico de Protocolos de Madrid. Comunidad de Madrid.

Miguel de Cervantes and Gaspar de Baeza shared a number of friends and acquaintances – Pedro de Padilla, Gregorio Silvestre, Hernando de Acuña, Luis Barahona de Soto – and a bookseller, Francisco de Robles, who sold the First Part of the *Quixote* in 1605 and who also, posthumously, held the rights to sale of the complete works of Gaspar de Baeza, at the request of the latter's brother, Melchor de Baeza (Tassa, *Opera omnia*).[48] The 'tasa' (fixed price mark) of that work states that Francisco de Robles was 'cesionario' of the jurist, that is, he inherited the printing rights from Baeza.[49] Robles is also identified as 'cesionario' of Miguel de Cervantes, in a document dated 28 September 1613.[50] Baeza dedicates his translation of Giovio's *Histories* to Francisco de Erasso (secretary to King Phillip II) and Antonio de Erasso, in the name of Phillip II, signs the licence granted to Miguel de Cervantes for the publication and sale of his *Galatea* (Sliwa 2005, 1584/02/22); it is also Antonio de Erasso who receives and rejects Cervantes' letter requesting a job in the New World (Sliwa 2005, 1582/02/17).

Gaspar de Baeza's work was well-known inside and outside of Spain. The jurist's *De inope debitore* was subsequently published in Venice by Franciscus Zilettus, as part of a prestigious collection of juridical works published from 1584 to 1586 under the auspices of Pope Gregory XIII.[51] The jurist's name is one of the many references found in later legal compilations, such as that of Augustin Barbosa, who lived from 1590 to 1649,[52] and Baeza's *Opera omnia* in the edition of Fernández de Castro, first published in Spain in 1592, was also subsequently published in a 1609 Frankfurt edition. Baeza is a key figure in Spain's sixteenth-century legal developments, as he rewrote the laws on debt and debtors with pertinent commentary on legal exemptions for nobles, clerics, soldiers, gamblers, lovers, thieves, and the insane, all preferred characters and themes in Cervantes' works. One of his legal tractates speaks to the laws on the amount of dowry parents could legitimately bestow on their sons and daughters. Titled *De non meliorandis dotis ratione filiabus*,[53] it specifically addresses a 1534 prohibition on 'excessive dowries' by the Catholic Monarchs, which reads:

> We order that no one give nor promise to give a third or fifth portion of their goods as dowry or for the marriage of a daughter ... And because those who get engaged or marry tend to give, at the time of their betrothal, excessive jewels and dresses to their wives and women, it is also necessary to put order and moderation in this: from now on no person, nor any person of our kingdoms may give to their wife and woman, when they become engaged or marry, such dresses and jewels, nor any other thing that amounts to more than the eighth part of the dowry they receive with her. (cited by Baeza 1592, fol. 1r–v)[54]

The law originated in Petition 101 of the Cortes de Madrid in the year 1534. That petition asked that dowries in excess of sums that would be accorded should the goods of a father be divided among all his children be prohibited.[55] In 1567 King Phillip II will uphold by reclamation the same law, as well as others from the 1505 Leyes de Toro that also speak to excessive dowries (Recop. V.2.1). In his gloss on the laws, Baeza cites in painstaking detail the specific places in Spanish and Roman law where other jurists have treated the question of dowries,[56] reviews the amounts allowed pursuant to laws of the Peninsula, and addresses particular questions such as whether grandfathers and brothers are to be held to the same limits on giving dowries to their granddaughters and sisters as are natural fathers to their own daughters (Baeza 1592, fols 63r–8r). The jurist also points out contradictions such as one law that orders compliance with promises [i.e., contracts] to bestow a 'third' or a 'fifth' while another expressly prohibits such large divisions of goods (Baeza 1592, fol. 7v). Baeza offers detailed philological study of words and phrases such as 'betterment' and 'his woman,' and he includes analysis of permutations of the norms, for example: 'Whether there is a prescribed solution in the law for the case of a daughter who promises herself without the knowledge or consent of her father. And second, whether the rapist of a deflowered virgin is entitled to receive the prescribed dowry sum' (Baeza 1592, fol. 83).[57] In addition to the legal citations and authorities, Baeza cites Plautus, Euripides, and Plutarch (Baeza 1592, fols 10v–11r), among other literary and philosophical figures, as well as Ovid's *Ars amandi* on love as the inspiration to giving and Erasmus on the virtue of parsimony, both of these last on the same page (Baeza 1592, fol. 12v). His scholarship is broad and meticulous.

In his *Novelas ejemplares*, Cervantes will address the same theme of dowries with a twist, as part of the set-up to the story of a returning Extremaduran who became wealthy during twenty years in Peru. The title *El celoso extremeño* refers to the sixty-eight-year-old gentleman who, on return to Spain, finds himself bereft of relatives or friends, all of whom have died while he was away. Cervantes' narrator sympathizes with the character, Carrizales, commenting that 'wealth is just as much a heavy burden to bear as is poverty to he who faces it on a regular basis,' and noting that 'in the few years that he [Carrizales] had been a soldier, he had learned to be generous' (Cervantes 1995, II.101).[58] Carrizales needs someone to inherit his wealth, but the mere thought of marriage is immediately accompanied by an overwhelming feeling of jealousy which, as it turns out, is just his nature, 'because his natural condition was to be the most jealous man in the world' (Cervantes 1995, II.102).[59] Carrizales prudently rejects in the abstract the idea of married life, recognizing that it will only exacerbate his jealousy but then, in a triumph of fate over will, he suddenly spots a beautiful 'thirteen or fourteen'-year-old girl in a window and falls in love. Carrizales convinces himself that the poverty of the house and the youth of the girl make her a perfect match for him, and he speaks directly to the matter of a dowry: 'Whether she has a dowry or not does not matter, because heaven gave me enough for all, and the wealthy should seek pleasure, rather than goods, in their marriages' (Cervantes 1995, II.102).[60] The protagonist's statement is a clear challenge to Spain's laws on dowries which, at the time, did let poverty prevent marriage. Cervantes' message, through his character Carrizales, is that those laws were socially and morally questionable.[61]

Carrizales speaks to the girl's parents who, as it turns out, are of the impoverished noble class; they take the time to assure themselves of his wealth and he of their nobility, and then Carrizales and the girl, Leonora, wed after 'he had given her as a dowry twenty thousand gold ducats ... [and] many ... so many and such beautiful dresses' (Cervantes 1995, II.103).[62] The 1534 law cited above specifically mentions that the monarchs had a problem with the 'excessive jewels and dresses' that fiancés were bestowing on their intended wives. It prohibits gifts of dresses and jewels worth more than the eighth part of what the fiancé receives with his betrothed as dowry from her parents (Recop. V.2.1), which would make both the 20,000 gold ducats and the dresses illegal, as Carrizales does not receive any dowry with Leonora. Carrizales constructs what he imagines to be an impregnable house in which to guard his wife, and then divides his wealth into three parts: 'one invested in diverse and good sources so as to provide a yearly pension, another to be held by the bank, and the last to spend as necessary' (Cervantes 1995, II.104).[63] Leonora sees her parents only on Sundays, but Carrizales gives them 'so many gifts' (tantas dádivas) that they do not complain (Cervantes 1995, II.105). The Recopilación forbids gifts from a spouse to his betrothed worth more than one tenth of all his worldly goods (Recop V.1.2),[64] and specifically prohibits an amount equal to one third or one fifth. Cervantes does not tell his reader how much of Carrizales' full estate is given to Leonora and her parents, but he does tell us that Carrizales divided his estate into three parts with one third 'to spend as necessary.' The Fuero Juzgo, after specifying that the husband may not give his wife as dowry more than a tenth of his full estate, further insists that for one full year after the marriage, he may not give her any more.[65] Carrizales, however, continues to bestow gifts on his wife throughout what Cervantes describes as the first 'year of their novitiate' (año de noviciado) or wedded bliss.[66] In *De non meliorandis,* Baeza offers a lengthy explanation of whether goods given prior to and after marriage can be identified as dowry, and analyses the use of the phrase 'his woman' for both pre- and post-marriage contracts (Baeza 1567, fol. 20v, numbers 18–19).[67] Cervantes' character repeatedly and openly violates the prohibitions.

Eventually, Carrizales' jealousy brings all his carefully wrought plans (and payments) to naught, and that is the side of the story on which Cervantes concentrates. Seen in conjunction with the laws as glossed by Baeza, Cervantes' backgound of legally violative detail resonates, as it would have for contemporary reader-listeners. The creative author uses the law as fictional fodder: his sympathetic character portrayal of the law-breaker obviates the logic of the legal proscriptions. Can it be wrong for Carrizales to be so generous? Should the law prohibit his liberal sharing of his own wealth? Cervantes' answer is clearly no, as he paints those details as almost insignificant, offers a sympathetic character portrayal, and then gets on to his prime consideration, which is Carrizales' emotional weakness, his human failing of unbridled jealousy. The background, however, to the author's study of jealousy is rife with legal particulars that inform the text and constitute the realist foundation of its telling. In seeing that basis, we gain another layer of understanding as to its creation and as to how it would have resonanted for readers in Cervantes' day.

Cervantes also addresses dowries in the entremés [one-act farce] *El juez de los divorcios,* in which the character Mariana petitions for a divorce and clarifies her knowledge of the divorce and dowry laws, first specifiying that she brought a fine dowry to the marriage and then responding to her husband's mention of his goods, 'Your goods? And what goods would you have that you did not earn by investments of my dowry? Half of the goods gained are mine, although you might not like it; and of those goods and the dowry, even if it means I die right here, I will not leave you even the value of one maravedí' (Cervantes 1970, 64).[68] The judge decides that he cannot grant the divorce, for 'lack of proper cause' (quia nullam invenio causam), and Cervantes shows us that his contemporary readers, like his characters, are quite cognizant of legal exigencies. Whether or not they are trained legal minds, and irrespective of their education, they know the law. Mariana is right on the equal division of goods upon the dissolution of a marriage, as per Recopilación V.2.4, and Cervantes' use of the specific legal details not only reflects his age's preoccupation with those matters but also gives him a very real basis for verisimilitude in a creative work.

In all his legal glosses, Baeza addresses the juridical issues in the full context of their social ramifications. In his tractate on debt, he references poverty as glossed by Hesiod: 'Poverty (so says Hesiod) is a miserable state for a man,' and by Chrysostom: 'Poverty is martydom, if one can patiently rise above it,' and then adds his own gloss: 'And paupers, everywhere, we call miserable,' following that up with further citations and references to Baldus, Aesdras, and Dominus Malachiae (Baeza 1592, 2.31, fol. 135r).[69] Baeza then proceeds to one-up them all by quoting from Seneca on poverty being a beatific thing to suffer.[70]

Baeza's thoughtful and detailed commentary on debt and legal exemptions for the insane, in chapter 9 of his *De inope debitore,* can be seen as a legal version of the 'cuerdo-loco' (sane-mad) running debate in *Don Quixote.* Baeza first states that the question is whether or not madness (*furor*) itself is an impediment to legal jurisdiction and determination either before or after the commission of the act,[71] then explains: 'First, it cannot be denied that madness (*furorem*) is an illness of not only the body, but also the soul: and so herein we will speak to those of ill mind (*male sanus*) and to those without mind (*insanos*), and what madness (*furiosus*) is thought and proven to be' (Baeza 1592, chap. 9.1, fol. 162v).[72] The jurist addresses previous authorities and their arguments on each point raised: recognition that commiting a crime is something that can only be adjudged the act of a sane mind,[73] the legal status of a self-induced insanity (i.e., by the ingestion of a drug),[74] whether the insanity took hold before or after the debt was incurred,[75] and whether the return to a sane mind would restore the indebted status.[76] Baeza considers the argument that the mute, deaf, and insane are to be similarly treated as incapable of rationally hearing and responding to charges against them.[77] The jurist also analyses whether the heat of a seductive passion excuses a crime,[78] whether one flaw can excuse another,[79] and then considers multiple authorities on the ill effects of love:

> Oldraldus [de Pointe] ... third point, as to consideration of serious crimes and the excuse of men desperately and miserably in love, influenced by women with recourse to demonic arts ... Aristotle in Book 7 of the Ethics ... [on] whether loving is insanity and, if its madness is punishment enough, whether to show pity with the mad ... [and] Virgil in Book 4 of the Aeneid ... Plato in the Phaedrus ... Cicero in the Tusculanarum [Disputations] (Baeza 1592, fol. 164r, 9.12)[80]

Baeza closes the chapter by arguing that the recklessly prodigal and extravagant spender, also unworthy of commiseration,[81] is a valid comparison, and he concludes: 'From this, it is evident that all insanity is to be questioned, including whether a destitute debtor or a reckless spender might be given over to his creditor ... this also might be the prodigal's flaw and while no one is exempting it, nor are they able to allege it in this instance: yet the prodigal and the insane are similar' (Baeza 1592, 9.13–14, fol. 164v).[82] These points are fictionally treated by Cervantes in *El licenciado Vidriera* (insanity by ingestion of a drug, women with recourse to demonic arts, heat of passion), in *El celoso extremeño* (reckless spending, the prodigal), and in *Don Quixote* (self-induced insanity, whether or not the insane can be held guilty for their crimes, rationally hearing and responding to charges). One twentieth-century legal scholar has commented that there is, in *Don Quixote,* a consistent recognition of legal indemnity as to damages caused being compensated, whether by the culprit (Maese Pedro's puppets, the enchanted boat) or by someone acting on his behalf (as when the priest pays the barber for his basin-helmet) (Alcalá-Zamora y

Torres 2001, 100–1). Baeza is the jurist who laid down these legal principles, in Spanish laws that would have governed Cervantes' own problems with debt, and that provided grist for the author's creative mill as well. Although Baeza wrote in Latin for a supposedly limited audience, Cervantes' own broad and wide classical erudition (Eisenberg 2006, Bowle in Cervantes 2006 [1781]), as well as his multiple personal experiences with debt would certainly have entailed his having knowledge of those principles, which are reflected in detail in his creative works. Cervantes stages the same legal concerns in the vernacular for a broader audience.

Other literary connections between Cervantes and Baeza include a circle of friends who show up in various roles in each other's works. For example, Cervantes refers to Angulo el Malo in *Don Quixote* (DQ II.11),[83] and one of the canine characters in his exemplary novel *Coloquio de los perros* refers to 'the other Angulo, not the author but the impresario' (Cervantes 1995, II.353);[84] the reference has been linked to a theatrical impresario named Andrés de Angulo but it is worth noting that in the exemplary novel, at the moment when the reference is made, the character's owner is a poet. Another contemporary of Cervantes and admirer of Baeza is Cordoban jurist Andrés de Angulo, author of *Commentaria ad leges Regias meliorationum,* published in Madrid in 1592 and reprinted in 1602 [the tasa seems to indicate another, earlier printing, in 1585].[85] In his legal gloss, this Andrés de Angulo refers to the work of Gaspar de Baeza, and a number of the poems included in various editions of the *Elogia* are by poet Andrés de Angulo.

The circle of jurist-poet friends frequently lauded each other in introductory poems. Gaspar de Baeza's posthumous *Opera omnia* is prefaced by his brother Melchor's dedication, then three poems, the first by Licenciado Fernández de Castro,[86] who ends his work:

> As much as Hercules wove complicated knots,
> You showed equally the clear power of intellect.
> Your talent has abandoned us, but we praise you
> As a great man, whose deeds will live forever. (vv. 11–14)[87]

The second of the three poems is by Luis Barahona de Soto, who Cervantes celebrates as 'one of the famous poets of the world, not just Spain' (DQ I.6), and 'distinguished, wise, and eloquent' (Cervantes 1999, VI, Canto a Calíope, stanza 65).[88] For Gaspar de Baeza, Barahona de Soto is similarly effusive in his praise:

> On the tomb of the brilliant jurist, Gaspar de Baeza, bringer of light
> A Tuscan epitaph to, as they say, guard your ascent

Sonnet

Behold the flesh with its divine spirit
Of perspicacious judgment and fine memory,
He flourished yet now, worthy of greater embellishment,
He lies without glory in this sarcophagus.
Here is covered Baeza, like Caesar
a pontifical jurist and orator,
Noble and known in Spanish history,
Accomplished in the Latin and Baetian languages.
You of the muses, and you of charity, you divine,
Herculean, during your lifetime
a laurel-crowned son of virtue,
You will live on in the present,
And Iberians will sing your high praise
On this, your tomb of purple and gold.[89]

Luis Barahona de Soto is a member of the same tertulia in Granada as Silvestre, Hurtado de Mendoza, Gaspar de Baeza, etc. The introductory poems of his own work *Las lágrimas de Angélica,* praised by Cervantes in the *Quixote* (DQ I.6), include one by another lawyer from the Audiencia de Granada. Cervantes' group of friends included a number of jurist-poets, many also connected in one way or another to Gaspar de Baeza.

In the *Histories* and the *Elogia,* Baeza makes numerous contributions as a translator. His lexical choices sound like Cervantes, with references to the 'rabble of peasants' (Giovio 1566, 17.2, fol. 137r), 'the town rifraff' (Giovio 1566, 13.5, fol. 98r), and 'the plebians (who know not how to control their appetites, nor have patience with troubles' (Giovio 1566, 13.5, fol. 98r).[90] Baeza defines and offers pronunciation tips, and there are multiple asides and parenthetical references, some found in Giovio's Latin original but others added by Baeza, who also speaks of the necessity of the history being 'verisimilar' as he translates the *Elogios.*[91] Cervantes will build on those concepts and formal aspects with his own highly expressionistic lexical twists and turns, add his own legal glosses, and make modern fiction.

Other Spanish writers of the late sixteenth century who offer practical advice and commentary on legal processes, or who write and gloss histories, will also be incorporated in what follows. In 1916 Rodríguez Marín noted that one detail of Spanish jurist Jerónimo Castillo de Bobadilla's *Política para corregidores* was pertinent to Cervantes' own legal troubles with appropriation of wheat from churchmen (Báig Baños 1916, 28–9), and that another might be related to Sancho Panza's commentary as governor on the gaming houses in Barataria

(Etienvre, 1987, 143). There are other points addressed by both Cervantes and Castillo de Bobadilla, although not always with a similar perspective. The jurist begins his manual for magistrates by comparing ideas on the constitution of a 'good republic,' specifically as to laws governing public versus private property. His own opinion is that only with private property can there be peace and justice, as man is naturally avaricious and ambitious, and yet his description of these republics includes: 'Plato wished ... that men would not have property, neither *mine,* nor *yours* but, rather, that all things would be common ... and Aristotle affirms, that men would live very peacefully in this world, if two words were no longer used: that is, *mine,* and *yours*' (1775 [1597], I.1.16, I:9–10).[92] In 1571 the author of an economic-juridical practicum, a treatise titled *Summa de tratos y contratos,* had signalled the beginnings of private property as the moment of man's expulsion from paradise: 'And so, having sinned, [man] lost this general and common empire, which was then distributed, with each man receiving his part as a legitimate inheritance: thus [private] property had its origin, and so began this language so common today of mine and yours' (Mercado 1571, fol. 18r).[93] We hear the echo in Don Quixote's discourse on the Golden Age: 'because those who lived then did not know the two words *yours* and *mine*' (DQ I.11)[94] although, as Cervantes' editors point out, this classical topos had been revitalized and was popular in Renaissance writings (DQ I.11, n. 14). Mercado and Castillo de Bobadilla opine on the impossibility of a return to the Golden Age, while Cervantes' protagonist laments it as a lost ideal. As he does so, we are told, Sancho Panza 'was eating acorns,' which is, perhaps not incidentally, also the sustenance proposed by Castillo de Bobadilla, who notes that the ancient poets who held these opinions pretended that men, living as solitary animals with the beasts, 'sustained themselves on acorns' (1775 [1597], I.1.3, I:6–7).[95] The echo is noteworthy but, more importantly, the contrasting perspectives highlight a fundamental difference: Mercado and Castillo de Bobadilla look to the past so as to justify and defend an economic-political reality that privileges only a few while Cervantes uses poetic detail of the past to model a genre that reflects the same reality, but privileges democratic ideals. Francisco Tomás y Valiente tells us that Castillo de Bobadilla was 'a fervent partidarian and defender of the basic postulates of the system' in which he lived (1975, 200).[96] To the contrary, Cervantes' criticism of that system is stinging and mordant, albeit hidden behind the mask of a 'fictional' narrative. The practical jurist sought stability in a chaotic environment, without concern for the attendant perversion of law and ideals that would entail. The creative writer highlighted those same processual perversions, and also appropriated many literal legal details not found in manuals like those of Castillo de Bobadilla, but only in the laws themselves and in the jurists' glosses.

History and Law in Cervantes' Works

Cervantes' first known works are in verse: a 1567 sonnet at the birth of the infant Catalina Micaela, daughter of Phillip II and his wife Isabel, titled *Serenísima reina, en quien se halla;* another sonnet, five *quintillas,* and an elegy included in a 1568 collection edited by humanist Juan López de Hoyos, who calls Miguel de Cervantes his 'dear, beloved' student (caro y amado discípulo);[97] and verse dedicated to Antonio Veneziano, penned while Cervantes was held captive in Algiers (Canavaggio 1998). From 1581 to1587, Cervantes wrote a number of theatre pieces: *Los tratos de Argel, La batalla naval,* and the *Numancia,* this last an epic that relates the heroism of a town holding out against invading Roman forces captained by Scipion. The *Numancia* ends with the sole surviving figure, a young boy, committing suicide so as not to provide Scipión with the hostage he desperately wants. Suicide, called 'the crime of desperation' in Cervantes' day, was illegal pursuant to Spanish law (Recop. VIII.23.8), although Cervantes presents the boy's act in a favourable light and as the means by which the enemy is truly defeated, with fame and eternal glory more crucial than the historical moment. Speaking of a town magistrate facing the same literal situation of surrender to an enemy and loss of his town, Castillo de Bobadilla also allows heroic suicide as admirable, using the 'Numantian Boy' as an example: 'and (so they say) he threw himself from the walls holding them [the keys to the town], falling dead at the feet of Scipión: because it is a glorious thing to die for one's Law, and for one's King' (Castillo de Bobadilla 1775 [1597], IV.3.5., II, 429).[98] Aaron Kahn points out that the Numantian Boy and his suicide in Cervantes' *Numancia* is 'a complete fictionalization of events by the playwright' (2007, 573). Castillo de Bobadilla's inclusion of Cervantes' fictionalization as feasible historical fact in his manual for magistrates highlights the porousness of the so-called border between fact and fiction. De Armas (1974) has studied Cervantes' play for its relationship to the classical Greek tragedy *Persae,* with a hero (Xerxes, Scipión) felled by pride, and a Christian catharsis that transcends the historical moment. De Armas's reading of imperial power humiliated by the powerless suggests a David versus Goliath approach by Cervantes, although it is also interesting to note that both sides of the Cervantine conflict see their intent as that of besting the pride of the other.[99] The pride of the weak wins out over the pride of the powerful in, as de Armas notes, a Christian catharsis, but it is a battle of two prides, two Achilles' heels, each weighed thoughtfully and respectfully by Cervantes in the work.

In 1585 Cervantes published a pastoral novel, *La Galatea,* in which a number of shepherds and shepherdesses celebrate and lament their love, but also kidnap and kill each other. The pastoral novels, made popular and codified by Jorge de

Montemayor's publication of his *Diana* in 1559–60, speak of romantic love in a bucolic setting, but Cervantes' version adds a level of reality not generally found in the genre.[100] It is frequently noted that Cervantes published nothing from 1585 to 1605, the date of the first edition of the *Quixote.* Although true as to published works, this is slightly misleading, as the author did continue to write during those years. Two theatre pieces from 1585 are noticed in documents, although not extant: *La confusa,* and *El trato de Constantinopla y muerte de Celín.* From 1587 we have poetry written in praise of various friends including López Maldonado, Alonso de Barros, and Pedro de Padilla; from 1592 there is a contract that has Cervantes promising 'six theatre works ... one by one ... and when each one turns out to be one of the best theatre pieces seen in Spain, you are obliged to give and to pay me for each, 50 gold ducats' (Sliwa 2005, 1592/09/05, Sevilla);[101] a 1593 romance titled 'Los celos' is part of an anthology;[102] in 1595 Cervantes wins a prize in a poetry competition; in 1598 he writes *Soneto al túmulo del Rey que se hizo en Sevilla,* at the death of Spain's King Phillip II. We know that the figure of Don Quixote existed as early as 1604, on the basis of an insult written by Cervantes' contemporary and rival Lope de Vega. The First Part of the *Quixote* was published in 1605 and earned its author immediate and wide-spread fame. Sabor de Cortazar and Lerner note that there were ten editions of the work by 1611, and that it was translated into English in 1612, then into French in 1614 (DQ II.3, notes 6 and 7). The burst of publications at the end of the author's life is impressive: Cervantes published his *Novelas ejemplares* in 1613, the *Viaje del Parnaso* in 1614 and, in 1615, both the Second Part of the *Quixote* and *Ocho comedias y entremeses.* Cervantes wrote his dedication of *Los trabajos de Persiles y Sigismunda* on 19 April 1616, and then passed away three days later, on 22 April 1616. This last work was published posthumously, in 1617.

All Cervantes' works show a keen historical consciousness, as is evident in the titles of the early verse and theatre works which mourn a death, celebrate a birth, and recount real battles and events. The author's earliest novel, *La Galatea,* includes some sprinkling of legal detail with its homicidal shepherds taking refuge in churches, but Cervantes saturates *Don Quixote* with juridical material, from the multiple law-breaking characters to their copious commentary on right and wrong. The *Quixote* is also a pointed and open exploration of the meaning of history in literary and preceptive terms. Various legal and historical connections, descriptions, and glosses will be discussed in detail in what follows, divided into two general sections on, respectively, jurisprudence (chapters 3, 4, 5) and historiography (chapter 6).

3 Jurisprudence in Spain, Seventh to Sixteenth Centuries

Starting in Bologna in the eleventh to twelfth centuries and continuing into the sixteenth, legal scholars in the various emerging countries of Europe began to explore the principles of classical-era Roman law, and to incorporate them into their local usage and customary laws. These are the earliest movements of what would come to be called the Renaissance, which began with the recovery of manuscripts containing legal codes, most importantly those of Roman Emperor Justinian.[1]

With methodical philological studies based on the trivium's arts of grammar, rhetoric, and dialectic, jurists learned and practised the law by glossing legal texts:

> Scientifically, the Gloss seems linked to the era's thinking, as would seem natural. To speak of science is to speak of a method, and the method employed by the glossers was no different than that used in scholastic thought which, generally speaking, found its inspiration in the liberal arts of the trivium: grammar, rhetoric, and dialectic. It is not insignificant that Irnerius, the founder of the school [of glossers], was a master at these three arts. As a consequence, the work of the glossers will present itself to us as the work of philologists and logicians. Philologists, in that they approach a text as such, that is, as *littera;* and logicians when they approach the content of said text. (Guzmán Brito 1978, 17–18)[2]

The glossers studied the literal constructions (grammar), and the artful language (rhetoric) of those codes, arguing with them so as to uncover their truths (dialectic), interpreting them both historically and in the context of their own circumstance: *verba, res,* and *mores.* For example, faced with Roman law's distinction between public and private law (*ius publicum, ius privatum*), the glossers attempt to explain it as general principle versus individual case or, alternatively, as custom versus statute (García Gallo 1967, 1:261, para. 521). Given the particular historical developments of the Iberian Peninsula, the situation in Spain took a specific form and focus.

The earliest extant written legal codes from the Iberian Peninsula are found in the seventh-century Visigoth Judge's Book (Forum iudiciorum), translated into Castilian as the Fuero Juzgo in the thirteenth century. It is described as 'a Roman-Gothic set of codes, for its mix of custom and law of both nations' (Fuero Juzgo 1815, Lardizabal y Uribe, IV).[3] Some of the laws are of unknown origin; some have notes identifying them as *antigua* and, of this latter group, a subset with the additional note *noviter emendata* are believed to be of Roman origin despite the Visigoths' prohibition against reliance on Roman law; yet other Fuero Juzgo laws are identified as having been promulgated by specific kings 'under their own authority and mandate'; and some were made by kings and ecclesiastics working together in council (Fuero Juzgo 1815, Lardizabal y Uribe, IV–V).[4] From the seventh through the fifteenth centuries, as Christian kings retook cities and towns that had been ruled by the Moors, they granted specific *fueros* (sets of laws, founding/legal charters) to the reconquered sites. The results, for the kingdoms of the Peninsula, would become a semi-haphazard system with multiple contradictions, even as to fundamental aspects like legal age (Byrne 2002). Consequently, from the thirteenth through the fifteenth centuries, in all likelihood following on the model of the Bologna jurists, rulers of the kingdoms of Castile attempted to incorporate the legal thinking and structures found in classical-era manuscripts into their own juridical norms, as a way to reconcile the various legal codes and charters.[5]

In the early thirteenth century, Kings Ferdinand III and Alphonse X 'the Wise' (el Sabio) of Castile were the first to ask their jurists to reconcile their local usage and customary laws, the *fueros,* with the Roman era manuscripts, but the results were not immediately successful. Both Alphonse's Fuero Real and his monumental Siete Partidas were fiercely resisted by the nobles, who stood to lose privileges with the changes. So Alphonse and his heirs partially withdrew those statute-based codes, establishing an order of applicable law that included them but only as a last resort, appellate source to be used in the king's court. The order of legal texts to be consulted in any given case stipulated that first, all were to abide by the laws in 'this our book' (este nuestro libro) – understood to mean whichever was being written at the time; in 1348 it was the Ordenamiento de Alcalá de Henares, in 1505 it was the Leyes de Toro, and in 1567 it was the Recopilación de las Leyes de estos reinos. If the answer to a case was not found in 'this book' then one should check the local *fueros* although, as the Catholic Monarchs Ferdinand and Isabel added in the late fifteenth century, 'only as to matters they have been used to decide before, and only if we have not altered them herein, in "this book," and only if they are not contrary to God and reason, or to the laws found in this book' (Leyes de Toro, law 1, included unaltered in the 1567 Recopilación, as Book II, Title I, law 3).[6] If the answer to a given case was not found after having followed those preliminary steps, then the Partidas could be consulted.[7]

This order of consultation seemed to guarantee that, over time, the Partidas would be incorporated in a sort of trickle-down fashion. Early in the fourteenth century, they were reformulated and deemed more a legal textbook than an applicable code but, in practice, they continued to be applied as law.[8] Referring to the late thirteenth and early fourteenth centuries, García Gallo explains that 'the Partidas, even without legal force, inspired the decisions made by the king's supreme tribunal, and so informed the legal thinking of upcoming jurists' (1967, 1:90, para. 188).[9] Jurists liked the scope and level of specificity of the Partidas but they also, as they copied the extensive codes by hand, intentionally altered the law to suit their particular needs; Ferdinand and his daughter complain in 1505: 'there is no reason for each and every one to delete and emend them [the Partidas] as they wish' and they order a set of amended and reconciled Partidas, to be kept and guarded, with 'seals of gold and lead,' in order that they might serve as the final unadulterated reference (Leyes de Toro, law 1).[10] However, this is said in another 'this book,' the Leyes de Toro, which, by the middle of the sixteenth century, would replace the Partidas as the favourite of many jurists, including Gaspar de Baeza, who declares that 'among ourselves, we hold the Leyes de Toro in higher regard than the other Spanish constitutions, because in the former we do not find anything that has not been much discussed, and considered with sound judgment as to its public usefulness' (Baeza, cited by Llamas y Molina 1853, 1:7).[11]

Gaspar de Baeza's opinion was shared by other jurists, including one named Antonio Gómez, who said that the Leyes de Toro should be the first laws consulted, and only then the Partidas. Only after those two collections does Gómez allow consultation of the local *fueros* and, failing all of the above, he then determines that 'sentencing should be [carried out] by the common laws of Roman and imperial jurisprudence' (Llamas y Molina 1853, 1:31–2 and para. 230), which greatly surprises his nineteenth-century editor who finds it contrary to an existing royal decree that prohibits the use of Roman law.[12] Gómez adds that when it is necessary to consult the Partidas, they should be followed 'even if it cannot be proven that they are in use' (Llamas y Molina 1853, 1:90, para. 229).[13] This last tells us quite a bit about the debates surrounding the Partidas: attorneys were undermining their authority with the legal argument that they were not even 'in use.' Concurrently, fans of the Partidas were trying to prove the same of the Leyes de Toro: the glosser of the 1555 text of the Partidas, Gregorio López, affirms that in his opinion, it is the Leyes de Toro that must be proven to be 'in use' (García Gallo 1967, 1:398, para. 752). In the same year (1555) that Gómez and López made those comments for their respective favourites, the royal charter (cédula) was granted to López's newly glossed edition of the Partidas, as 'revised and emended by the royal council.'[14]

By the late sixteenth century, the Partidas were in use, but it could be proven that they were not in use; they were obsolete, yet updated and official; they were taken seriously by some, but dismissed by others. Just like all the Peninsula's other legal compendia, the Partidas were competing for jurisdiction and authority. The seven centuries of Reconquest had led to a whole raft of legal charters, codes, and volumes, granted by one king after another to reconquered cities and towns, constantly augmented with new laws, without any old ones ever really being abrogated. In the various volumes, some laws disappear from one section only to migrate to another, or from one edition only to resurface in the next. This confusion would continue throughout the sixteenth century, by the end of which the Spanish legal system is in such a chaotic state that, much like Don Quixote, no one even bothers to abide by the laws. Early in the sixteenth century, Juan Luis Vives 'wanted to see the laws simplified, their number reduced, and the obscurities clarified' (Riveros Subizar 1951, 157),[15] and mid-sixteenth-century philosopher Pedro Malón de Chaide complains of the same problematic situation (Maravall 1976, 96). Twentieth-century historian I.A.A.Thompson quotes a solicitor who, in 1593, made 'a general supplication that the corregidores be ordered to keep the laws of the kingdom without dispensing with any of them, because it is a great absurdity that no law that is made is observed' (1976, 64–5). Sixteenth-century magistrate (corregidor) Castillo de Bobadilla is a fitting example of the complaint. In his manual for magistrates, he notes six specific reasons that allow a corregidor to go against the law with impunity in a broad sense (II.10.69–76, 1:386–7). Additionally, after each general rule duly noted, this magistrate lists the multiple doubts, occasions, amplifications, and limitations that contradict its stipulations. Tomás y Valiente calls Castillo de Bobadilla's reasoning 'casuistry on casuistry' (casuismo sobre casuismo), and points out that the exceptions are so numerous that they could constitute a general rule contrary to the general rule cited at the start (1975, 199).[16] Cervantes tells us that Don Quixote was engendered in a jail (DQ I, Prologue), making his a fit voice to comment on society's ills, a counterpart in counterpoint to magistrate Castillo de Bobadilla. Twentieth-century jurist Santos Manuel Coronas González speaks of complaints about the kings themselves not obeying the law (2005, 62–3), but sixteenth-century historian Cabrera de Córdoba had duly recorded for posterity those occasions when they, but no one else around them, did:

> the dresses and adornments worn by their Royal Highnesses and the happy couple were in conformance with the pragmatic, without any gold in the embroidery or passementerie trim, or any other thing of gold, although the gentlewomen and men who attended the ceremony wore much that had gold embroidery or passementerie. (Cabrera de Córdoba 1857, 5 January 1602)[17]

Throughout the sixteenth century, legal collections dating to the seventh, twelfth, thirteenth, fourteenth, and fifteenth centuries are all published in newly glossed editions, in volumes that contradict one another while all remaining in use at the same time, depending on the whims of judge, jurist and, sometimes, claimant. Kagan describes the situation: 'Castilian justice in the sixteenth and seventeenth centuries was a hodgepodge of confused laws and competing jurisdictions that crafty litigants exploited to their own advantage' (1981, 31), but blames the confusion mainly on 'the way courts … were organized and run' (37). His study leaves no doubt as to that source of confusion but, as he also notes, there was competition among the sets of laws themselves, with claimants choosing a court on the basis of the most favourable legal volume to the case they filed (32–7). Magistrates enforced the law, or not, as they saw fit. All the while, the monarchs continued to issue new pragmatics and orders on a regular basis. In the transition from manuscripts to printed volumes and from separate states to a centralized bureaucracy, juridical and humanist philological study led to examination, complaints, and (supposed) regularization of the legal tomes, a problematic process that only worsened the situation by multiplying the number of volumes and their contradictions.

In early seventeenth-century Spain, the 'ought to be' of the legal volumes was neither easy to figure out nor to follow. In 1619 Sancho de Moncada describes the dire situation in a discourse directed to King Phillip III: 'many complain that they cannot take even one step without falling into one denunciation or another of one of Spain's laws'; the jurist ennumerates a list of specific problems, beginning with the sheer quantity of tomes and laws, and then adds: 'there is no one in the kingdom who knows them all, and how could the labourer, or the non-learned know them, so as to abide by them and not fall victim to their penalties? Who has the money to buy so many and such enormous volumes, or time to read them?' (Moncada 1746 [1619], Discurso VII, chap. 6, pp. 117–22).[18] Moncada asserts that there are many abuses because no law is ever abrogated despite there being many that are not used, that many speak with confusing, polysemic words, and that, worst of all, the laws are not obeyed, which leads to deprecation and reprobation of the legislators themselves, and of the Republic.[19] The 'four cardinal points in Don Quixote's judicial weakness' pointed out by twentieth-century legal scholar Alcalá-Zamora y Torres (2001, 94–7)[20] are all a direct reflection, and should so be read, of that same set of circumstances and complaints by Cervantes' contemporaries about the very real judicial system itself: lack of clarity in the laws, lack of respect for the state when people seek private justice, failure of judges to be neutral and impartial, and failure to enforce decisions.[21] Cervantes' own commentary on that plethora of violated laws is clearly stated in Don Quixote's advice to Sancho on governing the Ínsula Barataria:

> Do not make many pragmatics and, if you do, make sure they are good ones and, above all, make absolutely sure they are observed and obeyed; for pragmatics that are not observed might as well have never existed and, even worse, they let it be known that the ruler who had the discretion and authority to make them did not have the valour to make people respect them. (DQ II. 51)[22]

Empirical confirmation of the problematic situation is found in a list compiled a little over three hundred years later, in 1935. Among the volumes of Spanish law published during the sixteenth and seventeenth centuries are found two editions of the Visigoth's seventh-century Fuero Juzgo newly glossed and published in 1600, six different editions of the thirteenth-century Fuero Real, eight editions of Alphonse X's Siete Partidas, nine of the Leyes del Estilo, fifteen of the Ordenanzas Reales de Castilla, twenty-eight of the Leyes de Toro, and various editions of Pragmáticas (Gil Ayuso 1935). Notwithstanding their differences and contradictions, all of these volumes were operative, with full force and effect depending on the particular judge, jurist, court, or case. Batiza points out that the 1567 Recopilación was promulgated and published when Cervantes was approximately twenty years old, and that it authorized its own content as well as application of the Siete Partidas, the Fuero Real, the Leyes de Toro, the Fuero Juzgo, the Espéculo, the Fuero Viejo, the Ordenamiento de Alcalá, and the Ordenanzas Reales de Castilla (Batiza 1964, 35). Tomás y Valiente (1969) situates the moment of greatest confusion and lack of respect for the law in the period beginning around 1580 and continuing into the middle of the eighteenth century,[23] that is, beginning when Cervantes was thirty-three years old, and then continuing throughout his lifetime and beyond. As a creative artist, Cervantes would filter a consensus view of cultural symbols through his own perspective; the moments of greatest social confusion and upheaval also tend to engender great art, as did this one.

Cervantes took the pervasive legal confusion and gave it a personal narrative voice, in both *Don Quixote* and his *Novelas ejemplares*, offering a fictional albeit realist gloss on specific content of the legal volumes, tailoring his protagonist Alonso Quixano in strict compliance with the Siete Partidas prescription for the perfect knight and then setting him loose like a bull in a china shop. Cervantes has squire Sancho Panza use outdated language from the Fuero Juzgo[24] but also make Solomonic decisions on legal matters, and the author paints exemplary law-breaking characters in his *Novelas ejemplares,* all the while commenting on the socio-historical criteria behind many of the legal volumes' conflicts and judgments. The civil and criminal violations of law by Don Quixote go for the most part unpunished, although they are all much debated by the protagonist and other characters in the novel. In this, it seems that Cervantes follows Baeza in finding for the Leyes de Toro, a legal compilation that addresses economic justice and dealings and that, as the jurist pointed out, does not contain anything that 'has not been much discussed, and considered with sound judgment as to its public usefulness' (Baeza, cited in Llamas y Molina 1853, 1:7). All of Don Quixote's reasonable discourses on arms and letters, the Golden Age, fathers and sons, personal liberty, etc., are of a piece with his era's filtering and sorting of legal values and norms.

4 Laws Broken, Glossed, and Made: Don Quixote

Tilting at Windmills

The most iconic representation of Cervantes' protagonist is the knight on horseback, defying a windmill with his sword. This episode in the novel, in which Don Quixote believes the windmill to be a giant whom he will take on in battle, is unfailingly read as imagination run wild and an outsized confidence in man's ability to defeat the odds, a tragic moment turned comically endearing by the protagonist's misreading of reality. However, when the protagonist tilts against windmills he is not just quixotic in the 'dream the impossible dream' sense; he is also breaking a very specific law that prohibits just such a 'breaking of mills.' The legal volumes use a word that had acquired, by Cervantes' day, enough acceptations to make it a fine candidate for parodic fodder.

Two of the oldest legal compilations in Spain, the seventh-century Liber iudiciorum and the fourteenth-century Fuero Viejo[1] prohibit the 'breaking' (quebrantar) of a mill: 'to any who break a garden, or mill, or winery press, or threshing floor, or noble's hunting ground, sixty days' pay' (Fuero Viejo I.6.1); 'if any man breaks a mill or fishing ground, all that he broke he restores within thirty days, and pays in addition twenty days' wages' (Fuero Juzgo VIII.4.30).[2] The verbs used for 'break' are the Latin derivative 'crebantar' with a 'c' in the Fuero Juzgo and 'quebrantar' with a 'q' in the Fuero Viejo. The Spanish dictionary for first uses, *Autoridades,* does not offer 'crebantar,' but defines 'quebrantar': 'To break, separate or divide violently the parts of a whole. Latin. Frangere, Effringere, Elidere' as well as a series of other acceptations:

> to crack or cleave . . . to pulverize or crush . . . to persuade, induce, or convince with cunning, clevernesss, and importunity . . . to cause pity or compassion . . . to violate or profane any sanctuary, safe place, or enclosure . . . metaphorically it means to

> violate any law, one's word, or an obligation… to break, overcoming certain difficulty… to bother, to irritate… to weaken, to diminish another's strength… in legal terminology, it means to disable or invalidate a testament. (*Autoridades*)[3]

Joan Corominas offers this etymology: 'from the Latin. crepare "to crush, to snap, to crack, to explode" and, in the later era to explode.'[4] Antonio de Nebrija's 1516 *Vocabulario* offers equally 'quebrar o quebrantar,' both of which are translated by today's dictionaries to mean 'to break; to crush, grind' although only 'quebrantar' also includes the meanings of 'to desecrate or defile' and 'to break out of prison' while 'quebrar' has taken on the commercial meaning of 'to go bankrupt' (Simon and Schuster). In *La lengua de Cervantes,* Julio Cejador y Frauca finds various forms of 'quebrantar' and 'quebrar' in the *Quixote:* 'quebrado(a),' 'quebradizo,' 'quebrantado,' 'quebrantamiento,' 'quebrantar,' 'quebranto,' with meanings ranging from 'broken' to 'tired' and, like Corominas, Cejador y Frauca (1906) offers the etymology of 'to crush = to explode' (crepare = reventar). The *Léxico hispánico primitivo* defines the verb with variations of the same Latin root *crepare:* 'crebantare, crepandare, crepantar, grebantare, krepantare. (Del lat. crepantare, der. de crepare) tr. "Quebrar,"' and offers a number of meanings as used in the early *fueros:* 'to break'; 'to raid, to trample'; 'to waylay on the road'; 'to oblige by force'; 'to break an agreement.'[5] The verb shows enough variety of uses that it could easily be one of those referred to by early seventeenth-century jurist Moncada in his 1619 complaint to King Phillip III about multivalence leading to confusion in laws that 'speak with ambiguous words, that allow for different meanings and interpretations' (Moncada, 1746 [1619], Discurso VII).[6]

Written when a mill was 'the old *aceña,* the paddle-wheel mill' (Aubrun 1986, 63), which could probably be broken or damaged without too much difficulty, and when the verb 'quebrantar' meant to break into or to steal from, the law was still on the books when the local mills grew into big windmills with giant arms, like those pictured with Don Quixote on Rocinante,[7] and when the verb had that whole series of possible meanings ranging from to break, to persuade, to violate by force, and to rob on the road. In Gaspar de Baeza's translation of Paolo Giovio's *Histories,* Gonzalo Hernández de Córdoba, whose 'history' is found in the inn in *Don Quixote,* is a hero who also goes out 'breaking the mills' (Giovio, 1566, 5.2).[8] Don Quixote's fight with the windmills is imaginatively quixotic but literally criminal. When his protagonist attempts to 'break' the mill, Cervantes paints him as a reader who, wild with images of adventure stories, has gone mad. This would, of course, exempt him from legal damages but only according to certain legal volumes out of the plethora of possibilities in late sixteenth-century Spain. In any case, Don Quixote did not 'break' the mill; it 'broke' him and then he, 'battered, went rolling across the field' (DQ I.8).[9]

Martínez Olmedilla notes that certain details of the novel bear a relation to specific laws but, like later twentieth-century jurists, advises against considering Cervantes himself a jurist, saying that since the novel has some of everything, 'it is only logical that it might also have some legal and juridical references' (1905, 20).[10] I would argue that Cervantes was quite conscious of his (ab)use of the laws as written, and had a specific parodic intent with regards to same. Seeing his creation as no more than that would be in error, but reading it in its full historical-intellectual context does not dilute but rather heightens the enchantment, while also offering a deeper appreciation of his creative daring. Tilting at windmills is just the beginning.

Don Quixote and the Partidas

The scene in Don Quijote I.3 in which Cervantes' protagonist is knighted by the ventero (innkeeper) has been analysed by a number of scholars, with opinions ranging from: 'historically and legally precise' (Martínez Olmedilla 1905, 20), to a 'cruel, ironic pastiche' of the *libros de caballería* (Pemán 1948, 9) or a farce, 'a dirty, miserable joke ... a grotesque imitation of the sacred ceremony' (Riquer 1967, 86–7).[11] An argument has been made in defence of its fictionality and right to be bound only by literary as opposed to positive law,[12] and in 1991 Augustin Redondo recognized the scene as an incisive parody not only of the *novelas de caballería* but also of very specific details of the proscriptions in law and in contemporary how-to manuals for such knightings.[13] The knighting ceremony takes place only after Cervantes has painted, in the first two chapters of the novel, a protagonist who embodies an incisive gloss on the ideal knight-defender-protector described minutely in Alphonse X's Siete Partidas. The ceremony, the knight himself, and the innkeeper's throw-away line about his demolished chapel are all glosses on specific prescriptions and proscriptions found in the Siete Partidas.

Cervantes' narrator tells us that the innkeeper, needing something to laugh about that night, concedes to Don Quixote's plea that 'tomorrow morning you will knight me,' but then demurs when confronted with the protagonist's plan that 'tonight in the chapel of this castle of yours, I will hold vigil over my arms'; substitution of a patio for the chapel is necessary, insists the innkeeper, because the chapel is 'knocked down so as to build it anew' (DQ I.3).[14] With his exact words, the innkeeper threads the thinnest of lexical lines between the law's proscriptions on the unmaking, remaking, and making anew of churches and chapels.

Prior to the thirteenth century, the laws of the Peninsula were not very specific as to knights or chapels, with the sole exception that some *fueros* exempted knights from paying certain taxes while others rescinded those rights. Even the twelfth century's Fuero de Molina, which was at one point retitled Fuero de Molina de los Caballeros,[15] does not specify who a knight is or how one is made, although, like some of the other legal codes, it does grant them freedom from taxes: he who has horse and arms 'pays no taxes' (nada non peche) (Sancho Izquierdo 64, quoting from cédula IV of the *fuero*). The seventh-century Liber iudiciorum of the Visigoths neither defines nor legislates specifically as to knights or chapels. Nor do the local *fueros* conceded to cities reconquered during the tenth through the fourteenth centuries. The Fuero Viejo accords all sorts of rights to noblemen, rich men, and 'gentry' (hijosdalgo), but does not address knights or chapels. Nor does the early to mid-thirteenth century Fuero Real, which had started to privilege the church over the nobles and, not surprisingly, was rejected by the latter who petitioned for, and were granted, a return to the Fuero Viejo and its judgments based on 'custom and deeds' (costumbre y hazañas).[16] Notwithstanding that concession, García Gallo points out that the Fuero Real continued to be granted as law to certain cities in the late thirteenth and early fourteenth centuries while, at the same time, the local *fueros* were reworked and given definitive form (1967, 1:390–1, para. 738).

Canon law of the fifteenth and sixteenth centuries refers to the proscriptions found in common law on the building of chapels, and says they should be respected (Pérez-Coca Sánchez-Matas 1994, 2:528). It also reprehends bishops who were allowing powerful persons to build churches and chapels 'with complete autonomy,' and attempts to restrict those abuses by prohibiting construction of new sacred places 'without a licence granted by the Diocesan prelate' (1994, 2:261, 262).[17] These citations are to documents from synods of the second half of the sixteenth century and, although the particular texts do not comment on the unmaking or remaking of sacred places, they do offer interesting details about certain abuses, especially by 'those who go into the churches to play, to blaspheme, or to perform other acts very unbefitting the sanctity and honesty of the church' (Pérez-Coca Sánchez-Matas 1994, 2:266).[18]

It is only in Alphonse X's Siete Partidas that the knight is fully described, and the process for knighting him is laid out in detail, and that is also where we find the laws about 'partially demolished chapels' (capillas derribadas). As indicated above, the Partidas came about as part of the reconciliation process of local customary law with Roman statute-based law, a regularization of the plethora of existing codes on the Peninsula. In the light of their legal proscriptions, the innkeeper's throw-away line about the chapel is charged with meaning, and Cervantes' description of Don Quixote in the First Part of the 1605 novel is better understood.

As to the place for the knighting ceremony, the Partidas stipulate that the day preceding the ceremony, the knight must keep vigil in a sacred place, for which the preparations are exacting: after bathing him and dressing him in the cleanest and best clothing,[19] his squires are instructed to bring him to the chapel or church, in order to parallel that cleansing of the body with a vigil to cleanse the soul.[20] As regards the bathing and fine, clean clothing, Cervantes' narrator has already described the peculiarity of Don Quixote's physical appearance when he arrives at the inn: 'raising the cardboard viser of his helmet, and showing his dry and dusty visage' (DQ I.2).[21] There will be neither bath nor clean clothing, and the narrator tells us that the quick-thinking innkeeper avoids another difficulty with his excuse of the chapel in repairs. The innkeeper assures the protagonist that the corral (or any place) is just fine for the vigil. His choice of words takes us to the Partidas, which prohibit construction of a sacred place without the specific mandate of a bishop, including 'if its foundation is knocked down with the intent to make it anew' (Partidas I.10.1).[22] In some editions of the legal code, there is a following law that allows rebuilding 'if some piece or part of it [the chapel] falls down, or if it is unmade by knocking it down bit by bit so as to remake it'; however, the newly glossed 1555 edition adds a footnote that contradicts that 'remake it' loophole: 'it cannot be made anew, not even if it is broken from within and remade' (Partidas I.10.1).[23] The chapel cannot be 'made anew' but, if one chooses to ignore the 1555 footnote only found in specific editions of the Partidas, it can be 'remade.' Cervantes gives the innkeeper a syntagm combining the phrases, with a chapel that is 'knocked down so as to build it anew,' but not to 'remake it,' thus posing a legal muddle. We can add 'demolisher of chapels' to the innkeeper's long list of known torts,[24] and an etymological debate as to the distinction between 'remaking' and 'making anew' for the night's entertainment at the inn.[25]

The Partidas also offer a complete template for Cervantes' description of his protagonist. The first eight chapters of the 1605 *Quixote* (the 'First Part' of the First Part) can be read as an insulting, tongue-in-cheek elogium of Spain's semi-legally prescribed ideal knight. Cervantes' protagonist is an anachronism that sixteenth-century pragmatics and ordinances kept trying and failing to recreate, on the basis of a model laid out in the Partidas, which not only define a knight: 'the knights are those called defenders by the ancients' (Partidas II.21, intro.), but also offer a history of professions once considered good training for the knightly calling: 'butchers, because they're accustomed to killing, and spilling the blood of live things,' or hunters, trappers, woodsmen, carpenters, blacksmiths, and stonecutters 'because they're strong of hand, and accustomed to wounding' (Partidas II.21.2).[26] The same legal compilation also addresses problems in relying on these types of strong men, most importantly that 'having no shame' they would lose the drive to win and, so, the battle.[27] Thus, 'the wise men, seeking those who might carry out these tasks,' concluded that the preferred choice for caballero is one who has 'natural shame' and one who is described physically, specifically, as 'a skinny, long-suffering sort of man' (Partidas II.21.2), 'measured' in his eating habits so that 'his flesh becomes tough and resilient' and, when it comes to sleeping: 'they should be accustomed to not sleeping a lot' (Partidas II.21.19).[28] The figure is clearly reflected in Cervantes' protagonist: skinny, long-suffering, and of measured habits or, as Cervantes describes him, 'of a tough complexion, with little meat on his bones, a long-drawn face, early riser, friend of the hunt' (DQ I.1).[29] Don Quixote himself explains the long-suffering part to Sancho: 'it is not given to knights errant to complain of any wound, even when their insides are pouring out through it' (DQ I.8).[30] The protagonist takes pride in not needing sleep, never backs down from a fight, and is mortified by even the slightest humiliation, that is, he has 'natural shame.'

The Partidas explain that 'natural shame' is found in 'men of good lineage … in the Spanish tongue … they are called nobles or gentry' and, they go on, the lineage should be proven 'gentry' (hidalgo) 'through the fourth generation, those called great-grandfathers' (Partidas II.22.2).[31] Cervantes' narrator specifies that Don Quijote's arms and shield 'had been those of his great-grandfathers' (DQ I.1).[32] The Partidas also specify that it is a good thing for the caballero to have a female friend to whom to dedicate his deeds: 'and so that they might exert themselves even more in battle, the ancients understood that it was a good thing that they have a female friend, whom they could name during the battles, so as to make their hearts grow stronger, and give them even more shame at the thought of failure' (Partidas II.21.22).[33] In Part I, chapter 13, Don Quixote defends the same practice when challenged by señor Vivaldo, using the legal formula 'usage and custom' (uso y costumbre):[34] 'it is established usage and custom for knight errantry that the knight errant, on performing some great feat of arms, should have his lady in front of him' (DQ I.13).[35] Another Partidas law specifies that the knight will not sit down to eat with his squire, but only with another knight of equal rank,[36] and Don Quixote says the same to Sancho (DQ I.11).

There have been a fair number of comments as to Don Quijote's 'advanced age,' but the legal age exemptions for knight service fluctuated.[37] The 1484 Ordenanzas de Castilla were neither sanctioned nor officially promulgated as law but they were, in practice, just like all the other legal compendia, applied as law throughout the sixteenth century.[38] They offer two different laws, one exempting only those over sixty, but the very next exempting all those over forty (Ordenanzas IV.1.4–5). King Phillip II's officially sanctioned and promulgated 1567 Leyes de recopilación restrict the exemption to those over sixty.[39] Cervantes' imprecise age for Alonso Quijano, who 'was somewhere around … fifty years old' (DQ I.1), keeps him in active service age.[40]

According to the Partidas, once Don Quixote is an armed knight he is exempt from the law, but that exception is not found in the rest of the legal texts.[41] The protagonist insists on this right in a flood of rhetorical questions full of legalisms:

> Who was the ignoramus who signed an order of imprisonment for a knight such as I? Who failed to recognize that knights errant are exempt from all judicial law, and that their law is their sword, their codes [*fueros*] are their courage, and their pragmatics are their will? Who was the idiot, I say, who does not know that there is no writ of execution against a noble with the privileges and exemptions granted to a knight errant the very day that he is armed, when he gives himself over to the harsh life of knight errantry? (DQ I.45)[42]

In one of their many pragmatics mandating 'cuantiosos caballeros' (literally, numerous knights) to defend Spain, Ferdinand and Isabel stressed the particular importance of knights and nobles having the proper horse and arms in order to protect 'the liberties, privileges and prerrogatives of their nobility and exemptions' (Pramáticas, fol 95, law 104).[43] I translate the 'cuantiosos caballeros' phrase literally, given the scope and mandate of those who were deputized so as to provide a more numerous and thereby effective defence. Although some sources allege that the 'cuantiosos' were limited to non-hidalgos (Thompson 1976, 132), and/or to property owners, the laws themselves make clear that these proscriptions were quite fluid, and even waived in the hopes of conscripting further numbers. Pedro Cátedra cites Covarrubias and mentions a few of the pragmatics promulgated in the sixteenth century, but not all of them (2007, 96–105). The full gamut of those legal proscriptions illustrates the confusion that must have reigned. Some legal texts exempted the 'cuantiosos' from paying taxes, but others rescinded those rights (Byrne 2007). The 1496 Pragmatic that called up the knights was directed to all those who lived in the cities and villages of Burgos and its provinces, irrespective of social status, although it based the need to maintain horse and arms on property owned, with certain arms for certain income levels (Pramáticas, law 104). In 1563, Phillip II recognized that the laws on the 'numerous knights' (cuantiosos) had been routinely ignored, and so he repromulgated them, adding that anyone who wished, even if they did not have the mandated quantity of property, could be a 'cuantioso' (Recop. VI.1.13). The only simple translation that can encompass the full range of legal manipulations and the basic intent of the 'cuantiosos' is,

I believe, 'numerous knights.' Thompson identifies the 'numerous knights' with, specifically, 'Andalusia and Murcia' (1976, 19). However, the 1528 edition of Pramáticas combined with the Leyes de Toro mandates horse and arms for the citizenry of 'all our reigns and holdings' and lists a number of places on the Peninsula that must comply with the provisions, beginning with 'Burgos, head of Castile our chamber' (Pramáticas, fol. 95, law 104).[44]

Those pragmatics address, among other things, late fifteenth- and sixteenth-century Spain's problems with a lack of armed knights. From the time of the Catholic Monarchs to Cervantes' day Spain's rulers tried, in essence, to draft them or, at the least, maintain them in ready reserve. Ferdinand and Isabel complain about this lack, which they attribute to their own divinely granted success in bringing peace to the land:

> We have been informed that due to the abundant peace and tranquility that divine clemency has allowed to exist in these our kingdoms since we have governed here ... there are not, nor have there been, offensive or defensive arms as there were before ... and so, when a situation calls for compliance with service to us in the execution of our justice or the prosecution of miscreants, when it is proper for citizens of a city, town, or place to pursue those miscreants, they go for the most part unarmed, which is dangerous and dishonourable for them. (Pramáticas, fol. 95, law 104)[45]

Cervantes will have Don Quixote respond to a question on the need for an armed knight like him 'in such a peaceful land' (DQ I.13).[46]

The same pragmatic also mandates the 'appropriate offensive and defensive arms' that all the crown's 'subjects and citizens of any law, status, or condition' must keep at the ready in their homes, with certain arms for each 'status or condition' (Pramáticas, fol. 95, law 103).[47] It is worthy of note that the first chapter of the *Quixote* is titled 'Which treats of the *condition* and practice of the famous gentleman Don Quixote de la Mancha' (DQ I.1, my emphasis).[48] The pragmatic on appropriate arms updates and expands the earlier calls for 'numerous knights,' who had to pass muster and swear twice a year that they were ready in case of need. First mandated in 1484 for Andalucía, as Thompson notes, the scope of the call was expanded in this 1496 pragmatic directed to 'all those who live and reside in the cities and towns free and exempt from taxation' of Burgos and its provinces, and also to 'all provinces and cities and towns and places of our kingdoms and holdings' (Pramáticas, fol. 95, law 104).[49] There had been similar, prior orders: starting in the second half of the tenth century, laws mandated that anyone with a horse had to be ready to be called into service – the 'village knights' (caballeros villanos) (García Gallo 1967, 2:578–9, para. 1071). Thompson notes that despite the general move to more modern military techniques, Phillip II authorized the Recopilación (1976, 1); this collection again insists on the need for the 'numerous knights' and includes some Partidas laws as to who they should be, and how they should come to be, but excludes others. In fact, one particular clause in the Recopilación removes the one condition – property ownership – that had previously defined all 'numerous knights': in this 1563 law, Phillip II declares: 'That all who wish of their own will to be a "quantioso" be admitted [to the ranks], even if they might have less than the declared sum of property, that is, the 1000 gold ducats mandated by the [earlier] provision' (Recop. VI.1.13).[50]

Notwithstanding the treatment Cervantes' narrator gives to the meagre means of Don Quixote's hacienda, which I believe can also be read as an ironic description of a gentleman very 'measured' in his eating habits, the protagonist's arms qualify him for one of the statute's 'most principle and wealthiest' for whom it is ordered 'that they have steel breastplate and a skirt of mail or cuirass [plate armour], and armature for the head that can be a casque with beaver, or a sallet with visor, and armpit guards or backplate, and a long lance measuring twenty-four spans [sixteen feet], and a sword and knife and helmet' (Pramáticas, fol. 95, law 104).[51] Cervantes scatters the description of Don Quixote's arms but, in the first three chapters of Part I, for various reasons, we hear about the 'lance, shield, sword, corselet, breast- and backplates, bridle, spurs, and helmet,'[52] with the only noted items lacking from the mandated list those which the protagonist himself notes, a chainmail sallet, for which he remedies his simple helmet with cardboard, and the 'skirt of mail' (falda de malla). By Part I, chapter 10, we get a reference to the 'cuirass skirt' (falda de loriga) as Sancho kisses it (DQ I.10).[53] That puts the protagonist in full compliance with the pragmatic's mandated arms for the 'most principle and wealthiest' men.

A later pragmatic (2 May 1493) mandates that all, 'even princes/or dukes/or marqueses/or counts/or any other man of greater or lesser status/or dignity' have a horse, and prohibits the substitution of a mule because, with this type of abuse, 'very quickly would be lost in these our kingdoms the nobility of the knighthood,' although there are exceptions for men of religion and academics: 'except for prelates and clergy who have taken sacred orders, and friars and doctors and licenciates and graduates in all and any sciences, who are not obligated' (Pramáticas, fol. 146, law 153).[54] Another 1499 pragmatic prohibits removing any horse from the kingdom and defines 'horse' as 'horse, or nag, or mare, or foal' (fol. 151), and another describes the necessary qualities of the caballero's horse: 'saddle horse or mare two years or older, such that an armed man might ride mounted on it and fight when necessary' (Pramáticas fol. 127, law 154).[55] Rocinante fits the bill.

Even when it comes to squires, the pragmatics prohibit the substitution of a mule for a horse (Pramáticas, fol. 146, law 104). Faced with Sancho accompanying him on an ass rather than a horse, Don Quixote tries unsuccessfully to remember 'if any knight errant had been accompanied by a squire mounted on an ass' and resolves to 'to find him [Sancho] a more honourable steed' as soon as possible (DQ I.7).[56] The pragmatic, however, fails to specifically prohibit riding an ass, although another does prohibit, for all towns south of the River Tajo, breeding a horse and an ass in order to get a mule: 'one should not nor ought to throw asses in with mares' (Pramáticas, fols 149–50).[57] Given that the squire is supposed to be on a horse, it does seem that Sancho and Don Quixote take full advantage of a loophole of omission in the law as written.

The Partida's blueprint for the nature of an ideal knight, combined with the pragmatics' legal dictates for the particulars of his arms, help us better understand the historical environment in which Cervantes and his 'idle readers' (desocupados lectores) found such pleasure in his protagonist. One final point needs to be made as to the late sixteenth-century's continuing calls to arms for such knights, which in all probability contributed to the genesis of Cervantes' protagonist. Between 1585 and 1595 'the government had to impose, for the first time, obligatory military service' (Ettinghausen 1996, 26).[58] According to Thompson, militia calls went out in 1596 and in 1598[59] and then again, in 1602 and 1603, another call to arms went out for the militia, and for volunteers to serve as captains, with a call-up area specifying various towns and villages in La Mancha, specifically in the Campo de Montiel, Don Quixote's particular stomping grounds: 'Villanueva de los Infantes and the rest of the towns of that area, Sigura de la Sierra and its surroundings, and the village of Torrenueva' (Thompson, personal communication).[60]

These continued calls for 'numerous knights' were coming long after the legal directives on knighthood had become formalities and /or exploited loopholes.[61] In the 1567 Recopilación de Leyes, Phillip II rescinded the knight status of certain 'brown knights' (caballeros pardos) who had been knighted by Cardinal Francisco Jiménez, archbishop of Toledo; the new law particularly revokes the non-taxpayer status that had been granted on the basis of that knighting. Both the Ordenanzas de Castilla and the Recopilación tried to revoke this exemption, which Don Quixote insists on: 'What knight errant ever paid income taxes, sales taxes, the queen's tax, or the statutory, tool, or ferry monies?' (DQ I.45).[62] Cervantes also speaks of secular and religious knights in *Don Quixote* (DQ II.13), with Sancho Panza distinguishing the sort of rewards that come to a squire on the basis of whether he serves a lay or ecclesiastical knight. In Paolo Giovio's *Elogios,* we read that the pope knighted two Aztecs brought back from the New World by Cortés.[63] Any of these knightings, the 'brown knights,' the 'religious knights,' and the 'Aztec knights,' are directly contradicted by another Partidas law, which says that a man of religion cannot be a knight, nor can they knight a man because they cannot 'meddle in disputes/ battles' (Partidas II.21.11).[64] That didn't keep them from doing it but, had they needed it, they could have found a legal defence in the Ordenanzas de Castilla, in which Ferdinand and Isabel simultaneously insist on and obviate the rules on the arming of knights: 'and it is our wish and will that they be knighted, with the solemnity and ceremonies that our Partidas laws mandate, or without them' (Ordenanzas IV.1.8).[65] It must be done by, or without, the Partidas rules. The 'without them' (sin ellas) loophole also provides cover for Don Quixote's status as a caballero, despite all the irregularities of his knighting ceremony. Riquer refers to the Partidas' proscription against a poor or crazy person, or anyone who has once become a caballero in jest, ever receiving the honour in serious terms (1967, 88), and both Gaos (Cervantes, 1987, I.3, n. 3b), and Marín Pina (1998, 23) have alleged the same: 'for having been knighted in jest, as well as for being crazy, poor, and having been armed by a pícaro, the gentleman Alonso Quixana, although he himself never doubted the validity of the ritual, can never be a true knight errant' (Marín Pina 1998, 23).[66] The 'with or without the rules' (con o sin ellas) phrase would seem to negate the problem, much as it negates the law itself.

The Galley Slaves, 'desfacer fuerzas'

Chapter I.22 of *Don Quixote* has been widely recognized for the legal transgressions of Cervantes' protagonist.[67] Rico's edition notes three general approaches to the episode: on the question of liberty, on the character Ginés de Pasamonte as a picaresque figure, and on the same character's relationship to an actual historical figure (Cervantes, 1998b, I.22, notes). It is generally recognized that Don Quixote's actions in the episode are illegal, with a protagonist who demonstrates a 'naturalist' ideal of liberty but is also 'anarchic' (Olmeda 1973, 175). Canavaggio has recapped various critical commentaries that he divides into two groups, those who read the episode as a serious attempt to render justice versus those who see it as a theatrical, burlesque farce; Canavaggio himself describes the protagonist's acts in the scene as 'incoherent' (1979–80, 31). Given that in this chapter Don Quixote interrupts the transport of prisoners to their mandated service in the galleys, it is impossible to miss the legal significance but, I would argue, the protagonist's acts are anything but incoherent.

Certain subtleties of Cervantes' legal commentary in the episode have escaped critical notice. By the end of the sixteenth century, juridical and historiographical preceptists who had been seeking the philosophical nexus of their respective fields began to differ on whether to include or exclude 'divine' matters. The jurists continued to speak of things 'human and divine' as a connatural pair in jurisprudence, but the historians had begun to divorce the two. In 1596 López Pinciano does not prohibit the mix of divine and human thematic materials in non-religious works, although he does raise the question, speaking of 'certain philosopher-poets' and 'whether religious and sacred histories might be fitting material for epic' (1953, 3:168).[68] His interlocutor Fadrique advises that 'imitation and fiction is better suited to non-religious material, because the poet is then more able to expand the history, and even to bring more amusing and delightful episodes to the listener's ear' (1953, 3:168).[69] Later, Fadrique will admit that some poets have dealt with religious matters but he repeats: 'to sum up, I would say that religious matters, being such, are not suited to imitation' (1953, 3:180).[70] Imitation, or Aristotelian mimesis, is here gently suggested as better restricted to human matters. Twenty years later, in 1616, Cabrera de Córdoba will write definitively that history is divided into two types: divine, further subdivided into sacred or ecclesiastical; and human, which includes natural and moral history. Cabrera de Córdoba also distinguishes the lessons of each: 'Divine history teaches religion; human history teaches prudence; natural history teaches science, and all history delights' (1948 [1611], Discurso VII, 34).[71]

On a date that falls basically mid-way between those two preceptive texts (López Pinciano 1596, and Cabrera de Córdoba 1616) Cervantes anticipates the definitive separation that will be made by Cabrera de Córdoba, although in practice he does not fully realize the schism. In the Prologue to the reader of the 1605 *Quixote,* the unidentified friend of the author comments that the knight's history should not mix 'matters human and divine, as that is a particular blend with which no Christian understanding should clothe itself' (DQ I, Prologue).[72] In I.13, Don Quixote compares the religious and knightly professions as to their respective importance in saving souls versus bodies. The Partidas had incorporated the same comparison,[73] which was omitted in the later Recopilación along with, ironically enough, the laws that said a knight should be intelligent, wise, of good customs, wily, skilful, and loyal (Partidas II.21.preamble and 5–10). Apparently, Cervantes thought the division of labour should be a part of the discussion, giving his protagonist a final gloss on the matter when he says: 'the religious ask the heavens for good on earth ... but soldiers and knights carry out that request by defending the earth ... without a doubt it [the knight's life] is harder, more wretched, and more louse-ridden, with more hunger, thirst, misery, and toil' (DQ I.13).[74] As we saw in the last chapter, here again Cervantes links Don Quixote to the legal perspective of the Partidas.

Cervantes insists throughout the novel that his text is a history, and human and divine categories do remain separated – at least to a certain extent. As for divine and human letters, the protagonist offers an echo *a priori* of Cabrera de Córdoba, dividing them into divine, which bring souls to Heaven, and human, whose goal is not to teach prudence as it is for jurist Baeza and historian Cabrera de Córdoba but, rather, 'to put distributive justice into place, and to give to each his due, understanding, and assuring that good laws are obeyed' (DQ I.37).[75] This statement is a gloss on distributive justice in consonance with the Aristotelian distinction made in the *Ethics,* but Cervantes also adds the final codicil limiting such justice to 'good laws' (buenas leyes).[76] Given the status of contemporary Spanish law when Cervantes wrote that, the phrase is a loaded one, although the specific placement of the adjective, as an epithet preceding the noun, also allows for a simple recognition that all laws are, of their nature, good. I would argue for specific ironic intent.

Contrary to historiographical preceptists, sixteenth-century jurists accepted a common goal for divine and human matters in rendering justice. The various legal tomes of the Peninsula, read chronologically, make quite clear the history of this mix and codification. The first title of the first book of the seventh-century Liber iudiciorum speaks directly to rulers and kings, and to a citizen's obligations to those monarchs. By the thirteenth century, the first title of the first books of the legal codes details a citizen's obligations to the church and it is only later, in the second or third books, that we find those matters related to the kings. Alphonse X's Siete Partidas incorporate canon and civil law (Pérez y López 1791, 7–8).[77] In the first half of the sixteenth century, Bartolomé de las Casas studies the same civil-canon law combination but highlights the over-arching supremacy of 'natural law' (Cárdenas Bunsen 2010). By the middle of that same century, Frenchman Françoise Baudouin will say that 'jurisprudence is, by definition, notice of things human and divine' and he will add that, as such, it must of necessity concern itself with ecclesiastical and civil matters (cited in Turchetti 1984, 156).[78] During those same years, Spaniard Gaspar de Baeza will write of the transcendent goal to be found in the historical study of laws, a way of preparing oneself for the future eternal life (see fig. 1). At the end of the same century, Spanish medical doctor Cristóbal Pérez de Herrera, in curious tractates advising Phillip II and Phillip III on social problems ranging from poverty to laziness to excessive spending and problematic lawsuits that spring from these 'disorders' begins one of his tractates: 'To comply with specific obligation, in conformance with divine and human law' (1598, 1v).[79] Castillo de Bobadilla not only mixes the two laws, but even sets forth biblical examples as evidence of the first civil laws, and the timelessness of the concept of private property: 'Cain founded cities that he enclosed in walls: maybe because of his fear over the death of his brother Abel, maybe for avarice, because there was already private property' (1775 [1597], 7); 'Jabet, son of Lamech, branded his cattle with his own mark, so as to distinguish and recognize them; so there was already mine, yours, and private ownership of things' (1775 [1597], 8).[80] Also recognized by Spanish monarchs were special intermediary categories, such as the 'tonsured monks' (clérigos de corona) who had taken just the first vows, signified by the crown shaved on their heads. The Recopilación recognizes that they are 'in between' civil and canon jurisdiction, with access to defence on the basis of the *fueros* only for criminal causes.[81] Today, jurists accept without questioning that 'jurisprudence, since Ulpian, has taken in knowledge of things divine and human' (Sánchez de la Vega 1987, 16).[82] In Cervantes' day, following on three centuries of mixing human and divine affairs in its legal codes, the burgeoning Spanish state had begun to assert separate secular control over civil law cases and procedures, albeit with continued ecclesiastical resistance.

The history of civil and ecclesiastical courts in Renaissance Spain reveals a constant effort on the part of the latter to hear cases related to civil matters, and the resistance of the monarchs who attempted to restrain the practice. Maravall notes that 'during the fourteenth and fifteenth centuries in Spain we frequently hear a popular clamor, given support from above, against the oversteppings by ecclesiastical magistrates who infringed on and resisted the authority of the king's judges and officials' (1972, 219), and the historian offers a list of the protests of those centuries, culminating in what he calls a key moment in 1491, when a particular civil case was appealed to Rome.[83] Maravall points out that from Ferdinand the Catholic to Phillip II, 'the state apparatus functioned more and more effectively to repulse this type of meddling' (1972, 220).[84] During the sixteenth century, multiple orders, pragmatics and laws forbade the ecclesiastical authorities from taking on any such cases. A noteworthy example is found in the Recopilación, in a law titled 'That one lay person may not subpoena another to appear before an ecclesiastical judge on a profane matter':

> We hereby order that no lay person dare to call, summon, or subpoena another in front of a church judge, nor shall they make nor grant any obligation to submit themselves to ecclesiastical jurisdiction regarding debt or other profane matters, which are not properly those of the church: if they do so, we hereby order that for having done so, the lay person who brought it loses said case, which is to be granted to the defendant: and if the claimant has an official post in any city or town or other place within our kingdoms, they lose it: and if they do not have such office, they are barred from ever having one and, in addition, they pay a penalty of ten thousand maravedis, half going to the accuser and the other half toward public works, such as repair of the walls of the city, town, or jurisdiction where the act has taken place. (Recop. IV.1.10)[85]

As if those remedies were not enough, the next law in the series adds: 'and any court clerk who draws up such a case also loses his job, and from then on his writing is not trusted as proof, and he loses half of all his goods' (Recop. IV.1.11).[86] Continued recalcitrance, on the part of the ecclesiastical authorities, to cede jurisdiction led the monarchs to attempt to put a halt to the mix by levying extremely severe penalties on those who brought the cases, and even on the clerks who penned them. The laws found in the Recopilación address the issue from a variety of perspectives, prohibiting the ecclesiastical judges from rendering a decision on any such cases, setting out specific penalties for those judges who disobey, and reordering compliance with existing law (Recop. IV.1). A very relevant example of the legal manoeuvrings is found in a case from 1532, when Cervantes' aunt María sued one Martín de Mendoza for monies promised and not delivered. Mendoza's original sworn document includes promises that his pledge will be honoured 'in front of all justices and judges and officials, ecclesiastical as well as secular,' and he specifically renounces:

> all and any rights under canon law, including bulls and apostolic indulgences and privileges and general and special exemptions that I might take advantage of … even those special ones conceded by the popes to protonaries and apostolic families and dignitaries … or earned by request of the Infante's duke my father as a favour to his chapel. (cited by Cortés 1916, 28, 29)[87]

Apparently, papal bulls did not just save one's soul in heaven, but could also be employed as legal manoeuvering for exemptions from certain civil law cases. The Cervantes' family was experienced enough in legal dealings to insist that all possible concessions be stipulated.

Cervantes' protagonist and his squire directly comment on the mix of 'human and divine' a number of times in *Don Quixote,* with messages that illustrate both the legal precepts combining the two laws and their specific differences. In the novel, we read about semi-religious figures – a priest who reads and writes books of chivalry, and of sacred places – 'we have come up against the church, Sancho' (DQ II.9), as well as descriptions of the knight's life as a 'military religion' (DQ I.49).[88] Nonetheless, Cervantes does not include in his novel hagiography, or ecclesiastical councils, or religion qua religion, although he does incorporate religious practices and identity as to their socio-legal import: Ricote and the expulsion of the Moors, Grisóstomo and pagan burials, 'old Christian' (viejo cristiano) Sancho. Don Quixote and Sancho comment at various moments on the mix of things 'divine and human' in regards to matters of justice. In the 1605 *Quixote,* Sancho bases his right to defend himself on 'divine and human' law (las divinas y humanas) (DQ I.8), but ten years later,

Don Quixote changes the pair of ideals that sustain that same right to 'natural and divine' law (natural y divina) (DQ II.27). When, shortly after that, the knight speaks of the combination of divine and human law, Sancho interjects: 'Well may the devil take me ... if this boss of mine is not a theologian; and if not, well he sure seems as much like one as one egg is like another' (DQ II.27).[89] These commentaries offer explicit and just slightly contradictory perspectives on temporal versus non-temporal justice, that of man versus God, but what we find in the episode of the galley slaves is an indirect and ingenious gloss on the procedural steps in Spain's civil versus ecclesiastical court struggles.

Critical study of the episode of the galley slaves has been directed to the social import of its thematic content as, for example, ideal justice coming face to face with social pragmatism (Canavaggio 1979–80, Benardete 1965), or for the author's introduction of his picaresque character Ginés de Pasamonte (Wiltrout 1978, Reed 1987, Colahan and Rodríguez 1990, González Echevarría 2005, Gaylord 1998). Riveros Subizar says that Don Quixote 'defies the king's inhumane and rigid justice, when he liberates the galley slaves' (1951, 142–3), and Américo Castro also believes that in this episode, 'Cervantes happily opposes a spontaneous, simple, equitable justice, that is, one that is mystically natural, to the legal justice of statutes; his doctrine is not formed dogmatically in any writing, but the acts he writes presuppose this justice with the greatest eloquence' (1972, 204).[90] I would argue that what the protagonist really does is point out that the king's justice in sending men to the galleys is not always in compliance with the selfsame king's justice, not at all 'mystically natural' but, rather, very clearly and dogmatically spelled out in writing in the legal volumes.

Even under the magnifying glass of specifically prescribed law, there are loopholes that, on the level of the letter of the law if not its spirit, might exonerate the protagonist for having freed the prisoners. The Ordenanzas Reales mandate that he who is charged with accompanying the prisoners and lets them go pays with the same penalty born by the released criminal (Ordenanzas II.14.12), but it is not Don Quixote who is charged with delivering the prisoners. Certain pragmatics of the Catholic Monarchs prohibit joining up with an ecclesiastical judge to free prisoners from those who are delivering them to a jail; strictly by the letter of these laws, Don Quixote's actions are, once again, defensible given that he does not join up with an ecclesiastical judge, nor are the prisoners en route to a jail. By contrast in the *Galatea,* Cervantes describes unnamed priests who help the character Timbrio, who is en route to be hanged for crimes he did not commit; he breaks out of his handcuffs and is helped by the priests who get him to the sanctuary of a church, sacred ground from which he cannot be removed by civil authorities (Cervantes 1999, 277–8). The Fuero Juzgo forbids taking someone from a church to which he has fled, unless he defends himself with arms (Fuero Juzgo XII.3.1), but also forbids that 'any man break into/out of a jail, or deceive the jailor, or that the jailor himself release prisoners,' with the specified penalty: 'in such a case, they will receive the punishment and reprobation that had been that of the prisoners' (Fuero Juzgo VII.4.3).[91] Again, strictly in the letter of the law, a literal 'jail' is not a factor in the galley slave episode, and Don Quixote does not deceive the guards but, rather, attacks them. Of course, there are laws under which Don Quixote's actions would be deemed illegal: those that prohibit interference with transport of prisoners (Novísima Recopilación XII.12.6), or, as cited above, those that prohibit 'breaking a jail' (fracción de cárcel) (Recop. VIII.16.8), although what Don Quixote does in the episode would seem to be best described as the crime of 'mutiny/agitating to riot ... or being the cause for a mutiny' (Recop. VIII.16.5).[92] These last two laws cited are found in sections of the Recopilación that specifically address extradition of criminals from the different kingdoms and Portugal. Don Quixote does seem to be guilty of violating them, but Cervantes gives his protagonist a very just cause.

On the details of transport of prisoners to the galleys, Cervantes alludes to the norms on describing the 'up to twelve' chained men on the road, the precise number mandated by the law on transport of galley slaves:

> with the sentences rendered in an adjudicated manner, or not pending any appeal ... when the number of those for transport as galley slaves has reached twelve condemned persons, from the lower court judges or from the High Court, they should be sent to Toledo passing through Villafranca, Valladolid, and Segovia. (Recop. VIII.24.9)[93]

In some cases, the number is raised to twenty, but twelve is the norm, and the 'about twelve' (hasta doce) by Cervantes acknowledges this detail. In another law, Phillip II complains that some jailors are not bringing the condemned to the galleys because the delinquents themselves lack the funds for transport, and the officials believe the king should make up this fault; since the monies do not arrive, those possible galley slaves 'remain in the jails without punishment, and are then released' (Recop. VIII.24.5).[94] This tells us that Don Quixote is not the only one in his day keeping the condemned from actually getting to the galleys. Further details as to matters of process are alluded to in other sections of the laws on galley slaves, which mandate that persons so condemned who request a copy of the order condemning them to serve be provided with one, so that they cannot be held for longer than they should: 'should they ask for a copy of their sentence ... it should be given to them ... and, having served the mandated sentence time, they are to be released and freed ... and no longer detained against their will' (Recop. VIII.24.3).[95] In *Don Quixote,* the guards of the galley slaves carry with them the papers detailing the sentences of each.

In general terms, beginning in the middle of the sixteenth century, various criminal offences (robbery, ruffianism) had their mandated penalties changed to time in the galleys, and sentences for certain crimes (corporal punishment such as the loss of a foot, or a hand, or perpetual banishment) were also commuted to time in the galleys.[96] Beyond those details, the author's obvious clues to the juridical reading hidden in the galley slave episode are two: first, Cervantes changes his protagonist's goal and second, in every sense what Don Quixote does in the episode is offer the galley slaves an appeal of their cases which, as noted above, is specifically called for in the law dealing with their transport, 'with no appeal pending' (Recop. VIII.24.3).[97] Three narrative layers are involved: the narrator informs the reader that Cide Hamete tells us that Don Quixote sees 'about twelve' chained men on the road, without recognizing them as prisoners. Sancho explains: 'This is a chain of galley slaves, persons forced by the king, going to the galleys' and Don Quixote asks incredulously: 'What do you mean persons forced? ... How is it possible that the king makes force against any person?' (DQ I.22).[98] The two keep playing with the phrase 'by force' and Don Quixote clarifies 'not of their will,' and then proclaims: 'herein lies the realization of the duties of my profession: to unmake forcings' (DQ I.22).[99] Don Quixote's 'and not of their will' might be read as a general statement, but can just as well be related to the law cited above, on galley slaves being held 'against their will' for longer than their sentence mandates (Recop. VIII.24.3). The more relevant and precise clue to Cervantes' legal gloss in this episode is his wording change on the protagonist's general goal.

I have literally translated the phrase 'make force' and 'unmake forcings' in the above, as they are key points in the era's legal wordings of laws on force. Don Quixote's statement on his mission to 'unmake forcings' (desfacer fuerzas) is a clear change from his standard 'to unmake torts' (desfacer tuertos), the phrase used both earlier and later in the novel. This one episode is the only one in which Cervantes changes the wording, which with a cursory reading would seem to be nothing more than a synonymous phrasing, a conflation by Don Quixote of forcings and torts, or legal wrongs. For the first and last time in the novel, Cervantes replaces 'to unmake torts' (desfacer tuertos) with 'to unmake forcings' (desfacer fuerzas), and modern editions gloss the syntagm 'to make force' with 'to attack or to harm someone.' This use is documented in the era and in the laws, to wit, in a section in the Recopilación that speaks to 'Forcings that men make one against another' (Recop. IV.13, VI.3, VIII.12),[100] but there was also another specific use for the phrase, directly related to justice, to ecclesiastical courts, and to appeals.

The 1567 Recopilación contains six laws with which Charles V and his mother Juana 'the mad' (la loca) had attempted to normalize a legal procedure called 'way of force' (vía de fuerza). The focus is strictly ecclesiastical lawsuits. The first law prohibits that the Chancillería de Valladolid hear cases appealed from such earlier suits if they proceed from Galicia (Recop. II.5.35). The second law seems to contradict the first, as it permits that the same High Court hear such cases although no specific mention is made of Galicia. That second law reads:

> In such cases, due to both law and immemorial custom it is our [royal] duty to lift the forcings that the ecclesiastical judges and other persons make in the cases they hear, when they do not allow appeals that are legitimately filed: for this we order the presidents and judges of our High Courts at Valladolid and Granada that, when someone comes before them with a complaint that a justly filed appeal has not been heard by an ecclesiastical judge, they will give our letters conceding such appeal in the accustomed form for our councils, granting the appeal ... so to unmake [literally, lift] the forcing. (Recop. II.5.36)[101]

Don Quixote is right: the king does not 'make force' against any of his subjects – to the contrary, his role since time immemorial is to lift the force imposed unjustly by another – and he does so by granting a properly filed appeal that has been denied by an ecclesiastical court. Cervantes signals the legal gloss with his protagonist's surprise that the king might 'make force' against anyone, and with the change in Don Quixote's goal, from his standard 'to unmake torts' (desfacer tuertos) to this only, and noteworthy, instance of 'to unmake forcings' (desfacer fuerzas).

For centuries, Spanish legal volumes used 'tort' (tuerto) for an injustice or the harm done by one person to another.[102] It is the word used in the books of chivalry: 'my lady might be avenged of the tort [insult] received' (*Palmerín de Oliva* 1996).[103] *Autoridades* confirms that this past participle of the verb 'to twist' (torcer), 'used as a noun, means harm, injustice, or injury done to someone,' and among the multiple acceptations of the verb is another related to justice or the lack thereof: 'It is also used to describe judges who incline more towards one party, thereby exhibiting less justice.'[104] The seventh-century Liber iudiciorum which, it is important to remember, was published in a newly glossed Spanish edition in 1600, offers two legal usages: 'tuerto' is the harm or injustice done (Fernández Llera 1929, 278), or it is a failure to fairly judge: 'The judge who judges 'tuerto' whether because he has been asked to, or due to ignorance' (Fuero Juzgo II.1.19).[105] Covarrubias says that the word is much used in old writings, and points particularly to the Siete Partidas.[106] Today, Spanish uses 'entuerto' with a meaning of 'tort' or 'harm' and 'tuerto' for 'the person or animal lacking an eye or blind in one eye' (Moliner 1997).[107] On the basis of the documentation in CORDE, the change in usage took place during the second half of the sixteenth century, when we read jokes such as the following: 'Be witnesses for me that this mister judge is suspicious and I fear that he will sentence me "twisted" (tuerto) as he looks at me with an evil eye' (Santa Cruz de Dueñas 1997).[108] Here, the acceptation that will take prominence in future, one who is blinded in one eye, is ironically combined with the former meaning of the judge who judges in a twisted (tuerto) manner. Throughout *Don Quixote,* Cervantes uses the phrase 'to unmake torts' (desfacer tuertos) as his protagonist's goal meaning to undo harms, legal insults, or injuries, although he also uses it for ironic wordplay in another episode, when the protagonist runs into twenty religious men on the road at night dressed in nightshirts. Don Quixote assaults the group and the majority flee but one remains, injured. The protagonist explains his goal of 'unmaking torts' and the injured man responds with a play on words that includes various double-entendres: 'of right … it will not be right' and 'in righting wrongs [tuertos] you have rightly wronged [twisted/vuelto tuerto] me, followed by three 'the aggrieving that you have undone has been to leave me aggrieved in such a way that I will remain forever aggrieved' (DQ I.19).[109] Cervantes highlights and emphasizes the polysemic quality of the word that, in the chapter on the galley slaves, will also be used in its acceptation of 'twisted judging' when the knight refers to the 'twisted judgment of the judge' (DQ I.22).[110]

As to the word 'force' or 'forcings,' the juridical processual usage in the galley slaves chapter is unique in the novel. In preceding and subsequent episodes, the characters have the necessary *force* to do something, feel their physical *force,* exhibit *force* of arms, *force* in rowing, and *force* at the rudder of a boat (DQ I.41). They even 'make *force*' against each other for one reason or another (DQ I.33) and, in certain instances, we read of someone rendering their will due to the *force* of love (DQ I.14, I.28). When Don Luis does not wish to return to his father's house, if those who come for him intend to *make force* against him, the others in the inn are well-disposed to help (DQ I.44). As governor, Sancho also uses the phrase but only so as to deny a woman who claims to have been violated the decision she hopes for: 'My good woman, if you had demonstrated the same energy and valour you just showed in defending that bag, or even half of it, to defend your body, the *force* of Hercules would not have been enough to *make force* against you' (DQ II.45, emphasis added).[111]

Autoridades does not include 'to make force' as a specific phrase, but for the word 'force' it offers a wide variety of meanings. Following is the one that ties the galley slave episode to a specific legal circumstance, and to the mix of human and divine laws:

> In legal parlance it signifies the wrong that a judge does to a party in hearing their case, or in disallowing an appeal. It is a common usage in those cases brought to the ecclesiastical tribunals, where one later has to remit to the council or chancillery by means of force, to there declare if the ecclesiastic judge made, or did not make, force against the party in hearing and proceeding with the case, or in refusing to grant an appeal. (*Autoridades*)[112]

Covarrubias defines the syntagm 'to make force' with a proverb: 'Where there is force, rights are lost,' and then explains:

> To these forcings are opposed justice and the power of kings, to whom it falls to defend and protect us. There are other forces that the judges themselves make against litigants, when they do not grant their appeals to a higher court, and the cases are then brought by 'way of force,' with which it is declared whether or not they are 'making force.'[113]

In the nineteenth century, legal dictionaries continued to use the phrase in the same sense: 'the harm an ecclesiastical judge does to a party, in hearing a case outside of his jurisdictional authority, in not following the rules of canon and civil law, or in unjustly denying the appeal,' and 'to lift or remove the force is when the Royal Tribunal removes, annuls, or relieves the effects of the violence done by the ecclesiastical judges' (Escriche 1852).[114]

We know that the episode with the galley slaves is a review, or appeal, of the condemned men's cases, and it is full of ironically employed ecclesiastical and civil forensic language that supports the reading of the scene as an ecclesiastical case appealed 'by force.' Sancho explains to Don Quixote that the men have been condemned for their 'crimes' but Don Quixote questions them as to their 'sins,' a word commonly used prior to Cervantes' time for both 'sin' and 'crime' but that, by the end of the sixteenth century, was giving way to 'offence' (delito) or crime in the juridical if not the popular lexicon. The Recopilación offers only two 'sins': the public sin and the nepharious sin.[115] After the fourth galley slave, Don Quixote also switches to 'offence' but then, on freeing them, resorts once more to liturgical language, calling them 'dear brothers' (hermanos carísimos) and saying: 'it seems to me a harsh case to make slaves of those whom God and nature created free' (DQ I.22),[116] a phrasing that omits mention of human law but does include those natural and divine. The knight ends by recapping the evils of the juridical system: 'it might be that the lack of spirit on the part of this one when tortured, the lack of money of this other, the little favour to be curried by another and, finally, the twisted judgment of the judge, might have been the cause for your perdition and for not having received the justice that your side deserved' and then ends with 'let each one go with his own sin: there is a God in heaven' (DQ I.22).[117] One of the guards describes the galley slaves with the liturgical phrase 'unholy [dishonest] persons' (gente non santa) (Cervantes 1998b, I.22, n. 24). The 'very genteel student of Latin' informs Don Quixote that there is no 'devil' capable of resolving the heredity of his multiple erotic adventures and assures the knight that 'if you have anything with which to succour these poor men, God will repay you in heaven, and we will on earth take care to beseech Him for your life and health in our prayers' (DQ I.22).[118] We hear from Don Quixote that 'one of the sins most offensive to God is ingratitude,' and Ginés asks that the imposed punishment of visiting Dulcinea be changed for 'some amount of Hail Marys and Creeds,' adding a commentary about 'the fountains of Egypt' that Sabor de Cortazar and Lerner note as an ironic twist on the proverbial biblical expression about the fountains of plenitude and of servitude (DQ I.22, and n. 38).[119]

In short, in the episode of the galley slaves there is no schism of divine and human matters but, rather, an ingenious combination of the two so as to comment on unjust procedures and doubtful laws. Tomás y Valiente details the particular manoeuvres outlined by Castillo de Bobadilla as the practical jurist plays one Partidas law off against another to allow for denying an appeal on the basis of no more than the personal decision of a judge (1975, 219–24). Don Quixote's role with the galley slaves is that of a king properly unmaking the force improperly imposed by an ecclesiastical court, or by just such a renegade magistrate. With his pseudo-juridical gloss, Cervantes anticipates Phillip III who, in 1611, will recognize the same problem of presumptive execution of sentences pending appeal:

> we have been informed that there have been certain inconveniences in granting freedom to those forced persons condemned to the galleys in our kingdoms due to different crimes and causes … many times it occurs that some are sent to the galleys with just the first sentence, without waiting for the review of their case. We hereby order that no one be sent to the galleys, or to the jails where they are normally conducted and held for this sentence, until they are condemned after appeal, and the sentence is upheld. (Recop. VIII.24.11)[120]

Even those forced by the king and courts deserve a just proceeding, including the proper review or appeal. Cervantes has used throughout the novel a goal for his protagonist that had an earlier meaning of 'undoing an injustice' (desfacer tuertos). Here in the episode of the galley slaves, the author decides to highlight the ecclesiastical-civil court split, placing his protagonist in the role of final arbiter, to unmake the unjust forcings of, specifically, ecclesiastical judges. The Partidas speak to how a knight should render justice: 'And justice, they [the knights] should render it directly' (Partidas II.21.4).[121] In the episode of the galley slaves, Don Quixote follows the mandate, by taking on the king's role and 'unmaking' the 'forcings.'

When it comes down to it, every reader of Don Quixote – sympathetic or not to the protagonist – recognizes that the sub rosa review of the galley slaves by Don Quixote is contrary to a juridical spirit that could not allow such interference in the transport of prisoners. Cervantes addresses this concern in a later chapter, again in a juridical-ecclesiastical manner. The galley slaves episode has its coda and final commentary in chapter 46, when the priest – an ecclesiastical person if not a judge, convinces the Hermandad with their arrest warrant to let Don Quixote go free on the basis of another loophole in the law: 'they had to release him due to insanity' (DQ I.46).[122] This petition is also contradictory to the law – as noted by the bounty hunters themselves in their response to the priest: they tell him that any judgment as to the protagonist's insanity is not theirs to make but, rather and properly, that of a court. Nonetheless, they accept the priest's counsel, and opt to not arrest Don Quixote. Cervantes gives the final word in the episode of the galley slaves to an ecclesiastical character who subverts the proper functioning of the legal system.

Legal Insanity

Spain's early legal codes on insanity add another layer of interpretation for the wordplay in Cervantes' description of himself as stepfather, rather than father, of Don Quixote (DQ I, Prologue). The *fueros* of Zorita de los Canes, of Plasencia, and of Teruel all disallow that a father might 'un-child himself' (desfijarse) from his insane offspring.[123] The meaning is not 'to disinherit' but, rather, 'to deny legal responsibility' for damages caused by a mad child. Similarly, although without use of the word 'desfijarse,' the Siete Partidas allow one 'to disinherit' a child but insist that a father is always responsable for damages caused by his mad offspring. We can read Cervantes' playful distancing of himself as 'stepfather' to the mad knight as an effort to deny legal responsibility for his mad protagonist's acts and/or words. Apart from that minor detail, the subject of insanity is addressed in a number of other legal volumes and codes, from various perspectives that offer further clues to Cervantes' literary and literal thematic gloss on 'madness' (locura).

Scholars have offered various interpretations of the knight's madness, and of Cervantes' use of the theme. For Olmeda, Don Quixote's insanity can only be read as a cover for Cervantes' social criticism, so as to allow him to clearly and plainly speak the unvarnished truth (1973, 243). Diego Martínez Torrón also sees the protagonist's insanity as a literary device to avoid censorship (1998, 34). Javier Rodríguez Pequeño attributes the change in Cervantes' representation of Don Quixote's madness, from 1605 to 1615, to the author's reaction to Avellaneda's apocryphal *Quixote* with its inept and obviously mad protagonist (2006, 515). Margit Frenk (2010) has suggested that Cervantes' interest is to leave the question open, even in the closing chapters of the 1615 *Quixote.* As a narrative strategy, Cervantes does exploit the imprecise nature of insanity and he does so, in part, by exploring his age's civil and ecclesiastical statutes and determinations on madness.

Right from the start, the narrator tells us that, having read so many books of chivalry, this 'gentleman' is 'irremediably out of his mind,' and that he has come to the strangest decision 'that any madman had ever come to' (DQ I.1).[124] This confident summary judgment will be reinforced at times: the innkeeper tells the muleteers that, no matter the charge, Don Quixote 'will be let go because he is mad' (DQ I.3); Vivaldo and his companions listen to a little of what Don Quixote has to say and 'take him for mad' (DQ I.13).[125] However, the same judgment is alternatively questioned by other voices that tell us the knight shows both 'insanity and ingeniousness' (locura e ingenio) (DQ I.44), and that he is both 'discrete … and foolish' (discrete … [y] mentecato) (DQ II.59). Most if not all of the other characters in *Don Quixote* offer their opinions on the protagonist's madness, and Cervantes lets the reader know that there is constant doubt as to whether or not the knight should be considered sane or deranged.

These doubts reflect general legal ideas on madness in Cervantes' day. The early *fueros* accept a regular vacillation between states of sanity and insanity. In the Fuero Real we read: 'If any absent-minded madman brings a legal case, while his insanity lasts, the case is not recognized. However, if he later recovers his sanity and sense, the case that he brought in that time is recognized, even if [although] he later goes mad again' (Fuero Real VI).[126] In the second half of the sixteenth century, Gaspar de Baeza will accept the same vacilation in mental state in his tractate on debt and debtors. Baeza analyses the case of one who is of 'sound mind' (mente sana) and commits a crime but then goes mad, a state that will absolve the debtor of not only the criminal penalties, but also repayment of the debt: 'the *furor* excuses the *furioso* from the deserved penalty for his crime and also from the penalty and service owed: given this, the debt is not satisfied' (Baeza 1570, 9.6, fol.75v).[127] Baeza specifies 'furor' and 'furioso,' and adds that this decision stands only so long as the insanity lasts: '*Furioso* is an absolute juridical finding: but if the person returns to a sane mind, the creditors can petition that he repay the debt' (Baeza 1570, 9.9, fols 74v–5r).[128] For the jurist, even a definitive finding of insane is merely the recognition of a temporary state, or an accident. In *Don Quixote,* Cervantes paints momentary lapses in judgment for his protagonist while simultaneously questioning any definitive finding.

In the 1615 *Quixote,* Sancho Panza exemplifies the vacilations in judgment: as he debates whether or not to go to Tobosa in his ironic Hamlet-like soliloquy outside the forest, Sancho calls Don Quixote 'the kind of madman who should be tied up' (DQ II.10); shortly after, the squire defends the knight: 'he is not mad … but daring' (DQ II.17); then again, he opines that Don Quixote is 'out of his mind and mad on all counts' (DQ II.23).[129] Darío Fernández-Morera tells us that the Gentleman in the Green Coat, AKA Don Diego, clearly judges the protagonist mad, but a late sixteenth-century court would reject this critical assessment, as Don Diego himself expresses doubt; finding Don Quixote 'a sane madman and a madman who acts sane … he took him for sane at moments but then at others, for mad' (DQ II.17).[130] Although Don Diego does not speak aloud, Don Quixote notes the moment and offers: 'I want your grace to take notice that I am neither as mad, nor as foolish as I might have seemed to you' (DQ II.17).[131] Don Diego asks his son Don Lorenzo for his opinion and the responses are various: 'So far … I cannot judge you [Don Quixote] mad'; 'he is a strange madman'; 'he is off and on mad, with many lucid intervals' (DQ II.18).[132] The doubts expressed by other characters in the novel as well as the 'lucid intervals' prohibit a definitive finding on the protagonist's madness. As we saw in the legal citations, during moments of sanity even the 'furioso' is considered liable for his actions.

In a general sense, the early juridical volumes classify the insane with the infant, the deaf, and the mute: all are seen under the law as those who do not have sufficient control over logical language.[133] However, Gaspar de Baeza distinguishes among them, saying that as far as debt is concerned, the deaf and the mute are to be held liable but the insane, though juridically classified with the others, cannot be held to the same for the duration of their state, or 'accident' of insanity. For Cervantes, too, insanity is an 'accident,' a 'state,' or a 'humour' and, as is evident throughout the novel, the protagonist has a fine command over logical language. All those who doubt his mental state simultaneously praise his rhetorical skills. In both parts (1605 and 1615), concomitant with the multiple references to the knight's insanity, we hear that he 'speaks with beautiful clarity and reason … a fine understanding in everything … as long as no one mentions chivalry' (DQ I.30); 'Don Quixote was expressing himself so well, and in such fine words, that none of those who were listening could consider him mad' (DQ I.37); 'in all that he commented on and responded to he showed such a fine understanding' (DQ I.49).[134] In the fourth part of the 1605 novel, various characters doubt the knight's insanity, as he speaks so convincingly on war and peace that 'none of those who heard him thought he was crazy' (DQ I.37).[135] These and further indications of the knight's sanity keep the topic open and debatable. Throughout the novel, the narrative voice and other characters question the 'type of madness' (género de locura) and the 'strange madness' (estraña locura) evidenced in Don Quixote's acts. The knight's verbal prowess, however, always gives pause and introduces doubt in the minds of those other characters. This point has a clear basis in the legal particulars; Cervantes has his protagonist speak as a juridically adjudged madman would not.

Cervantes' preferred lexical description of his protagonist's state of mind is not the juridically condemning 'furious' or 'insane' but, rather, the maddeningly obtuse 'loco' (nuts, crazy, mad). The Peninsula's early *fueros* show a variety of uses for the word 'loco.' In 1611, Covarrubias complained that trying to disentangle the etymology of this word 'would make any sane man mad,'[136] as the gaps in explicable usage switch-over were impossible to fill. Nor have I found any particular moment to fill in that etymological gap, but the early legal codes of the Peninsula do show the move from *locus-lugar* (place) to *loco-insane,* with some volumes offering both uses. This is the case, for example, in the Fuero de Madrid, which dates to 1141–1235, and finds against 'any man who pulls the beard of, or who wounds, another man in a tavern or in a plaza or on a road or in any other place (loco)' (Fuero de Madrid, IV, p. 44) in one section, but then also stipulates: 'He who pulls the beard of, or wounds a man who is mute or deaf or mad (loco) and out of his senses, does not pay the legal penalty' (Fuero de Madrid, XLVII, p. 55).[137] Both usages seem to be commonplace already by the given date for the Fuero de Madrid. In the late sixteenth century, the official juridical finding would have been 'loco' (mad) in Castilian legal volumes but 'furious' (furioso) in Latin. The earliest volume I have found to offer both terms as synonyms for a legal finding is Alonso de Villadiego's 1612 *Instrucción política,* which reads: 'and the same applies to the *furioso* or *loco* who cannot be castigated for a crime to which they confessed while the madness was on them, but only if it were committed during a sane interlude' (Villadiego 1612, fol. 57v).[138] Obviously, this volume postdates the First Part of the *Quixote* and precedes the Second Part.

In the Prologue of the 1615 *Quixote,* Cervantes uses the word 'mad' (loco) eighteen times within fours paragraphs of text, telling the stories of two madmen who mistreat dogs, and then one wealthy madman who complains that his relatives had him condemned as insane so as to take his money. Don Quixote asks Sancho what is being said of the two of them, and the response is: 'the common opinion finds your grace really mad and considers me no less a fool,' but then adds: 'as to your valour, courteousness, deeds, and affairs ... some say mad but funny, and others valiant but unlucky' (DQ II.2).[139] Sansón Carrasco's squire Tomé sees the former bested by Don Quixote, tells him he deserved it, and points out: 'Don Quixote is mad, but we are sane; yet he goes off healthy and laughing, while your grace lies here beaten and sad. Let's see, then, who is more mad: he who is so for not being able to help it, or he who is so by his own will?' (DQ II.15).[140] Various phrases are used in these commentaries: Don Quixote is 'out of his mind' (I.29); 'broken and out of his mind' (DQ I.32); he is 'mad' (loco) and performs 'mad acts' (locuras).[141] In *Autoridades,* 'mad' (loco) is 'he who has lost his judgment, lacks reason, and does and says foolish things,' or 'someone with little judgment, unsettled, absurd, imprudent.'[142]

Gaspar de Baeza begins his chapter on insanity as a legal exemption from debt by stating that 'it cannot be denied that *furor* is an illness of body and soul' and then specifying three words used for the legal status: *furiosus, insanus,* and *male sanus.* The jurist calls only the first an 'absolute juridical finding' (Baeza 1570, 9.1, fol. 75r).[143] Classical juridical writings tell us that 'the *furious* can never conduct business' (Paulus), 'the *furious* is prohibited from managing his own properties, because he lacks will' (Pomponius), and 'the *furious,* even if physically present during an event, is considered as if he were absent, because he lacks any juridically relevant will' (Paulus, cited by García Sánchez and García Fueyo 2007, 79, and notes 161–2).[144] Cervantes commonly uses 'loco' to describe his protagonist, but he also has Don Quixote consider and specifically reject the idea of becoming *furious.* The scene is presaged in two of the preliminary poetic works of the 1605 *Quixote.* In his dedicatory sonnet, Amadís de Gaula says to Don Quixote:

> You, who imitated the tearful life
> that was mine, alone and scorned on
> the grand slopes of Peña Pobre,
> reduced from happy to penitent,
> you, whose eyes offered a drink
> of liquid, although salted, in abundance,
> and lifting its own silver, tin and copper
> earth gave you herself as sustenance, (DQ I, p. 18, vv. 1–8)[145]

The emphasis in these verses is on tears and crying, that is, the melancholic madness, distinguished in both legal and medical treatises of the era.[146] In another preliminary sonnet, Orlando the *furious* says to the protagonist:

> I cannot be your equal; for this deference
> is owed to your feats and your fame,
> although you, as I, did lose your mind. (DQ I, p. 22, vv. 9–11)[147]

Neither of the two accuse Don Quixote of being *furious,* that definitive juridical finding.

In the Sierra Morena, the protagonist first tells Sancho that he will imitate both of these heroes: 'I want to imitate Amadis, by being desperate and silly, and also furious by imitating simultaneously the valiant Don Orlando' (DQ I.25).[148] Orlando is the furious madman and Amadís, the melancholic. Don Quixote tells Sancho how Orlando uprooted trees and killed people, and then compares him to Amadís, who was also 'mad' (loco) but 'without performing damaging mad acts, rather only weepings and grievings' (DQ I.25).[149] Once alone in the Sierra Morena, Don Quixote again debates which of the two figures he should imitate: 'Orlando in his madnesses contrary to the *fueros* (desaforadas), or Amadis in his melancholy' (DQ I.26).[150] Here, Cervantes employs the particular legal term 'desaforadas,' literally, 'contrary to the *fueros,*' or law books. Don Quixote decides not to commit 'a manifest grievance' – again, a specific legal term – against Dulcinea by going 'mad with Orlando's type of furious madness' (DQ I.26).[151] He decides to imitate only Amadís, rejecting the status and acts of a furious madman. The scene ends with the narrative voice speaking of the 'strange madness' (estraña locura) of the knight, apparently leaving the question to be resolved by the reader, but with those clear signals of legal liability: this madman is strange, but not furious and, as we see in the same scene, Don Quixote manages his financial affairs – the promise of the donkeys to Sancho – and he exercises his will in, literally, deciding not to be a contrary-to-the-*fueros* furious madman. These acts would negate a definitive juridical finding of insane.

In the same scene, we also have commentary on another of Baeza's legal exemptions, regarding someone who deliberately goes mad. On self-induced insanity, Baeza says: 'But now, one who takes it on himself to become furious (for example, by ingesting a strong medicine) so as to not repay his creditors … this debt is considered a crime' (Baeza 1570, 9. summa.7, fol. 74v).[152] Don Quixote pointedly decides to go mad in the Sierra Morena. Sancho Panza questions the validity of the act: 'the knights who did those things were provoked and had cause to do those foolish things and penances; but your grace, what cause is there for you to go mad?' (DQ I.25), but Don Quixote insists: 'That is the point … and that is the beauty of my plan; for a knight errant to go mad with cause is neither notable nor worthy; the thing is to lose one's mind without reason … just to do it' (DQ I.25).[153] The knight insists: 'I am mad, and will be mad until' you, Sancho, return with a reply from Dulcinea, which Don Quixote hopes to be such that 'my foolishness will end' but, 'if it is other, I will really go mad' (DQ I.25).[154] The narrative voice describes the knight here 'as if he had lost his mind' (DQ I.25),[155] again seeding doubt as to his actual status.

In accordance with Baeza's exemptions, for having purposefully gone mad, he cannot be adjudged mad.

The points raised and contested by Baeza in his legal gloss on exclusions for the insane include a number of those also debated by Cervantes' characters, such as whether the commission of a crime can only be adjudged the act of a sane mind;[156]or whether insanity that prefigures or postdates a criminal act exempts debts incurred by that act.[157] Baeza also analyses in detail the case of an amorous passion leading to insanity. On this last point, Cervantes specifically distinguishes Don Quixote from Cardenio, who is described as having suffered a 'momentary madness' (accidente de locura) but who, once cured, is 'in his right mind, free of that furious accident' (DQ I.27).[158] Cardenio does cause physical harm to the shepherds and his type of love-induced insanity, with all its legal exemptions, is dealt with at length by Baeza. The jurist reviews earlier opinions, including Oldraldus, who had excused a debtor whose debt was due to the 'demoniacal arts' (demoniacas artes) of a woman, and Aristotle, who had asked if love itself was a type of insanity and questioned if the furious lover should be punished or pardoned (Baeza 1570, 9.12, fol. 77r). Baeza cites Virgil, Plato, and Cicero, among others, on one who is furious for love, and points out that 'the effect of Venus is more than vehement' (Baeza 1570, 9.13, fol. 77v).[159] In this last, Baeza's Latin can be read literally as 'one very much without his mind': Moliner offers the etymology of 'vehemente,' with the privative prefix 've' followed by 'mind' (mente), and Baeza emphasizes with the suffix 'very much' (issimus). However, the jurist follows that statement by noting that Aristotle also spoke of drunkenness and asserted that a man can choose to not become drunk (Baeza 1570, 9.13, fol. 77v).[160] Baeza concludes that, in general, all insanity should be doubted and questioned,[161] much as Cervantes does in *Don Quixote* by putting the legal arguments into play through his characters' actions and words.

In classical juridical texts, the only mention of insanity is referenced in the need to deny the insane control over financial matters, as we read in the first chapter of the 1615 *Quixote,* with the anecdote of an insane man in the Seville madhouse who claims that his relatives have put him there for their own greedy motives. In Don Quixote's case, it is worthy of note that despite his tendency to sell off his inheritance so as to purchase more books of knight errantry, no one in the novel ever attempts to deny him control over his property and finances. Additionally, the knight's debts are always paid, although not always by him, at least in the 1605 *Quixote:* Don Quixote's refusal to pay for a night's stay in the inn means that Sancho is obligated to be tossed in a blanket, paying the debt, as he says, 'at the expense of his customary creditors ... his back' (DQ I.17).[162] Toward the end of the 1605 *Quixote,* the priest and Don Fernando pay further debts related to Don Quixote's adventures in the First Part of the novel (DQ I.46). We can relate their generosity, as well as that of the shepherds with Cardenio, to one of Gaspar de Baeza's precepts: 'while a temporary insanity is in effect, Christians should show mercy and compassion by offering alms to their brothers' (Baeza 1570, 9.11, fol. 77r).[163] In the 1615 *Quixote,* the knight himself arranges payment for all damages caused to Ginés de Pasamonte for the destruction of his puppets (DQ II.26), and to the fishermen for the destruction of one of their boats (DQ II.29), while Sancho Panza acts as his banker, carrying and providing the funds. In late sixteenth- and early seventeenth-century Spain, these would not have been the acts of one legally adjudged insane.

At the end of the novel, Don Quixote declares 'I was mad, and now I am sane' and 'I have my wits again, free and clear, without the caliginous shadows of ignorance' (DQ II.74).[164] Critical commentary has accepted that Cervantes wished his knight to die so as to prevent another apocryphal volume, such as that of Avellaneda in 1614. However, from a literary standpoint, the force of the protagonist's rejection of his knightly profession comes as a shock to the reader, who for something on the order of 1000 pages, has happily shared in the character's dreams. I believe that, as he penned those pages, Cervantes had further specific legal arguments in mind, both civil and ecclesiastic.

Without return to a sane state of mind, Don Quixote's final will and testament, in which he rectifies his debts with Sancho Panza and others, would not have been recognized by either civil or canon law. Also, as per Phillip II's Recopilación, any Christian who failed to confess before dying lost half of his goods to the state (Recop. I.1.5). To confess, one had to adhere to the canons of the Council of Trent, which spoke at length about the sacraments (Redondo 2006). Particularly, there was much debate on the question of penance, including whether it should be accorded to an infant, that is, to the legal category of persons that also included the insane. The question was not resolved by the Council but, in *Don Quixote,* Cervantes covers all contingencies.

Responding to the Reformers, the Council of Trent condemned as anathema anyone who dared to assert that faith alone was sufficient to receive the Eucharist, and insisted on a confessor and penance, with the latter to take place prior to granting of the Eucharist and Extreme Unction. In order to receive penance, the Council mandated will and desire, two qualities lacking in the insane, as we also read in Baeza's exemptions: 'And so it is a matter of insufficiency, because the law mandates will: if the mind is lacking, as a consequence, disposition is also lacking' (Baeza 1570, 9.1, fol. 75r).[165] The madman cannot commit a crime, nor be penitent and confess, both of which must be free and voluntary. The Siete Partidas also deny Extreme Unction to a 'madman' (loco) unless 'he might recover his senses after having lost them, and demand it [the sacrament]' (Partidas I.4.71).[166]

Cervantes' protagonist has to recover his senses before receiving, as his author tells us, 'all the sacraments' (todos los sacramentos) (DQ II.74).

The Council of Trent also mandated that the penitent feel 'hate' (odio) for his previous sins, and this we hear clearly in Don Quixote's voice: 'I am an enemy of Amadís of Gaul and of all that gang of his; all the profane histories of knight errantry are now hateful to me ... I abhor them' (DQ II.74).[167] For confession, the Council mandated that the penitent enumerate one by one their mortal sins, although it did accept that this might be done in secret. We do not know exactly what takes place between the priest and Don Quixote during the latter's confession, given that it is done 'in secret' (en secreto), but we can be sure that the knight would have at least had to be forgiven his sin of 'having put his hands on a sacred thing' (DQ I.19)[168] in the 1605 *Quixote,* an act for which he had been excommunicated by the religious bachelor. As de Armas has noted, the words 'refer to a decree from the Council of Trent' (2006, 91), that had used the word 'thing.' The Council had also forbidden that a 'serious and manifest' sinner receive the Eucharist, specifically anyone who had been excommunicated. Cervantes allows his knight to die only 'after having received all the sacraments, and after having expressed, in many and no uncertain terms, loathing for the books of chivalry' (DQ II.74),[169] with a scribe as witness to the very 'Christian' manner in which Don Quixote died. Cervantes' literary treatment of insanity is clearly of a piece with his era's legal norms and precepts. It is to be questioned at every turn, it is not a permanent state, and it is nearly impossible to adjudge with certainty. As to the much-debated question of an insane man being knighted, the Partidas do state that a 'madman' (loco) cannot be a knight (Partidas II.21.12). But unlike all the other legal compendia, they alone add a condition to the legal exemption, saying that it only applies to 'he who is so mad, that he does not know what he is doing' (Partidas I.1.21), and Don Quijote himself has told us all along that he knows exactly what he is doing, at one moment emphasizing in three verbal tenses: 'everything that I have done, am doing, and might do is very reasonable' (DQ I.25).[170] In his final moments, he declares himself cured of his madness, takes care of business matters, recants his sins, and acts quite reasonably. Legally, we cannot declare him insane. That generations of readers have so determined is testament to Cervantes' masterful exploration of the subtle legal limits and exemptions.

5 Laws Broken, Glossed, and Made: Sancho Panza et al.

Critical commentary on Sancho Panza has ranged from a perception of the character as the standard comical type (gracioso), to his roots in folklore, his surprisingly astute legal decisions as governor, and as comic foil to Don Quixote's quirky gravity.[1]

In what follows, I would like to add Sancho Panza's role as representative of the contemporary populace who, as Sancho says about himself, is formally illiterate and has never read a history but, nonetheless, frequently references the laws and their penalties; for example: 'I know the Holy Brotherhood deals with those who fight in the countryside' (DQ I.10).[2] Spain's laws specified that all had to know them (Fuero Juzgo II.1.3), they were proclaimed openly and repeatedly in the public squares, they were published and sold, and there were even special penalties for those who claimed ignorance of the law. Convicted of violating a law of which they claimed to be ignorant, the guilty suffered all the regular penalties 'plus one hundred lashes in public, and for eternal infamy, their head is to be shaved misshapenly' (Fuero Juzgo VI.4.5).[3] One scholar of French medieval literature has said that even 'the rudest medieval audience' (Bloch 1977, 5) would have been aware of the law's proscriptions, and García Gallo notes that some ancient nations wrote their laws in verse so as to make them easy to learn, and to be certain of their communication (García Gallo 1967, 1:288). From the middle of the sixteenth century onward, collections for *escribanos* (amanuensis) offered templates of legal forms along the lines of: 'Let all know that so-and-so, a resident of [fill in town], on such-and-such a date came to such-and-such a place' (Díaz de Valdepeñas 1554), for everything from standard contracts to a husband's letter forgiving his wife and her lover for a cuckolding (Díaz de Valdepeñas 1554, Perdón de cuernos, folio XLII). This group of writings is a fine example of the ubiquitousness of the legal system in everyday life. The plethora of pragmatics issuing from Spanish monarchs in Cervantes' day meant that market days in most towns were also proclamation days, and the published pragmatics and laws all bore signed, notarized statements as to when and where they had been publically proclaimed with the theatrical accompaniment of bells and whistles. It is not at all surprising that Sancho can make astute declarations as to penalties, loopholes, and injustices, and he does so frequently with a comic twist as, for example, his declaration that a wild boar might be a bother but has not committed any crime (DQ II.34).

Omecillos

Spanish legal texts explain a word substitution made by Sancho, and mistakenly glossed by most modern editions of the *Quixote* as a misunderstanding. Sancho responds to Don Quixote's use of 'homicide' (homicidio) with 'omecillo' (DQ I.10), and modern editions gloss this 'misuse' by assuming that Sancho really meant to say 'rancour' (rencor).[4] However, the Fuero Viejo lists 'omecillo,' spelled as Cervantes does with a 'c,' as one of the prohibited words that can only be used as an insult if the person who says it has five witnesses ready to testify as to the act having occurred (Fuero Viejo II.1.9). The Partidas define 'omezillo' with a 'z': 'Homicide is a thing that men do sometimes wrongly [con tuerto], but other times with right [con derecho],' with the etymological roots: 'Homicide in Latin, just as in Romance, means the killing of a man. And from this root was taken "omezillo" as used in the Spanish language' (Partidas VII.8.1).[5] In the first half of the sixteenth century, Juan de Valdés commented on the polysemic nature of this word:

VALDÉS: This seems too much; if I stop on every little thing like this, we will never finish. We have let 'omezillo' come to mean 'rancor'; I would still use this word, but only in the right circumstance, and not in any other way.
MARCIO: Do you think it is an Arabism or Latinism?
VALDÉS: I think it is a corruption, from homicide, omezillo (1999, folio 70)[6]

Valdes' twentieth-century editor, Antonio Quilis, notes the use of 'omezillo' with an explanation of the word's etymology in dictionary uses: 'rancour' (homecillo) in *Autoridades* and 'murder' (homicidium) in Nebrija. *Autoridades* postdates the *Quixote* by a century, and shows the eventual common acceptation for the word while Nebrija, writing one hundred years before Cervantes, offers only the original meaning. In between those two, Valdés offers commentary on the dual acceptations. By the end of the sixteenth century, real-life magistrate Castillo de Bobadilla continued to use only 'omecillo' (1775 [1597], II.21.177, 1:827), citing to the Recopilación (Recop. 4.10.3). Sancho Panza shows enough knowledge of the law to use the term as found in the Fuero Viejo and the Recopilación, and to insist: 'I know nothing of homicides ... nor have I ever seen one in my life' (DQ I.10),[7] removing himself from any possible witness list. In the same chapter, Sancho will advise Don Quixote against illegally imposing a second penalty for a crime that has already been judged: 'Take note, your grace mister Don Quixote, that if this knight has complied with what was ordered, that is, presenting himself to my lady Dulcinea de Toboso, he will have already complied with what he owed, and he does not deserve further penalty unless he commits another crime' (DQ I.10).[8] As Márquez Villanueva has pointed out, Sancho is not just an innocent rustic along the lines of literature's 'fool' character but also, 'as Hendrix saw, a web of contradictions: simple, yet sharp, materialist in one sense, dreamer and un-self-interested in another' (1973, 84). The squire is also an astute wordsmith and, apparently, a foil for a few hidden commentaries on certain very specific laws and linguistic usage. Sancho again echoes Castillo de Bobadilla when he advises Don Diego that Rocinante is harmless, as the horse has been threatened with a penalty 'multiplied by seven' (de setenas) for any attempted disobedience (DQ II.16). Magistrates were liable for charges of abuse of power after their terms in office, with the imposition of seven-fold (de setenas) penalties, and Castillo de Bobadilla notes that he has seen them applied in cases where a magistrate improperly carried out the penalty of 'homicide' (omecillo) (1775 [1597], V.1.233, 2:558).

La ínsula Barataria

As he tries to convince his neighbour Sancho Panza to accompany him on his adventures, Don Quixote tells Sancho of the rewards that come to squires who faithfully serve their knights, including the possibility that the knight could win an 'ínsula' (island-region) in battle, to which he would name Sancho as governor (DQ I.7).[9] Sancho accepts, and Cervantes' narrator then describes the two characters setting out for adventure, with Sancho riding on his mule: 'Sancho rode seated like a patriarch on his mule ... with much desire to see himself already governor of the *ínsula* promised by his master' and reminding Don Quixote: 'Look here, your grace, mister knight errant, do not forget about the *ínsula* you have promised me, which I will know how to govern, no matter how large it might be' (DQ I.7).[10] This promise is a running commentary throughout both parts of the novel until finally, in the 1615 *Quixote,* the duke grants Sancho Panza a governorship over the *ínsula* Barataria.

Cervantes' narrator explains that the name Barataria has two possible interpretations: 'It was given as understood that the place was called "Baratario" and so, the *ínsula* would be called Barataria, or maybe it was so named because of how cheaply Sancho had come by the governorship' (DQ II.45).[11] Of those two reasons, the first offers the masculine-feminine variant of the word, in conformance with standard Spanish usage of an adjective modifying a feminine noun with modification of the final letter, from 'o' to 'a.' The second possibility is wordplay on the adjective 'barato,' which means 'cheap' or, here as an adverb, 'cheaply.' Scholarly studies on the name have turned up a few other connections: the term 'barato' was used for the tip given to the look-outs who protected gaming houses, 'barato' is also related to fraudulent sales locales, and there is a possible real-life identification with Alcalá de Ebro, in Zaragoza (Cervantes 1998b, I.45, n. 9). There is another contemporary legal usage that warrants examination.

In 1612 Alonso de Villadiego Vascuñana y Montoya published *Instrucción política, y práctica iudicial,* a guide to the political and juridical practices of Spain's tribunals, councils, and courts. In his prologue, the author says that his volume is a useful compendium of the works of other erudite thinkers, and explains why he has not written the work in Latin:

> And due to being written in Romance this book has a particular grace and utility, in that those who do not know Latin will not be deprived of these materials which are such common things that it is convenient for all to know them. This does not mean, however, that the science of jurisprudence is lessened or profaned especially given that, among all the vulgar tongues, ours is the most abundant [in words], vigorous, and resonant, as well as the most commonly used in diverse nations of the world. For the most part, royal laws according to which lawsuits and cases are litigated, supported, and adjudged, pass first through common laws which are, as we know, written in our spoken romance tongue, which is as it should be. And so it also seems that the practices and procedures for those laws should also be in the same Castilian tongue. (1612, Prologue, no page numbers)[12]

Villadiego, who had also prepared the newly glossed 1600 edition of the Fuero Juzgo, includes an explanation of 'Barateria,' a term for bribe-taking by judges, taken from the Latin 'Baratarius.' The item reads, in part: 'A judge may not receive any thing intended to make him bring about, or not bring about, justice. This is called barratry, and it carries the same penalty whether the sentence given has neither harmed nor prejudiced anyone, because selling that which should be free (gracioso) is corruption, and barratry' (1612, fol. 117r).[13] Castillo de Bobadilla had used the same language in 1597, while distinguishing 'bribery' (cohecho) from 'barratry' (baratería) and pointing out that the former perverts justice for money while, with the latter, the judge merely receives payment for justice, which should be 'free' (gracioso) (V.1.228, 2:556–7). The intent behind the use of the word 'gracioso' was obviously the selling of something which is supposed to be free, 'gratis,' but the word was also used for 'funny' and for 'beautiful' (*Autoridades*). It is another of those polysemic etymological developments in the move from Latin to Spanish: the same Latin root, *gratia,* will evolve, in Spanish, into 'thank you' (gracias) and 'funny' or 'comical' (gracioso), which was also commonly used as a noun for the comical character type in theatrical works. This last, of course, is a use directly related to Cervantes' presentation of Sancho Panza throughout the novel. Cervantes has his *gracioso* Sancho Panza go off to govern an *ínsula* named for an illicit judicial practice, *Baratarius,* described in this official legal tome as 'the selling of something which should be free / funny.' The irony is rich, and the joke seems to be very much an inside one, which again attests to Cervantes' intimate knowledge of legal affairs although, as Villadiego states, it is quite useful for all to know these things and as we have already seen with 'omecillo,' even the non-readers in the society did know the laws.

Spain was rife with legal writings, concerns, and actions, and from the middle of the sixteenth century jurists began to switch to Castilian and write for a more general public. Spanish laws had been written, proclaimed, and published in the vernacular for a few centuries, but jurists like Baeza who glossed those laws continued to do so in Latin. The new group of 'practical' jurists writing in the vernacular frequently faced diffulties in getting their works published (Tomás y Valiente 1975, 180). In 1595 Castillo de Bobadilla's request for a licence to publish his *Política para corregidores* was denied on the basis of its having been written in the vernacular; it was suggested that he rewrite the work in Latin (Tomás y Valiente 1975, 180–3). The jurist appealed to the courts, the licence was eventually granted, and his treatise, still in the vernacular, was published in 1597. The *Política para corregidores* was a popular work, and subsequent editions were published in 1608, 1616, 1624, 1649, 1704, 1750, 1759, and 1775 (Tomás y Valiente 1975, 186). Later practical juridical volumes in the vernacular would follow, in 1612 (Bermúdez de Pedraza, Villadiego) and in 1613 (Pradilla Barnuevo). Some of Cervantes' work faithfully reproduces and echoes, at least in part, those volumes. The 1612 *Arte legal para estudiar la jurisprudencia* by Bermúdez de Pedraza begins with a chapter titled 'On the obligation of parents [fathers] to teach their sons the science to which they most incline,' and includes advice on teaching them well 'from the first years on, so that they are directed down the straight path towards virtue' (1992 [1612], 6, 8).[14] Cervantes' readers will remember Don Quixote's advice to Don Diego, regarding his son Don Lorenzo's studies: 'from the first years on, in the direction of virtue … I would think that they [the parents] should let him [their son] pursue the science to which he is most inclined' (DQ II.16).[15] Bermúdez de Pedraza expands on the topic to point out to his public of legal students that torturing a son in the presence of his father is sure to get information quickly, while Cervantes will segue from the same topic of fathers and sons into praise of poetry. The juridical volumes attest to popular interest in the thematic and practical aspects of jurisprudence, and their authors, for the most part, seek stability in solid, prescriptive formulae. In certain cases, Cervantes puts that same status quo to a test with mordant between-the-lines commentary on both the legal and practical processual tomes, to reflect the same unstable situation but project it into a new and different realm: fictional realist writing. Barataria, for example, is an invented place named for a real practice.

In his *Instrucción política, y práctica iudicial,* Villadiego insists that there is nothing worse than selling justice, and that any judge who has received something is obliged to return it, with one exception: 'unless the judge is not receiving a public salary' (1612, fols 117r–18v).[16] The rules dictate that all legal cases must be dispatched in the order filed, with special attention to those of the poor or foreigners, and they specify that any judge who accepts, whether 'tacitly or expressly' a promise of recompense is guilty of 'baratería' unless he returns the gift, in which case the sentence is excused (1612, fols 117r–18v). The instructions then refer the reader to the Partidas and the Recopilación, among other juridical references. Castillo de Bobadilla's distinction between 'bribe-taking' (cohecho) and 'barratry' (baratería) would seem designed to further protect a magistrate from the charge. This practical jurist states that Doctors in Law use the two terms as synonyms, but he believes they should be distinguished in that 'bribery' implies a corruption of justice for monetary gain, while 'barratry' is to gain from the position without corrupting justice itself (1775 [1597], V.1.228, 2:556). This very subtle distinction infers the need to prove intent on accepting monies, and intent is a notoriously difficult thing to prove. Castillo de Bobadilla, who frequently counsels hearings in secret (1775 [1597], II.5.60, 1:325), adds a layer of protection for the magistrates but apparently, by 1612 other practical jurists were not following suit. Villadiego calls barratry corruption.

The verb for this illicit judicial activity is 'baratar' and in the 1567 Recopilación it appears under the general heading of 'payments' where it is part of a triplet of suspicious activities: *barato, trato,* and *contrato,* all referring to bribe-taking by accountants, treasurers, and tax collectors (Recop. IX.16.17).[17] A second item includes the term under 'residences' (residencias), in the law directed to legal magistrates such as Castillo de Bobadilla, governors (like Sancho Panza), and their assistants (Recop. III.7.17).[18] A third listing, under 'mayors' (alcaldes) prohibits this last group from fraudulent sales of state property (Recop. VI.5.5).[19] Given Sancho's duties and judicial decisions while he is governor of Barataria, Cervantes' use of the word is richly resonant.

Two other legal uses might also be in play in the naming. Contemporary with Cervantes, English usage of the term 'barratry' adds another lexical dimension. Today's law dictionaries define the crime of barratry as 'vexatious incitement to litigation, especially by soliciting potential legal clients,' and note that those lawsuits are 'typically groundless' (Black's 2004). Oxford offers uses dating as far back as 1427, and notes that the Provençal term is 'Barataria,' exactly as Cervantes names Sancho's *ínsula. West's Encyclopedia of American Law* (2005) notes that barratry 'has today, due to our own highly litigious atmosphere, for the most part ceased to be charged and is considered an "archaic crime."' As Kagan (1981) has noted, Cervantes' contemporaries were equally, if not more, litigious, and Sancho's court in Barataria hears multiple cases, some of which he finds groundless.

Another use of the term, noted in the 1550 edition of the Partidas, is also noteworthy, as it clarifies a reference found in Spain's epic poem, the *Cantar de mío Cid*:

> Baratarians and cheaters are those men who want to pretend to another that they have something, and so they touch on a closed sack, bag, or chest that is full of sand, or rocks, or some such thing, and pretend that it is gold or silver coins, and then leave the sack or bag under guard in the office of a church sacristan, or in the house of an honourable man, pretending it to be a treasure, and borrowing against it. (Partidas VII.16.9)[20]

The ruse is one used by Spain's national hero, the Cid, when he borrows from the two Jews Rachel and Vidas, against a chest full of sand. The Cid never repays the loan. This use is that offered by *Autoridades:* 'fraud or cheating in sales or trades,'[21] which identifies the 1567 Recopilación de leyes as the first usage, although the referred law (Recop. III.7.17) seems to have been first promulgated in 1525, and the Partidas pre-date that by over two centuries. This is also related to a ruse used by one of the inhabitants of Sancho's *ínsula* Barataria, who hides coins in a cane, then hands off that cane to someone else so as to be able to swear that he is not holding the plaintiff's money. Sancho sees through the ploy and breaks open the cane to reveal the coins. In all legal acceptations of the word, there is fodder for comic effect and Cervantes took full (and fair) use of the word's possibilities.

As readers of Don Quixote are well aware, once ensconced as governor of Barataria, Sancho Panza shows himself the wisest and most intelligent of judges, seeing through excuses, uncovering lies, and rendering justice speedily. The twentieth-century legal scholars who uniformly find fault with Don Quixote's justice also consistently acknowledge Sancho's aptitude with legal matters. Alcalá-Zamora y Torres praises the squire's 'qualities of expeditious and correct judgment' and his 'plain, simple and certain administration of justice' (2001, 106).[22] Sancho Panza is neither susceptible to bribery nor partial to one complainant over another, and he dismisses goundless lawsuits with dispatch. On returning to the castle of the duke and duchess, he assures them: 'I went to govern your *ínsula* Barataria, in which I entered with nothing, just as you find me now, nothing lost, nothing gained' (DQ II.55).[23] The declaration would seem to preclude, or at least offer a first defence against, any charge of barratry.

Sancho Panza and Cristóbal Pérez de Herrera: *protomédicos and pragmáticas*

As governor of Barataria Sancho Panza is, much to his surprise, placed on a diet by his court *protomédico.* Both this episode and Sancho's written constitutions offer commentary on one of the contemporary Spanish court's very real *protomédicos* and his own written constitutions.

The title *protomédico* was used for the king's doctors, and also for those who were part of a licensing board charged with evaluating future medical doctors. In the year 1610, the publisher of the First Part of the *Quixote,* Juan de la Cuesta, published a collection titled *Notebook of Laws added to the Recopilación ... in which are contained the laws made up to ... and since ... the 1598 publication of the Recopilación, up to 1610. And some others from prior years that were not included in the Recopilación.*[24] In this collection is a law dating from 1589, which mandates that instead of the existing single court *protomédico,* there would in future be three, 'so that what should be done in the ministry be done better and more carefully' (Quaderno 1610, added law 9 to Recop. III.16).[25]

One of the Spanish court's own *protomédicos* under Phillip II was named Cristóbal Pérez de Herrera (1566–1620) and his requests for dietary restrictions for the entire populace would seem to be the model for Sancho's nemesis. In 1610 Pérez de Herrera published a program for state reform which included a section titled 'Remedies for the good of the health of the body of the Republic.'[26] The original idea dates to 1563, when it was one of a series of questions identified as those not answered in that year's court session in Madrid. Chapter 105 of that session reads in part: 'And another thing, it is notorious that there is much excess and disorder regarding meals and banquets and spending ... resulting in much disservice to God because from this are born vices and other sins of the republic' (Quaderno 1563, fol. 35).[27] The unidentified writer of this request at court in 1563 asks 'that at no table of any quality, there be more than two fruits to start, and two more to finish, and four dishes each of its own foodstuff, and no more' (Quaderno 1563, fol. 35).[28] Apparently a hard sell, Phillip II had responded: 'we shall speak about this, so as to see what order and remedy might be convenient,'[29] but the monarch did not ever, apparently, try to promulgate such a law. A brief biographical sketch of Pérez de Herrera identifies him as part of a late sixteenth-century reform movement at the Spanish court, and dates his first written requests to remedy social ills to 1595 (Caporossi 2004, 847–9). In his 1610 request for *Remedies* ... Pérez de Herrera is more specific in his dietary advice than the 1563 author, stating that to remedy the ills of the republic, it will be necessary:

> to put order in the overwhelming disorder that exists as to foods and meals, which cause so much sickness and need ... of souls and bodies, as well as dire needs and lacks in domestic matters, as alluded to by Plutarch, Pliny, and Seneca when they said: 'large amounts of tastes and condiments are dangerous and pernicious, as diverse foods in the stomach are very damaging, and even worse is the variety of condiments with which they are prepared.' So it would be good to have a pragmatic (and all would obey it very willingly) that permits four or six dishes at most, with a similar number of appetizers and pastries, as is the norm in Portugal. (Pérez de Herrera 1610, fol. 15)[30]

Although published by its author, this 1610 attempt seems to have been as fruitless as the 1563 request at court, and the Recopilación of 1640 does not include any such law. Caporossi makes clear that, with the court shift from Phillip II to Phillip III in 1598, Pérez de Herrera lost influence which he would try, unsuccessfully, to recoup (Caporossi 2004, 849).

However, in 1615 Cervantes will put the food-loving Sancho Panza, governor of Barataria, into the hands of a court *protomédico* who enforces Pérez de Herrera's mandates. After one bite of a plate of fruit, the rest of the sumptuous dishes arrayed on the governor's table are declared off-limits by *protomédico* Pedro Recio de Agüero, with the exception of some salad greens and a few slices of quince. Cervantes' *protomédico* echoes Pérez de Herrera: 'the diversity of foods in the stomach is very damaging, and even worse is the variety of condiments with which they are prepared,' and explains his own role: 'to disallow that which I imagine will be damaging and noxious to the stomach,' including foods that are 'too hot, with too many spices' such as 'that veal, that would be fine were it not roasted in a seasoned sauce' (DQ II.47).[31] Sancho reacts by dismissing the *protomédico*, even threatening to throw a chair at him despite any possible resultant legal damages and defence. Cervantes' commentary indicates that, contrary to Pérez de Herrera's expressed belief, Spain's populace would not willingly follow his proposed dietary restrictions. The author makes another veiled commentary to this type of unsolicited advice in the first chapter of the 1615 *Quixote,* when the barber asks Don Quixote if his advice to the king was such that it should be put 'on the list of the many impertinent pieces of advice that people tend to give to kings and rulers' (DQ II.1), followed by brief comments on Spain's many *arbitristas.*[32]

There is a second episode during Sancho's governorship that relates in part to Pérez de Herrera, as well as to a more general Cervantine legal commentary. While the squire is in Barataria, Don Quixote writes to him with advice on legislative matters:

> Do not make many pragmatics and, if you do, make sure they are good ones and, above all, make absolutely sure they are obeyed; for pragmatics that are not observed are like those that never existed, and they even let it be understood that the ruler who had the discretion and authority to make them did not have the valour to make people respect them. (DQ II.51)[33]

On leaving his governorship, Sancho assures Don Quixote, the duke and the duchess that he complied with that particular advice: 'And although I considered making some useful ordinances, I did not do so, for fear that they would not be observed, given that making them is the same thing as not making them' (DQ II.55).[34]

The references to unobserved pragmatics and ordinances would have been quite significant to Cervantes' contemporaries. In his twentieth-century listing of legal volumes published in the sixteenth century, Gil Ayuso describes the pragmatics, which 'regulated everyday life – not only actions and obligations, but also things and the use of things,' and notes that 'satirical writers abused them, taking them in jest,' adding, 'it is easy to see the connection between [Cervantes' character] Ricote's voyage and the pragmatic of the pilgrims' (1935, 9).[35] Gil Ayuso does not explain further but, in Cervantes' text, we hear Ricote himself comment on the legal situation, as he says of the 'edict and proclamation' (bando y pregón) that exiled the Moors from Spain: 'because I understood, as did our old wise men, that those proclamations were not just threats, as others tried to say, but real laws which would be acted on at a certain moment' (DQ II.54).[36] Cervantes has Ricote comment on one contemporary dilemma engendered by the flood of daily issued and mostly unobserved pragmatics: how to decide which laws must be obeyed. With his advice to Sancho, Don Quixote warns against failure to enforce laws that have been promulgated, and Sancho reduces the argument to say that making them is just the same as not making them. Neither of these sharp commentaries seems to have been noted by the censors, who might have accepted these statements by a 'mad' knight and a rustic labourer as non-problematic.

Contrary to Don Quixote's advice and to his own later assurances, however, Cervantes also tells us that as governor, Sancho did promulgate certain regulations: 'Sancho spent the afternoon drawing up some ordinances' (DQ II.51) that included allowing the import of wine, contrary to Castile's laws of the time. Beginning in 1339 monarchs had prohibited just such transport: 'we order that no wine from Aragon, Navarre, and Portugal, or from any other place, be brought to, or sold in, our kingdoms' (Ordenanzas VI.9.37); 'let no one dare bring wine into the cities of Segovia, Zamora, Salamanca, Córdoba, or Cuenca, or into any other place of our realms' (Ordenanzas VI.9.45).[37] In 1532 Charles V will add must, vinegar, and salt to the prohibited items (Recop.VI.18.31). Cervantes' narrator assures the reader that Sancho's ordinances, titled *The Constitutions of the Great Governor Sancho Panza,* were considered so wise that they continue to be observed in Barataria to this day (DQ II.51).[38] Among those governor's ordenances is the creation of a specific justice for the poor, 'not to follow or harass them, but just to investigate to be sure they are truly poor: for under the guise of a pretended disability or falsified wound are found the arms of thieves and those drunk on spirits' (DQ II.51).[39] This is a direct echo of Pérez de Herrera's 1597 tractate titled 'That which is convenient to arrange, for the aid of poor beggers, and the reform of those who are not'; Pérez de Herrera had been seeking those reforms since 1595, although his proposed remedies are a bit more explicit and draconian. Like Sancho, he recommends a general examination of all those who ask for alms, to be sure they are truly needy, and he adds that, found to be truly poor, they should be granted a one-year licence to beg (see fig. 4, full transcription in note).[40]

Those who refuse the examination are to be put to work, and those who receive the licence must carry a rosary of specific design, and live in a designated poorhouse where they sleep in spartan beds, with men separated from women. Should the poor already have their own house, they must assist at Mass in the poorhouse on Sundays and feast days, and attend catechism classes. Excluded are those on pilgrimage, and poor students. There is no named authority on the 1682 edition of the treatise held by the Hispanic Society of America (fig. 4), which simply lists it as 'A very rare and interesting proclamation.'[41] Other editions make clear that the author was the same *protomédico* who wished to limit the number of dishes and regulate the diets of his fellow citizens (Pérez de Herrera 1598). Through Sancho, *Don Quixote*'s author ridicules Pérez de Herrera's proposed restriction on diets but then has his narrator praise his reforms for the poor. Cervantes' legal gloss is selective, ergo intentional.

Lo que parece que es conueniente proueer, para el amparo de los pobres mendigantes, y reformacion de los que no lo ſon, es lo ſiguiente.

1 QVe ſe haga viſita general de todos los que piden limoſna mẽ digando, y ſi pareciere que lo hazen con neceſsidad, o cauſa baſtante, ſe les dè licencia por eſcrito, poniendo en ella nombre propio, y apelatiuo, naturaleza, edad, y ſeñas corporales, y ſi es ſoltero, o caſado, y que hijos tiene, con las edades, y ſeñas dellos, y q̃ èſta licencia ſea limitada por vn año, que comience deſde Paſcua de Reſurrecion, haſta el ſiguiente.

2 A los que no vinieren a eſte examen, o que en el parezca q̃ no tienen cauſa legitima de mendigar, ſe mandarà que no lo hagan, ſo pena que paſſados veynte, o treynta dias, ſeran condenados por la primera vez, a que ſiruan en las fabricas de los miſmos Aluergues, y en otros ſeruicios dentro dellos, y por la ſegũda vez ſeran caſtigados en la pena de vagamundos.

3 Que a los que ſe diere la dicha licencia, para que puedan vſar della, ayan de traer vn Roſario hecho en vna cadenilla de hierro fuerte, donde corran las cuentas, y al cabo della trayran vna inſignia cõ la Imagen de Nueſtra Señora de vna parte, y de la otra las armas de la Ciudad, o villa dõde el pobre huuiere ſido examinado: y eſta ſeña del Roſario parece ſer mas conueniente, por ſer honroſa, y deuota, y de ninguna nota.

4 Que para eſtos pobres aya vna Caſa o Aluergue de patio y ſitio eſpacioſo con pieças largas, y portales al rededor, y en ellas lamparas encendidas toda la noche, y camas, que ſolamente tengan xergones con paja, o heno, y vna manta groſſera, pues han de ſeruir para que los que aora duermen por las calles y portales, ſe recojan alli.

5 Que los que tuuieren otra Caſa o Aluergue conocido, donde los recojan, no ſera neceſſario que vayan al Aluergue general, ſino los Domingos, y fieſtas de guardar, para que los vnos, y los otros, eſtos dias oyan alli Miſſa, y los Domingos la doctrina Chriſtiana, y eſto hecho, ſaldran a pedir limoſna como en los otros dias de la ſemana, haſta la noche, o pueſto el Sol, que ſe han de recoger.

6 En eſta caſa aura vn Rector ſacerdote de confiãça, que los dichos dias les diga Miſſa, y enſeñe la doctrina Chriſtiana, cõ tres, o quatro hombres

Fig. 4 'Lo que es conveniente …' 1597. Ms. HC 398/1642. fol. 1r–v. Courtesy of the Hispanic Society of America, New York.

hombres de ſeruicio, que ſeran bien meneſter para tener cuenta con las luzes que ſe les hã de dar, y con las dichas camas, y agua, y de inuierno fuego.

7 Con interuencion del dicho Rector han de hazer las juſticias ordinarias el examẽ de los que han de quedar por pobres verdaderos, y ambos firmar las dichas licencias, que como eſtà dicho han de valer por vn año, y èſte acabado, las han de reualidar los meſmos, cõſtandoles que el pobre que la tiene, ſe ha cõfeſſado y comulgado en el tiempo que manda la Igleſia, y no de otra manera.

8 Que el dicho juez ordinario haga q̃ el eſcriuano del Cabildo tenga libro donde ſe pongan los examenes, y el Rector liſta de los nombres: y ninguno deſtos pobres ſe pueda auſentar ſin licencia de la juſticia, y Rector, la qual ſe les dara por eſcrito cõ qualquiera juſta cauſa, borrando de los libros al que ſe le diere.

9 Aunque ſean ciegos, coxos, o mancos, o tullidos, han de traer el Roſario, y efigie de Nueſtra Señora, como dicho es.

10 Los del mal de San Lazaro, y Santo Anton, y de otros que inficionan, ſe han de curar en ſus caſas, y no ſe ha de conſentir que ſalgã fuera à mendigar.

11 Eſta orden no ha de comprehender a los peregrinos, yendo o viniendo recta via, y ha ſe de guardar cõ ellos lo proueydo por leyes, y prematicas. Tampoco ha de comprehender a los eſtudiantes pobres que ſuelen acudir a pedir limoſna, como tengan licencia para pedir, la qual ſe les ha de dar por tiempo limitado.

12 Con los pobres vergonçantes, que por ſerlo, no mendigan por las caſas, y con eſta orden eſtaran mas preciſamente neceſſitados, ſe tenga particular cuenta con que ſean ſocorridos, tomando eſte cargo el Cura de ſus perrochias, ayudandoſe para ello de algunos de los Regidores, que ſeran nombrados cada año, y de perſonas virtuoſas de las meſmas perrochias.

13 Entiẽdeſe que en eſte Aluergue, han de eſtar apartados hombres de mugeres, aunque ſean caſados, y podran el padre, o la madre tener y acoſtar conſigo a ſus hijos, que ſe preſupone han de ſer niños, y que en ſiendo algo crecidos, ſe los han de quitar, y que ſiruan, o ſe ocupen en algun miniſterio. En Madrid a diez y ſeys de Enero, de mil y quinientos y nouenta y ſiete años.

(Fig. 4 continued)

Sancho and *señoría*

Speaking of Cervantes' *Rinconete y Cortadillo,* Antonio Bañón Hernández mentions without further exploration a possible connection between the opening dialogue of the two protagonists and a pragmatic on 'forms of address and courtesies' (tratamientos y cortesías) (2001). His intuition was right. First published in 1586, the pragmatic was repeatedly proclaimed in 1593, 1598, 1600, 1604, 1611, and 1623 (Gil Ayuso 1935, number 472.1). It regulated spoken and written forms of address and the opening dialogue between Rincón and Cortado would seem to be a general mockery of such a law although, as it turns out, the phrases used by the two lads – your grace, mister gentleman, and mister nobleman – are not found among the forms prohibited by the pragmatic. However, we can find in that law a precise clue to another dialogue, between Sancho Panza and his wife Teresa in the 1615 *Quixote.* Excited by the idea of further adventures with Don Quixote, Sancho informs Teresa that when he is governor of his *ínsula,* he will marry their daughter Mari Sancha to someone of such a high rank that 'they will have to call her señoría' (Cervantes 1998b, II.5).[42] Some but not all modern editions change the spelling to 'señora' instead of 'señoría' when the word is first employed in the novel, apparently following the 1637 Madrid edition.[43] However, in the 1586 pragmatic on treatments and courtesies, we read that the appellative 'señoría' is only to be used for archbishops, bishops, grandees, ambassadors, marqueses, counts, commanders, and keepers of the keys in the orders of Santiago, Calatrava, and Alcántara, the knight-commanders of the order of San Juan, the priors of Uclés and San Marcos de León while they are in office, foreign princes, dukes, and marqueses, virreys and generals of the army, navy, and armed forces, and for those of 'Tusón, camp officers, generals and governors of armies, vizcounts, and heads of cities of the kingdom, and of villages that have a vote in the courts, and of guilds and metropolitan churches, where such titling is customary' (Recop.VI.12.1).[44] This offers a general idea of the reach of Sancho's dream, and contradicts Moncada's opinion on the difficulty of legal interpretation for the common labourer. In Sancho Panza, Cervantes paints a worker who knows and understands even the most intricate of Spain's confusing laws.

Loopholes in *Rinconete y Cortadillo*

In his exemplary novel *Rinconete y Cortadillo,* with other very specific lexical details, Cervantes flaunts loopholes in the laws on illegal groups of persons. At the start of the novel, we read that two young lads 'somewhere in the range of fourteen to fifteen years old' but specifically 'not older than seventeen' meet up in front of an inn.[45] Dressed in rags described in painstaking and hilarious detail by the author, the two address each other in an unexpectedly courtly manner, become fast friends, and continue on to Seville, where they come to know the thieves' underworld of that city. For the novel's theme, language, characters, and acts, there can be no denying its connections to the legal world. Cervantes describes various criminal acts on the part of his characters Rincón and Cortado, right from the start: they cheat a muleteer at cards, and then cut open the travel bag of a Frenchman to rob him of two good shirts, a watch, and a notebook. Once in Seville, the two learn the arts of a man named Monipodio and his gang of thieves. Cervantes paints the brotherhood of Monipodio's house as one that is obviously illicit yet simultaneously and contradictorily, as we will see, strictly compliant with the law. To do so, the author takes advantage of two loopholes in the legal prohibitions against brotherhoods and monopolies, beginning with the name Monipodio.[46]

For this central figure, father of the confraternity of thieves, Cervantes uses a corruption of monopoly that is first found in a 1390 law (*Autoridades*). Spain's first ordenance prohibiting vagabonds dates to 1387, when Juan I of Castile ruled that any authority who found an idler could 'on their own authority … take them and make them work for one month without pay, providing that they give them food and drink' (Recop. VIII.11.1).[47] The 1387 law was subsequently grouped with other laws against groups forming so as to subvert the crown's justice. Later, in the 1567 Recopilación, the prohibitions against vagabonds had grown into a full section, a series of laws prohibiting 'thieves, ruffians, vagabonds and Egyptians [aka Gypsies]' (Recop. VIII.11, title epigraph), and the prohibitions against such groups were contained in another section of law dedicated to 'leagues, monopodies [*sic*], and brotherhoods' (Recop. VIII. 14, title epigraph).[48] This 1567 title epigraph repeats the corruption of the word monopoly that is first found in the 1390 law on illicit groups. In *Rinconete y Cortadillo,* Cervantes will first present the two lads as vagabonds, and then join them up to a league of thieves whose leader is named for that corruption of the word.

In the laws regulating these groups, the monarchs specify that no persons are to join up to protect each other 'under guise of doing good' (Recop. VIII.14.1) as, despite pledges to 'advocate or take the name of a saint' (Recop. VIII.14.3), and supposed 'honest statutes to be shown publicly' (Recop. VIII.14.3), the groups are not believed to have 'good intentions' (Recop. VIII.14.1).[49] Seemingly a description of Monipodio's lair with its brotherhood of thieves who also, as described by Cervantes, have their 'statutes … good ordenances' (estatutos … buenas ordenanzas) and 'tariffs' (aranceles) (Cervantes 1995, 2:217, 227), the actual laws had quite a different type of group as their primary focus. The first prohibition, dated 1390, identifies as its focus 'princes, dukes, counts, magistrates, masters, priors, marqueses, rich men, knights and squires' although it adds 'and other singular persons of any state or condition' (Recop. VIII.14.1).[50] Those listed are prohibited from making any type of 'sworn union or league … in which they pledge to defend each other against any other person,' and the statute closes by formally disbanding any such group already formed, adding the word 'monipodios' to the list of prohibited groups, with the particular plea that 'prelates … archbishops and bishops, and any other ecclesiastical person refrain from making or consenting to such leagues' (Recop. VIII.14.1).[51] During the last half of the fifteenth century, Enrique IV would further mandate that 'bishops and abbots, and all other ecclesiastical persons, from this moment on, shall not dare to scandalize the cities, villas, and places of our kingdoms, nor show themselves part of nor partial to any faction, nor join in leagues or monipodios, nor give advice, favour, or help to the same' (Novísima Recopilación XII.12.3).[52] Obviously, these laws address the potential problem of nobles and ecclesiastics who, as the various kingdoms and central authorities were gaining and consolidating power during the Reconquest, had attempted to join forces so as to defend their inherited rights against the encroachment of a centralized state. In 1597 Castillo de Bobadilla offers a political twist on the word, as he describes the first of three types of republic: 'Aristocracy, which is free government by wise and powerful men, as today in Venice: due to man's evil inclination, we see that this type of government easily turns into *monipodio,* ambition, and pretension, called oligarchy by the Greeks' (Castillo de Bobadilla 1775 [1597], 1.1.13, 1:9).[53]

By Cervantes' day, the nobles had lost this battle and, as we saw above with the ecclesiastical versus civil court exchanges, sixteenth-century churchmen were losing theirs. Spain's legal history tells of both groups, nobles and ecclesiastics, rejecting the newer legal compilations and insisting on the restitution of prior versions that protected their usage and customary laws (Martínez Marina 1808, García Gallo 1967). Enrique IV's 1473 law is the last in the series of legal dictates prohibiting such groups to include the word 'monipodio,' but both it and its fourteenth-century predecessor offer an exception for certain *monipodios* and 'leagues.' In the specific language of *Rinconete y Cortadillo,* Cervantes takes clear advantage of that loophole for his fictional group.

Shortly after meeting Cortado, Rincón says: 'I think that we will be, from here to the last day of our lives, true friends' (Cervantes 1995, 1:194), and Cortado also blesses their acquaintance: 'and so that our friendship … will be perpetual, let us begin it with sainted and praiseworthy ceremony' (Cervantes 1995, 1:198).[54] Once in Seville, Rincón and Cortado become acquainted with Monipodio's gang of thieves and ruffians, and we read that the 'the constable of the vagabonds … is a friend' (Cervantes 1995, 1:217) of Monipodio's group.[55]

In his description of a fight that Chiquiznaque and Maniferro, two bullies of Monipodio's gang, have with tough guy Repolido, and then its reconciliation, Cervantes puts the word 'friend' in the mouths of his characters eleven times within nine lines of prose, first with Repolido: 'Friends never have to anger friends, nor make fun of friends, and even more so when friends get angry' (Cervantes 1995, 1:230).[56] Maniferro responds: 'There is no friend here ... who might wish to anger nor make fun of another friend; and since we are all friends, let's shake hands as friends,' and Monipodio steps in to codify the reconciliation: 'All of you have spoken as good friends, and as such friends should shake hands as friends' (Cervantes 1995, 1:230).[57] Still in the gang's lair a short time later, Monipodio speaks with a gentleman who is thinking about not paying his bill for a contractual debt. A member of the gang had slashed the face of a man fourteen times with a knife, as planned, but had mistakenly attacked the servant of the intended target instead of the man himself. Monipodio tells him: 'one does not quibble over such small points with one's humble servants and friends' (Cervantes 1995, 1:234).[58]

Cervantes leaves no room for doubt that all in this thieves' lair consider each other friends. With his overuse (abuse) of the single word and its permutations, the author takes full advantage of a loophole in the previously cited laws prohibiting 'leagues and *monipodios*.' In 1392 Enrique III affirmed and upheld the 1390 law, but added a codicil: 'but by this law we do not mean to legislate against good friendships, and all should be friends and live in peace' (Recop. VIII.14.2).[59] That is to say, a *monipodio* is licit if it is just a matter of friends and friendships. Apart from Cervantes' patent glee in describing Monipodio's house and its inhabitants, we can also read between the lines to appreciate his clear commentary on the lack of efficacy of a law that does not prohibit the obviously criminal acts of this group of thieves. The legal gloss is specific and pointed.

The next laws in the same series prohibiting groups are four pragmatics that issued from the Catholic Monarchs Ferdinand and Isabel. They order that no one join up with the ecclesiastical judges to interfere with 'our justices' and 'the encarcerated who are being taken to jail' (Novísima Recopilación XII.12.6),[60] and they further prohibit helping the captured delinquents by declaring them to be relatives or friends. In the sixteenth century, Charles V and Phillip II promulgated four more laws against groups described thus: clerical or ecclesiastical convocations of relatives, friends, or allies; confraternities of officials; persons who make pacts among themselves so as to 'defraud the Crown of income ... by forming a league or a monopoly and promising to not sell or put out for contract those things that they produce or own' (Recop. IX.8.5).[61] It is only in the last law of this series, dated 1566, that the word 'monopoly' is used, and the wording makes clear that the focus of the legislation is commerce.

Despite that official change in wording, a subsequent treatise on merchants still uses the corruption 'monipodio' for this commercial focus which its author calls an 'abominable and hateful vice' (vicio abominable y aborrecible) (Mercado 1571, fols 50–1). None of the laws in the series specifically mention groups of thieves, although the inclusion of phrases such as 'and any other persons' would obviously expand the scope of the law to include them.[62] A comprehensive list of the prohibited groups includes leagues, unions, allegiances, sworn pledges, contracts, signings, *monipodios,* confederations, bands, partialities, last-name, lineage or military allegiances, guilds, promises, capitulations, chapter councils, and, finally with Charles V and Phillip II, monopolies.

The various ways in which Monipodio's group of thieves refer to themselves include order, guild, company, congregation, brotherhood, confraternity, community, and, at the end of the novel, one more phrase added by Rinconete: 'the infamous academy' (la infame academia) (Cervantes 1995, 1:240). Apart from *monipodio,* which Cervantes uses as the name of the group's leader but not for the group itself, the only other word from the list of prohibited types is guild (cofradía). As with his use of 'friend,' Cervantes seems to have employed 'guild' for the group with ironic intentionality, on the basis of yet another loophole found in the specific pragmatics against guilds.

In 1534 Charles V affirmed certain fifteenth-century laws that prohibited guilds but pointedly exempted those made 'solely for pious and spiritual causes' (Recop. XII.12.12).[63] As the reader of *Rinconete y Cortadillo* cannot help but notice, Cervantes' description of Monipodio's house is that of a guild so pious and spiritual that it is a complete mockery of the concept. The guildsmen-thieves invoke various saints and the Virgen Mary, Monipodio is 'father, teacher, and protector' and the gang is itself 'so very sainted and good … we pray our rosary … many of us do not steal on Friday, nor have conversation with any woman named Mary on Saturday' (Cervantes 1995, 1:208).[64] Monipodio speaks of 'masses for our souls' (misas por las ánimas) and 'charitable donations' (limosna) (Cervantes 1995, 1:212). An elderly guildswoman prays devoutly and places 'little candles for Our Lady of the Waters and the Sainted Crucifix of Saint Augustine' (Cervantes 1995, 1:219).[65] Monipodio's pious, spiritual, and friendly guild is specifically written so as to take advantage of both loopholes.

In further details of *Rinconete y Cortadillo,* we again find Cervantes winking an eye at the pragmatics, for example, those that prohibit men from wearing 'collars, or wristguards with any decoration whatsoever' (*Premática en que se manda guardar*).[66] The collar worn by Rincón, Cervantes tells us, is 'one of those called VanDykes' (Cervantes 1995, 1:192).[67] Those specific collars are prohibited, given that the VanDyke is an 'adornment' worn at the neck (*Premática en que se manda guardar*).[68] A 1594 version of this pragmatic, mandating that the earlier, 1586 pragmatic be complied with, is signed by Juan Gallo de Andrade, apparently the same person who signed the tasa on the 1605 *Quixote*. The same bookseller, Blas de Robles, and his son Francisco, owned the rights of sale of both the pragmatic and the 1605 *Quixote*. The pragmatic's signed proclamation (Pregón) details exactly how the public was made aware of the latest law: 'In Madrid ... in front of the Palace and Royal House of His Majesty, and at the Guadalajara entryway to the same villa, in the place of trade and commerce of merchants and officials ... By town criers with trumpets and bells, the pragmatic was published and cried out, in loud and intelligible voices' (*Premática en que se manda guardar*).[69] Cervantes' defiance of such open proclamations makes his texts not only literarily, but also socially, quite anarchic. Of course, the fancy collar is threadbare and worn by a ragamuffin scamp, whose other crimes also go unpunished, as do most of those by Cervantes' characters.

Everyone Breaks the Law

In each of the above sections, we have seen Cervantes offer a gloss on a certain aspect of the law: a process (to unmake forcings, barratry), a loophole (friends and pious guilds), a description (ideal knight), outdated terminology (tilting at windmill, omecillos), or legal exemptions for insanity. Taking a broader perspective, it is evident that almost all the characters in *Don Quixote* and the *Novelas ejemplares* are breaking one law or another. In 1593 Phillip II complained of just this problem:

> Because we are informed that many laws and pragmatics that we have made for the good governance of our kingdoms have not been, and are not being, observed: this is due to our justices taking little care to act on them and impose the legislated penalties, or using diverse means and inventions so as to defraud the provisions of those laws: we mandate that from here on, said laws and pragmatics are to be observed and obeyed inviolably, on penalty of the punishments contained in those laws. (Recop. VIII.26.21)[70]

This law continues with a list of particular laws and pragmatics that have not been observed, including many of those parodied by Cervantes. For example, on the list are the 1565 laws on vagabonds, and the 1586 prohibitions on excessive collars and forms of address, all three the target of Cervantes in *Rinconete y Cortadillo* and in *Don Quixote*. Many more pragmatics on Phillip II's list are also among those slyly alluded to by Cervantes, whose characters in the *Quixote* and in the *Novelas ejemplares* are, frequently, in violation of these same specific laws. Following are some of Cervantes' glosses.

The women who cover their faces with veils in the 1605 First Part of the *Quixote:* Luscinda (DQ I.36) and Zoraida (DQ I.37), are in violation of the 1588 pragmatic against 'veiled women' (mujeres tapadas): 'We order, that no woman in all our kingdoms, no matter her status, quality or condition, may cover her face in any manner at all but must, rather, be uncovered' (Recop. V.3.11).[71] Golden Age theatre offers multiple examples of veiled woman 'misbehaving' in various ways. Calderón de la Barca's *La dama duende,* for example, is titled for its female protagonist, a widow in the house of her brothers who covers herself so as to move freely in the court. The violations of this particular pragmatic were ubiquitous enough that, by 1641, Antonio de León Pinelo writes *Ancient and Modern Veils on the Faces of Women, Their Advantages and Disadvantages: Explanation of the Real Pragmatic on Veiled Women.*[72] León Pinelo covers every contingency, from historical uses (chap. 1) to particular fabrics (chap. 2), and from biblical references (chaps 6, 7, 9) to Saint Thomas and natural law (chap. 15). The author also addresses cross-dressing, another common practice in Golden Age theatre and in Cervantes' novels, and León Pinelo specifies that such an act can be seen in one of three ways: 'if it is done only for diversion, it is a venial sin. If to a specific end or means, which is in itself a mortal sin, then so, too, is the cross-dressing whether by a man or a woman. And [But] if it is out of necessity, then there is no blame whatsoever, according to Saint Thomas' (1641, II.304).[73] With León Pinelo's three-part division, the protagonist in Calderón's *La dama duende* would have to be seen as guilty of a venial sin, as she specifically covers her face for amusement and recreation, whereas Cervantes' veiled / disguised women and men always seem to have a legitimate need, whether hiding from an irate relative, pursuing a lover, or travelling in hostile terrain. In this protection of his characters, Cervantes differs from the authors of the picaresque, who fail to justify with causality the acts of their law-breakers. Like those authors, Cervantes uses the law as a springboard or foundational material but, unlike them, he simultaneously glosses it by, for example, providing his characters with justification for breaking it. Cervantes probes beyond the obvious and, so, strengthens the fictional portrait. With justifiable causality and character motivation, his realism is, simply, more real.

In the episode of twenty religious men out at night dressed in nightshirts, carrying candles as they transport a corpse from one town to another (DQ I.19),[74] the violated laws include one that prohibits the religious men from being out at night dressed in nightshirts,[75] another that bans moving a corpse from one town to another (Pérez-Coca Sánchez-Matas 1994, 270–3),[76] and a third that declares it illegal to carry so many candles lit at one time, as part of the laws regulating the wearing of mourning clothes and the ceremonies and rituals for the dead: 'And as for burials, rituals and ceremonies, we order that no one ... may carry ... or put ... more than twelve torches or wax candles' (Recop. V.5.1).[77] There is an exemption, specifically for the clergy, friars, or children who are accompanying a corpse to its burial place but, given that Cervantes' group of twenty are already out at night illegally dressed and in the middle of an illicit transport, that exemption on the number of candles would seem to be moot.[78] Another legal compilation from the year 1600 is less forgiving on the prohibition: 'And no person except for the grandees may light themselves with more than two torches, and the grandees may only have four, and no more, under penalty of one hundred gold ducats for each instance to the contrary' (Ordenanzas fols 86v–7r).[79]

A series of laws found in the Partidas includes one that parallels Cervantes' gloss on the venerable galley slave, the 'go-between' (alcahuete) who denies his conviction as a magician. Fortune telling and the reading of omens are prohibited, but

> those who practise enchantment with good intention, so as to exorcise demons from the bodies of men, or to dissolve the bonds between husband and wife who cannot live together, or to break up the clouds that might throw hailstones or fog that will ruin a crop of fruit, or kill the locusts or plant louse that will damage cereal grains or grape vines; for these or any other beneficial reason like them, they should not be punished but, to the contrary, rewarded. (Partidas VII.23.3)[80]

Notwithstanding the Partidas' stipulations, Castillo de Bobadilla tells his readers that both 'go-betweens' (alcahuetes) and 'magicians' (hechiceros) should be thrown out of a city by a good governor (V.1.259, 2:569). To the contrary, Don Quixote echoes the sentiment of the Partidas: 'the profession of go-between is one of discrete men, and is very necessary in a well-ordered republic' (DQ I.22).[81] Cervantes' *alcahuete,* punished and sent to the galleys, is one of the few characters not in violation of the law, at least as stated in the Partidas. This would, apparently, make him the victim of a renegade magistrate like Castillo de Bobadilla, and well-deserving of Don Quixote's efforts to 'unmake' that 'forcing.'

Cervantes' legal parody is intensified in the 1615 Second Part of the *Quixote,* in which the author paints a whole cast of richly dressed characters: Quiteria, whom Sancho Panza describes as adorned in 'rich corals ... golden rings, and really golden ones ... each one must be worth an arm and a leg' (DQ II.21), the enchanted-by-Sancho Dulcinea who is, as he says, along with her servant girls, 'dressed all in gold, with strands of pearls, diamonds, rubies, and brocades of the richest sort' (DQ II.10), Don Diego de Miranda whose velvet clothing is inlaid with gold thread (DQ II.16), the duchess who rides on a 'silver saddle' (DQ II.30), the duke and duchess's palace with walls adorned in 'rich, sumptuous fabric of gold-threaded brocade' (DQ II.31), the nymph dressed in 'one thousand veils of silver cloth, each one glittering with infinite leaves of filigreed silver-inlaid gold' (DQ II.35), and the sixteen-year-old girl in Barataria dressed in 'red silk stockings, and white taffeta garters with flecks of gold and seed pearls, green, gold-threaded breeches, and a scarf or overshirt of the same fabric ... and a shirt of a very fine white-gold cloth' (DQ II.49).[82] All these characters are in violation of the sumptuary laws, which legislate to an extraordinarily specific degree the use of certain cloths, fabrics, and adornments. Prohibited are any brocades or silks adorned with gold thread, any cord, backstitching, or passementerie that is edged, raised, or embroidered in lace containing gold or silver, whether fine or false, and any use of pearls, seed pearls, or other stones, as well as any adornment of beads or silk.[83] In the 1605 First Part of the *Quixote,* only Zoraida is described as similarly dressed: 'more pearls were hanging around her neck, ears, and hair than the number of hairs on her head ... two bracelets ... of pure gold with so many inlaid diamonds which she later told me her father valued at ten thousand *doblas,* and then an equal amount on her wrists' (DQ I.41).[84] This, however, is a description of the first sighting of Zoraida by the captive, when both were in Algiers and out of the reach of Spain's sumptuary laws. Cervantes will have the captive state specifically that this is customary dress among the Moors.

On the same legal note, I would add one small detail to the Green Knight episode (DQ II.16). Fernández-Morera has studied earlier uses of green knights in medieval stories, and points out that Cervantes' character is different in that 'rather than wildness, the clothes suggest a foppish concern with sartorial detail' (1993, 532). Fernández-Morera does not elaborate on that point, but Spain's sumptuary laws had very specific details as to colour. The Recopilación's title on the preparation of fabrics specifies that only a *veyntiquatreno* cloth, that is a fabric of 2400-thread (or closer) warp, could be dyed dark green, blue, or copper (Recop. VII.13.79). First it had to pass through two blue dye-baths and be so stamped with the requisite quality seal. Contradictorily, the law then says that if the desire is for a more perfect green, one can use only as much blue as required for the desired green colour.[85] The Green Knight would seem to be the carrier of two legal messages: the judge of insanity (see above) and the arbiter of a properly dyed green cloth. The Ordenanzas Reales add one more possibility, in that they mandate, for all male Moors, the wearing of a 'green hood / cape, or Moor's cloak over their clothing or, at the least, a crescent marking' (Ordenanzas 8.3.27).[86] The colour carried a variety of social messages, and Cervantes could have been referring to any, or to all, of them.[87] A good reason for Cervantes' sartorial commentaries can be deduced from the sheer number of regulations governing dress, a total of 230 laws on what can be worn by whom, and on how the cloth had to be prepared, all found in Book VII of the Recopilación, in titles twelve through seventeen. That quantity makes Cervantes' ironic commentaries seem understated.

Other legal glosses by Cervantes include, as we have seen, allowing wine to be transported from one place to be sold in another, as per Sancho's constitutions; this contradicts laws in the Recopilación (Recop. VI.18.30 and 32) that prohibit such transport and sale in a confusing mishmash of laws retained from the years 1339 through 1532. Sancho decides to allow wine from any place at all to enter Barataria, and adds what seems to be a Cervantine innovation, the wise addition of consumer protections against the watering down of that wine, on penalty of death (DQ II.51).[88]

The actors in masks on the road (DQ II.11) are in violation of a 1523 law against the wearing of masks in public (Recop. VIII.15.7). The enchanted head (DQ II.62) and even Sancho's refrains would seem to be prohibited by the Siete Partidas, which mandate against 'fortune telling on the head of a dead man' or 'by using words (called proverbs)' (Partidas VII.23.1).[89] Magistrate Castillo de Bobadilla would not prosecute in this case, however, as he allows such law-breaking if done by *caballeros* or other privileged persons, in their houses, for amusement (Tomás y Valiente 1975, 210). It has been noted that Sancho's proverbial torrents increase in the 1615 *Quixote.* That, and the increased violations of the sumptuary laws, tell us that by the 1615 Second Part of the novel, Cervantes had less fear of censorship in this regard. We know that the sumptuary laws were routinely ignored, but we can also read the greater willingness on the part of Cervantes to openly defy legal prohibitions as a greater recognition, in the 1615 *Quixote,* of what would come to be called realist fiction as a reflection on and incorporation of, but also a model outside of, the parameters of reality. For Lerner, Cervantes' parody in the 1605 *Quijote* was an 'antagonistic re-writing' of the books of chivalry invaded by the quotidian; in the 1615 Second Part, the author has to 'continue but also change the First Part and, so, the genre,' and Cervantes does so with a 'reflection on the text itself, one that moves away from genre and meditatively focuses on the First Part' (1990, 821).[90] González Echevarría emphasizes that 'self-reflexiveness is the hall and hallmark of Part II, the overarching structure and theme under which all others fall' (2005, 117). By 1615 Cervantes was exercising greater freedom in this self-reflexive fictional space, blatantly instead of covertly flaunting reality's legal, social, and literary constructs, as he created new ones within the pages of his history. His ironic legal gloss reflects a fairly absurd reality: in 1590 a pragmatic had been published in Alcalá mandating 'that merchants and businessmen be imprisoned until their lawsuits are finished' (Pérez Pastor 1970, 176, no. 343).[91]

The legal reality, like the literary creation, was a world unto, and concentrated on, itself.

Cervantes' perspective on that reality is reflected in his creation, with a protagonist who purports to restore justice with quick, pragmatic steps. However, he too, like the real-world judges and kings, operates with an outdated manual. Real-world magistrate Castillo de Bobadilla advises that, once 'the truth is known' (la verdad sabida), a magistrate is free to act with complete impunity which, as Tomás y Valiente notes, 'signals the unlimited independence of the inquisitorial process, and the elimination of all or almost all feasible defences of the person charged,' leading to 'true judicial absolutism' (1975, 230, 231).[92] Don Quixote also acts with impunity in his quest to restore the rights of the wronged (desfacer tuertos), defending them against renegade magistrates, abusive bosses, and each other. In his actions he privileges the ideals of the law in a mirror image version of Castillo de Bobadilla. Cervantes' protagonist praises the Golden Age as a time when 'capricious law' (ley de encaje) such as that exercised by contemporary magistrates did not exist (DQ I.11), and advises Sancho to avoid governing Barataria in such a manner (DQ II.42). However, the knight also recognizes the law's failure to treat all fairly and recommends equity in penalties meted out (DQ II.42). Castillo de Bobadilla, placing order over rights, used equity as a means to find 'modifying circumstances' (causas) that would allow greater judicial rigour, assuring his reader that he had 2000 such extenuating circumstances and would shortly publish a book on them (1775 [1597] II.21.147, 1:821). To the contrary, Don Quixote recommends compassion and lighter penalties (DQ II.42).

Frequently, Cervantes' glosses are subtle, seemingly throw-away lines in a text full of them. Anthony Close has pointed out that 'a large amount of Cervantes' poetics of comic fiction consists not in formal pronouncements, but in more or less incidental comments' (2000, 8–9). On legal matters, Cervantes gives us an ironic, fictionalized commentary on the social realities behind the plethora of Spain's Partidas, Ordenanzas, *fueros*, and pragmatics, outdated and 'ignored' (no guardadas). It is a fictionalized compendium of justice, individually conceived and /or altered at will by almost every character in the novel. In addition to the large number of operative legal compendia, there was an even greater number of glossers of those volumes, each interpreting the law as he saw fit. Magistrates then decided cases according to their own very independent readings of fact and, sometimes, law. Cervantes' multiple voices in the *Quixote* parallel those conversations, debates, and difficulties.

Within a couple of years of the publication of Part II of the *Quixote,* there would be a new law, disbanding forever the 'numerous knights.'[93] Cervantes had called up the ideal knight from the Partidas to render justice in a world in which legal stipulations were routinely ignored. In the guise of this invented character who purports to 'undo torts' in general wherever they are found, Cervantes highlighted the reality of living in a society overwhelmed by laws that no one observed. Don Quixote was both an old-style, and a new, knight errant for an age that celebrated his anachronistic ways, but he was also a fictionalized legal commentator who spoke for the public mind, in a parody whose referent is, frequently, not a book of chivalry but a legal text, whether *partida*, pragmatic, order, or magistrate's manual. We can read Cervantes' protagonist as just answering a call to duty – the 1602 call to arms – while, at the same time, offering an incisive critique of the outdated legal underpinnings of that particular call to duty, which had become as passé as a book of chivalry.

When Cervantes was writing *Don Quixote*, the chaos in the Spanish legal system had reached an apex and, as we know, Cervantes experienced it personally throughout his lifetime. The author commented on the law in a gloss that both ridiculed and praised it.[94] Contemporary censorship would not have perceived the work as a threat because it was, after all, only a critique of the silly books of knight errantry. This red herring in the best legal sense, insisted on by Cervantes in his prologue to the 1605 *Quixote*, was a cover for an incisive legal gloss.

Another facet of Cervantes' creative appropriation of the juridical-historical debates and texts is his equally skilled and polished rhetorical strategy in adapting historical and semi-historical texts. Kagan explains that official chroniclers for Spanish monarchs worked much like lawyers, impugning the opposition's evidence while insisting on their own reading of facts in their 'histories' (2009, 6–7).[95] Cervantes' *history* of Don Quixote, as the knight's author himself calls it, can be directly linked to those polemical histories of his time.

6 History and Historiography in the *Quixote*

In the movement from late Middle Ages to Renaissance, as law was using the tools of the trivium to reformulate and redefine itself, history broke out of its subservient role to the same scholastic triad. During the Middle Ages, history had come to be seen not as a genre but, rather, as a way to learn grammar, with its exempla being used to understand rhetoric (Cortijo Orcaña 2000, 15). Early Renaissance study of classical legal manuscripts was followed, in short order, by research, translation, and study of classical works from multiple fields, including history. Humanist scholars of history added the lessons of those classics to medieval conceptual modes: 'The conjunction of both tendencies, classical and medieval, came to constitute during the Renassaince a new historical genre, flourishing and splendid' (Montero Díaz 1948, 14).[1]

Cotroneo finds in the 1560 work of Francesco Patrizi the first formulation of the 'philosophical problem of what history might be' (1971, 6–7), although Montero Díaz notes that albeit 'dispersed in various writings,' Spaniard Juan Luis Vives was 'the first to articulate a systematic thought … on the fundamental problems of history' (Montero Díaz 1948, 22), and to affirm its 'profound unity … [in] the permanent identity of man throughout the ages and nations, a single and universal human essence' (1948, 17).[2] Grafton studies the evolution of historiographical approaches by sixteenth-century scholars who commented and 'rationalized' history (Robortello 1548), attempted 'a full history of culture' (Milieu 1551), and otherwise 'made multiple efforts to formalize inquiry into the past' (Grafton 2007, 23, 25–6). Kagan signals that by the 1660s, 'a new generation of scholars, now known as the *novatores* … declared open war on the "fictions and fables"' of earlier chronicles (2009, 290). Cervantes wrote *Don Quixote* as these pitched polemical battles over what Kagan studies as 'perfect history,' 'official history,' and 'politic history'[3] were being waged.

Prior to this time, philosophers and theologians had been unappreciative of history, which they had restricted to 'allowing the narrated events to be known without seeking, generally, relations of cause and effect' (Orcástegui and Sarasa 1991, 17).[4] Orcástegui and Sarasa note changes in attitude in the fifteenth century, when documents begin to refer to professional historians (1991, 22–5). Early in the sixteenth century Paolo Giovio chose the profession of historian over his original training as a medical doctor. Giovio, who had a 'strong sense of the interdependence of heroes and historians,' recognized that 'the humanists had no interest in history and the diplomats and generals had no interest in writing, leaving him the opening he wanted' to 'seek the illustrious friendship of great commanders as a means of satisfying [my] [his] urge to know the real truth of events and plans' (Zimmerman 1995, 6, 24, and n. 30). In the mid-sixteenth century, with the works of Frenchman Jean Bodin, history 'liberates itself' to join with 'philosophy, given that both seek the truth, not doubt or deceit as does oratory, nor the fabulous invention of poetry' (Cortijo Ocaña 2000, 16).[5] Bodin's *Methodus ad facilem historiarum cognitionem* (1566) 'is not so much a "method" for reading or writing history, but more … a truthful and appropriate philosophical discourse on history' (Cotroneo 1971, 15–16).[6] Zimmerman points out that Bodin differed from Giovio in his approach to history, and notes the impact on the Italian's reputation as a result: 'Venality aside, Bodin preferred the archival scholarship of Guicciardini to the eyewitness methods of Giovio, and his aversion formed the basis for the overwhelmingly negative entry on Giovio in Bayle's *Dictionary*' (1995, 264, n. 12).

Spaniard Juan Páez de Castro (c. 1512–70/ 1580?) also wrote of method, criticism and philology, trying to 'explain the genesis of events' and 'identify causality and motivations' (Montero Díaz 1948, 23), while proposing that history should be based on documents.[7] Páez de Castro describes the pitfalls of the historian, in the words of an unidentified poet: 'Writing history, said a poet, is like walking on burning coals hidden under a white ash that deceives us' (Páez de Castro 1892, 28).[8] Páez de Castro's work was not published until 1892 but Cervantes, who counted among his acquaintances a number of contemporary historians, was obviously aware of and a participant in these debates. Forcione notes that Cervantes 'exploits' the 'flexibility with which the term *historia* was used in the sixteenth century' (1970b, 19, n. 14), and Gaylord sees *Don Quixote* as part of the 'very real, and often very serious national and cultural historiographic project' of the fifteenth through seventeenth centuries (1998, 127). On the basis of personal contacts, expressed interests, and specific mentions in Cervantes' own works, Eisenberg includes in a probable library of *Don Quixote's* author Garibay y Zamalloa's *Compendio historial de todas las historias de los reinos de España,* and Juan de Mariana's *Historia general de España,* as well as Pedro de Mantuano's critical rewrite of the latter work (Eisenberg 2002, nos. 78, 119, 117), along with a number of other histories and chronicles. Wardropper notes that by the late sixteenth century, 'a whole generation had lost its respect for historical truth' (1965, 9), and Cervantes was squarely in the middle of those debates.

Cervantes' narrator assures the reader of his history's documents, which the 'second author' of *Don Quixote* thinks must be hidden in the archives of La Mancha or neighbouring towns. While this nod of the head to archival sources might comport with the Gucciardini / Bodin preferred method, Cervantes' archives will turn out to be a lost manuscript recovered in a Toledo marketplace. Following on this wink and nod to other well-known forgeries of his day, the apocryphal documents of Granada's Sacromonte,[9] *Don Quixote*'s 'second author' has the manuscript translated, and Cervantes hides 'original historian' Cide Hamete Benengeli under layers of multi-voiced commentary [white ash] which includes the apocryphal nature of certain episodes, the translator's doubts as to some events, and the author's masking of himself as a 'second author.'[10] It is the reader of *Don Quixote* who sorts out ash from burning coals as he follows the history, deciding the truth of what was written. Cervantes' pointed commentary, with Don Quixote's fictional 'history,' pits readers and characters of the novel wresting for control as did the official chroniclers (and enemies) of Spanish monarchs (Kagan 2009). In the 1615 Second Part of the *Quixote,* various characters comment on their acceptance, or rejection, of the events of the 1605 First Part.[11] The legal decision of the earlier judge or king is now that of the reader, and the archives include the inventions of the enchanter who writes the history, debating voices who offer simultaneous yet contradictory testimonies, and interviews within the text as, for example, when Don Quixote himself asks Sansón Carrasco for his opinion of the history's related events. Law, testimonial account, and archival as well as eyewitness history converge to become novel.

Aristotle may have separated history and poetry for the truth of its content, but the Iberian Peninsula has a tradition of combining epic-historic material in both verse and prose forms.[12] A reading of the various chronicles and verse on Visigoth king Rodrigo is a fine example. According to the earliest known chronicle source (*Crónica mozárabe,* year 754), Rodrigo disappears on the battlefield. Later Romancero versions begin to introduce the supposed violation of an enemy's daughter and then, by the last of the prose compositions (*Crónica sarracina,* year 1430), Rodrigo is castigated for his concupiscence by having the offending member eaten by serpents in a cave in Viseo, Portugal. Rodríguez Pequeño speaks of the *Quixote* as a denunciation of intentional falsifications such as Pedro del Corral's *Crónica sarracina* (2008, 267). I would dispute only the characterization 'denunciation' as it seems limiting, much as does seeing the *Quixote* as a mere denunciation of the books of chivalry. Cervantes' work is more a celebratory creation that acknowledges its debt to the earlier forms (and forgeries) while synthesizing them into a new model. Forcione says that Cervantes puts 'certain types of literature on trial in the scrutiny of Don Quixote's library' and 'certain literary theories on trial' in other episodes of the *Quixote* and the *Novelas ejemplares,* as the author tests 'the freedom of the creative imagination' and refuses to 'impoverish the realm of art by tethering the artist to the stake of factual accuracy' (1970a, 254). As we have seen, this is how Cervantes also appropriates legal thought, precept, and actuality. His treatment of his age's debates on history and historiography are equally innovative.

Developments in historiographical trends in Spain from the thirteenth through the sixteenth centuries detail the combinations and permutations of truth and invention, and have been studied by both historians and scholars of literature. Diego Catalán studies Spanish fourteenth-century rewritings of earlier histories and tales 'novelizing historiographical recreations' (2000, 340). Domingo Ynduráin (2006) describes the movement from the thirteenth-century's 'scientific historicism' to a 'novelesque and fabulous history' in the fourteenth century, and then speaks of prose developments in history and chronicle through the fifteenth century. Cátedra (1989) details the increase and importance of verse historiography under the Catholic Monarchs. Kagan (2009) offers a comprehensive and compelling account of the development of various types of history in Spain in the relevant time frame for Cervantes' work, from Nebrija's celebrated recommendation for a history written in Castilian, through Count Duke Olivares's use of a propaganda machine described as 'a diverse group: jurists, dramatists, painters, poets, historians' who not only took liberties with the historical record, but even 'reinvented history for political ends' (Kagan 2009, 223, 227). These studies of official Spanish historiographical practices throughout the sixteenth century are crucial to an understanding of the environment in which Cervantes wrote *Don Quixote.*

From the differing [i.e., competing] versions of battles, to laudatory chronicles and criticisms of the same, to competition for the post of royal chronicler, to limitations on access to archives, and what Kagan calls tit-for-tat history: the points raised in Kagan's work are all reflected in *Don Quixote.* Cervantes will employ multiple voices who literally 'see' the same event differently: a windmill for Sancho Panza is a giant for Don Quixote, ergo the historian's crucial 'eyewitness' account is unreliable. Cide Hamete both praises and undermines the deeds of Don Quixote; the novel's internal voices [first author, second author, translator] quibble over details of the story; the continuation of the history is discovered in Toledo, and then purchased and zealously guarded by the 'second author,' who has it translated. It is noteworthy that this 'second author' had no luck finding the 'archives' which, he insists, must exist as, judging by the books in Don Quixote's library, his history must be a modern one. This detail is of a piece with the late sixteenth-century move away from ancient history and toward more contemporary chronicling of the present, a development presented by Kagan with multiple examples from the same decades. The out-of-reach archives can be read as an echo of Simancas, created by Phillip II as an archival repository for historians, but inaccessible to most. Kagan points out that Phillip II denied access, specifically, to any recent materials (2009, 104); Don Quixote's history is a modern one, ergo out-of-reach. The full irony of Cervantes' work is only heightened with the knowledge that the 1605 *Quixote* was submitted for approval to, and read by, censor Antonio de Herrera y Tordesillas, also the official Head Chronicler of the Indies (Bouza and Rico 2009); that is, a historian was charged with judging the appropriateness of Cervantes' 'history' of Don Quixote (Kagan 2009, 151).[13] The overarching categories of *historia pro patria* versus *historia pro persona* studied by Kagan are painstakingly reflected in Cervantes' *persona* Don Quixote and his *patria* La Mancha. Cervantes celebrates the most unlikely of historical heroes in one of the most remote and uncelebrated regions of Castile.

During this same century, the chroniclers of the Indies vehemently debate history and historians, and later writings in Latin America will continue to incorporate that mix of myth, archive, and invention (González Echevarría 1990). Montero Díaz notes 'the vivacity, realism, and extraordinary inventiveness of the historians of the Indies, gifted with a prodigious flexibility on coming face to face with unheard-of situations and unexpected problems,' and adds that these historians 'were constantly pushing further than the fixed models of rhetoricians' (Montero Díaz 1948, 16).[14] Adorno studies the use of those histories of the Indies for political manoeuvrings, and speaks of the 'nexus of law and history in the "true history"' of Bernal Díaz, for whom 'historical authority rested on sworn testimony ... eyewitness validation and ... the resultant actions of the emperor favouring his petitions' (Adorno 2007, 174). Gaylord has related *Don Quixote* to that polemical historiography of the American conquest, which 'resembled a courtroom' with voices 'in adversarial fashion, trading claims and counterclaims, accusations and defenses related to matters large and small' (1998, 134). Grafton explains the wide scope of historical tradition in late sixteenth century: 'the *ars historica* provided a shell, a portable house and carapace, which any hermit crab of a humanist could inhabit and move about in, safely, as he explored strange and dangerous intellectual spaces' (2007, 181). Herrera y Tordesillas offers a range of options as to why one might write history: to please a patron, to demonstrate one's eloquence and so gain glory, to relate an event as eyewitness, to reveal a truth that would otherwise remain hidden (1615, dedication). This was the environment in which Cervantes wrote the history of Don Quixote, the *res gestae* of an unlikely hero whose legally proscribed acts are described with consummate poetic licence. *Don Quixote* is tongue-in-cheek panegyric, invented history, chronicle written by an enchanter, and polemical narrative of a criminal record. It shares multiple elements with another popular pseudo-historical genre of the day, the elogium.

Ynduráin (2006) has studied elogia being written to relate, yet also to embellish historical feats in the service of both an incipient nationalism and the formation of a rhetoric in the developing Castilian language. Gaspar de Baeza calls Paolo Giovio's *Elogios* a good read for their brevity and variety of materials, as well as their combination of prose and verse and, in them, the jurist does not distinguish apocryphal from empirical detail.[15] In his dedication to King Phillip II, Baeza insists that the volume is judged to be 'in the opinion of serious men, the most excellent and prudent book of history written in our times' (Baeza, 1568, 'Dedicatoria,' *Elogios*).[16] For the seventh book of the *Elogios,* Baeza painstakingly annotates each elogium with references to Giovio's full *Histories,* which he had translated two years earlier. The jurist sees both works as history.

Cervantes will take this model and develop it further, writing brief, episodic chapters, incorporating a variety of materials, having his characters comment on the link between prose and verse (DQ I.47), stressing truth and truthful histories while incorporating names and places from real and invented sources, and offering fictional testimony on a plenitude of legal details and scenarios. Cervantes persistently and insistently calls his work a history which thereby makes everything in it true, following on his own dictum in the *Persiles:* 'an excellent characteristic of history is that everything written in it can pass as truth' (Cervantes 2003, III, 10, 527).[17] Cervantes joins the literary debates, but he also incorporates his era's philosophical questions on the meaning of law and history, and on the latter's development as a genre,[18] at a time when history was not seen as truthful, despite the Aristotelian precepts that so defined it. Montero Díaz describes Fox Morcillo's motivation for the historian as a sort of Darwinian struggle to survive: 'There is in man a thirst for immortality put there by Nature herself, in which is found the historical drive and activity' (Montero Díaz 1948, 29–30).[19] The appetite for immortality is also a running commentary in *Don Quixote,* with Cervantes' protagonist hoping for a trustworthy chronicler, worrying who he might be, and doubting his veracity if he truly is a Moor as described. Richard Predmore sums it up: 'In Part I they [Don Quixote and Sancho] anticipate the immortality of bookish fame; in Part II they face the achievement of that fame' (1973, 15). Cervantes explores the fine line separating truth from lie in the historical drive and activity, and explodes the underpinnings of that distinction (and deception) in history, law, and literary works. Riley has noted that with *Don Quixote,* Cervantes 'blew the doctrine [of literary decorum] to pieces and reassembled them in a new artistic form' (1962, 135). I would expand the description to include legal, philosophical, and historical decorum, that is, the precepts and the practicum of all written disciplines, including Giovio's *Elogios* as translated by Gaspar de Baeza.

Cide Hamete and the Elogios

In chapter 9 of the First Part of *Don Quixote,*[20] Cervantes introduces 'Cide Hamete, Arab *historian*' and repeats almost as a mantra the word 'history' with varying adjectives: 'this *history*'; 'such a juicy *history*'; 'such a spirited *history*'; 'his *history* must be a modern one'; 'this agreeable *history*'; 'this narrated *history*' (DQ I.9).[21] The narrative voice describes Don Quixote and the Basque in the same stances as 'told in the *history*' in a painting labelled with their names as given in 'the *history,*' and three ideal concepts of history are laid out, all stressing truth: the 'true telling of the *history*'; 'punctual, truthful, and in no way passionate *historians*'; and 'truth, whose mother is *history*' (DQ I.9).[22]

Apart from the Prologue, which by all measures was written after the 1605 novel was finished, the word 'history' is found with relative infrequency in Don Quixote, especially in comparison with the fourteen uses of history and historian in chapter 9, in which Cervantes also introduces his historian and the painted image of his protagonist in medias res.[23] These details of chapter nine suggest a connection between Cervantes' novel and Giovio's elogium of Muley Hamet, the same historical figure described in the 'Captive's History' in *Don Quixote* (DQ I.39–41). According to official histories, there was a succession of kings in the throne of Tunis: Muley Hasan, followed by his son Muley Hamida, followed by Uluj Alí (the Uchalí of the 'Captive's History'), followed by Muley Hamet, brother of Hamida and son of Hasan. In the father Muley Hasan's elogium, Giovio reports the historical facts while adding just a few dubious details, such as Muley Hasan being 'very learned in scholarly disciplines, specifically in philosophy as according to Averroes' (Giovio 1568, fol. 203r), which we can read to identify him as a 'Mohammadan philosopher' like Cide Hamete (DQ II.53).[24] However, in narrating the elogium of the historical son Muley Hamet, Giovio changes fact for invention, switches the name of the elder brother from Muley Hamida to Mohammed, and introduces a completely fictional father named Zidamet. The elogium begins with demonstrative adjective and description that link painting to writing:[25]

> This long linen cloak is worn by the Sharif, and his head is covered with a single linen cloth that ends (after curling around his right ear), by draping over his shoulders and falling all the way to his heels. In the old days, Egyptian priests used a

similar vestment, and I believe that this is the origin of the robes our own priests wear when saying Mass. Muley Hamet was also known as Sharif, as he is descended from the lineage of the false prophet Mohammed, and Cyrif (which is how it should be pronounced) means sainted one in the Arab tongue, that is, one given to contemplation of the mysteries. (Giovio, 1568, fol. 217r)[26]

Like Cervantes, Giovio paints a description in such a way that the reader feels they are actually seeing the figure, while hearing in person the intimate tone of the storyteller whose added comments, such as the origen of the priest's robes, link the tale to the reader-listener's world. Translator Baeza follows Giovio's text but also, at times, adds information; in this case, he is responsible for the detail as to the correct pronunciation of 'Cyrif.'

The description of the portrait is followed by a narrative transition and expansion: 'the way in which this man (in a sort of modern miracle), went from simple teacher to leader of powerful kingdoms, I will tell as succintly as I am able, so that all might understand that predictions of astrologers are not always illusory' (Giovio, 1568, fol. 217r).[27] Included along with the details of the brothers' lives are descriptive passages on Fez, Sufa, and Morocco. Of particular interest for readers of Don Quixote are two specific elements of these topographical descriptions: first, that from Sufa come certain 'princely lions, of a generous sort, who do not harm men' (Giovio, 1568, fol. 217v).[28] This calls to mind Don Quixote's battle with the lions, although the details are a bit different in that Giovio also states clearly that if the lions do not have 'beasts to eat' (bestias a comer), they will harm man. Cervantes' lion tamer warns Don Quixote that the animals have not eaten, yet they do not harm the protagonist. Another Cervantes' contemporary, historian Luis del Mármol Carvajal, also tells of tame lions that come from Oran, but describes them a bit differently: 'brown ... and very strong and cruel, but they do no harm to men, except for when they do them harm' (Mármol Carvajal 1573, I.18, fol. 26v).[29] While the actual reading is 'they do them no harm except for when they do them harm,' the passage can also be read as 'the former do not harm the latter except for when the latter harm the former.' Those specific demonstrative pronouns are not found in the text, but they can explain a detail of Don Quixote's lion episode: the lion tamer refuses to follow the protagonist's order 'that he irritate the lion by striking at it' (DQ II.17).[30]

Also of interest in Giovio's elogium is Baeza's translation of Giovio's conjecture about Morocco: 'it is *verisimilar* that, in the Roman era, it was governed by King Bogudis' (Giovio, 1568, fol. 217v, emphasis added).[31] Both Giovio and Baeza highlight the uncertain nature of the detail; in Giovio's Latin it reads *coniectari licet,* which Baeza translates with 'it is verisimilar.' Cervantes' narrator, speaking of Don Quixote, takes both Giovio's subtly questionable noun 'conjecture' and Baeza's adjective 'verisimilar,' and combines them: '[Other historians] want to say that his last name was Quixada, or Quesada, but in this there is some difference in the authors who write about his case, although a verisimilar conjecture gives us to understand that he was called Quexana' (DQ I.1).[32] Francisco Rico offers the spelling variants in the princeps edition: 'Quixada, o Quesada ... Quexana,' disputes that the trope might be related to the books of chivalry as 'I am not aware of anyone having found analagous vacillations in such works,' and relates Cervantes' use of the phrase 'verisimilar conjecture' to humanist philological trends (2005, 449–50).[33] Such 'analogous vacillations' are directly related to the historical works and, with particular intensity for Spaniards of the era, to those of Paolo Giovio. Jiménez de Quesada invokes Quixada as a witness to his version of events, versus that of Giovio (1952, 475). Cervantes' verisimilar conjecture, it seems to me, comes with a very deliberate wink of the eye to Jiménez de Quesada, a historian not at all like those counselled by Don Quixote's creator in chapter 9, that is, 'punctual, truthful and in no way passionate' (DQ I.9). Jiménez de Quesada insists that Giovio's negative portrayal of Spanish soldiers during the Sack of Rome is untrue and that events did not occur as described by the Italian historian, but then adds: 'as if it were not known to everyone that such sacking of cities will take place during a war' and 'as if it were some great evil, while sacking a town, taken by force of arms (speaking of during a war, of course), to take every advantage that comes to one. That is why they are called Sacks' (1952, 220).[34] The debates over 'punctual, truthful, and in no way passionate' historians, histories, and historical truth were quite polemical in sixteenth-century Spain. Flores (1997) has studied orthographic changes introduced into the *Quixote* by text compositors, as well as subsequent editors and critical commentary, in relation to one historical figure, a Jewish convert from La Mancha, as a possible model for the name-play regarding Cervantes' protagonist. These other two historical and historiographically literary figures, author Jiménez de Quesada and his dedicatee Luis Quixada, in the contemporary context with the polemic surrounding true histories and debates over real names, offer another facet in the prism of possible readings of and commentary by Cervantes. Twentieth-century historian Víctor Frankl, editor of Jiménez de Quesada's work, keeps the debate going in his introduction to the *AntiGiovio,* painting Jiménez de Quesada as a modern day Quixote and drawing an analogy that is surprising in its conflation of the real and the fictional: 'and so, as Don Quixote wishes to heroically reform the world ... so does Quesada wish to restate the original truth of the history' (Frankl in Jiménez de Quesada 1952, 679).[35] Frankl then links the *AntiGiovio* and the *Quixote* in literary terms due to the representation in both of an ideal figure who wishes to reform the world: Charles V for Jiménez de Quesada and

Don Quixote in Cervantes' text. An inversion of Frankl's thesis has equal merit, with Cervantes using books of chivalry, real historical figures, and real histories like that of Jiménez de Quesada, as material for parody. The realism of the *Quixote* comes from this type of borrowings and glosses by its author.

In Giovio's elogium, Muley Hamet's apocryphal father is a rich merchant named Zidamet who sells 'dates and other things' (Giovio 1568, fol. 217r), and 'was considered a prudent and well-informed man ... principally, a great astrologer' (Giovio 1568, fol. 217r),[36] who predicted that his two sons, Mohammed and Muley Hamet, would be kings. The younger, Muley Hamet, also goes by two nicknames: Hamete and Sharif. The two brothers, 'learned in Arab letters, opened a school and taught young men' and thus 'earned a good living, and became well known in the environs' (Giovio 1568, fol. 217r).[37] At one point their father Zidamet advises them that 'so as to get to know the world, and the customs of foreign lands, they should go on a pilgrimage to Arabia, to revere Mohammed's tomb in Mecca and in Talnabi' (Giovio 1568, fol. 217r–v).[38] The brothers go to Cairo, Jerusalem, and Constantinople, and then return to Africa, and spend a few days in Tunis, after which, becoming friends with 'certain Arab gentlemen,' they decide 'to take up arms' and so they join up

> with the vagabond Arabs, who in Africa, with no particular residence, move from one place to another, from the Nile to the Canarian Sea, insisting that the various kings pay them ransom, and they wage war against those who refuse their venal friendship, as they were doing with great strength and force at this time, against Bucentufo, king of Morocco. (Giovio 1568, fol. 217v)[39]

With the brothers, the Arabs conquer Morocco and fictional elder brother Mohammed becomes king. The younger, now called Hamete Sharif, conquers and rules over two other towns, Sufa and Tarodenta (Giovio 1568, fol. 217v). These ahistorical details of the elogium now become an illogical mishmash in and of themselves: Sharif is jealous of Mohammed, takes Morocco from him, and then, with 'insatiable greed, he sets his cap for Fez and making use of his wiles and his lucky weapons, he beats King Muley Hamet and throws him out of the kingdom' (Giovio 1568, fol. 218r).[40] With this series of events, the author seems to have forgotten that the same Muley Hamet is the only one in this story with the nickname Sharif. Giovio's text then reads that after the victory, Sharif ordered that Muley Hamet become king of Morocco 'although he had just beaten him, and was a short while ago his enemy' (Giovio 1568, fol. 218r).[41] The character Muley Hamet, with nickname Sharif, has been split into two characters, one with the name and the other with the nickname, he has beaten himself in battle, then taken pity on himself, and he has gained the kingdom of

Fez (as Sharif) and that of Morocco (as Muley Hamet). The illogical leaps could be explained by the tradition of giving the nickname Sharif to, as yet another sixteenth-century historian tells us, 'all of the relatives of Mohammed ... [who] are known, by a green cloth that they wear on their head, and they are all called Sharif' (Haedo 1612, 33),[42] but in this short, three page elogium, Giovio has not introduced any other Sharif. In other histories of Cervantes' day, similar slip-ups are frequent, and in those texts, with their detailed intrigues, name changes, and multiple Sharifs, the reader easily becomes completely confounded. But in a text this short, the illogical leap is surprising, and should also be read as a model for what is, in my opinion, Cervantes' deliberate carelessness with detail in *Don Quixote,* including the name changes, the lapses in logic in the storyline, etc. All are common features of the chronicles and histories of his time, and Cervantes' 'true history' incorporates and develops that narrative model.

Muley Hamet's elogium ends with one of the conquered kings, 'wounded and blinded in his right eye,' fleeing to 'plead for help from the emperor' (Giovio, 1568 fol. 218v).[43] He begs Charles V to avert the danger that Sharif 'in time not come to Spain, to conquer Granada' because 'should he desire to do so, and to make war so as to extend his law, he would be joined by an infinite host of Moors, and Arabs' even though

> in truth, he is already a very old man of eighty years, and while he keeps himself strong and fresh, drinking a lot of camel's milk, his fate will do him in, or God will not permit that he make it into Spain – and if he does, the Spaniards (true soldiers that they are) will come out to meet him and they, being accustomed to valiantly conquering all over the globe, will either kill or capture him. (Giovio 1568, fol. 218v)[44]

In short, Giovio invents the apocryphal father Zidamet, fills the brothers' history with minutiae and intimate details illogically and ahistorically confounded at will, narrates a life of study converted into one of arms, and ends with the threat of an eighty-year-old Arab, still fresh and strong thanks to camel's milk, who might invade Spain to retake Granada. In later editions of the *Elogia,* there would be woodcuts reproducing the portraits from the museum. Figure 5 is Muley Hamet, as Giovio described him, from a 1571 edition with portraits in woodcuts.

The reader's imagination will match the earlier citation, with the long linen cloth draped around the right ear, although Giovio failed to mention that enigmatic, almost Mona Lisa smile. This is the threat, the eighty-year-old drinker of camel's milk who might retake Granada. The literary attractiveness of this last is fairly obvious from the standpoint of the Spanish public in Cervantes' day. A little over one hundred years before Cervantes published *Don Quixote*

LIBER VII. 381

Muleamethes Cognomento
SCYRIFFI,
Magnus Rex Mauritaniæ.

HAC talari linteaque toga induitur Scyriffus, & oblongo linteolo ſimplicibus ſpiris ita caput inuoluit, vt eius extrema pars inſtar ingentis caudæ à dextra aure per humeros & crura ad talos vſque diffundatur. Hoc habitu Sacerdotes Aegyptios olim vſos fuiſſe conſtat, ſic vt facilè rear ſacrificuli cultũ inde acceptũ, quem noſtri ſacra facientes ſuperinduũt, & Camiſum vocãt. Muleamethes ſiquidẽ ob id Scyriffus vocatur quod ſacratæ ſit ſtirpis, & Mahometis pſeudo prophetæ ſanguine progenitus. Ea vox enim Arabicè virum ſanctimonia pollentem, & ſacris myſterijs deditum

Fig. 5 Woodcut of Muley Hamet in Paolo Giovio, *Elogia*. Basel, 1571. Courtesy of the Beinecke Rare Books and Manuscript Library, Yale University.

the Reconquest ended, and so came to a close seven centuries of what has been called 'convivencia' or 'coexistence' in the eyes of some, but which was also a time of city-by-city conquest and changeover in control. In 1492, the Catholic Monarchs Ferdinand and Isabel officially retook Granada, the last of the Peninsula's cities held by the Moors. Throughout the next century, the fear of a re-invasion was prevalent, for fairly obvious reasons given geographical proximity and historical relations. As we have seen, during the 100-year period prior to the appearance of Cervantes' novel, Spanish monarchs continued to issue calls-to-arms for knights to defend the countryside.

Rumours of another invasion by the Moors were commonplace in Spain, and the Catholic Monarchs and their successors placed the responsibility for defending against such an eventuality in the hands of two groups: landowning nobles along the coast, and the 'numerous knights' deputized as necessary. In the years immediately preceding the publication of *Don Quixote,* there were specific calls-to-arms for numerous knights in La Mancha, and specifically from the very area around the campo de Montiel where Don Quixote roams in the novel: 'In both 1602 and 1603, the marquis of Los Vélez compelled various militia units from the Adelantamiento de Murcia to serve on the galleys of Spain'; 'In 1611 and 1618 the marquis of Los Vélez again called out the militia of Murcia and La Mancha' (Thompson 1976, 129, 130).[45] The call-up area specified various towns and villages in La Mancha, specifically in the Campo de Montiel: 'Villanueva de los Infantes and its surrounding towns, Sigura de la Sierra and its surroundings, and the village of Torrenueva' (Thompson, personal communication).[46] Cervantes answers those call-ups with a protagonist who, as we have seen, embodies an ironic gloss on the ideal knight as depicted in the only Spanish legal text to describe and prescribe how, and who, a knight should be, the protector and defender of the thirteenth century's Siete Partidas. Cervantes dedicated the 1605 *Quixote* to the duque de Béjar who, according to Kagan, had so many legal cases going at once that he maintained twenty legal counsellors in his employ and, in 1640, had at least twenty-nine lawsuits in process at the same time (Kagan 1981, 12, and n. 24). One of those lawsuits was against the crown for forcing him to finance the turrets to protect the coastline (Thompson 1976, 24). Giovio comically paints the coastal threat in his elogium of Muley Hamet, and Cervantes purports to cede control of Don Quixote's history to a similarly iconic and ironic figure, Cide Hamete Benengeli.

Control of a history, however, always falls to he who wields the pen and not just at the composition stage, but also in later editions, translations, and readings. In Muley Hamet's elogium, translator Baeza amends Giovio's text, which in its original reads simply 'his fate will do him in' (Giovio 1568, fol. 218v) before its praise of the Spanish soldiers.[47] In his prologue to the *Elogios,* Baeza takes issue with Giovio's use of the words fate and fortune: 'in this book it is said that fate and fortune are words that are used, without the author making it clear that there is no such thing but that, rather, all is governed by God's infinite providence and will' (Baeza 1568, Al lector).[48] In Muley Hamet's elogium, Baeza faithfully translates Giovio's 'fate' (hado) but then adds in the phrase 'or God will not permit' (o Dios no permitirá). It is interesting to note that in *Don Quixote,* Cervantes completely eschews use of the word 'fate,' and opts for 'destiny' on only two occasions, both related to love. Marcela speaks of her freedom not to love just because she is loved by another: 'Heaven has not yet wished on me the destiny of loving someone' (DQ I.14), and Sansón Carrasco, disguised as the 'Knight of the Forest' (Caballero del Bosque), tells Don Quixote of his own amorous destiny: 'I want you to know that my destiny or, better said, my choice, brought me to love the incomparable Casildea de Vandalia' (DQ II.14).[49] For Cervantes, 'free will' (albedrío) is the determining factor in human affairs, as it is in narrative control. A translator may interrupt to gloss a historian's text but that interpolation will subsequently be re-interpreted by yet another voice, whether a different character or, eventually, a reader's 'I' with its own free will. Cervantes develops the multi-voiced historical yet apocryphal elogia structure with paintings in words that allow those with imagination to fill in the blanks, from Muley Hamet to Zidamet to Cide Hamete.

True Histories and Names

Related to Cervantes' insistence on the word 'history' and, particularly, 'true histories,' is Jiménez de Quesada's accusation that Giovio does not tell the truth but, rather, selectively edits the facts, as seen in 'the suspiciously abbreviated nature of some of Giovio's books' (1952, 80) which he attributes to Italian hatred for 'the Spanish empire' (1952, 27).[50] Cervantes opts for a more long-standing enemy figure, telling us that Don Quixote's original author Cide Hamete is 'an Arab author, and it is very common for those of that nation to be liars; although, given that they are such enemies of ours, it is more likely that the history will be lacking in detail instead of containing an overabundance of it' (DQ I.9).[51] Taking the complaints of his contemporaries about the unjust perspective of Italian historians, Cervantes proposes an original author / chronicler / historian who is an enemy and a liar, only to wryly insist on the truth of his story,[52] just as Jiménez de Quesada insists on the truth of his version of events, versus that of Giovio. Jiménez de Quesada takes issue with many of the particulars of Giovio's *Histories,* frequently minor details such as a mistaken date, or the wrong number of ships in an expedition, and they include having named 'Hamete' someone whose real name was 'Cara Hacén' (1952, 332). The section begins with the general idea: 'And now I'll speak of Giovio's errors about Harradin himself,' and then gets to the particulars of the mistaken name: 'pursued by one Cara Hazen, his captain (and not Hamete, as our author [Giovio] calls him), nor an Arab, either, because he was not one' (1952, 332).[53] Jiménez de Quesada had already disputed the identification of another figure as a 'father' instead of a 'stepfather,' due to a scruple about the role of a priest as physical, earthly father: 'This Mahomedin, once grown into a fine lad and being of the right age, came to live in Meteleno and settled in the city of Bonaba, where he married a Christian widow, although he was a Turk; she had been the woman of a Greek priest named Alexander, and she even had sons of this priest, who Giovio calls father but I say stepfather' (1952, 316).[54] Cervantes, as we know, tells his reader that he is stepfather, not father to Don Quixote (DQ Prologue and I.7), as we have already seen also a possible legal stand. The specific roles have been discussed by scholars in terms of their literary import (Haley 1965, Avalle-Arce 1976); both the legal codes and the polemical histories offer further subtleties for interpretation.

As to the name switching, confusing one name with another is something very common in the histories of the time, and in the work of another Cervantes' contemporary, we find yet another figure whose name is similar to that of Cervantes' historian: Cid Amet Benelcadi, named as the son and heir of the king of Cuco, handed over 'in chains' (por rehenes) (Haedo 1612, 62) at the age of fifteen to the king of Algiers Asán Agá [Hasan Agha]. It is the only mention of Cid Amet Benelcadi in Diego de Haedo's text.[55] In his *AntiGiovio*, Jiménez de Quesada also speaks of a Cide Benalchade, with the honorific Cide but without the first name Amet and, instead of a son handed over in chains, the name belongs to one of Red Beard's captains (1952, 317). For Giovio, Hamete Alárabe was an enemy of the same Red Beard and it was this latter who trounced Bençayde 'the most principal of all the Alárabe leaders' (Giovio 1566, 23.1).[56] Writing in the year 1731, historian J. Morgan says that Aben al Cahdi was king of Cucco, and chief of the Zwouwa; he claims to have the information from a number of sources, including the works of Mármol [Carvajal] and Haedo. Writing in the twentieth century, John Wolf says that during the years 1520–30, the chief of the tribe Koukou was Ben-al-Kadi, another possible variant spelling of the name Benalchade (Giovio) and Benelcadi (Haedo). With Ben-al-Kadi, the Koukou joined with the Tunisians to take Argel, but chief Ben-al-Kadi died at the hands of Kheir-el-din (Haradín Barbarroja / Red Beard). Wolf says that his information comes from Spanish historian 'Marmols' [Mármol Carvajal] and that, after the defeat, the Koukou tribe sought peace with Kheir-el-din by sending him the head of Ben-al-Kadi (Wolf 1979, 14–15).

Each retelling, or translation, will multiply the chance of errors in transmission of the details of any 'true history.' Cervantes was obviously aware of this and used it to great effect. His 'errors' (descuidos) are just like the unavoidable variants in spelling of names that were provided by returning soldiers who had heard a story, or met an enemy on or off the battlefield, and then returned and told their story to someone who wrote down the most logical spelling according to their own language's phonetics and orthography. However, the historians of the sixteenth century used the variants to accuse each other of mistakes. On that model, Cervantes creates a narrative voice for a 'history' that reflects those of his day, with all their supposedly actual, but quite confusing, historical sources and Cides, Ametes, and Benalchades. For this, Cervantes did have a model in Giovio, who invented the apocryphal father Zidamet and included him in what the Italian historian considered to be an explicitly non-historical text. Cervantes takes the appropriated name as that of the apocryphal author of his novel, the father of Don Quixote, for whom Cervantes will only accept the role of stepfather. Cide Hamete's true history consistently and insistently debates its own truthfulness, as the reader hears other narrative voices who, with malevolent criticism and insinuation, introduce doubts and questions, and edit that true story. For example, Cervantes' narrators add 'deeds never seen' (DQ I.9); delete 'a couple of other minor things should be said, but they're all of little importance and don't really matter to the true telling of the story' (DQ I.9); and comment en route, for example, on a conversation between Sancho and Teresa that the translator 'thinks must be apocryphal ... but he didn't want to leave it out, so as to comply with what he owed to his position as translator' (DQ II.5).[57] In translating his own history from Latin to Castilian, Juan de Mariana called history 'the mother of all arts' and truth its 'first law' but, nonetheless, noted that with the language change, he had also freely altered content, 'as some things are appropriate for learned persons, and others for the non-educated' (1617 [1601], Prologue).[58] The *Quixote* is not only the first modern novel, but also a companion text to all sixteenth-century polemical preceptive writings about histories, chronicles, and truths.

Cervantes' Elogia

In the prologue to his *Novelas ejemplares,* Cervantes will let us know that the historiographical debates also included discussion on the *Elogios.* In 1611 Cabrera de Córdoba defines 'elogium' as a 'brief discourse or narration in praise,' that 'is difficult to do well,' and that is written 'only for captains, generals, or other serious persons' (1948 [1611],108).[59] This model conforms to that of Papire Masson, a law student under Françoise Baudouin who also wished to combine 'his theological and historical knowledge and method with the study of law,' but who was 'first and foremost a biographer' and who wrote both vita and elogia, distinguishing between them in considering the elogia 'a discourse sharply focused on the hero and composed of undiluted praise' and 'posthumous praise in declamatory form' (Backus 2008, 174). As stated above, Giovio used elogium in quite a different sense, along the lines of Roman legal usage in which it was conceived of as more or less a criminal record (Zimmerman 1995, 206). González Echevarría has noted that the damages caused by Don Quixote are akin to a 'criminal record' (2005, 61), and the jurists who have commented on the text unfailingly fault the protagonist for 'real' criminal acts.

It is Giovio's elogium-criminal record model that Cervantes adopts for his own elogia, those to Sancho Panza and Dulcinea at the end of the 1605 *Quixote,* as well as the author's own self-elogium in the prologue to the *Novelas ejemplares.* Supposedly written by a friend, this last is even accompanied by the portrait that would have been necessary for inclusion in Giovio's museum.[60] Baeza points out in his prologue that Giovio would only write the elogia for those whose portraits hung in his museum and tells his reader not to be disappointed that many famous Spanish kings, princes, and knights are not included in the volume.[61] As does Giovio in the *Elogios,* for his own self-elogium Cervantes begins with a demonstrative that links portrait to writing: 'this one pictured here, with the aquiline face, chestnut-brown hair, smooth and clear forehead,' and then adds his own preceptive comment: 'because to think that such elogia state to an exact truth is poppycock, for neither praise nor vituperation is final or determinate' (Cervantes 1995, 1:51).[62] Cervantes uses the same model, in ironic verse instead of prose, at the end of the first part of *Don Quixote,* in two sonnets by the Academics of Argamasilla, one to Dulcinea: 'This one pictured here with the brutish face, / arrogant breast and spirited gesture' (DQ I, p. 451, vv.1–2), and another to Don Quixote's sidekick: 'Sancho Panza is this one, small in body / but great in valour, a rare miracle!' (DQ I, p. 453, vv. 1–2).[63] Both of these latter elogia are related to those mentioned in a general sense in the prologue to the reader of the 1605 *Quixote,* when Cervantes' friend counsels him not to worry about a lack of introductory 'sonnets, epigrams, or elogia' (sonetos, epigramas o elogios), because he can either just make them up or ask 'some pedants or baccalaureates' (algunos pedantes y bachilleres) to write them (DQ I, Prologue). In general, Cervantes paints his characters with a combination of physical and character traits similar to that of Giovio in the *Elogios.* For example, the innkeeper in Don Quixote 'because he was fat, was also very calm-natured' (DQ I.2), and Sansón Carrasco is presented first with a physique that contradicts his name: 'although named Sansón, he was not very big,' and then with a facial description: 'a round face, a pug nose and a large mouth,' factions that are 'all signs of a malicious manner, a friend of jokes and jibes … traits he proved as he arrived' (DQ II.3).[64] Whereas Giovio fictionalized one detail or another about an actual portrait so as to create his elogia (Zimmerman 1995, 206), Cervantes took the next step, painting with historical verisimilitude both the praise of the elogium and the vituperation of the criminal records of his fictitious characters.

Neither Giovio nor Baeza had the funds to reproduce the museum's portraits in the published *Elogios.* Giovio reproduces just the text, but Baeza adds the wonderfully creative touch of an empty frame at the start of each elogium, telling the reader that he has done so in order that they might 'suffer more easily' the lack of the actual portrait, and fill the empty frame by imagining the figure as they read the text (see figure 6).

Baeza provides a formal space on the page for the reader's imagination to fill in the factions as he reads the description. This is a new step in ekphrasis, a painting with words that creates a visual impression in the mind of the reader who will need a blank space in which to place the results of his own imagination. De Armas (2006) studies the many forms of ekphrasis in Cervantes' *Don Quixote,* linking the author's use of the classical rhetorical technique to his time in Italy (2006, 9–13). Ana Laguna signals the combined influences of Northern Flemish art and Italian art models, and offers contemporary commentary that recognizes a different, more 'moral' ideal in the former, as well as a negation, by Cervantes in his *Coloquio de los perros* (Dialogue of the Dogs), of our 'ability to judge moral intentions through external appearances' (Laguna 2009, 94). Giovio's *Elogios* offer a model for moral commentary through description that links physical traits to actions, that is, a moralizing narrative ekphrasis. In his *Persiles,* Cervantes specifically comments on the connections between the artistic practices: 'History, poetry, and painting all represent [things] in a similar way and they are so alike that, when one writes history, they are also painting and when they paint, they are composing history' (Cervantes 2003, III, 12, 570).[65] Like Giovio, Cervantes paints character sketches / criminal records in words, along with the details of causality so as to better understand and explain the reality behind the described acts. The exposition of ironically real, or at least verisimilar, reasons for characters' actions brings them to life in realistic portraits that explore morality without rendering unidimensional judgments. A model for the possibility of appearance that does not reveal but, rather, masks and ironizes further enigmas of appearance and action is found in Giovio's works.

Cervantes' preceptive comments on how an elogium should be read, as well as his own written elogia, make clear that he knew Giovio's *Elogios.*[66] In *Don Quixote* (DQ I.32), among the books found in Juan Palomeque's inn is the *Historia del Gran Capitán Gonçalvo Hernández de Córdova,* which Eisenberg (2002, no.54) identifies as an edition that included Giovio's elogium and certain

Libro Quarto. 120.

CON ESTE esclarecido y heroyco rostro, dignissimo verdaderamente de vn gran Capitan, se mostraua a los Napolitanos Gonçalo Hernandez, quando hauiendo ganado muchas vitorias, acabo felicissimamente la guerra de Francia. Siendo a juyzio de los soldados, y clamor del pueblo, tenido por digno de corona triumphal, si el con gran modestia no la rehusara. Escriuo le este breue Elogio, por que su vida y hechos, E escripto en vn particular libro. Por que no puede justamente caber en poco papel, este capitan, que por merito, sobrenombre y conformidad de casi todas las naciones, es llamado Grande, y sin que en ello aya contradicion, excedio en grandeza de animo y valor de guerra, y gloria de toda humanidad y prudencia politica, casi a todos los capitanes de nuestro tiempo, siendo tan excelente, y de nombre tan sublime, que el rey Luys de Francia (que aun en los enemigos estimaua el verdadero valor) dixo publicamente, que selo auia embidia al Rey don Fernando de España. Por que comiendo ambos reyes juntos en Saona, Gonçalo Hernandez fue por honrra sentado à la mesa, donde el rey Luys, hauiendo lo alabado infinito, se quito vna cadena de oro, y se la echo al cuello. A

Todas las hazañas del gran capitan estan muy copiosamente escriptas por Paulo Iouio en la hystoria añadida.lib.5. cap.1.y lib.6. cap.1.y lib.8.dende.c.1. hasta.ca.10. y lib.9.cap.1.y su muerte esta.lib.15.cap.5.

De Gregorio Syluestre.

El gran Capitan soy si lo as oydo
Que te espantas de mi que miras hombre
De Turcos y Franceses fuy temido
Y Goncalo Hernandez es mi nombre
A mi grandeza solo fue deuido
Por capitan insigne el gran renombre
Si quieres saber mas de mis vitorias
Al Iouio lo pregunta en sus historias.

De George de Mōtemayor.

Mis grandes hechos veran
Los que no los han sabido
En que solo he merecido
Nombre de gran capitan
Y tuue tan gran renombre
En nuestras tierras y estrañas
Que se tienen mis hazañas
Por mayores que mi nombre.

Del Licenciado MACIAS BRAVO.

El gran

Fig. 6 Elogium of Gonzalo Hernández de Córdoba in Paolo Giovio, *Elogios*, 1568. Trans. Gaspar de Baeza. Courtesy of the Beinecke Rare Books and Manuscript Library, Yale University.

poems in praise of the Great Captain penned by Cervantes' contemporaries and friends. As seen in figure 6, in Baeza's translation of the *Elogios,* the Great Captain has a shortened elogium because, as it reads, his 'full life' has been written by Giovio as a separate work, and Baeza also provides bibliographical detail linking the elogium to Giovio's *Histories.* The first two poems in praise of Hernández de Córdoba are by Gregorio Silvestre and George de Montemayor, friends of both Cervantes and Baeza (see fig. 6).

In another elogium, echoing the very last lines of *Don Quixote,* one of the three poems praising Emperor Charles V's elogium ends with the first person poetic voice of the subject praising himself, then historian Giovio, and then the latter's pen:

> My good luck was combined
> with Giovio having understood
> how to exalt my role.
> His pen makes me strong
> against the river of forgetfulness
> against the power of death.
> Well we might conflate
> and even prefer
> we two to those two without equal
> Myself to Caesar in acts
> Giovio to Homer in words. (Giovio, 1568, fol. 209v, vv. 73–83)[67]

At the end of the Second Part of *Don Quixote,* the first person poetic voice of Cide Hamete's pen sounds in echo: 'For me alone was Don Quixote born, and I for him / he knew how to act and I, to write' (DQ II.74).[68] Cide's pen substitutes Don Quixote for Charles V and Caesar in the line of those who act, and itself for the pens of Giovio and Homer who write.[69] The difference is that Giovio's pen made Charles V 'strong / ... / Against the power of death,' whereas Cide Hamete's exhorts other authors to not resuscitate Don Quixote for another adventure 'against all the *fueros* of death' (DQ II.74).[70] Cervantes substitutes the poem's word 'power' (poder) for a legal image and instrument – the *fueros* which are Spain's law charters, and a word also used for laws and rules in general. Cervantes' narrative voice also links the lack of a specific origin for the protagonist with Homer's text, saying that Cide Hamete wished that all towns and cities in La Mancha might compete for the honour of claiming Don Quixote as their own, much as the seven cities of Greece did for Homer (DQ II.74). The verses in praise of Charles V from Baeza's translated *Elogios* are not found in Giovio's first edition, nor in the later editions in Latin, or Italian, all of which contain

Charles V's prose elogium followed by one poem. Apparently, translator Baeza added two more, one titled *Habla la Fama* (Fame speaks), anonymous in the *Elogios* but today included among the works of Spaniard Hernando de Acuña, and the other, cited above, which was written by Cervantes' friend Gregorio Silvestre. The parallel verses in the *Quixote* leave no doubt that Cervantes knew Baeza's translation of the *Elogios* or, at the very least, the poem his friend had written for that work.[71] We can read Giovio's *Elogios* as a point of departure for Cervantes who, in Don Quixote, inverts the historian's proportion of apocryphal detail sprinkled into historical narrative, borrows and adapts certain characters, and offers multi-voiced praise and vituperation in prose and in verse.

Giovio's Histories

Like the *Elogios*, Giovio's *Histories* have a decidedly unique literary flair. Giovio did not write a dry, dispassionate retelling of events, nor a chronicle that conformed to the image-building standards of the powerful but, rather, stories filled with information gleaned from interviews with returning soldiers and emissaries, in conformance with his eyewitness approach. His sources were varied: 'Giovio was ahead of most Europeans in his knowledge of the Turks, gained from extensive reading and questioning of travelers and merchants'; 'While he used archival documents when necessary, he preferred the oral interview, which allowed him to probe one witness with information extracted from another' (Zimmerman 1995, 29, 267). Giovio allows history's characters a certain freedom to speak for themselves, filtering their voices into his story line and vouchsafing for their veracity, albeit with certain caveats. For instance, in relating the history of Preste Juan, Giovio demurs when it comes to the magical powers of the unicorn's horn, admitting to having seen two of the horns sent as presents, but 'of the virtuous powers of this animal, I cannot affirm more than that of which public fame persuades those who wish to believe it. Because none of the ancients (whom I have read), mention this admirable virtue of the unicorn, with the exception of the Greek Heliano' (Giovio 1566, 18.8).[72] Giovio makes his own opinion clear, but allows the reader leeway to decide, as does Cervantes, who has his narrators, characters, translator, and 'second author' comment on events in the novel. Speaking of the development of fiction in the sixteenth century, Fernando Lázaro Carreter points out the novelty of a character's freedom to direct his own story, one recognizable to the reader as real life. For Giovio and Cervantes, however, as we have seen, those characters do not always have the last word. Cervantes' contemporary Páez de Castro combines Giovio's historiographical method with archival searches, saying that history is invention, wit, hard work, interviews, and reading of public memorials, gravestones, old notarial registries, and lawsuits, wills, and testaments, as well as investigations in libraries, archives, and old lawbooks.[73] The early narrative forms of legal volumes, archives, and lawsuits are adapted by both Giovio and Cervantes, who filter multiple testimonial voices but privilege the reader's role as narrative judge and ultimate arbiter of truth.

After speaking of the importance of history in his dedication of Giovio's translated *Histories* to Francisco de Erasso, Baeza also defends the art of translation:

> Others may find translation to be a humble occupation but, for me, there is nothing that is too humble. Cicero translated one of Plato's books. Saint Jerome translated many things, and in his day the Greek tongue was more 'of the people' in Rome than Castilian is today in Valencia. Erasmus, Angelo Poliziano, and Theodore Gaza, as well as many other erudite gentlemen of eternal fame, all translated. (Baeza, 1566, 'Dedicatoria,' *Histories*)[74]

Once published in Castilian, the *Histories* became more accessible, and so more polemical, as they reached more readers. In his own ironic gloss on the same ideas and ideals in the *Quixote,* Cervantes comments on translation, histories, trustworthy chroniclers, and the role of the reader.

Interrupted Histories

In the First Part of *Don Quixote,* Cervantes' first narrative voice moves from chapters 8 to 9 relating details of the search for an end to the protagonist's interrupted history with its battle between the knight and the Basque. The narrator thinks it must be in the archives and annals of someone around La Mancha, in part because 'his history must be a modern one' – an echo of Baeza's translated title for Giovio's *Elogios,* with its 'knights ancient and modern' – and then Cervantes' narrative voice tells his reader that after finding Cide Hamete's original text in the marketplace in Toledo, he instructed a Moorish translator to put the pages of the history's Arabic into Castilian, 'without deleting from or adding anything to those pages' (DQ I.9).[75] The translator does, however, become one of the voices privileged enough to comment, add, and delete material from Cervantes' text, despite this original exhortation by the 'second author.'

On returning to the history of the battle between Don Quixote and the Basque, Cervantes again echoes the *Elogios,* making the transition back into his history with a painting found in the folder of papers, what de Armas calls a 'metaekphrasis' (2006, 10). The painting is described in detail, although in past tense and without the introductory demonstrative pronouns found in

Giovio's *Elogios*. The narrative voice of he who now identifies himself as the 'second author' tells the reader that the painting was in the first sheaf of papers, describes the labels with inconsistent characters' names, and then states that there is more information but he has decided it is not crucial enough to include for the reader: 'a couple of other minor details should be taken into account, but all are hardly important, and do not come into play for the truthful telling of the history' (DQ I.9).[76] The painting's details are alluded to but hidden, both mentioned and masked as some of them, at least, are judged not important to the writing. This eyewitness account states boldly to having omitted at will. The history has been adapted by the second author, and the philosophical-historical primacy of first-person visual testimony and faithful recording of detail is denied. The reader has to be content with the story as told, or use his own imagination to fill in explicit blanks in the interrupted and redacted history. Giovio used detail from unreliable sources; Cervantes makes the detail itself illusive.

Like Don Quixote's battle with the Basque, Giovio's *Histories* were also interrupted. In Giovio's case, it was by the Sack of Rome and the actions of two Spanish soldiers, one from Córdoba and the other, a Basque. Both searched high and low in the Church of Santa María de la Minerva, tormenting the sacristans they found cowering there until they finally uncovered a lead box into which Giovio, fleeing the sack with Pope Clement, had placed his precious *Histories* along with a good quantity of silver. The way Baeza tells it, the Basque was content with the silver, and 'threw the books from him as he would a useless prisoner' but the Cordobés, 'no fool he,' took those books which had already been bound, so as to ransom them to Giovio and the pope. He left behind the unbound manuscript pages, which ended up 'ripped to shreds' (Baeza 1566, Summa, Book V).[77] Those missing chapters were never fully rewritten by Giovio, who only briefly recapped them on publishing the *Histories*. In the second edition of his translation, Baeza tells the reader that he is tired of hearing complaints about Giovio's partisanship against the Spaniards, and so he has restored the missing sections of what he calls the 'interrupted history' (historia interrumpida), but only those parts that involve the praiseworthy deeds of his countrymen and he insists: 'there is not even one word that is not taken directly from Giovio.'[78] The jurist adds, however, that those additions from Giovio's other works include some from the semi-apocryphal *Elogios* which, as Baeza made clear in his dedication of the volume, he apparently takes as fully consistent with history: 'in the judgment of serious men, this volume is the most excellent and prudent book of history that has been written in our time' (Baeza 1568, 'Dedicatoria').[79]

As did Giovio and Baeza, Cervantes also mixed real history with apocryphal elogia, description, and competing eyewitness testimonies.Those elements are key components of not only histories and elogia such as Giovio's, but also of legal glosses and cases. For example, one case in the archives of the Chancillería in Granada deals with a man named Gutiérrez from La Mancha who has sued to prove his nobility. The file for the case is enormous, with hundreds of folios of testimony from dozens of witnesses, all of whom were interviewed in La Mancha. Each witness statement begins with: 'In the villa of La Mancha on the ninth day of the month of November of 1598,' followed by the answers to a series of questions: 'says he does not know'; 'says he knows, and it is true', etc. ('En la villa de La Mancha ... ' 1598).[80] There is an echo in Cervantes' imprecise and ironic opening to the 1605 *Quixote:* 'In a place in La Mancha, the name of which I do not wish to recall' (DQ I.1).[81] All legal cases share the formal aspect of a multiplicity of voices relating the 'same' history, with contradicting versions of a debated truth. This is also how Giovio wrote his *Histories,* probing one eyewitness with the testimony of another (Zimmerman 1995, 267). Cervantes develops this pattern with additional, intentional lapses, using diverse layers of real and unreal historical voices to paint multiple legally compromised acts while filtering them through the memory of a character and narrators who selectively and pointedly see and remember as they choose to do so. One voice is never enough to relate a true history and, in Cervantes' work, the acts themselves as well as the precepts and philosophy of the disciplines are put to the test.

Don Quixote and the *Histories*

The 1605 *Quixote* was first published with four internal divisions, each bearing an epigraph identifying it as a 'part' of what we today consider the full First Part, published as one volume in 1605. Studies of the typographical composition of the first and subsequent editions of the 1605 *Quixote* note the insertions made by the press (Flores 1975), but the internal divisions seem to be those of Cervantes himself. That makes the slightly altered epigraph in some editions of the fourth part noteworthy. Whereas parts one, two and three are inscribed, respectively, 'The first / second / third part of the ingenious Don Quixote de la Mancha,' the fourth epigraph reads 'Fourth part *of the history* of the ingenious gentleman Don Quixote de la Mancha' (Cervantes 1998b, emphasis added). The fourth part of the 1605 *Quixote* is also where the reader finds mention of a number of (pseudo)historical characters also encountered in Giovio's *Histories.*

In his prologue to the 1605 *Quixote,* Cervantes' friend tells the author to invent sonnets, epigrams, and elogia for his work, relating them somehow (ahijándolos) to Preste Juan de las Indias or to the Emperor of Trapisonda (DQ I, Prologue), both of whom, as he has heard, were famous poets. Trapisonda is mentioned again when the narrator tells us that Don Quixote imagines he will be granted the empire of Trapisonda in recognition of his valour (DQ I.1), and Preste Juan has a second mention when the priest, speaking with the barber, likens books of chivalry to Milesian tales, that is, 'ridiculous stories,' given that the knights can be in Lombardy today, then tomorrow in 'the lands of Preste Juan of the Indies' (DQ I.47).[82] Cervantes' editors gloss the references with actual place names,[83] but deny a real existence to the characters themselves, saying that both are 'fabled characters' (personajes fabulosos) frequently mentioned in the books of chivalry.[84] In Giovio's *Histories*, both are real, and both do have a connection to the world of letters.

For the Emperor of Trapisonda, Giovio's version of the history begins with Caloyanes, the Christian king of Trapisonda, who for political gain marries his daughter Despina to the Moor Usuncasano, on the condition that he allow her to continue practising her Christian faith. Their daughter Marta, raised by her mother as a Christian, marries Harduel, who gains followers by publishing a new interpretation of Mohammed's law. Marta gives birth to Hismael, who will come to be known as Hismael Sofí and who, raised by his mother and grandmother, honours the Christians and never reproaches their law. Usuncasano's son Jacob succeeds his father, fears Harduel's power, and sends men to kill him, which they do, 'thus freeing Jacob's heart of its vain fear' (Giovio 1566, 13.5).[85] However, Harduel's disciple Tequel escapes, and becomes a hermit in caves along the river Euphrates known by the inhabitants as 'red heads' (cabezas rojas), which will also become his nickname.[86] Tequel lives there alone, away from human conversation and occupied in high contemplation of divine things. For the shepherds and labourers who come to know him there, he seems more than human, and he answers their questions as would a prophet; the fame of his saintliness extends widely (infinito) and, against his wishes, the curious bring him to towns and cities to show him off; eventually all Armenia is filled with admiration for his fame. At some point along the way, Caloyanes is killed and his 'Empire of Trapisonda' (imperio de Trapisonda) is reduced to no more than a province.[87] Giovio puts Trapisonda in the history books (which makes it true), says it was an empire, names the leaders, and tells the story of their rise and downfall. The prophet-like character, taken despite his wishes to the contrary to towns and cities to spout wisdom can also be seen as a precursor to Cervantes' Tomás Rodaja in *El licenciado Vidriera* and, in the story of a Christian mother keeping her faith alive although married to a Moor while teaching her daughter to follow suit, we read a non-clandestine version of a common Cervantes' intrigue.

Preste Juan de las Indias is given an even fuller treatment in the *Histories*, with author Giovio vouching for his real existence on the basis of informants, archives, histories, and a portrait. How he tells the story is, in itself, a structural tie to Cervantes' intercalated stories. In the 1615 *Quixote,* Cervantes has his protagonist reject the intercalated stories of Part I, when the character Sansón Carrasco informs Don Quixote and Sancho of complaints that the inserted story *El curioso impertinente,* no matter its own merits, should not have been included in the First Part as it was not integral to Don Quixote's history. The protagonist responds by saying that he has no idea what would have led his historian to include extraneous material: 'In truth, offering only my thoughts, sighs, tears, desires, and deeds would have made for a better work' (DQ II.3).[88] Paolo Giovio offers a narrative model for intercalated stories, identified as such by the historian as he narrates. On writing of Tunis: 'Well, since we are at this point it seems to me that it would be convenient to dedicate a few words to what I have learned about the kingdom of Tunis, and of Moorish custom. Given that I write history, I have come to know with the emperor's victory about many things that for a long time were known only to merchants' (Giovio 1566, 33.6); or of Gonzalo Hernández, who has just taken Ostia from the corsair Mena. Following the pope's pardon of Mena, we read: 'The deeds of the Spaniards and Gonzalo Hernández during the war of Granada, when the Catholic King Ferdinand won that powerful kingdom, were great and memorable, and it will not be a bother to the readers if we tell them briefly here and then later return to the history' (Giovio 1566, 5.2).[89] These extended asides offer a model praised by Cervantes in the 1605 *Quixote,* where we read that, thanks to Don Quixote's decision to become a 'caballero andante,' 'we enjoy now, in our own day which needs happy entertainments, not only the sweetness of his true history, but of all its stories and episodes, no less enjoyable and creative and true as the history itself' (DQ I.28).[90]

The narrative model developed, from the Giovio-Baeza example with its numerous and very digressive internal asides, through the 1605 *Quixote* with just a few intercalated stories, and then to the 1615 *Quixote,* with no material not tied directly to the main plot structure. The four internal parts of the 1605 *Quixote* can be read as one ironic elogium (first part), followed by a series of legal commentaries-through-adventures (parts two and three). In part four we have an incorporation of multiple (actual) historical characters and subplots linked mostly by happenstance, such as meeting at the inn or hearing the story of a captive, who are only tangentially tied to the main storyline. This last section of the 1605 *Quixote,* with its digressive narration, has its model in Giovio's *Histories.* The stitching together of the four parts, each tied in one way or another to Gaspar de Baeza, is a weave of the legal and historical narrative traditions that, combined, created a new form. In 1615 Cervantes perfected the form by omitting the digressions, and accepting the literary criticism incorporated in the voice of Sansón Carrasco, a Salamanca graduate who offers the opinions of the university's readers. These latter had found the intercalated tale to be misplaced, as it did not 'have anything to do with the history of Don Quixote' (DQ II.3).[91] Cervantes took the model, adapted and used it, then reworked and perfected it.

Preste Juan de las Indias

In Giovio's *Histories* Preste Juan's story begins with the Turks en route to Suez, marching up the coast 'to the confines of the kingdoms of David, the very powerful king of Ethiopia, whom our people call Preste Juan' (Giovio 1566, 18.5).[92] Then we read:

> Since we have mentioned Preste Juan, it seems to me that the reader will not be bothered if (after so many and such bloody battles and sad events in all the foregoing), I slightly digress here with more agreeable material, so that those who are tired of reading might rest. The digression will be pleasant, as it will include the description of Ethiopia, and things that many perceive to be fable will be seen to be true, and written in a true history. (Giovio 1566, 18.6)[93]

As in the earlier example, we see that the historian recognizes the value of a break in the main action, so that those who are tired of reading of bloody battles and sad events might rest. Interestingly, he does not say 'read or listen' – his assumption is a reader. Also noteworthy is the assertion that writing something in a true history will make it true. This is also what Cervantes says about history: 'It is a fine point of history that anything written in it can pass as true, for its proximity to the truths it accompanies' (Cervantes 2003, III, 10, 527).[94]

In Giovio's text as translated by Baeza, there is a very poetic description of Africa and its geography, including the 'great daring' of the Portuguese in sailing the waters where the Indian Ocean 'fights back the waves of another sea' that 'seems like another, different ocean' (Giovio 1566, 18.6); in this last, we hear the historian filtering his informant's voice in as his own conjecture on that other, different ocean, and then we read that Preste Juan's kingdoms are full of riches, and that he lives in the richest part, called Sceva, which is very specifically located: 'below the Antarctic Pole, at 22 grades' (Giovio 1566, 18.7).[95] There are details as to how long it takes to get there via different routes, and on the variety of peoples: Guineos, Mandinga, Manicongo, with the particular characteristics of each. Together, the general name of the 'vassals of Preste Juan' (vasallos del Preste Juan) is Abyssinians, and they are ingenious, with solemn customs; they govern themselves with very just laws, as do 'gracious Venetian men' (los gentiles hombres Venecianos) and they celebrate the Christian rites, even as to the use of organs during Mass (Giovio 1566, 18.7). Finally, Giovio justifies the real existence of Preste Juan:

> But because I would like to briefly say some things about Preste Juan's nobility, and his magnificence, and the customs of his court, and of his armies and his war material, and deeds, and of the birth of the Nile and the lakes of the moon, and of various types of beasts, it seems to me that it would be wise to say from whom I came to know this, so that the ignorant will not take as fable that which, on the basis of the testimony of many, is seen to be certain and notorious. I want all the credit to go to those who (following on my long and curious questions) told me these things. Among them was the Portuguese Pedro Álvarez, who was sent with Don Rodrigo de Lima as an embassador to Preste Juan. (Giovio 1566, 18.7)[96]

That first-hand informant Pedro Álvarez came back to Rome and presented a gold cross from Preste Juan to Pope Clement but then, sadly, died although 'he left some written commentaries, in which day by day he tells of his route and the events' (Giovio 1566, 18.7).[97] The Hispanic Society of America in New York holds a copy of those commentaries, in the form of a report and letter, published in 1533, from Pedro Álvarez addressed to Pope Clement VII (see fig. 7).

Contained with the report is a letter identified in *Hispaniae illustratae* as from Preste Juan himself to Pope Clement VII, translated from Ethiopian into Latin by Paolo Giovio (Schottus et al. 1603) (see fig. 8).

In case the spoken and written testimony of Pedro Álvarez, and the written letter to the pope from Preste Juan David himself do not suffice to convince his reader, Giovio adds another testimonial source: 'And after Pedro Álvarez, Pedro Abissino, a man of genteel and prudent wit, who had spent much time in Preste Juan's court, told me with great humaneness and truth of the notable things of the Abysinnians' (Giovio 1566, 18.7).[98] Peter the Abyssinian now teaches that language, which is also found in certain 'printed material in Rome, in Chaldean script,' to 'some of the curious' in the Eternal City (Giovio 1566, 18.7).[99] Giovio follows by explaining the origin of the name Preste Juan, giving his reader the Abyssinian word, and its meaning:

> This great king of Ethiopia, and of the Abyssinians, who our people, with a corruption of the real word call Preste Juan, is called in his land Belulgian, an ancient last name of his ancestral kings, which means 'pearl of immense value and incomparable excellence.' He who reigns today is named David, with the last name Atanadidinghel, which means 'incense of the virgin.' (Giovio 1566, 18.7)[100]

There's a little bit about Preste Juan David's parents, and then his unquestioned nobility: 'the uncorrupted nobility of his royal blood is proven with

Legatio Dauid Ae
thiopiæ Regis, ad Sanctiſſi-
mum D.N. Clementem
Papam VII. vnà
cum obedientia,
eidem ſanctiſ.
D.N. præ-
ſtita.

Eiuſdem Dauid Aethiopiæ Regis Le
gatio, ad Emanuelem Portu-
galliæ Regem

Item alia legatio eiuſdem Dauid Ae-
thiopiæ Regis, ad Ioannem Por-
tugalliæ Regem.

De regno Aethiopiæ, ac populo, déq;
moribus eiuſdem populi, nonnulla.

Antuerpiæ apud Guilelmum
Vorſtermannum.
Anno. 1533.

Fig. 7 Title Page of Report on Preste Juan David and the Aethiopians, by Pedro Álvarez addressed to Pope Clement VII. 1533. Courtesy of the Hispanic Society of America, New York.

LITERAE SERENISSIMI IOAN-
nis Regis Portugaliæ ad Sanctiſ
ſimum. D.N. Clementem
PP. VII.

Sanctißimo in Chriſto Patri, atque beatißimo do-
mino. D. Clemēti Papæ Septimo Diuina prouidentia
uniuerſæ Eccleſiæ dei præſidenti, &c.

SAnctißimo in Chriſto patri, atque
Beatißimo Domino, eiuſdem ſan-
ctitatis deuotißimus filius Ioan-
nes dei gratia Rex Portugalliæ,
& Algarbiorum citra ultraque
mare in Africa Dominus Guinæ,
Expugnationis, Nauigationis, Commercij Aethio-
piæ, Arabiæ, Perſidis, atque Indiæ, poſt humillima
ſanctorum pedum oſcula. Sanctißime in Chriſto Pa-
ter, & felicißime domine. Rex dominus, & pater
meus, cum animaduerteret, quam gratum Deo eſſet
futurum, ſi Aethiopiæ, atque Indie remotißimæ regio
nes, quæ fama tantum, atque ea quidem ambigua au-
ditæ fuerant, ſolerti nauigatione Chriſtianorum claſ
ſibus adirentur, ſtatim ab ipſo ſuſcepti regni initio
complures duces & ſubditos ſuos ad perſcrutanda
cognoſcendaque earum terrarum littora, inſtructis
ualidißimis claßibus miſit, ſcilicet ut Mauri gētiles
earū regionū populi ueritatem Chriſtianæ religionis
agnoſcerēt, Atq; obiter patefacto itinere, alij etiā po
puli reperirētur, qui deū Chriſtum colerēt, ſicut opi-
nione hominum eos inueniri poſſe ferebatur, Itaque
uolente deo tota Guinæ regio feliciter peragrata eſt.
In qua Rex de Manicongo cum ingentibus populis
ipſi ſubditis, qui ſe ad eius authoritatem ac obedien
tiam contulerat ſacro baptiſmate ſuſcepto Chriſtia-
nus effectus eſt, & complures aliæ gentes ex regio-
nibus Indiæ, Perſidis & Arabiæ ad Chriſtianam fi-
dem noſtrorum pietate & diligentia ſunt perductæ,
& quotidie aliæ atq; aliæ nationes, quæ tardius ueri
tatem agnouerunt exemplo aliarum ad Chriſtum con
uertuntur. & quanquam in his expeditionibus gra-
uiſſima amiſſarum nauium & Ducum, itemque nobi-
lium Equitum, & ſubditorum ſuorū detrimenta rece
piſſet, Tamen ab hoc eximiæ pietatis conſilio non
deſtitit, uti pium & Chriſtianum regem decebat. Ita
que eodem curſu mare Rubrum penetrante claſſe no-
ſtra repertum eſt, nunquam antea Chriſtianorum claſ
ſibus nauigatum. Nam fere totum in poteſtate Tur-
carum erat, & demum poſt diuturna atque aſpera
bella inuentum eſt iter, quod ad uulgo Preteian
nuncupatum Aethiopiæ Regem potentißimum du-
cit, qui cum uniuerſis regnorum ſuorum populis
Chriſtum colit. Ad hunc extemplo Rex pater meus le
gatum deſtinat, ut ad obedientiam ſanctæ ſedis Apo
ſtolicæ pertraheretur, oportunaque narrando, &
aperiendo certior redderetur tuam ſanctitatem in ſe
de Petri reſidere, & unicum eſſe in terris Chriſti ui-
carium, cui omnes Chriſtiani reges obedientiam cum
ſumma ueneratione præſtare conſueuiſſent. Nec mul
to poſt idem Aethiopiæ rex quum legatum remitte-

Fig. 8 Letter from Preste Juan to Pope Clement VII, translated from Ethiopian into Latin by Paolo Giovio. 1533. Courtesy of the Hispanic Society of America, New York.

the testimony of histories, because among his people, the memories of events, heredity, and royal succession are faithfully written down as law' (Giovio 1566, 18.7).[101]

To sum up, Preste Juan's real existence has been verified by a Portuguese and an Abyssinian, as well as attested to with the former's written diary, and Preste Juan's own letter; further, his language is found in the Chaldean letters of published works in Rome, and his nobility is codified as law in the written histories of his own people. If that is not enough, part of his kingdom includes the famous city Siene, celebrated by poets and known as the place in which 'are born the stones of the obelisks' (Giovio 1566, 18.9), and Giovio even has Preste Juan's portrait. He ends the history with the most recent information:

> Wishing to publish this work, I learned that Preste Juan David had passed away. He reigned after having been under the tutelage of his mother for twenty-six years, and he lived forty-eight in all. He was a most virtuous man, with a clever and lively mind for all the business of war and peace, and very learned, so much so that he knew astrology. He was of medium build. His face was round and the colour of a quince fruit when it has been toasted under embers. Lively eyes. Not matted hair, like black men (as can be seen in his portrait, which I have from when he was alive). (Giovio 1566, 18.9)[102]

The conflation of the real and the not-so-real in Cervantes' work had a clear precedent in Giovio's *Histories* and, even more so, in the Italian historian's *Elogios*. Cervantes took the next step, the creation of a portrait in words of an invented verisimilar character. At least some seeds of the creation of the alternate reality that we call the modern novel are in the Italian historian's works. Giovio justified the existence of Preste Juan with documents, and Cervantes followed suit for his Don Quixote, albeit with invented documents, paintings, and archives that 'must exist' but are hidden, somewhere in the annals of the towns and cities of La Mancha.

Etc.

There are numerous other elements in Cervantes' work that seem to relate directly to Giovio's *Histories* and *Elogios*. For Giovio, Cachadiablo and Manicongo are real people; for Cervantes, they are the authors of the elogia to Sancho Panza and Dulcinea with which he ends the 1605 *Quixote*. Giovio tells of hero Diego García de Paredes whose melancholy causes him to lose his mind from time to time and throw rocks at people (Giovio 1566, 8.4); Cervantes' lovelorn Cardenio will do the same. Giovio tells of knights being armed 'with the ordinary words and military rites, that is, striking him lightly on the left shoulder with an unsheathed sword' (Giovio 1566, 15.12),[103] and he even describes how the pope knighted two Aztecs brought back from the New World (Giovio 1568, fol. 198); Cervantes sends out Alonso Quixano, an unlikely knight errant who is armed with a blow to the neck followed by one to the shoulder (DQ I.3). In Giovio's work, the Turks hang the heads of their fallen enemies from palm trees 'so as to amuse the eyes of their boss when he passed by with the novelty of such a terrible spectacle, representing the victory they had gained' (Giovio 1566, 17.8); Cervantes will have Sancho Panza note that the trees are 'full of human feet and legs' (DQ II.60) when he finds the enemies of Roque Guinart hanging from the branches.[104] Giovio tells of the great Captain (gran capitán) Gonzalo Hernández who goes out 'breaking down the mills' (quebrando los molinos) (Giovio 1566, 5.2); Cervantes has Don Quixote imagine the mills to be giants, ready for battle (DQ I.8). In the 1615 *Quixote,* the protagonist tells Sancho about 'famous men' (famosos varones) slandered in histories, among them Alexander the Great of whom it is said 'that he was, to a certain point, a drunkard' (DQ II.2).[105] The same detail is found in the verse that accompanies Giovio's elogium of the same figure, where we read that although he overcame many peoples and kingdoms, he himself was overcome and 'brought down by wine' (del vino y rendido) (Giovio 1568, fol. 4). The palace parties in Giovio's elogium of Ippolito de' Medici share the extravagance and settings of those of the duke and duchess in the 1615 *Don Quixote.* In the exemplary novel *El celoso extremeño,* Cervantes' character Loaysa speaks of the 'the great Sophi Tomumbeyo' (gran sofí Tomunibeyo) whose songs are sung by his people (Cervantes 1995, 2:109), a description matched by that of Giovio in the *Histories* (Giovio 1566, 18.1).[106]

In addition to the multiple voices, truths, inventions, and digressive intercalations, there is another shared formal aspect in the reliance on the prudence of the reader: Giovio's narrator offers two choices and allows the reader to decide: 'Because he traitorously killed twenty-two brothers or (what is even worse than death), he blinded them, burning their eyes out' (Giovio 1566, 33.4).[107] He killed them, or what is worse, he blinded them: you decide, reader. Cervantes frequently offers two options: 'male, or female, donkeys' (pollinos, o pollinas) (DQ II.10); only, in this last instance, he seems to then say that it does not really matter. Leaving it up to the reader, he continues the history. Cervantes, like Giovio, recognizes that in a true history, multiple perspectives allow valuable space for a reader's own imagination. Giovio offered details that were both historically true or at least verisimilar, and fabulously attractive. He accepted the reports of returning soldiers and created the full stories by fleshing them out and combining them. For Cervantes, too, a reader is the judge of the true history an author (witness) purports to tell, and multiple versions add depth and credibility to that narration.

Close describes Cervantes' 'radical refusal of omniscience. He assumes that what we read is what a witness saw or heard or heard from someone else, "more or less" as originally seen or heard or reported. The "more or less" is a qualification used by him [Cervantes] to suggest a plausible margin of error between the immediate act of hearing or seeing and subsequent recollection or transmission' (2000, 68). Close describes both Cervantes and his characters as 'focalizers' through whom the reader gets the information. To a certain extent, Cervantes only allows those other witnesses to speak through his own filter (pen), making him a sort of, to borrow Close's term but with a slight modification 'superfocalizer,' much as were the historians like Giovio who got their information from returning soldiers and emissaries. All histories are, ultimately, written through the perspective of one person, but that writer may, as did Giovio and Cervantes, insert other 'I' figures who believe, doubt, confirm, or negate each other's testimony.

In the 1605 *Quixote* Cervantes pretends to cede control to a previous author (Cide Hamete) who, like Paolo Giovio, is purported to be an enemy of the Spaniards, that is, one who cannot possibly tell the whole truth about them. Cervantes also invents a translator, adding the same layer that Baeza added to Giovio's texts. Cervantes' translator provides what turns out to be unreliable access to Cide's text, adding and deleting after having promised not to do so. Protagonist Don Quixote discusses in detail his expectations for the fame that will result from his life and deeds, recounted by a reliable 'historian.' By the 1615 *Quixote,* Cide and his translator are positioned as the arbiters of all truths, as they censor and comment, while real-world author Cervantes fashions around and through them a more perfect, sophisticated version of a 'truthful history,' and the character Don Quixote is in the hands of other inventors of stories. The protagonist has not read the most recent history, that of his own adventures. This places him in a precarious position as his inventions are now fodder for others to weave their own version of his entertaining history.

For Friedman, Cervantes' work 'justifies the study of literature on its own terms, not as the stepchild of other disciplines' (1994, 120). I agree with the spirit, if not the letter, of the statement, as historically, 'literature' as such did not exist in Cervantes' day. We can and should study the text on its own terms, but also in the context of other disciplines at the moment of its writing. In so doing, we can recover more of the original meaning of the author's creation, that sense the text 'would have had for its first readers' (Lerner 1996, 64).[108] All late sixteenth- and early seventeenth-century writers were 'men of letters,' and many of them were also jurists and historians. Reading the legal and historical tomes alongside the creative works elucidates that relationship, and improves our understanding of the genesis of the creative genre.

Parr suggests that acknowledging Cervantes' subversive discourse in the novel 'better reflects the richness of the work and of Cervantes's genius by showing how his talent permitted him to express subversive ideas, threatening to the established order, within a highly repressive socio-political milieu' (1988, 164). Parr is absolutely right on the subversive aspect, but the socio-political milieu was anything but orderly, particularly when it came to legal and historical truths. So as to communicate his message in that disorderly world, Cervantes creatively put the literary precepts, legal exemptions, historical 'facts,' and literal and philosophical definitions in full living-colour context, debating and resolving them in the court of public opinion, that is, by his protagonists, his characters, and his reader-judges. Speaking of the history of narrative development, Friedman points out that '*Don Quixote* is an experimental work; it brings theory into the practice of writing at the moment that praxis is being formulated and tested' (1994, 113) and Cervantes' 'ludic approach to the theory of the novel makes the work a theoretical treatise within its practice' (1980, 206).[109] We see this clearly in the 1615 Second Part of *Don Quixote* when the protagonist, who created his own adventures in the First Part on the basis of his reading of certain books, is out-invented by those who are most up-to-date in their reading, as they have read the First Part of *Don Quixote*. With that, Cervantes tells us that readers are always, and ultimately, in control of history.

7 Cervantes' *mos hispanicus*: Considerations and Conclusions

Miguel de Cervantes was a writer of 'good letters' in an era when that rubric was used for writing in all disciplines. The enormous bibliography on Cervantes and his works includes a number of studies related to the author's use of legal language and detail, as well as his commentary on the concept of history as a genre. With few exceptions, most of those studies have seen Cervantes' work through the lens of literature, literary artifact, and /or development. That restricts the work to a later model for literature, and misses much of the author's message. On the other hand, legal scholars who have commented Cervantes' use of juridical detail have failed to see beyond the argument of the work. The author's gloss on the contemporary legal situation through his portrayal of characters whose acts defy societal norms constitutes another layer of ironic commentary, missed by the legal scholars. By his own criteria, Cervantes did not write a novel but rather a history. His inclusion of such a wide range of incisive juridical commentary in that history calls for a perspective on his work that appreciates its place in the juridical-historical debates of his day.

In the full environment in which history and law were being hammered out of their medieval and into their modern forms, Miguel de Cervantes used the precepts, elements, and details of those two disciplines to create the contours of a new genre. His appropriation of juridical elements could have been for personal reasons, such as pertinent legal glosses on debt for a man whose family had recurring problems with it; or for social concern, in reflecting an ideal of justice at a historical moment when surrounding reality was sorely lacking in it. It is crucial to recognize that the creative impulse that inspired Cervantes to weave from almost-real character portrayals, muddied historical detail, and legal chaos a new type of work incorporated a wide range of intellectual precedent. The full background of Cervantes' creation should take into account all of those factors, fields, and disciplines. The result was a new genre, the modern novel, and specifically one text whose resonance would outlast the particular and enrich the universal in its portrayal of an idealist and a pragmatist who live out their dreams together while they exemplify reality's difficulties in living up to its own ideals in a pragmatic way.

Cervantes' work followed, and developed out of, a few centuries of humanist thought that had opened up the parameters of the fields of law, history, theology, politics, and philosophy, with a concomitant reworking of the limits and preceptive norms of each, and the resulting recognition that their strictures did not cover all contingencies. Within the full range of the liberal arts, Cervantes found seeds for creative thought, and he used certain paradoxes in his surrounding reality to fashion, and then to perfect, a new genre. As Barry Ife said of the picaresque, writers of literary texts abuse the conventions of linguistic rules 'in order to tap the anarchic creative potential of the medium' (1985, 45). The fictional text allows for contradiction and paradox.[1] However, *Don Quixote*'s author did not merely reflect reality's paradoxes, as did the anonymous author of the *Lazarillo,* by giving voice to a puzzlingly silent real person. Cervantes illustrates the paradoxes inherent in ideals as well as reality by appropriating the rhetorical strategies of 'fictional,' 'fantastical,' and very 'real' juridical and historical texts. While legal scholars attempted to peacefully resolve conflicting arguments, and writers of historical texts battled for supremacy in the spurious realm of pure objectivity, Cervantes moved the debates forward in a new form whose parameters he himself established.

Over the past twenty years, there has been a lot of work done on law and literature. The critical mass of those studies constitutes a burgeoning field or discipline that identifies itself as 'Law and Literature.' Scholars researching the relationship between the disciplines have for the most part concentrated on the eighteenth century forward, and studied the connections between the fields as coincidence in two written intellectual products that both evidence similarities such as ambiguities of interpretation (Hanafin et al. 2004, 1–2). One of the early collections of articles in the field speaks to the 'stories, explanations, performances, linguistic exchanges' of legal discourse and to the inherent rhetorical properties of language but, again, with a modern focus (Brooks and Gewirtz 1996, 2, 14–22). Recently, some of that scholarship has taken the *Quixote* and quixotism as an abstract ideal incorporated into later texts in service of other crucial historical movements. Wendy Michiko Motooka, for example, offers the character Don Quixote as 'a prime example of irrational power' at the service of England's 1688 Revolution: 'Quixotism, as a reminder that reason is a fiction, suggests the arbitrariness and instability of constructs supposedly authorized by reason, including philosophy, history, morality, gender, and government' (1992, abstract).[2] That later use of quixotism takes the arguments full circle:

Cervantes contained an irrational reality in the pages of a book that became an example of the irrationality of reason.

My hope in the preceding has been to explore the sixteenth-century historical roots of the combined questioning on the philosophical nexus between history and law, and to highlight its treatment by Cervantes, who synthesized the intellectual turmoil of his era into a new aesthetic product, a new genre. In the sixteenth century, the literature component of today's Law and Literature studies was, like history, in a stage of infancy. Today we study medieval and Renaissance texts as literature but for those who wrote them, they were 'good letters' with a specific agenda: draw more converts to the church, tell the stories of a battle, offer examples on moral behaviour, celebrate heroes, etc. In sixteenth-century Spain, the word 'literature' was any and all writing down of letters: that is how one Latin-Spanish dictionary defines it in the late fifteenth century (Palencia). Another, compiled in 1611, does not even include the word (Covarrubias). In tractates written in the sixteenth century, there are references to 'Christian literature' meaning the Bible, or to 'Mosaic literature' meaning the Koran; in both of these cases, the religious word (and law) is literature because it is written down. Up to and throughout the sixteenth century, writing was 'good letters' with a meaning of 'moral learning' or 'literacy' in phrases such as 'good letters and learning'; 'good letters and disciplines'; 'good letters and philosophy'; 'the doctrine and erudition of good letters, whose practice and use ...' (CORDE).[3] In the year 1600, Spaniard Gaspar Gutiérrez de los Rios wrote a work titled *General notice of estimation of the arts* (*Noticia general para la estimación de las artes*) in which, after writing about the history of letters and learning as he saw it, he offers this description of the art of writing:

> the art and exercise undertaken by writers of good letters and teachers of reading and writing, who are also called grammarians, primary school teachers, antiquarians, scribes, stenographers, and men of letters or chroniclers; they practise a profession also called literature, which jurisconsult Ulpian excluded from the liberal arts. Maybe because it is the fundamental base of grammar, or maybe because it imitates the liberal arts in its use of letters, Ulpian also conceded that custom has it that salaries of school teachers are, extraordinarily, the same as those of professors of liberal arts. With time, this art became so esteemed that it entered into the number of the liberal arts by an imperial decree which specified that the art of reading and writing well is one of the greatest virtues to be had among all studies and liberal arts, etc. Today, this art has so increased in importance that one can more easily and more assuredly by the pen than by the sword become a noble man. (1600, 92–3)[4]

This is 1600, and Gutiérrez de los Ríos accepts second-century Roman jurisconsult Ulpian's definition and description of 'literature' as the teaching of reading and writing, while noting the importance and respect to be garnered by those skills in his own day and time. Legal writings, histories, theatre, poetry, and every other type of writing were 'good letters' and all of the other writers of Cervantes' day – historians, jurists, philosophers, poets, soldiers, and theologians – saw their own field of 'good letters' as the most important one: for historians, history was the 'science of all sciences'; for the jurists, law was the 'science of all sciences.' Cervantes has Don Quixote say that chivalry is the 'science of all sciences.' My reading of that is that Cervantes saw the fallacy in thinking that any one thing was everything. His perspective is both synthetic and forward-looking, and he was going to replace the idealism of the past with one that looked clearly and realistically, albeit ironically, at man and his present. In Spain, this is the moment when Renaissance hopefulness gives way to pragmatic realism, a move we see highlighted in the differences between the 1605 First Part and the 1615 Second Part of the *Quixote*. In 1605, Don Quixote is the resurrected memory of a past ideal, created as part of a full discussion and debate on law, history, politics, philosophy, and religion. In 1615 he is a literary character and Cervantes will, in a stunning statement of creative autonomy, kill his protagonist so as to retain creative copyright over him. This is a legal stance and assertion of an entirely new legal right – creative copyright of a character, unheard of in Cervantes' day and still contentious in our own.

Cervantes solidified the parameters of a new written art form. His modern concept of novel accommodates both truth and non-truth (as did history), both cause and result (as did law), and both hero and comic foil in a thoughtful dialogue on life and literature. While the preceptists proceeded to sort it all out, Cervantes juggled history as record of events, as archive, as documentary trail, and as translated retelling with multiple voices in prose and verse, while showing how all of those are unreliable. He put the precepts themselves into action. Part of what makes him modern is that he recognized that there is no historical truth, just as there is no perfect justice. The ideals are laudable but reality, even an alternate reality, is something else entirely. By putting 'on stage' in his prose all of these contemporary, very real debates, Cervantes struck a chord. He put his precepts for literature and life in action, as part of a wider debate. His contemporaries were rewriting the laws on legal exemptions for the insane, and rewriting Aristotle's genre distinctions in preceptive works, while they constructed and cemented the boundaries of those forms and their formulas. Cervantes had the stroke of genius to act out both the concerns and the precepts of multiple disciplines in the pages of a book written in prose and verse, a new type of hero-creating epic. The character Don Quixote is dramatic and mimetic, tragic and comic, real and imaginary; and his history is a new genre, a modern novel capable of doing all that. The *Histories* and *Elogios* of Paolo Giovio, in Baeza's translation, were very popular works and Cervantes' gloss on them includes their incorporation into a chivalric 'history' that serves as a mask for an ironic social and juridical commentary. As Anthony Close (2000) has made clear, Cervantes' goal in writing seems most obviously to have been to entertain. We know from his own comments that he thought to solidify his literary legacy with a masterpiece epic, his *Persiles,* which is, by rights as Armstrong-Roche (2009) has pointed out, both a backward-looking epic and a forward-looking novel. It is not surprising that Cervantes wanted to write a new version of a form that had both created eternal heroes and solidified the reputations of authors whose names outlived their historical moment. After centuries, epic still entertained and educated (enseñar deleitando). What happened instead is that Cervantes, as a creative filter for the multiple intellectual and artistic threads of his era in his own hard-lived actuality, created an ironic epic character in Don Quixote.

If we think of Cervantes' protagonist as a personification of the fears of the *mos gallicus,* that is, as an ahistorical misapplication of Roman statues in a contemporary setting, and Sancho Panza as a personification of the usage and custom based Fuero Juzgo, with its judgments based on past deeds brought to bear on contemporary circumstances (*mos italicus*), we can better understand Cervantes' gloss. The Partidas model is admirable in its principles, but in reality it acts like a bull in a china shop, while the plain, simple, and certain justice of the Fuero Juzgo renders a practical but unworkable righteousness. Neither is adequate in the modern environment in which Cervantes and his contemporaries found themselves. As jurists like Baeza and Baudouin sought to read the lessons of law in its history, Cervantes tried to move the discussion back to the underpinnings of the law, to its origin in reasonable social discourse. The amount of legal commentary in Cervantes' *Don Quixote,* and the subtlety with which it is addressed make a strong case for the author having had some legal training. Lacking empirical evidence to confirm this, we can nonetheless appreciate the masterful use Cervantes made of the juridical-historical polemic as a set piece for commentary, and as a foundation on which he ended up building another type of writing, one that both was and was not history. In so doing, Cervantes created a new form that addressed the philosophical concerns with history, justice, and truth by putting them in an ideal context, a form removed from reality and its problems with accommodating paradox and expecting perfection.

Cervantes has Don Quixote come down on the side of the kings, in recognizing the separate goals of church and state, but also insist on the combination of natural and divine law which allows a man to defend himself, his dreams, and his beliefs. The protagonist opposes the abuses of ecclesiastical judges who force men against their will, and demands that the king exercise his proper role in protecting his subjects against such injuries. However, like Spain's kings, Don Quixote is unable to enforce his decisions; Philip II repeatedly issued pragmatics recognizing that his previous orders had gone unobserved, a process most clearly seen in the constantly reissued sumptuary laws. In the 1605 *Quixote,* the protagonist advocates forthrightly but the result is a scattershot justice: Andrés' whipping stops but only briefly and while Don Quixote is in sight; once he has left, the abuse resumes and worsens (DQ I.4). In the 1615 *Quixote,* Sancho Panza is a non-reader who cuts through the confusion in written statutes to uphold an honest, forthright version of justice.[5] The collective memory of Spain's early constitutions is reflected in Sancho's decisions and laws, but Sancho cannot bear the demands of the office. The old guard, whether that represented by Sancho Panza and the Fuero Juzgo or Don Quixote and the Siete Partidas, is not the answer to the modern state's demands. A return to either of those collections is not the answer, but Cervantes' fictional *mos hispanicus* does accord each its due in terms of the history lesson they provide, and the opportunity to use those lessons so as to better approach a future just state. It is a creative juridical-historical stance, with its insistence on the inviolable freedoms of natural law, and its recognition that each and every individual, and each and every law, must be fully re-interpreted in what will always be ever-changing circumstances. Cervantes does not shy away from any facet of his era's legal discourse, but rather takes it head-on, albeit frequently sub rosa, and subversively.

Cervantes takes the creatively relevant parts of literary preceptives, as well as the contentious contemporary developments in history and law, and combines them in a multifaceted gloss. His quixotic *mos hispanicus* does not dismiss out of hand the old laws, as did the *mos gallicus.* Nor does it follow the *mos italicus* with an automatic assumption of the viability of those earlier codes in a contemporary context. However, it does pragmatically and prudently admit their solid principles as a history lesson, as did Baeza in his manuscript gloss to Spain's Ordinances (see fig. 1). In their Pragmatics, Ferdinand and Isabel had explained why new laws were sometimes necessary: 'man, with his nature and shrewdness, invents new things and exquisite cunnings every day' (Pramáticas, fol. 36, law 42, dated Madrid 4 dic. 1502).[6] Of Cervantes's cunning and inventive mix of characters, storytelling, history, and law, a new and exquisite form was born – a modern novel, that has spoken clearly ever since, to all those who read it with prudence and discretion, of what justice and history really are – the parents, or step-parents if you will, of fiction, because a true history is as illusory as perfect justice, but all history and justice contains some hidden truths. As concepts, ideals, and stories, all will be judged and rewritten by their readers, we the vulgo.

Notes

Introduction

1 'una de las más violentas polémicas que acaso recuerde la historia jurídica de occidente' (Guzmán Brito 1978, 11).

2 De juris interpretibus dialogi sex. 'sint veteres interpretes plebei, nocui, inepti, sophistae, barbari, suum cibus, benarum omnium artium imperiti, serviliter, sordide nostram tractantes disciplinam, rixantes de lana caprina, sycophantae, vitiligatores, pestes ingeniorum, lacunae, sentinae foedissimae, tortores, cornifices studiosorum, rabulae, praestigiatores, ad aratrum nati, non bene de mente constituti' (Alberico Gentili, cited in Guzmán Brito). Here, I have translated to English from Guzmán Brito's Spanish: 'los antiguos intérpretes son plebeyos, funestos, ineptos, sofistas, bárbaros, alimento de cerdos, ignorantes de todas las buenas artes, sórdidos y serviles tratadistas de nuestras disciplinas, dispuestos a la pendencia por cualquier fruslería, sicofantas, picapleitos, pestes de los ingenios, huecos, escorias repugnantes, torturadores, verdugos de los estudiosos, rábulas, impostores, nacidos para el arado, no bien constituidos de mente' (Guzmán Brito 1978, 12).

3 For the ubiquitousness of legal proceedings in Cervantes' day, see Kagan (1981).

1. History, Jurisprudence, and the Creation of the Novel

1 'sine bonis literis ceca et manca et omnis eruditio simulam memineris sine virtute' (Baeza undated, gloss to Ordenamientos reales). The full text of this hand-written note penned on the last folio of a manuscript held by the Escorial library can be seen in figure 1.

2 'si la obra literaria es un producto de un momento histórico y cultural determinado, tiene que responder a la coyuntura histórico-social en la cual se produce' (Sabor de Cortazar 1979, 41); 'observaciones que difícilmente pueden entenderse fuera del contexto histórico' (Ettinghausen 1996, 27).

3 Wardropper says 'the novel has its roots in historiography' and suggests that Cervantes was preoccupied with 'historical truth and its cognition' due to 'the crisis being undergone by the historian's art' (1965, 3, 7). Gaylord asserts that *cervantistas* have not taken into account that 'Cervantes might be engaging, in *serious* fictional dialogue' with the historians of his day, and asks that we see his 'fictional representation' as 'deeply engaged with history' (1998, 127).
4 'deslizamiento de códigos lingüísticos' (Lerner 1998, 210).
5 'nuestro derecho, de donde depende la buena administración de la república todo vino de la historia' (Céspedes 1965, 228).
6 'Celtiberae, ad quam descendens cum vidisset locum ubi Barcanona erat, valde pulchrum, & deliciosum, Civitatem hercules ibi dificavit, quam ex Barca, nona barcinonam appellavit, Et sic tempore, quo Hercules predictus, renavit, aedificavit in Hispania Civitates Scilicet, Sibiliam, Tarraconam, Balagarium, et Barchinonam, usque ad hoc tempus, quo currit anno. Christi, Millesimo, cc lxviiii, sunt. anni duo Mille, trecenti.&octuaginta, quibus fuit civitas Barchinonae edificata. Et fuit antequam Roma construeretur. cccclx annis. Et haec civitas Barchinonae: fuit constituta ante adventum Christo. Dcclii.annis. Et capta Hispania fuit in eadem Rex per Herculem constitutus nomine hesperiam grecus. & ab eo voluit nominari hispaniam.& fuit hispania sub dominio grecorum, usque ad tempus sonsulum romanorum' (Usatges 1544, law numbers 11–13, fol. 3).
7 'Decidir lo que se va a contar es, irremediablemente, inventar el pasado' (Lerner 1991, 125). Kagan points out that 'even the most high-minded and scholarly early modern historians had a nasty habit of "cherry-picking" their evidence so as to achieve a particular reading of a given personage, era, or event' (2009, 5).
8 One of the authors proposed as the anonymous source of the *Lazarillo* is Diego Hurtado de Mendoza, who studied civil law at the University of Salamanca. Francisco Rico disputes this proposed authorship, saying that it is not certain that Hurtado de Mendoza did study law and that, if he did, it would have been at a much earlier date than the 1554 publication of the novel (Rico 2002, 36, n. 13). He also disputes the possibility of Alfonso de Valdés as author, for similar chronological reasoning (39). The series of pragmatics pre-date the novel, and would easily allow for either man to be the author. It is not my intent to join the debate on who the anonymous author of the *Lazarillo* might be, but only to point out the dates which also conform to events in the novel, such as the battle of Guelves.
9 It is noteworthy that the Monarchs direct most of the blame to the women, for not being content with their status of 'mancebas públicas.' The pragmatics referred to here are found in law number 96, parts 1 (1487) and 2 (1502) and law 97, parts 1 (1491) and 2 (1503). In the first, the clergy complain that the justices show a lack of respect for them by arresting the women and falsely making them confess: 'las fazen confessar que son mancebas públicas de los dichos clérigos no lo seyendo'; in the

third, the Monarchs allow the arrests with sufficient proof: 'si la dicha información fuere bastante para que por ella según las leyes de nuestros reinos y lo que por nos está mandado: la tal manceba de clérigo debe ser presa'; and in the fourth, they express outrage at the new loophole of marrying the women to other servants: 'E agora somos informados que lo susodicho ha tenido mucho inconveniente: porque algunos de las mancebas de los dichos clérigos y beneficiados no contentas de estar por mancebas públicas de los tales clérigos, por encubrir el delito que en ello cometen se casan con algunos criados suyos' (Pramáticas 1528, fol. 89). The earlier Fuero Juzgo prohibits any priest, deacon, or subdeacon of the church from having 'fornicio' (sexual relations) with a widow, virgin, or any other woman, whether within marriage or in an adulterous relationship (Fuero Juzgo III.4.18), although other laws on 'barraganas, barraganería' (concubines, concubinage) make clear that the practice continued. In what follows, I use Pramáticas for the 1528 volume, in which the Bulas y pramáticas are followed by the Leyes de Toro.

10 González Echevarría has noted that stories drawn from legal cases 'emerge in Spain from *La Celestina* and the picaresque on' (2005, xv), and that 'law saturates the Spanish literature of the Golden Age and is a determining factor in the origins of the novel' (1990, 51).

11 'A través de los textos literarios—especialmente los de índole narrativa y dramática—en que el autor se propone reflejar la actividad social que le rodea y el ambiente en que vive, podemos percibir cómo las normas jurídicas eran entendidas por los contemporáneos e incluso cómo eran burladas; cómo la realidad reaccionaba contra las leyes y cómo en muchos casos estas eran impotentes para conseguir el fin que el legislador se propuso al dictarlas. Los textos legales nos dicen lo que debía ser; los textos literarios lo que realmente era' (Ossorio Morales 1949, 18–19).

12 'se muestra partidario del matrimonio por amor' until speaking of his own daughter's marriage (Ossorio Morales 1949, 36–40). Ossorio Morales is correct on the source, although the Fuero Juzgo is not as clear-cut as he states; there are caveats on the idea of marriage for love. The second law of the section on marriages and births specifically prohibits a daughter from marrying, or having relations with, one man while her father has already chosen another for her, and renders both offending parties to the power of he who was originally promised the woman's hand in marriage: 'Si alguno desposar[e] la manceba de voluntad de su padre, e la manceba contra voluntad de su padre quisiere casar con otro, e non con aquel a quien la prometió su padre, aquesto non lo sofrimos por nenguna manera que ella lo pueda fazer'; 'ambos sean metidos en poder daquel con que la desposaran de la voluntad de su padre' (Partidas III.1.2). Rabell focuses on Spanish novels that fictionalized laws issuing from the Council of Trent, and mentions that Cervantes' *Las dos doncellas* can also be linked to laws from the Siete Partidas (2003, 44).

13 See Alfonso García Gallo, volume 1, chapter 7, 'La recepción del Derecho común.'
14 See Brundage 2008.
15 See Aguilera Barchet 2006.
16 Álvarez Vigaray offers an extensive list of studies of law in Cervantes' works (1987, 16–30). Batiza points to Antonio Martín Gamero's 1870 study as the first (Batiza 1964, 24).
17 'los textos literarios nos dicen acerca del Derecho algo que silencian y no pueden decir los textos legales'; 'no fue un profesional al que se pudiera exigir originalidad de ideas y pensamientos jurídicos, una técnica precisa ni conceptos depurados' (Álvarez Vigaray 1987, 16, 42–3).
18 'el anacronismo de la institución de los caballeros andantes, y la inocencia, candor y locura de don Quijote' (Castro Dassen 1953, 114).
19 'muestra en toda la novela dominio de nociones y de tecnicismo'; 'cuatro puntos cardinales en la flaqueza judicial de don Quijote' (Alcalá-Zamora y Torres 2001, 86).
20 'no confunde verdad y ficción; las funde' (Cervantes 1987, III.121). For more on Cervantes' mix of fiction and history, see also Castro (1972 [1925]), Bell (1947), Wardropper (1965, 2005), Forcione (1970a), Guillén (1971), Close (1994), Quint (1997), Gaylord (1998), Friedman (2006), Mercedes Rodríguez Pequeño (2008).
21 Riley offers an extensive list of examples of Cervantes' 'all-pervasive claims of truth' in the novel (1962, 128–9).
22 In Spanish, the word history did not split into history versus story, as English usage did. One twentieth-century Spanish legal dictionary offers for 'history' a range of acceptations from 'Historia. Narración fiel de los principales acontecimientos del pasado' (faithful narration of past events) to 'Mentira, cuento, embuste, falsedad' (Lie, story, deception, falsity) (Cabanellas 1976, 2:216).
23 Riley has pointed out that sixteenth-century uses of *inventio* often differed little from those of '*imitatio, fictio,* and *fabula,*' and that 'the crux of the matter [in the development of imaginative literature] was the problem of history and poetry' (Riley 1962, 58, 162). Wardropper notes the era's use of 'poetry' for lies or imagination and 'prose' for truth or history, and says that with *Don Quixote,* Cervantes 'does not disentangle the story from the history, but points its telescope at the ill-defined frontier itself' (Wardropper 1965, 4, 7, 5). James Parr finds that in *Don Quixote,* Cervantes subverts the very idea of trustworthy narrations and *auctoritas,* bringing 'the writing of history … to the zenith of absurdity with the introduction of that paragon of creative chroniclers, the mendacious Moor' Cide Hamete Benengeli (Parr 2005, 48).
24 See the elogium of Egidio Viterbo, in *Le Inscrittioni* (Giovio 1558).
25 For example, 'fiction' is used by Pedro Mexía for certain details of Ovid's tales, and Las Casas uses 'fiction' when speaking of Saturn's consuming his children to speak

of cannibalism. *Corpus Diacrónico del Español:* http://corpus.rae.es/cordenet.html. In what follows, CORDE.

26 I cite from a copy in the Beinecke Library, Yale University, ms. 978 57.

27 I cite to the 1953 Carballo Picazo three-volume edition, by volume and page.

28 'ánima y parte esencial' (López Pinciano 1953, 2:7); 'las ficciones que no tienen imitación y verisimilitude, no son fábulas, sino disparates' (2:8).

29 'fición pura ... todo es imaginación'; 'sobre una mentira y fició[n] funda[n] una verdad ... muestran vn consejo muy fino y verdadero'; 'sobre vna verdad fabrican mil ficiones, tales son las trágicas y épicas' (López Pinciano 1953, 2:12–13).

30 'conviene guisar sus acciones con tanta puntualidad y gusto, y con tanta verisimilitud, que a despecho y pesar de la mentira, que hace disonancia en el entendimiento, forme una verdadera armonía' (Cervantes 2003, III.10, 527). Cervantes ends his theatre piece *El gallardo español* with a statement as to its mix of truths and fables: 'No haya más, que llega el tiempo / de dar fin a esta comedia, / cuyo principal intento / ha sido mezclar verdades, / con fabulosos inventos' (Cervantes 1997, 139–40).

31 Montero Díaz notes the source as W. Dilthey 1929, *Weltanschauung und Analyse des Menschen,* Leipzig, Teubner, page 423.

32 For E.M. Forster, causality is the key element of plot in a novel: 'A story is a narrative of events arranged in their time sequence. A plot is also a narrative of events, the emphasis falling on causality' (Forster 1927, 130).

33 'Assí como entre todos los géneros de letras ninguno ay más agradable ni más suaue que la hystoria, assí entre todas las hystorias Griegas, Latinas, y Bárbaras, que en tantos siglos passados nos han sido escriptas, ninguna (a mi parecer) ay, que deua ser preferida, y si miramos la disciplina militar de nuestro tiempo, no sé quál merecer [*sic*] ser comparada conlas hystorias que el doctíssimo varón Paulo Iovio Obispo de Nochera nos dexó escriptas. Ora miremos la graueded, elegancia, y magestad de palabras de que están ordenadas. Ora el ingenio, diligencia, y rara erudición del autor. Ora la verdad, variedad, y grandeza delos casos y successos que enellas se escriuen. Ora los consejos, ingenios, vicios, y virtudes delos Príncipes y Capitanes, de que este varón excellente para vtilidad incomparable delos lectores hizo con admirable diligencia particular mención' (Baeza 1566, 'Dedicatoria,' *Histories*).

34 'Ahora algunos, que tengan por cosa ajena de mi profesión escribir historia. Y cierto se engañan: porque de más que todas las ciencias son unas, es certísimo que ninguna cosa hay que tanto acresciente la prudencia humana como la historia, pues los juristas bien saben que para la gobernación de la república y ejercicio de las leyes es necesaria prudencia. El jurisconsulto Modestino abrevió la historia de la Aeneida de Virgilio. Celio Antipatro jurisconsulto escribió largamente historia. Alciato varón doctísimo en derechos ilustró las historias de Cornelio Tácito. Zazio jurisconsulto escribió sobre

las epístolas de Cicerón. Plutarcho filósofo escribió divinamente historia. El sancto Hierónymo escribió historia de varones ilustres. La historia del rey don Juan escribió el doctor Carvajal' (Baeza 1566, 'Dedicatoria,' *Histories*).

35 'FONTECHA 1606: *fronesis,* prudencia, discreción, sabiduría.' Cited in the *Nuevo tesoro lexicográfico del español: (S. XIV–1726),* referring to Alonso Ruyzes de Fontecha, and his *Diccionario de los nombres de piedras, plantas, frvctos, yervas, flores, enfermedades,* published in 1606 as part of a volume titled *Diez privilegios para mugeres preñadas.*

36 'Por Dios, hermano, que agora me acabo de desengañar de un engaño en que he estado todo el mucho tiempo que ha que os conozco, en el cual siempre os he tenido por discreto y prudente en todas vuestras acciones' (DQ I, Prologue).

37 'el discreto se admire de la invención, el grave no la desprecie, ni el prudente deje de alabarla' (DQ I, Prologue).

38 Speaking of the development of the novel as a genre, Wardropper notes Cervantes' insistence that the reader be the final judge of the 'uncertainty of truth' told in a fictional work (1965, 5).

39 'dice el que tradujo esta grande historia del original' (DQ II.24).

40 'Tú, letor, pues eres prudente, juzga lo que te pareciere' (DQ II.24).

41 T. Price Zimmerman (1995, 267) offers the reference and reading of prudence, but not the actual quote from Giovio's *Dialogo de viris …* which reads: 'Sciebam enim conscribendae historiae gravissimum semper munus vel divinis ingeniis extitisse [constitisse] quoniam tanta res invidiae exposita, et praeparatum ocium, et non exiguum tempus, et singularem prudentiam cum eloquentia coniunctam requirere videretur' (Giovio 1984, 255).

42 'uno de los medios más importantes para alcanzar la prudencia tan necessaria al príncipe en el arte del reynar, es el conocimiento de las historias' (1948 [1611], Discurso I, 11); 'No es escriuir las cosas para que no se oluiden … sino para que enseñen a viuir con la esperiencia, maestra muda, que hazen los particulares que perficionan a la prudencia. El fin de la historia es la vtilidad pública' (Discurso IX, 35). Cabrera de Córdoba cites Aeneas Silvius: 'Nec ab re, siquidem prudentia est, quae vitam ducit prudentia vero multarum et magnarum rerum, cognitionem parit, quam nemo inter scriptores melius historico tradit' (Discurso IX, 35). Forcione speaks to the difference between *discreción* and *sabiduría* in Cervantes' episode of Sancho Panza telling a story and Don Quixote interrupting: '*discreción,* the product of study and art, and *sabiduría,* the product of experience, common sense, and nature' (Forcione 1970a, 248). Ergo, progression leads to prudence and/or discretion, with history the written expression of that process.

43 'Françoise Baudouin, teorizzando la *coniunctio* fra la storia e la giurisprudenza, indicherà una prospettiva affatto nuova, approfondendo i problemi inerenti alla

critica delle fonti, scoprendo definitivamente i nessi fra la storiografia e la politica' (Cotroneo 1971, 15).

44 Variants in spelling include Françoise or François, Baudouin or Bauduin and in Spain, the jurist-historian is also sometimes indexed as Balduini. For clarity, I add [o] and [e] to quotes from others who do not include the letters, and use Françoise Baudouin in my own references.

45 'Conditi a Deo sumus & collocati in hoc mundo, tanquam in amplissimo quodam amphitheatro, primum ut spectatores, deinde ut actores, atque etiam ut iudices quodammodo simus. Spectatores dico, non earum modo rerum, quae in oculos nostros incurrunt: sed & earum, quas memoria nostra comprehendit, & iam olim praeteritas nobis tanquam praesentes sistit. Non possumus, si oculos habemus, non spectare res naturales: quas & orbium caelestium assidua conversio, & hic telluris globus immobilis quotidie spectandas, contuendasque nobis, vel inuitis, offert, admirabili quidem varietate differentes, sed constanti tamen & perpetua vicissitudine recurrentes: quarum quidem certe considerandarum causa natos etiam homines esse magni olim Philosophi dixerunt' (Baudouin 1561, chapter 1, after the dedication, no page or folio numbers).

46 For example, the Fondo Antiguo of the University of Salamanca holds nineteen volumes with Baudouin's name as a primary or secondary author.

47 As a wonderful aside, Luis Cabrera de Córdoba dedicates his *De historia para entenderla y escribirla* to the Marquis of Denia, Don Francisco de Sandoval, and then offers a short opening to his reader, 'the theatre': 'Luis Cabrera de Córdoba al teatro. Escrivo la importancia de la historia, la del buen historiador, las partes que ha de tener, las de legítima y perfect historia y como se hará tal. Vale.' (1948 [1611], 9). Ernst Cassirer notes that the topic of 'theater as a symbol and simile of the human life' was developed by the Stoics (Marcus Aurelius, Epictetus) and by the Neoplatonists (Plotinus Ennead iii.2) (Cassirer 1948, 385).

48 'Per legi omnes constitutiones seculum illud incultum et impexum re[s]pientes. Utilis tamen est earum cognitio ad parandam antiquitatis noticiam. Vix enim constitutiones vulgari Hispanorum lingua proditas int[elli]gimus neque sine horum codicum presidio intelligemus unquam. Q[ui] lector venerare antiquitatem et in tanta ingeniorum ac literatum suo [?] quantam n[uest]ra tulit etas natus. Bonas horas noli male perdere sed quan avidus negociator para tibi xpianam [christianam] eruditionem cum meliorum terrarum notitia coniunctam. nanque sine bonis literis ceca et manca e[st] omnis eruditio simulam memineris sine virtute. ad beatam vitam qu[?] tum vis doctissimis, nullam patere viam non enim superciliosa erudition[is] sed charitatis oficiis paratur regnum celorum ubi Paulus ille mag[ister] gloriatur se municipat[i]um habere. adquorum hereditatem misericordia ac bonitate christiani omnes cum eo asciti ac vocati sumus. El Licenciado gaspar de baeca' (Baeza undated, gloss, Ordenamientos reales, Escorial, ms. Z.I.10, last folio).

2. Giovio, Baeza, History, and Law in Cervantes' Works

1 Martín Fernández de Navarrete's 1819 *Vida de Cervantes* seems to have been the first full-length biography of the author, although Bowle includes in his edition of the *Quixote* a short biographical sketch by Juan Antonio Pellicer y Saforcada dated to 1778 (Cervantes 2006 [1781] III, 8–13). The list is extensive, and I offer just a few names, with titles for those not specifically referenced in my text and bibliography: Díaz de Benjumea 1878; Astrana Marín 1948; Bell 1947; Navarro y Ledesma 1905, *Ingenioso hidalgo Miguel de Cervantes Saavedra; sucesos de su vida contados;* Schevill 1919; Díaz-Plaja 1969, *Cervantes: la desdichada vida de un triunfador;* Byron 1978, *Cervantes, a biography;* Canavaggio 1986, *Cervantes;* McKendrick 1980, *Cervantes;* McCrory 2005, *No Ordinary Man: The Life and Times of Miguel de Cervantes;* Manuel Lacarta 2005, *Cervantes: biografía razonada.* Some recent biographies speak particularly to Cervantes' legal problems: for example, three sections of Manuel Fernández Álvarez's 2005 biography of the author are titled: 'Fugitivo de la Justicia' 56–60, 'Cervantes cautivo' 149–73, and 'De cómo Cervantes conoció de veras la cárcel' 329–35; see also specific legal-biographical references in Francisco Javier Blasco Pascual 2006, chapters 8, 9, and 17, and in Álvar Ezquerra 2004, 36–40 and 259–77.

2 For example, a baptismal certificate dated 7 October 1547 leads us to believe that the author was born on 29 September, St Michael's day, given Spanish custom in naming a newborn for the saint's day of the birth, and a baptism that followed shortly thereafter (Canavaggio 1998).

3 Boccalini's 'Dispatches from Parnassus' had an obvious impact on Spanish writers after Cervantes (Williams 1946) but, although Rodríguez Marín accepted connections between that work and Cervantes' *Viaje del Parnaso,* the publication dates would require that any influence would have to have been on the basis of pre-published manuscripts, as the *Ragguagli* were published in 1612–13, and the *Viaje del Parnaso* in 1614. Vicente Gaos accepts Cervantes' own statement that the inspiration and model for his *Viaje* … was that of Cesare Caporali, which Gaos also sees as the model for Boccalini (Cervantes 1984, 31–5).

4 For the multiple authorial voices and narrators of the *Quijote,* see Flores (1982), Stagg (1956), and Weiger (1996). López Navia (1996) points out the same multiplicity of voices as a noteworthy aspect of the twelfth-thirteenth-century *El Lanzarote del Lago,* in which each knight offers his own version of events, and the author includes the process of compilation and sorting of those voices as a part of the text itself. Scholars have long argued, without resolution, about the exact number of narrative voices in the *Quixote.* See, for example, Spitzer 1948, Rivers 1982, Fernández Mosquera 1986, Martínez Bonati 1992.

5 Anderson (1994) comments on the same translated structure and narrative masking of voice in Ginés Pérez de Hita's *Guerras civiles de Granada.* Parr has noted that the

Quixote is 'a potentially subversive document because it calls into question not only the authority of books of chivalry, but also of translations and, equally important, of history itself as a reliable medium for truth (2005, 48). Menéndez y Pelayo (2008) related the structure to the falsifications of chronicles and pious frauds common in the era. With Giovio's work in translation, we have another, and highly-polemical, comtemporary layer in that chain.

6 'varon doctíssimo (a quien todas las naciones de conformidad llaman padre de la hystoria)' (Baeza 1566, 'Dedicatoria,' *Histories*).

7 Francisco Márquez Villanueva cites the verses on his page 135, speaking of the link between Zapata and Cervantes, and of the former being marked with 'the stamp of Italian humanism' (sello italiano) (Márquez Villanueva 1973, 135).

8 'De los cuales yo sumé y recogí lo que diré; señaladamente seguí a Paulo Jovio en un tractado que hizo particular deste mismo argumento' (Mexía 2003, 116).

9 As testament to the popularity of Giovio's works, in 1562 two different Spanish translations of the *Histories* were published, Gaspar de Baeza's and another by Valencian medical doctor Antonio Ioan Villafranca. Baeza's translation was expanded and reprinted in 1566. Unless otherwise indicated, I cite Baeza's 1566 second edition of the work.

10 Ballesteros Gaibrois, who writes the preliminary study to the *Antijovio,* not published until 1952, says that Jiménez de Quesada used, in all likelihood, Baeza's 1566 translation of the *Histories,* and points out that Jiménez de Quesada was one of the soldiers who took part in the Sack of Rome (Jiménez de Quesada 1952, 56).

11 'el traductor guardó bien el decoro, usó de limpios vocablos y muy significativos a lo moderno de lo que quería dezir, y la verdad del latín muy castamente puesta en el castellano'; 'su traslación tan bien y aventagadamente, que es una de las cosas que he visto mejor trasladadas de latín en romance' (Jiménez de Quesada 1952, 7–8, 197).

12 'serpiente ytaliana'; 'cosas ymaginadas de su caveça, como de la de Medusa'; 'Pues por eso se llama saco' (Jiménez de Quesada 1952, 298, 193, 455).

13 'el retirar no es huir, ni el esperar es cordura cuando el peligro sobrepuja a la esperanza' (DQ I.23).

14 'los *historiadores* puntuales, verdaderos y no nada apasionados' (DQ I.9); 'de algunas de sus cosas, me espanto y de otras me río; pero de otras singularísimamente me enojo y tomo cólera' (Jiménez de Quesada 1952, 101); '¡O palabra italiana, y a italiano propósito dicha!' (1952, 163).

15 'Paolo Iobio contra los españoles y florentines tiene pecho lleno de ira y malenconía'; 'por más que dizen éstos que un médico suyo conocedor de su humor le purgó con oro envolsable, medicina conveniente a su enfermedad' (Cabrera de Córdoba 1948 [1611], 92).

16 'El Jovio desta vez se desengaña, / Que la ignorancia celebró española; / Cosa que allá se tiene por hazaña' (Vega 1968–1971, carta 343, p. 428).

17 'The extant portraits often reveal that many of Giovio's descriptions are embellished or intentionally artful, a kind of literary illusion contrived to enhance the conceit of gazing on a painted image' (Klinger 1991, 214). 'The "certain license" Giovio allowed himself in the elogia has been the bane of scholars seeking to verify details which appear nowhere else' (Zimmerman 1995, 206).

18 'Erat distortis saepe moribus, uti facie nequaquam ingenua et liberali ab enormi praesertim naso subluscoque oculo perabsurda' (Giovio 1999, 116). Klinger notes the use without citing it specifically (1991, 209).

19 'ciertos ginetes Españoles'; 'a rienda suelta por desiertos arenosos, y yua derramando doblas, para detener a los Españoles' (Giovio 1568, fol. 192r). The title of the first Latin edition, published in 1551, reads: *Elogia virorum bellica virtute illustrium supposita quae apud Musaeum spectantur. Volumen digestum est in septem libros. Florentiae, In officina Torrentini Dvcalis Typographi, MDLI.* Another volume of elogia, dedicated to men of letters rather than war, was published in Venice in 1546, and is titled *Elogia veris clarorum virorum imaginibus apposita quae in Musaeo comi spectantur.* Klinger compares the volumes and says that the 1551 volume of men of war, 'is an altogether more thoroughgoing attempt to integrate the literary and visual components of the biographies and to heighten the reader's awareness of the portrait' with the use of demonstratives such as 'this countenance' (1991, 209, 210).

20 This elogium is not in Baeza's translation, which only includes the elogia of men of war. Zimmerman uses Viterbo's elogium as an example of the 'certain liberty' that Giovio allowed himself in the elogia, hoping that they might illustrate 'a rounded picture of the actual human character, not an idealized *exemplum* … Thus, even if Giovio had no proof that the cardinal inhaled fumes of smoldering straw, the tale would have illustrated the streak of hypocrisy in his overly severe bearing' (1995, 206–7).

21 'liberal claro, nunca engañoso. Pero era deshonesto, burlando con mugeres, y assí andando de una en otra se hinchió de bubas (que en aquel tiempo comenzaban) y triste y miserable, murió mal logrado, fatigado de grandes dolores' (Giovio 1568, fol. 131v).

22 The number of editions testifies to Márquez Villanueva's claim that, in the sixteenth century, there was a reading public avid for 'lo anecdótico … lo pintoresco y, sobre todo … lo divertido' (1973, 195), which had been all but ignored by the historians of the day. Michael Armstrong-Roche links this same 'larger and more heterogenous reading public' to the successful revival and vernacular translations of Heliodorus's *Ethiopica,* and to the welcome reception given Cervantes' *Persiles* (2009, 5–6). See also Kagan 1974.

23 The title change is not found in the royal privilege granted to the 1568 publication, which offers a more literal translation: *Elogios de varones Illustres* in one reference and the variant *Elogios y vidas de varones Illustres* in another. In all fol-

lowing references, *Elogios* refers to this volume translated by Baeza, and *Elogia* to the published works in a general sense, that is, the various volumes of men of war, letters, etc.

24 Alexander the Great (DQ I, poem by Urganda la desconocida, and chapters 1, 6, 39, 48, 49); Red Beard (DQ I.39); Hernán Cortés (DQ II.8); Hannîbal (DQ I, poem by Urganda, and chapter 49); Charlemagne (DQ I.48 and 49; DQ II.24 and 26); Preste Juan de las Indias (DQ I, prologue, and chapter 47).

25 See Joost-Gaugier (1982) for a study of the history and tradition of compilations of famous, illustrious men.

26 'una obra en que se representa al biuo, y casi se ve con los ojos la mudança de la fortuna y inconstançia de las cosas humanas, para consuelo de los desdichados, y para que los dichosos no se ensoberuezcan con su felicidad'; 'Quita el fastidio la breuedad y variedad y yr el libro en prosa y verso' (Baeza 1568, 'Dedicatoria,' *Elogios*).

27 'la épica también puede escribirse en prosa como en verso' (DQ I, 47). For Riley, 'the chief importance of the passage lies in the attempt to raise the novel to the level of the most esteemed form of poetry' (1962, 49). Forcione studies the relation of the phrase in its context to Tasso's theories on the heroic poem (1970b, 99, n. 17).

28 The description from Zimmerman refers to Giovio's *Libellus de legatione Basilii magni Principis Moschoviae,* for which the Italian historian prepared by speaking daily with the Russian ambassador to the papal court.

29 'lo mató una mujer de Argos dándole con una teja en la cabeza' (Giovio 1568, 4v); 'fue vencido de vn viejo Eunucho tamaño como tres palmos' (Giovio 1568, 9v).

30 Zimmerman links the Giovio family's fondness for chivalric romances to 'not only Giovio's keen appreciation of Ariosto but also his salient qualities as a narrative historian, particularly his unwearied enthusiasm for describing battles and individual deeds of valor, his admiration for knightly virtues, and his sense for military pageantry and the drama of events' (1995, 6).

31 For Díaz de Benjumea, the idea negates the author's talent and beliefs, which 'fueran ridículas si su objeto hubiera sido acabar con una literatura ya cadáver' (would be ridiculous if his objective had been to put an end to a literature that was already a cadaver) (1878, 218). Díaz de Benjumea also dismisses other single-motive inspirations, such as vengeance for the author's arrest in Argamasilla, or faithful description of a real person from La Mancha, and asks that readers and critics look at the varied messages in the context of the author's life as a way to understand the full import of the literary work (1878, 230–1). Astrana Marín echoes the sentiment: 'Lo que no puede admitirse es que se reduzca y rebaje la alteza del poema [i.e., DQ] a una triste y pobre sátira de libros de caballería' (What is unacceptable is to reduce the beauty of the work to a poor, sad satire on books of chivalry) (Astrana Marín 1948, 1:65).

32 'aquestos endemoniados instrumentos de la artillería … diabólica invención, con la cual dio causa que un infame y cobarde brazo quite la vida a un valeroso caballero' (DQ I.38).

33 'contentóle Florencia en extremo, así por su agradable asiento como por su limpieza, sumptuosos edificios, fresco río y apacibles calles' (Cervantes 1995, II.49).

34 'Natural de la ciudad de este nombre famosa en toda la región andaluza, de la que tomó su apellido, habiendo caído en la cuenta de que estaba dotado de un gran talento, ambicionó la fama de las letras emprendiendo el camino regio que conduce a aquélla, es decir, la conveniencia de marchar a la Universidad de Salamanca para estudiar el derecho civil. Allí escuchó las lecciones de Juan de Orozco que gozaba de un gran prestigio en su cátedra y que era famoso por sus comentarios *Ad duos priores Digestorum*. Después de haber estudiado filosofía, y teología, así como geografía e historia, pertrechado con los mejores criterios de todo el campo de las letras se dedicó a escribir. Y si la muerte no le hubiera arrebatado en plena juventud, aún no había cumplido treinta años, sin embargo, su prudencia, amor a Dios y sus ideas sobre las cosas divinas e imperecederas eran propias de un hombre maduro, habría llegado a ser un gran especialista en Derecho Civil y en las demás disciplinas' (N. Antonio 1999, 1.526–7). Another source contradicts N. Antonio on this point, saying that Baeza was born in Granada, and 'probably' studied at the University of Granada (Montells y Nadal 1870).

35 'Por desgracia, este amigo del padre de Cervantes y del de fray Luis de León, acabó suicidándose cuando apenas había traspasado los umbrales de la juventud' (Astrana Marín 1948, 2:530–1, n. 5). Astrana Marín cites Pérez Pastor's *Bibliografía madrileña* as his source although on consultation, I failed to find the information in that text.

36 For sources, the Biblioteca de Andalucía cites the Archives of the Real Chancillería of Granada and of the Universities of Granada and Salamanca.

37 One other tantalizing document held by the Archives is the 1592 naming of a 'licentiate Cervantes,' who was one of the Chancillería's judges, as 'visitador' (inspector) of the monks of the High Court (sign. 4437/38). The archive folder is missing all but the identifying cover information. Further, given that Cervantes never identified himself as 'licentiate' it does not seem possible to relate this Cervantes to the author.

38 'Por quanto por parte de vos Rodrigo de Baeza vezino dela ciudad de Granada nos fue hecha relación diziendo, que el licenciado Gaspar de Baeza vuestro hermano ya defuncto, avía scripto un libro intitulado declaración de la ley del fuero, que trata de los deudores pobres, si an de ser entregados a sus acreedores' (Baeza 1570, Privilegio).

39 'Ad trigesimum sextum accesserat annum quae aetas laborum omnium longe est tolerantissima' (Baeza 1570, 'Dedicatoria').

40 'Acceserat nondum frater meus charus ad trigessimum aetatis annum' (Baeza 1592, fol. 5).

41 Pérez Pastor, vol. 1, document 13, dated 25 February 1577. On examination, the protocol, for which Sliwa offers a full transcription and also dates to 1577 (2005, 396–7), is dated 1577. The power of attorney is found at folios 196r–7r, of the Protocolo of Rodrigo de Vera, Archivo Histórico de Protocolos, Madrid, and reads in part: 'Let all who see this document know that I, Rodrigo de Cervantes ... give and cede ... power ... to Gaspar de Baeza, resident in Granada ... to recover ... from Licentiate Pedro Sánchez de Córdoba ... eight hundred gold ducats in Castilian reales' (Sepan quantos esta carta de power vieren que yo, Rodrigo de Zervantes ... doy y otorgo ... poder ... a Gaspar de Baeza, vecino de la cibdad de Granada ... cobrar ... del licenciado Pedro Sánchez de Córdoba ... ochocientos ducados en reales castellanos) (Sliwa 2005, 396–7).

42 On the basis of another document in which the jurist sold his publication rights to the translated *Histories* to bookseller Francisco de Robles, Astrana Marín says that Gaspar de Baeza was in the court in 1566. Apparently unaware of Baeza's translation of Giovio's *Histories*, Astrana Marín assumes the copyright sale is for an earlier edition of the translated *Elogios* (1948, 3:13–14).

43 'Fray Luis de León es el que digo, / a quien yo reverencio, adoro y sigo' (Cervantes 1999, VI, Canto de Calíope, stanza 84).

44 'ingenio vivo, veloz, pronto y agudo'; 'un torrente oratorio enérgico, vehemente, jugoso, elegante y ameno'; 'León, engendraste un León cuya voz (si no engañan las apariencias) oirá también la posteridad' (León 1891–5, 7:285–7).

45 The relevant documents signed by both Andrés de Cervantes and Rodrigo de Baeza (as notary, witness, or found in his Protocolo, i.e., collection of his notarized documents) are dated 4 February 1568 through August 1593 (Sliwa 2005).

46 The three documents are found in Sliwa 2005: 'viuda' (1575/05/16 Cabra); 'hermana y heredera' (1602/01/13 Cabra); 'suegra' (1602/12/05 Cabra). The Luis de Baeza connection to the other Baeza brothers (Gaspar, Melchor, Rodrigo de Baeza) is yet to be determined. Another doña Leonor de Fernández de Torreblanca was Miguel's grandmother, wife of Juan de Cervantes, and some documents refer to her as doña Leonor de Torreblanca – she died in 1557 (Canavaggio 1998). There are three Rodrigo de Cervantes – it is the name of Miguel's father, of his brother, and of his cousin, son of Andrés.

47 For this family connection, Astrana Marín refers the reader to a discourse read by 'don José de la Torre y del Cerro en el acto de su recepción como académico numerario de la de Ciencias, Bellas Letras y Nobles Artes de Córdoba, el día 4 de noviembre de 1922' which studies a particular document from the Cabra collection. Miguel's aunt Leonor de Torreblanca, who married Luis de Baeza, is also noticed by Astrana Marín (1948, 'Árbol geneológico secundario,' Appendix 2, 7:586).

48 Cervantes praises Padilla in *Don Quixote* (DQ I.6), writes him a 'pompous elogium' in *Canto de Calíope,* and wrote verses to Padilla that were published with the latter's works (Fernández de Navarrete 1819, 396–402). Padilla's name figures a number of times in the lists of texts that Eisenberg (2002) finds mentioned, referred to, commented on, etc., in Cervantes' works. Sabor de Cortazar and Lerner identify certain verses in the *Quijote* (DQ II.18, n. 18) as a gloss by Silvestre. In his introduction to Silvestre's works, Cáceres y Espinosa lists Silvestre's friends, including Gaspar de Baeza and Pedro de Padilla. Acuña translated the *Orlando enamorado* of Mateo Boyardo, mentioned in *Don Quixote* I.6. The Tassa, later spelled 'tasa,' was the book's price-mark; it specified the legally set price of a book.

49 'Yo Gonzalo de la Vega escrivano de camara del Rey nuestro señor, doy fe, que por los señores del Consejo fue tassado a tres maravedís y medio cada pliego, del libro intitulado, opera omnia Gasparis Baeza, que con su licencia le ha impreso Francisco de Robles, librero de su Magestad, como cesonario de Gaspar de Baeza' (Baeza 1592, Tassa).

50 The final document in the collection organized by Baztán and Mariño. See Baztán 2001.

51 *Tractatus illustrium in utraque tum Pontificii, tum Caesarei iuris facultate Iurisconsultorum. De Iudiciis. Ex multis in hoc volumen congesti, additis plurimis, etiam nunquam editis, hac * nota designatis; & multo, quam antea, emendatiores redditi; Summariis singulorum Tractatuum locupletissimis illustrati. Indices accessere ita locupletes, ut omnes materiae, quae sparsim leguntur, facillime distinctae Lectoribus appareant.* Vol. 3. Part 2. Venice, 1584.

52 Augustini Barbosae, I.V.D. Lusitani, protonotarii apostolici ... & a Consiliis D. Philippi IV ... *Collectanea in codicem justiniani, Ex doctoribus tum priscis, tum neotericis.* Vol. 1. Lyon: Petri Borde, & Ioannis Arnaud, 1701.

53 First published by Hugo de Mena, Granada, 1567, with licence to print dated 1566. I cite here from the 1592 *Opera omnia* edition.

54 'Y mandamos que ninguno pueda dar ni prometer por vía de dote ni casamiento de hija, tercio ni quinto de sus bienes ... Y porque los que se desposan, o casan, suelen dar al tiempo que se desposan, o casan a sus esposas y mugeres, joyas y vestidos excessivos. Y es cosa necessaria que assí mesmo se ordene, y modere: añadamos, que de aquí adelante ninguno, ni algunos destos nuestros Reynos, que se desposaren, o casaren lo pueda dar, ni dé a su esposa y muger en los dichos vestidos y joyas, ni en otra cosa alguna más de lo que montare la octava parte de la dote que con ella recibiere' (cited by Baeza 1592, fol. 1r–v).

55 'Otrosí, suplicamos a V.M. que las dotes que enestos Reynos se dieren, no puedan ser más de la legítima que le vendría a la dotada, si entonces se partiessen los bienes del dotador' (Baeza 1592, De non meliorandis, chap. 1, fol. 2r).

56 Baeza includes a wide range of previous opinions, from Alexander, Salic law [Brundage – law of the Franks], Bartolus, Baldus, Deci. [Decemviri], Raphael Comensis, Curtius and Curtius Junior, Trebel[lianum], Fulgencio, Paul, Belon, Doctísimus Antonius Padilla, Alciato, Bosquus, Aretino, Aristotle, Ioannem Lupum, vir doctissimus Ferdinandus Vasquius, Bernardus Díaz, and more, including Gregorio López's glosses to the Siete Partidas.

57 'An praefinitio huius legis locum habeat, quando filia se ipsam dotat inscio aut invito patre. Et an dos quam constuprator dat virgini deflorare possit excedere summam hic praefinitam' (Baeza 1592, De non meliorandis, chap. 18, fol. 83).

58 'que tan pesada carga es la riqueza al que no está usado a tenerla ni sabe usar della, como lo es la pobreza al que continuo la tiene'; 'porque en algunos años que fue soldado aprendió a ser liberal' (Cervantes 1995, II.101).

59 'porque de su natural condición era el más celoso hombre del mundo' (Cervantes 1995, II.102).

60 'De que tenga dote o no no hay para qué hacer caso, pues el cielo me dio para todos y los ricos no han de buscar en sus matrimonios hacienda, sino gusto' (Cervantes 1995, II.102).

61 In 1621 Phillip IV upheld the laws limiting dowries but added that public monies would be spent to provide dowries for orphans and the poor so as to allow them to wed, since poverty and necessity were preventing their marriages: 'Y porque demás de las causas referidas de excesso en las dotes, y gastos, suele serlo la pobreza, y necessidad de que muchas mugeres están sin disposición de poderse casar, desseando disponerles algún socorro: Ordenamos, y mandamos, que de aquí adelante los bienes que huviere mostrencos en cada lugar, sirvan, y se apliquen para casamiento de mugeres pobres, y huérfanas' (Recop. V.2.5).

62 'habiéndola dotado primero en veinte mil ducados … [y] muchos vestidos … que fueron tantos y tan ricos' (Cervantes 1995, II.103).

63 'dio parte de su hacienda a censo, situada en diversas y buenas partes, otra puso en el banco, y quedóse con alguna, para lo que se le ofreciese' (Cervantes 1995, II.104).

64 'Que no se pueda renunciar la ley del Fuero, que dispone, que no se pueda dar más de la dézima parte en arras' (Recop. V.1.2). The 'ley del Fuero' or Fuero Juzgo, states: 'si quier sea virgen, sequier viuda, non le pueda dar más por arras que la décima parte de todas sus cosas' (Fuero Juzgo III.1.6).

65 'Doncas si el marido después que un anno oviere que es casado, por amor o por grado quisier dar alguna cosa a la muier, puédelo fazer libremientre. Mas ante que el anno sea passado, ni el marido a la mugier, ni la mugier al marido non puede dar más de las arras' (Fuero Juzgo III.1.6).

66 'se entretenía en relagar a su esposa y acariciar a sus criadas, que todas le querían bien, por ser de condición llana y agradable, y, sobre todo, por mostrarse tan liberal con todas. Desta manera pasaron un año de noviciado' (Cervantes 1995, II, 106).

67 Baeza specifies: 'Sic & arra non potest excedere decimam partem bonorum, sive ante matrimonium sive post constituatur' (Baeza 1592, Do non meliorandis, 5.15).

68 '¿Hacienda vuestra? y ¿qué hacienda tenéis vos, que no la hayáis ganado con la que llevastes en mi dote? Y son míos la mitad de los bienes gananciales, mal que os pese; y dellos y de la dote, si me muriese agora, no os dejaría valor de un maravedí' (Cervantes 1970, 64).

69 'Pecunia (enim iuxta Hoesiodum) est anima miseris mortalibus'; 'Paupertas est martirium, si patienter tolleretur'; 'Et pauperes, ubisque, miseros appellamus' (Baeza 1592, 2.31, fol. 135r).

70 'Beatissima (inquit) res est paupertas' (Baeza 1592, 2.32, fol. 135v).

71 'Rvrsus quaero an furor excuset a dispositione huius legis. Haec quaestio duo habet capita: primum, vtrum debitor incidens in furorem sit addicendus creditori iuxta dispositionem huius legis. Secundum vtrum furor superueniens post addictionem eximat debitorem a potestate creditoris' (Baeza 1592, chap. 9, introduction, fol. 162v).

72 'Primo, negari non potest furorem infirmitatem esse, non solum corporis, verum etiam animi: unde furiosos malesanos & insanos appelamus, & quod furiosus censeatur esse' (Baeza 1592, 9.1, fol. 162v). Baeza's exemptions from debt due to insanity are all in chapter 9 of *De inope debitore.* When citing from the summa preceding the chapter, I so indicate with the additional word 'summa' between chapter and number indications.

73 'Committens delictum, dum est sanae mentis: si postea in furorem incidat parcitur ei' (Baeza 1592, 9.summa. 6, fol. 162v).

74 'Etiam si propria culpa quis in furorem incidat (puta medicamina accipiendo) non addicitur suo creditori. Etiam si debitum descendat ex delicto' (Baeza 1592, 9.summa. 7, fol. 162v).

75 'Si furor superveniat debitori postquam est addictus creditori eximitur a manibus creditoris: sicuti ratione senectutis' (Baeza 1592, 9.summa. 8, fol. 162v).

76 'Furiosus sententia iudicis absolutus: an sit reddeat an sanam mentem possit a creditoribus peti ad servitium' (Baeza 1592, 9.summa. 9, fol. 162v).

77 'Mutus, surdus, & furiosus, aequiparantur' (Baeza 1592, 9.summa. 11, fol. 162v).

78 'Ardor illiciti amoris, an excuset a delicto commisso' (Baeza 1592, 9.summa. 12, fol. 162v).

79 'Unum vitium aliud non excusat. Libido vitium, & blanda malorum pestis, & alia libidine' (Baeza 1592, 9.summa. 13, fol. 162v).

80 'Oldraldum ... tertia consideratio. excusat hominem, qui, vt potiretur foemina, quam misere deperibat, ad demoniacas artes confugit quod reputatur crimen gravissimum ... Aristoteles.7. Ethicorum ... quod si amans insanus est, satis suo furore punitur, vtimur enim misericordia cum furiosis ... Vergilius.lib.4.Aeneidos ... Idem significat.Plato.in Phaedro ... Et Cicero Tusculanarum' (Baeza 1592, 9.12, fol. 164r).

81 'Inopia vitio prodigalitatis contracta est indigna miseratione' (Baeza 1592, 9.summa. 14, fol. 162v).

82 'Ex his apparet insanum omnino esse dubitare, an debitor inops, ex prodigalitate sit addicendus creditori ... Cum autem prodigalitas vitium sit, nemo excusatur vitio prodigalitatis, neque hoc casu allegare potest: quod prodigus, & furiosus equiparentur' (Baeza 1592, 9. 13–14, fol. 164v).

83 The scene is the encounter with the theatre troupe en route from one performance to another, still in costume. It is illegal for them to be so dressed on the road (see below, chapter on laws broken).

84 'otro Angulo, no autor, sino representante' (Cervantes 1995, II. 353).

85 Rodríguez Marín tells us that Andrés de Angulo, of Córdoba, received his licentiate in law at the University of Osuna on 22 November 1584 (1947, 23).

86 Any relationship between this Fernández de Castro and the Conde Pedro Ruíz Fernández de Castro y Osorio, conde de Lemos, to whom Cervantes dedicates the Second Part of the *Quixote,* would be at this point conjecture.

87 'Et quantum Alcides nodoso stipite, tantum / Praestitit hic clari, viribus ingenii. / Ingenium tibi deficiet, si dicere laudes / Fore viri immensas, longius ausus eris' (Baeza 1592, preliminaries).

88 'uno de los famosos poetas del mundo, no sólo de España' (DQ I.6); 'varón insigne, sabio y elocuente' (Cervantes 1999, VI, Canto a Calíope, stanza 65).

89 'Lucinensis Gasparis Baetii Iurisconsulti clarissimi tumulum Epitaphium Toscana scansione conditum, quod vulgo dicitur. SONETO. Ecce membra, quae spiritu divino, / Perspicaci iudicio, alta memoria, / Viguere quondam, iacent sine gloria: / Sarcophago maiori ornatu digno. / Hoc tegitur Baetius, Caesarino, / Pontificioque iure, & oratoria, / Magnus, & magnus in hispana historia, / Magnus sermone Betico & Latino. / Vos Musae, vosque charites, vos Divae, / Dauricolae, quae tempora viventi / Virtutum filio redimistis lauro, / Estote modo numine praesenti, / Tuque eliberius bonos laude vive / Quae in tumulo est praestantius ostro & auro' (Barahona de Soto in Baeza 1592).

90 'chusma de villanos' (Giovio 1566, 17.2, fol. 137r); 'la canalla del pueblo' (Giovio 1566, 13.5, fol. 98r); 'el vulgo (que no sabe refrenar sus apetitos, ni tener paciencia en los dolores)' (Giovio 1566, 13.5, fol. 98r).

91 Rabell points out that Cicero used the concept of verisimilitude for legal oratory, and that sixteenth-century Italian preceptist Bonciani linked verisimilitude to Aristotle's precepts for history (Rabell 2003, 24–5).

92 'Platón quiso ... que los hombres no tuviesen propriedad, ni mío, ni tuyo, sino que todas las cosas fuesen comunes ... y el Filósofo afirma, que los hombres vivieran quietísimamente en este mundo, si se quitaran dos palabras: es a saber, *mío, y tuyo*' (Castillo de Bobadilla 1775 [1597], I.1.16, I:9–10). I cite book, chapter, and number, followed by volume and page number of the 1775 edition.

93 'Mas en peccando perdió este general y común imperio y se repartió por partes, aplicándose a cada una la suya como legítima y herencia: y tuuo principio, y origen la propriedad, y comenzóse a introduzir este lenguaje tan común de mío y tuyo' (Mercado 1571, fol. 18r). The frontispiece to this work refers to the 1571 edition being revised, which would indicate an earlier printing. The 1571 edition bears eleven different censors' approvals, including one from Fray Luis de León.
94 'porque entonces los que en ella vivían ignoraban estas dos palabras de *tuyo* y *mío*' (DQ I.11).
95 Sancho Panza 'comía bellotas' (DQ I.11); 'sustentándose de bellotas' (Castillo de Bobadilla 1775 [1597], I.1.3, I:6).
96 'un ferviente partidario y defensor de los postulados básicos del sistema' (Tomás y Valiente 1975, 200).
97 The work prepared by Juan López de Hoyos is titled *Historia y relación verdadera de las … sumptuosas exequías fúnebres de la sereníssima Reyna de España*, and was published in Madrid in 1569 (DQ I, Estudio preliminar, XIV).
98 'como hizo (según dicen) el Muchacho Numantino, que con ellas [las llaves] se despeño, y cayó muerto a los pies de Scipión: porque es cosa gloriosa morir por su Ley, y por su Rey' (Castillo de Bobadilla 1775 [1597], IV.3.5., II, 429).
99 Friedman (1977) puts Cervantes' *Numancia* in the context of other Spanish tragedies of the era, in a study of how each dramatist achieves dramatic unity. It is noteworthy that another work, *Tragedia de la muerte de Ayax Telamon sobre las armas de Aquiles* by Juan de la Cueva, also ends with a suicide, and that the topos of the phoenix who dies only to be reborn is specifically noted in the verse of each work.
100 For the pastoral in Cervantes' works, and in the era, see Finello 1994 and 2008. Finello speaks of a pastoral novel written by González de Bobadilla, a law student at the University of Salamanca, who addresses in his novel various 'casos' (cases) taken from his surrounding reality (2008, 40–3).
101 'seis comedias … una a una … y paresciendo que es una de las mejores comedias que se han representado en España, seáis obligado de me dar e pagar por cada una de las dichas comedias cincuenta ducados' (Sliwa 2005, 1592/09/05, Sevilla).
102 First published in *Flor de varios y nuevos romances* … in Valencia in 1593, the work is included in Gaos' two-volume *Miguel de Cervantes, Poesías completas* (Cervantes 1981).

3. Jurisprudence in Spain, Seventh to Sixteenth Centuries

1 Brundage points to a legal case in 1076, in which a *legis doctor* name Pepo cites a passage from Justinian's Digest as 'the earliest individual who can reasonably be associated with the revival of the study of Roman law' (2008, 80–1).

2 'Científicamente, la Glosa aparece vinculada con las concepciones de la época, como tenía, por lo demás, que resultar natural. Hablar de ciencia es hablar de un método; y el método que los glosadores emplearon no difirió del usado por el pensamiento escolástico, que, en sus líneas generales, se inspira en las artes liberales del *trivium:* gramática, retórica y dialéctica. No en vano Irnerio, el fundador de la escuela, había sido maestro en estas tres artes. En consecuencia, el trabajo de los glosadores se nos presentará como un trabajo de filólogos y lógicos. Filólogos, en cuanto se acercan a un texto considerado como tal, es decir, como *littera;* y lógicos en cuanto se acercan al contenido de ese texto' (Guzmán Brito 1978, 17–18).

3 'un código gótico-romano por la mezcla que en él hay de costumbres y leyes de entrambas naciones' (Fuero Juzgo 1815, Lardizabal y Uribe, IV). See Fuero Juzgo in bibliography. Lardizabal y Uribe writes the introductory Discourse to the legal volume.

4 'por su propia autoridad y potestad' (Fuero Juzgo 1815, Lardizabal y Uribe, IV–V).

5 See García Gallo 1967, vol. 1, chapter 7, 'La recepción del derecho común.' See also Madden 1930, who notes complaints in verse about the plethora of authorities and interminable lawsuits by Fernán Martínez de Burgos in his *Crónica de Don Alonso VIII*: 'Alcaldes, notarios, é aun oidores / Segund bien creo, pasan de setenta, / Que están en trono de emperadores / A quien el rey paga infinita renta; / De alios doctores hay ciento y noventa / Que traen el regno entero burlado / E en quarenta años non es acabado / Un solo pleito mirad si es tormento // Viene el pleyto a disputación, / Alto es Bartolo e Chino Digesto / Juan Andrés e Baldo, Enrique; de son / Más opiniones que ubas en cesto / E cada abozado es ni mucho presto / E desque bien visto bien disputado / Faltan el pleyto en un punto errado / E tornan de cabo a question por esto' (cited by Madden 1930, 71–2).

6 'establescemos e mandamos, que los dichos fueros sean guardados en aquellas cosas que se usaron, salvo en aquello que Nos fallaremos que se deben enmendar e mejorar, y en lo al que son contra Dios y contra razón, e contra las leyes que en este nuestro libro se contienen' (Leyes de Toro, law 1, and Recopilación, II.1.3).

7 See García Gallo 1967, 1:394–5, paragraph 745, 'El orden de prelación de fuentes.' García Gallo also notes that this ordering of sources, as first specified in the Ordenamiento de Alcalá, remained unaltered until the nineteenth century.

8 García Gallo 1967, 1:392–3, para. 741 and 1:91, para. 188.

9 'las Partidas, aun sin fuerza legal, inspiraron las decisiones del tribunal supremo del rey y formaron la mentalidad de los nuevos juristas' (García Gallo 1967, 1:90, para. 188).

10 'no hayan razon de tirar y enmendar en ellas cada uno lo que quisseren'; 'uno sellado con nuestro sello de oro, é otro sellado con nuestro sello de plomo' (Leyes de Toro, law 1).

11 'Entre nosotros las Leyes de Toro son estimadas más que las otras constituciones de España, porque creemos no hay en ellas cosa alguna que no se hubiese discu-

tido, y con mucho juicio considerado para la pública utilidad' (Llamas y Molina 1853, 1:7). The reference is to Gaspar de Baeza, translated into Spanish by Llamas y Molina, who also offers the original quote in Latin: 'Ibi apud nos leges Tauri supra caeteras Hispaniae constitutiones in pretio sunt, nihil in eis crecimus esse, quod non discussum, ac magnopere consideratum ad publicam utilitatem fuerit' (Llamas y Molina 1853, 1:7).

12 'se han de sentenciar por el derecho común de la jurisprudencia romana y emperadores'; 'Todavía es más digno de notarse que suponga como una consecuencia deducida de la ley, que cuando no basten los expresados cuerpos legislativos nacionales para la determinación de las causas, se deben juzgar por el derecho común de los romanos, no haciendo la ley la más mínima mención de tal derecho, y antes bien virtualmente prohibe que se pueda hacer uso de él, cuando después de referir las leyes que se deben usar y guardar, añade: «y no por otras algunas»' (Llamas y Molina, 1853, 1:31–2 and para. 230).

13 'aunque no se pruebe que estén en uso' (Llamas y Molina 1853, 1:90, para. 229). Llamas y Molina calls this an inversion of the order of consultation, and says that it is 'more than a little surprising' (causa no pequeña admiración). The inversion of order of laws to be applied is not that surprising, given that the first law of the Leyes de Toro specifies the same order of consultation, as did every 'this book,' after referring to the local *fueros* and saying they should be used and applied as they have been unless changed in 'this book': 'por las cuales leyes de este nuestro libro mandamos que se libren primeramente todos los pleitos civiles é criminales; é los pleitos é las contiendas que se no pudieren librar por las leyes de este nuestro libro é por los dichos fueros, mandamos que se libren por las leyes de las Siete Partidas, que el rey don Alfonso, nuestro visabuelo, mandó ordenar' (Llamas y Molina 1853, 1:31–2).

14 'revisada y enmendada por el Consejo real.' The royal charter's letter of privilege, dated 7 September 1555, is headed with the customary 'El Rey' and then signed by 'La Princesa, por mandado de … Juan Vázquez.' It reads: 'por nuestro mandado los del nuestro consejo, con asistencia del dicho Licenciado Gregorio López, la vieron y entendieron [la obra], y por muchos días platicaron sobre ella: y con gran deliberación y acuerdo examinaron la dicha letra, y e[n]miendas por el hechas, y determinaron como quedassen.' In subsequent references, Partidas.

15 'desea ver simplificadas las leyes, disminuida su multiplicidad, y aclarada la obscuridad de su redacción a fin de que sean accesibles a todos' (Riveros Subizar 1951, 157).

16 Moliner (1997) defines casuistry in a general sense as a 'collection of cases or examples with which a treatise or theory, etc., can be illustrated' (conjunto de casos o ejemplos con que se ilustra un tratado, una teoría, etc.), notes a connection to moral theology and cases of conscience, and as for the casuist, says it is he 'who adapts the moral principles to each individual case, at times for his own benefit'

(que acomoda los principios morales a cada caso particular, a veces según su conveniencia). This last describes the approach of Castillo de Bobadilla. See also González Echevarría on casuistry and literary prose that, from the particulars of legal cases and 'the prose of the law,' weaves a concrete narrative blending of morals and acts (2005, 31–2). Castillo de Bobadilla's narrative is more a search for loopholes so as to evade the legal dictates.

17 'los vestidos y galas que sacaron sus Magestades y los novios fueron a la premática, sin bordados ni pasamanos, ni otra cosa de oro, aunque las damas y galanes que estuvieron en la boda, llevaron muchos bordados y pasamanos de oro' (Cabrera de Córdoba 1857, 5 January 1602).

18 'Muchos se quexan que no puedan assentar el pie sin incurrir en alguna denunciación contra alguna de las Leyes de España'; 'y si bien se advierte, las Leyes de España deben de passar de cinco mil, porque solas las de la Recopilación son tres mil, y fuera de ellas hay las del Estilo, Partidas, Ordenamiento Real, Fuero Real, y Fuero Juzgo, Leyes de Toro, y Pragmáticas, que salen cada día, sin todo el Derecho común. Los daños de tantas Leyes son muchos. El primero, que oprimen el Reyno'; 'y no hay en el Reyno persona que las sepa todas, ¿cómo las ha de saber el Labrador, y el ignorante para guardarlas, y no incurrir en pena? ¿Quién tiene dineros para comprar tantos, y tan grandes tomos de ellas, ni tiempo para leerlas?' (Moncada 1746 [1619], Discurso VII, chap. 6, pp. 117–22).

19 'El segundo daño es que muchas de ellas no se usan, y dexan la puerta abierta a Jueces, para que aprieten a quien quisieren, diciendo que no están abrogadas y disimulen con quien quisieren, diciendo que no están en uso, como ponderó Navarro. El tercero es, que hablan con palabras equivocas, que admiten diferentes sentidos, y declaraciones, de que se ocasionan tantas denunciaciones, y pleytos, fin de tantas honras, vidas, y haciendas. El último, y principal daño es, que no se guardan [las leyes], en desprecio de la autoridad de los Legisladores, y gran perjuicio de la República' (Moncada 1746 [1619], Discurso VII, chap. 6, pp. 117–22).

20 'Los cuatro puntos cardinales en la flaqueza judicial de don Quijote: reflejo inevitable sobre el fondo de su lógica extraviada, intrusiones profesionales en la jurisdicción, apasionado atropello del trámite, y coacción ilusoria' (Alcalá Zamora y Torres, 2001, 94–7).

21 Moncada's discourse is published along with another he wrote, which takes the form of a vicious diatribe against the gypsies, and Ricapito mentions a study by Bernard Leblon on the connections between Cervantes' *La gitanilla* and that discourse (Ricapito 1996, 11–15).

22 'No hagas muchas pragmáticas; y si las hicieres, procura que sean buenas y, sobre todo, que se guarden y cumplan; que las pragmáticas que no se guardan lo mismo es que si no lo fuesen; antes dan a entender que el príncipe que tuvo discreción y autoridad para hacerlas no tuvo valor para hacer que se guardasen' (DQ II.51).

23 'La situación de mayor delincuencia, más abusos de los encargados de combatirla y menos respeto a la ley real y a sus representantes, se acentuó claramente hacia 1580; y desde entonces en adelante, hacia la segunda mitad del S. XVIII todo fue mal en peor en casi todos los sentidos' (Tomás y Valiente 1969, 44).
24 Most of Sancho's 'prevarications' are comic in nature and, as Ángel Rosenblat (1971) and Amado Alonso have stated, they also offer serious social commentary on the particular situation of language development and 'purification' that marked the transition from Latin to the use of Castilian as a norm: 'el lector moderno ... ya no oye las voces implícitas en ellos, ni siente funcionar en ellos los graves intereses culturales que realmente funcionaban (sí; materia grave, humorísticamente tratada; ahí su eficacia cómica') (A. Alonso 1948, 20).

4. Laws Broken, Glossed, and Made: Don Quixote

1 I accept García Gallo's 1356 date for this compilation prepared by an anonymous jurist (1967, 1:265–6, para. 527). Martínez Marina (1808) offered a probable date of 1155 (32–3), and the prologue to the 1847–9 edition of the Fuero Viejo dated the work to 1250.
2 'a quien quebranta guerto, o molino, o cavaña, o era, o monte de Ynfanzón, a sesenta sueldos de caloña' (Fuero Viejo I.6.1); 'si algún omne crebantar molinos o las pesqueras, todo que crebrantó refágalo fasta treinta días, e demás peche veinte sueldos' (Fuero Juzgo VIII.4.30).
3 'Romper, separar u dividir con violencia las partes de un todo. Lat. Frangere, Effringere, Elidere'; cascar o hender ... moler o machacar ... persuadir, inducir o mover con ardid, industria y porfía ... causar lástima o compasión ... violar o profanar algún sagrado, seguro o coto ... metafóricamente vale violar alguna ley, palabra u obligación ... romper, venciendo alguna dificultad ... molestar, fatigar ... debilitar, disminuir las fuerzas ... n lo forense se decía por inutilizar e invalidar el testamento' (*Autoridades*).
4 'del lat. crepare "crujir, chasquear, castañetear, estallar" y en la baja época reventar' (Corominas).
5 'quebrar'; 'allanar, atropellar'; 'saltear un camino'; 'obligar por fuerza'; 'quebrantar un pacto' (*Léxico hispánico primitivo*).
6 'hablan con palabras equivocas, que admiten diferentes sentidos, y declaraciones' (Moncado, 1746 [1619], Discurso VII).
7 Clemencín points out that the windmills were likely introduced shortly before Cervantes' day (Cervantes 1910–13, I:8, n. 1).
8 Baeza translates with 'quebrar' instead of 'quebrantar' which exemplifies the fluidity of the definitions and offers good reason for the polemic. I cite the two-volume

Histories by Chapter, then paragraph, as chapter numbering from one volume to the next is continuous.

9 'fue rodando muy maltrecho por el campo' (DQ I.8).

10 'lógico es que encierre algunas referencias legales y jurídicas' (Martínez Olmedilla 1905, 20).

11 'histórica y legalmente era exacto' (Martínez Olmedilla 1905, 20); 'cruel pastiche irónico' (Pemán 1948, 9); 'una burla soez y miserable … una grotesca imitación de la sagrada ceremonia de la vela de las armas' (Riquer 1967, 86–7).

12 Gregorio B. Palacín takes issue with Riquer's conclusion, differentiating between military knighthood and knight errant, noting Cervantes' word play on 'never before seen ceremonies' (las hasta allí nunca vistas ceremonias) and stressing the fictional nature of a knight errant (1971, 2, 6).

13 Marín Pina (1998) notes the quality of farce in the parody, and Clemencín (Cervantes 1910–13) offers various points of contact to the ceremonies as portrayed in books of knight errantry (libros de caballerías).

14 'mañana en aquel día me habéis de armar caballero'; 'esta noche en la capilla deste vuestro castillo velaré las armas'; 'derribada para hacerla de nuevo' (DQ I.3).

15 Miguel Sancho Izquierdo dates the added title phrase 'de los caballeros' (of the knights) to Francisco Díaz's 1474 edition of the legal codex (1916, 44–7).

16 According to García Gallo, this request by the nobles 'makes sense in the light of the Speculum, which regulated public law, but not that of the Fuero Real that only dealt with private and penal codes' (tiene sentido frente al Espéculo que regula el Derecho público, pero no frente al Fuero real que sólo trata del Derecho privado y penal) (1967, 1:390–1, para. 738).

17 'con plena autonomía'; 'sin licencia del perlado diocesano' (Pérez-Coca Sánchez-Matas 1994, 2:261, 262).

18 'los que en ellas entran juegan, blasfeman y hazen otros atos muy desconvenientes a la santidad y onestidad de la yglesia' (Pérez-Coca Sánchez-Matas 1994, 2:266).

19 'desde el medio día en adelante, han los Escuderos a bañar, e lavar su cabeza, con sus manos, e echarle en el más apuesto lecho, que pudieren aver. E allí le han de vestir, e de calzar los Cavalleros, de los mejores paños que tovieren' (Siete Partidas II.21.13).

20 Some of the laws specify church and others, chapel. In the introduction to his 1555 edition of the Partidas, jurist Gregorio López defines church in three ways: 1) a sacred place with walls and roof, where Christians go to hear the hours and to beg God's forgiveness for their sins; 2) the Christians themselves, the 'faithful'; and 3) the prelates and clergy of each place. The laws on churches and capillas are contained at Partidas I.10.1–20.

21 'alzándose la visera de papelón y descubriendo su seco y polvoroso rostro' (DQ I.2).

22 'si fuese derribada de cimiento et la quisiesen facer de nuevo' (Partidas I.10.1). López adds a note referring to the proscriptions for construction of churches laid out in Exodus 25–6.

23 'si cayese alguna partida della, o la desficiesen derribando poco a poco para refacerla' (Partidas I.10.2). 'Et ecclesia pro ut primo modo sumitur, non potest fabricari de novo, neque si sit penitus dirupta refici, sine mandato Episcopi dioecesani, & alias non celebratur in ea sine eius consensu hoc dicit' (Partidas I.10.1).

24 The innkeeper's brief description of his life in I.3 has been noted for its picaresque and criminal qualities (DQ I.3, notes).

25 For 'rehacer' *Autoridades* offers: 'Redo that which had been undone' (Volver a hacer lo que se había desecho); 'Reinforce that which is deteriorating' (Vale también añadir nuevas fuerzas a lo que está deteriorado); 'Augment or add to a thing' (Vale asímismo aumentar o añadir el peso o la cantidad a alguna cosa) with Latin roots of 'Reficere, Reparare, Augere, Addere, and Superaddere.' For 'de nuevo': 'Adverb that means newly' (Modo adverbial que vale lo mismo que nuevamente). Lat. Denou. Ordenanzas de Castilla'; Corominas finds 'de nuevo' earlier, in Berceo. The distinction 're' v. 'de nuevo' does get muddied if one includes one of *Autoridades*' multiple meanings for 'new' (nuevo): 'Also taken to mean repeated, or done again so as to renovate' (Vale asímismo repetido, o reiterado para renovarlo) which sounds a lot like 'to redo' or 'to remake' (rehacer). Sevilla Arroyo's edition of the *Quixote* glosses the phrase 'hacerla de nuevo' with: 'newly: new, with new materials' (de nuevo: nueva, con materiales nuevos) (Cervantes 1998a, I.3, n. 7).

26 'son los Caballeros, a quien los antiguos dicen Defensores' (Partidas II.21, intro.); 'los carniceros, por razon que usan matar las cosas bivas, e esparzar la sangre dellas'; 'porque usan mucho a ferir, e son fuertes de manos' (Partidas II.21.2).

27 'E esta manera de escoger usaron los Antiguos muy grand tiempo. Mas porque estos atales vieron despues muchas vegadas, que non aviendo verguenza, olvidavan todas estas cosas sobredichas, e en logar de vencer sus enemigos, vencianse ellos' (Partidas II.21.2). Maravall cites various fifteenth-century texts whose writers complain about another, probably related reason for military losses, avarice and greed among the soldiers (Maravall 1976, 41).

28 'los sabidores, que catasen omes para estas cosas'; 'verguenza naturalmente'; 'el ome flaco, e sofridor' (Partidas II.21.2); 'mensurado'; 'les fiziessen las carnes recias, e duras'; 'Otrosi los acostumbraban, que non fuessen dormidores' (Partidas II.21.19). The extended section explains in detail that shame assures the knight will not flee or allow himself to be beaten, and that a skinny, suffering type is less likely to flee than a strong man (Que la verguenza vieda al Cavallero, que non fuya de la batalla, e porende ella le faze vencer. Ca mucho tovieron que era mejor el ome flaco, e sofridor, que el fuerte, ligero para fuyr. E por esto, sobre todas las cosas, cataron que fuessen omes de buen linaje, porque se guardassen de fazer cosa, por que podiessen caer en verguenza) (Partidas II.21.2).

29 'era de complexión recia, seco de carnes, enjuto de rostro, gran madrugador, amigo de la caza' (DQ I.1). Sabor de Cortazar notes that 'hunting was a gentlemen's sport' (la caza era el deporte de los señores), the poor menu described for Alonso Quijano is typical of a noble of modest means, and that this 'social type had become a literary type' ([el] tipo social se ha transformado en tipo literario) in Spanish letters (Sabor de Cortazar 1979, 44, 47).

30 'no es dado a los caballeros andantes quejarse de herida alguna, aunque se le salgan las tripas por ella' (DQ I.8).

31 'omes de buen linaje ... en lenguaje de España ... los llamaron Fijosdalgo'; 'fasta en el quarto grado, a que llaman bisabuelos' (Partidas II.22.2).

32 'habían sido de sus bisabuelos' (DQ I.1).

33 'E aun porque se esforzassen más, tenían por cosa guisada, que los que oviessen amigas, que las nombrassen en las lides, porque les creciessen más los corazones, e oviessen mayor verguenza de errar' (Partidas II.21.22).

34 Castro Dassen points out that reference to usage and custom, as well as other formalistic legal language, themes, and characters, are frequent in the *Quixote* (1953, 41, 20–111). Close finds in Don Quixote's language 'a host of comic species and colloquial or technical registers (thieves' slang; proverbs; the commonplaces of everyday speech; notarial, commercial, liturgical terminology; and so on)' (2000, 115).

35 'ya está en uso y costumbre en la caballería andantesca que el caballero andante que al acometer algún gran fecho de armas tuviese su señora delante' (DQ I.13).

36 'al comer, non deve asentarse con ellos escudero, ni otro ninguno, si non Cavallero, o ome que lo meresciesse por su honra, o por su bondad' (Partidas II.21.23).

37 Don Quixote volunteers at an age when, as Redondo points out, 'he is already old, at fifty years of age, which only accentuates even more the burlesque character of his gesture' (está ya en la vejez, a los cincuenta años, lo que acentúa todavía más el carácter burlesco de su gesta) (1991, 31).

38 All towns were mandated to have a copy and, by 1567, there had been twenty-eight editions of this 'unofficial' compendium, which continued to be cited, argued, and commented on: 'Aunque no recibe sanción oficial, su utilidad es sin embargo tan grande que los Reyes Católicos mandan a los pueblos tengan un ejemplar de ellas ... y los juristas las citan, alegan y comentan como si fuesen obra legislativa. Hasta 1567 se hacen veintiocho ediciones de ellas' (García Gallo 1967, 1:396, para. 747). In subsequent citations, Ordenanzas.

39 'pero que el Cavallero, que fuere de edad de sesenta años arriba, no sea tenudo de ir por su persona a la guerra' (Recop. IV.1.1).

40 'frisaba ... los cincuenta años' (DQ I.1). Thompson speaks to problems with the advanced age of the earlier militias of *cuantiosos caballeros* (1976, 21), who continued to be called up all throughout the sixteenth century.

41 'los caballeros que han a defender la tierra, e conquerirla de los enemigos de la Fe por las armas, deben ser escusados, por no entender las leyes ... ca bien es derecho

y razón, que aquel que su cuerpo aventura en peligro de prisión, o de muerte, que nol[e] den otro embargo, porque aquello se estorbe … fueras ende si el caballero ficiese traicion, o falsedad, o aleve, o yerro, que otro home debiesse entender naturalmente que mal era' (Partidas I.1.21).

42 '¿Quién fue el ignorante que firmó mandamiento de prisión contra un tal caballero como yo soy? ¿Quién el que ignoró que son esentos de todo judicial fuero los caballeros andantes, y que su ley es su espada, sus fueros sus bríos, sus premáticas su voluntad? ¿Quién fue el mentecato, vuelvo a decir, que no sabe que no hay secutoria de hidalgo con tantas preeminencias ni esenciones como la que adquiere un caballero andante el día que se arma caballero y se entrega al duro ejercicio de la caballería?' (DQ I.45).

43 'las libertades privilegios y prerogativas de sus hidalguías y esenciones' (Pramáticas, fol 95, law 104). The spelling varies in documents of the era, with 'pragmática,' 'pramática,' and 'premática.' A 'pragmática' (pragmatic) in general is spelled thusly, today.

44 'todos los de nuestros reynos y señoríos'; 'Burgos cabeza de Castilla nuestra cámara' (Pramáticas, fol. 95, law 104).

45 'nos fue hecha relación diciendo que por la mucha paz y tranquilidad que mediante la divina clemencia en estos nuestros reinos ha habido y hay después que nos reinamos aca … no ha habido ni hay armas ofensivas ni defensivas como solía … por tal manera cuando que para alguna cosa que cumple a nuestro servicio y a la ejecución de nuestra justicia o para prosecución de algunos malfechores conviene que salga alguna gente de alguna ciudad o villa o lugar: aquella va por la mayor parte desarmada con mucho peligro: mengua y deshonra suya' (Pramáticas, fol. 95, law 104).

46 'por tierra tan pacífica' (DQ I.13).

47 'armas convenibles ofensivas y defensivas'; 'súbditos y naturales de cualquier ley y estado o condición'; 'estado o condición' (Pramáticas, fol. 95, law 103).

48 'Que trata de la *condición* y ejercicio del famoso hidalgo don Quijote de la Mancha' (DQ I.1, my emphasis).

49 'todos los que viven y moran en las ciudades y villas francas y exentas'; 'todas las provincias y cibdades y villas y lugares delos dichos nuestros reynos y señoríos' (Pramáticas, fol. 95, law 104).

50 'Que sean admitidos por quantiosos todos los que quisieren desu voluntad, aunque tengan menos de los mil ducados de hazienda, que enla prouisión declara' (Recop. VI.1.13). This collection is known as Nueva Recopilación or, alternatively, as Recopilación de leyes and in what follows, I use Recopilación or Recop. for the 1982 facsimile edition of the 1640 printing. A later and somewhat different edition called the Novísima Recopilación was published in 1775, then republished in 6 volumes from 1805–1829, and is herein cited with that title.

51 'más principales y ricos'; 'que tengan unas corazas de acero y falda de malla o de launas/ y armadura de cabeza que sea capacete con su babera/ o celada con su barbote y más gocetes o musequíes y una lanza larga medida de veinte y cuatro

palmos: y espada y puñal y casquete' (Pramáticas, fol. 95, law 104). The mandate for those of 'mediano estado y hacienda': 'que ayan de tener y tengan corazas y una armadura de cabeza aunque sea casquete/ y espada y puñal/ y una lanza larga ... o lanza común y medio pavés o escudo de pontevedra o de oviedo' and, for those of 'menor estado': 'que tengan espada y casquete y lanza larga de veinte y cuatro palmas y dardo con ella: o en lugar de lanza larga una lanza medina medio pavés o escudo de pontevedra o de oviedo' (Pramáticas, fol. 95, law 104).

52 Don Quixote is 'un hidalgo de los de lanza en astillero, adarga antigua' (DQ I.1); on leaving the hacienda 'se armó de todas sus armas ... puesta su mal compuesta celada, embrazó su adarga, tomó su lanza' (DQ I.2); he is seen approaching the inn: 'armada de armas tan desiguales como eran la brida, lanza, adarga y coselete' (DQ I.2); when the 'doncellas' (young lasses) help him disarm, they are able to remove 'el peto y el espaldar' but not the 'contrahecha celada' (DQ I.2); after the ceremony, the ventero orders one of the doncellas 'que le ciñese la espada', following which 'le calzó la espuela' (DQ I.3).

53 Translated into Cervantes' terms in the novel: the steel armour includes his mentioned 'peto, espaldar (musequíes), y coselete' (breastplate, backplate and corselet) (DQ I.2); the skirt of mail is a 'falda de loriga' (skirt of cuirass) (DQ I.10); the casque with beaver / sallet with visor is the 'morrión simple' (simple helmet) with its cardboard additions (DQ I.1).

54 'aunque sea infante / o duque / o marqués / o conde / o otro de mayor o menor estado / o dignidad'; 'muy prestamente se perdería en nuestros reinos la nobleza de la caballería'; 'excepto que los perlados y clérigos de orden sacra y frailes y los doctores y licenciados y bachilleres en cualesquier ciencias no sean obligados' (Pramáticas, fol. 146, law 153).

55 'cavallo / o rocín / o yegua / o potro' (fol. 151); 'caballo o yegua de silla sea de arriba de dos años: y tal que en el pueda andar un hombre armado y pelear en el cuando fuere menester' (fol. 127, law 154).

56 'si algún caballero andante había traído escudero caballero asnalmente'; 'acomodarle más honrada caballería' (DQ I.7).

57 'no se pueden ni deben echar asnos a las yeguas' (Pramáticas, folios 149–50).

58 'el gobierno tuvo que imponer, por primera vez, el servicio militar obligatorio' (Ettinghausen 1996, 26).

59 'In September 1596 modified instructions were issued for the registration of all male Old Christians aged between eighteen and forty-four, and a further effort to get the militia under way followed at the beginning of 1598' (Thompson 1976, 128).

60 'Villanueva de los Infantes y las demás [villas] de su partido, Sigura de la Sierra y las demás del suyo, & la villa de Torrenueva.' I am indebted to Professor Thompson for this information, which he kindly provided from notes taken for his *War and Government in Habsburg Spain 1560–1620*, published by the Athlone Press of the University of London in 1976.

61 Redondo calls Don Quixote's decision to become a knight a 'significant usurpation of social status, given the term's use beyond that of the books of knight errantry, as used for an authentic aristocrat' (significativa usurpación de *status social.* En efecto, el término *caballero,* más allá del significado que cobra en los libros de caballerías, al designar al que ha recibido la orden correspondiente, se aplica, a principios del siglo XVII, al auténtico aristócrata) (1991, 31).

62 '¿Qué caballero andante pagó pecho, alcabala, chapín de la reina, moneda forera, portazgo ni barca?' (DQ I.45). Both legal compendia include one 1317 law specifying that if one is a pechero (taxpayer) before being knighted, the granted order of caballería does not excuse that taxpayer status, but also a 1417 law that does provide an exemption from taxpayer status to caballeros as to all taxes except those paid by 'gentry' (hijosdalgo) (Ordenanzas, IV.1.3–5).

63 'Estas cosas obraron tanto con los Mexicanos, que como Cortés por mano de predicadores intérpretes, les dixiesse mucho, de las cosas divinas, y del autoridad del Papa, y grandeza y valor del Emperador don Carlos, príncipe soberano, determinaron por determinación pública embiar por embaxadores dos illustres señores de su nación, que viniessen a España, y hiziessen reverencia al emperador, y venerassen al Papa Clemente, Yo vi a estos embaxadores en Roma, y en color, cabello, y alegre condición, parecían a nuestros mulatos, y presentaron al Papa, unas pequeñas ymágenes de oro, y él selas pagó bien, mandando les dar sendos vestidos de brocado. Y haziéndolos armar cavalleros, dio les dos taluartes, y dos espadas, y dos dagas doradas, y sendas cadenas de oro' (Giovio 1568, fol. 198).

64 'meter las manos en las lides' (Partidas II.21.11).

65 'y en nuestro querer, y voluntad sea que sean armados, y con solemnidad, y ceremonias, que las nuestras leyes de las partidas disponen, o sin ellas' (Ordenanzas IV.1.8).

66 'por haber recibido la caballería por escarnio, amén de estar loco, ser pobre y haber sido armado por un pícaro, el hidalgo Alonso Quijana, aunque nunca dude de la validez del rito, jamás será un verdadero caballero andante' (Marín Pina 1998, 23).

67 Basave Fernández del Valle finds a lack of true understanding of the necessity of positive law in the character's act of freeing the galeotes: 'La libertad que dio Don Quijote a los galeotes es un verdadero atentado contra la seguridad jurídica y contra la cosa juzgada … Si don Quijote hubiera comprendido la dignidad y la necesidad de la ley positiva, habría aceptado, como consecuencia, la coacción. Pero él sólo entendía la ley como un ordenamiento de la razón al bien común, privado de fuerza coercitiva' (1968, 199).

68 'algunos philopoetas'; 'si puede la historia religiosa y sagrada ser materia buena de épica' (López Pinciano 1953, 3:168).

69 'cae mucho mejor la imitación y ficción sobre materia que no sea religiosa, porque el poeta se puede mucho mejor ensanchar y aún traer episodios mucho más deleytosos y sabrosos a las orejas de los oyentes' (López Pinciano 1953, 3:168).

70 'en suma, digo que la materia de religión, por ser della, no parece tan bien en imitación' (López Pinciano 1953, 3:180).

71 'La divina enseña religión; la humana, prudencia; la natural, ciencia, y todas deleitan' (Cabrera de Córdoba 1948 [1611], Discurso VII, 34).

72 'lo humano con lo divino, que es un género de mezcla de quien no se ha de vestir ningún cristiano entendimiento' (DQ I, Prologue).

73 In Partida II, Title 21 'Of knights ...' we read that 'Defenders are one of the three civic states ... those who pray to God for the people ... those who work the land for the people ... and those who defend the people ... ' (Defensores son uno de los tres estados ... los que ruegan a Dios por el Pueblo ... los que labran la tierra ... los que han a defender a todos ...) (Partidas II.21, preamble).

74 'los religiosos ... piden al cielo el bien de la tierra; pero los soldados y caballeros ponemos en ejecución lo que ellos piden, defendiéndola ... sin duda es más trabajoso y más aporreado, y más hambriento y sediento, miserable, roto y piojoso' (DQ I.13).

75 'poner en su punto la justicia distributiva y dar a cada uno lo que es suyo, entender y hacer que las buenas leyes se guarden' (DQ I.37).

76 Cervantes' statement here in is consonance with other European writers of the time, as studied by Ullrich Langer, who finds an echo of Aristotelian and Ciceronian ideas on justice in Italian, French, and German short stories of the Renaissance. To that effect, Langer cites a 1581 French work: 'Distributive justice consists in giving to everyone what he deserves, either honor and status, or punishment; commutative justice consists in keeping, and causing others to keep, faith in things promised and contracted, and to do to others only as we would like to have done to ourselves' (Langer 1999, 316, citing *La Primaudaye* 119).

77 Pérez y López (1791) specifies that Partidas I and IV have their origin in canon law.

78 'la jurisprudencia es, por definición, noticia de lo divino y lo humano' (Baudouin, cited in Turchetti 1984, 156).

79 'Por correr obligación precisa, conforme a ley divina y humana' (Pérez de Herrera 1598, 1v).

80 'congregó poblaciones, y las cercó de muro: ora de miedo que tenía por la muerte de Abel su hermano, o por avaricia, porque ya usaban de proprios'; 'Jabet, hijo de Lamech, señaló los ganados con señal conocida, para los distinguir, y conocer: de manera, que ya entonces havía mío y tuyo, y propriedad en las cosas' (Castillo de Bobadilla 1775 [1597], I.1.10, I:7, 8).

81 'Recop. lib. I. tit. 4. l.2. Los Clérigos de corona y menores órdenes, que conforme al decreto del Sacro Concilio, y la ley antes de esta, pueden gozar del privilegio del fuero, sea y se entienda tan solamente quanto al privilegio del fuero, en las causas criminales' (*Autoridades*).

82 'la jurisprudencia, desde Ulpiano, comprende el conocimiento de las cosas divinas y humanas' (Sánchez de la Vega 1987, 16). Ulpianus was a Roman jurisconsult who lived from 170 to 228 A.D.

83 'nuestros siglos XIV y XV escuchan en todo momento un clamor popular, alentado desde arriba, contra las extralimitaciones de la jurisdicción eclesiástica que invade y resiste a la de los jueces y oficiales del rey' (Maravall 1972, 219). Maravall lists the dates of those protests, beginning in 1301, and occurring repeatedly in 1307, 1315, 1318, 1322, 1325, 1345, 1351, 1371, 1386, 1401, 1425, 1430, 1432, 1433, 1435, 1436, 1438, 1422, 1451, 1453, 1455, 1462, 1476, until the historian finally just adds 'etc.' (1972, 219–20).

84 'el aparato estatal funciona cada vez más eficazmente para repeler las intromisiones de este tipo' (Maravall 1972, 220).

85 'Que el lego no emplace al lego ante el juez Eclesiástico sobre cosas profanas. Ordenamos que ningún lego sea ossado de mandar, citar ni emplazar a otro lego delante el juez de la Iglesia ni hazer, ni otorgar obligación sobre sí a que se someta a la jurisdicción Eclesiástica, sobre deudas, o cosas profanas, a la Iglesia no pertenescientes: y si lo hiziere, mandamos, que por el mismo hecho pierda la acción, y sea adquirida al reo: y si tuviere oficio en cualquier de las ciudades, villas y lugares de nuestros Reynos, pierda el oficio: y si oficio no tuviere, que dende en adelante no pueda aver otro, y demás que caiga en pena de diez mil maravedis, la mitad para el acusador, y la otra mitad para el reparo de los muros en la ciudad, villa o lugar do esto acaesciere' (Recop. IV.1.10).

86 'que el escribano que lo signare pierda el oficio, y dende en adelante su escritura no haga fee, ni prueva, y pierda la mitad de sus bienes' (Recop. IV.1.11).

87 'a todas e qualesquier justicias e juezes e oficiales qualesquier, ansy eclesiásticos como seglares'; 'todos e qualesquier derecho [*sic*] canónicos y bulas e yndultos apostólicos e previllejos y esenciones generales y especiales de que en qualquier manera me pudiese aprovechar ... aunque sea de las especiales concedidas por los summos pontífices a los protonotarios e familiares apostólicos o dignidades ... o ganada a pedimiento del duque del ynfantado mi señor en fabor se su capilla' (Martín de Mendoza, cited by Cortés 1916, 28, 29).

88 'con la Iglesia hemos dado, Sancho' (DQ II.9); 'religión militar' (DQ I.49).

89 'El diablo me lleve ... si este mi amo no es tólogo; y si no lo es, que lo parece como un güevo a otro' (DQ II.27).

90 'desafía la justicia del Rey, inhumana y rígida, al liberar a los galeotes' (Riveros Subizar 1951, 142–3); 'Cervantes se complace en oponer la justicia espontánea, sencilla, equitativa, en suma, místicamente natural, a la legal y estatuida; no se formula dogmáticamente esa doctrina en ninguna parte, pero los hechos la presuponen con la mayor elocuencia' (Américo Castro 1972, 204).

91 'algún omne crebanta cárcel, o enganna el guardador, o el guardador mismo suelto los presos'; 'cada uno destos deve recivir tal pena e tal damno qual deven recibir los presos' (Fuero Juzgo VII.4.3).

92 'bolleciendo ... o siendo causa de la bollecer' (Recop. VIII.16.5).

93 'siendo las sentencias passadas en cosa juzgada, o no aviendo lugar apelación ... aviendo número de doze galeotes, assí de los condenados por los juezes inferiores, como en la dicha Audiencia, se embién a la Ciudad de Toledo por Villafranca, Valladolid y Segovia' (Recop. VIII.24.9).

94 'se quedan en las cárceles sin castigo, y se sueltan' (Recop. VIII.24.5).

95 The full quote reads: 'Y si por alguno, o algunos de los dichos delinquentes condenados a las galeras fuere pedido traslado de la sentencia contra él dada, o sentencias, para le tener en su poder, para que cumplido el término lo suelten, el dicho Corregidor, o su Teniente se le hagan dar. Y mandamos al Capitán de las nuestras galeras, o a su lugarteniente, que aviendo servido los tales condenados el tiempo en las dichas sentencias contenido, los suelten y dexen ir libremente, conforme a las dichas sentencias, y no los detengan contra su voluntad, y les den fe y testimonio de como han servido el dicho tiempo en las dichas galeras' (Recop. VIII.24.3).

96 'Mandamos ... [que] seyendo los tales delitos de calidad, en que buenamente pueda aver lugar comutación, sin hazer en ello perjuyzio a partes querellosas: seyendo condenados en penas corporales, o en cortar pie, o mano, o destierro perpetuo, o otras penas semejantes ... los comutéys ... en mandarles ir a servir a las galeras por el tiempo que os pareciere' (Recop. VIII.24.4).

97 'no aviendo lugar apelación' (Recop. VIII.24.3).

98 'Esta es cadena de galeotes, gente forzada del rey, que va a las galeras'; '¿Cómo gente forzada? – preguntó don Quijote. ¿Es posible que el rey haga fuerza a ninguna gente?' (DQ I.22).

99 'no de su voluntad'; 'aquí encaja la ejecución de mi oficio: desfacer fuerzas' (DQ I.22).

100 'Fuerzas que hazen unos hombres a otros' (Recop. IV.13, VI.3, VIII.12).

101 'Por quanto, assí por derechos, como por costumbre inmemorial nos pertenece alçar las fuerças, que los jueces Eclesiásticos, y otras personas hazen en las causas que conocen, no otorgando las apelaciones que dellos legítimamente son interpuestas: porende mandamos a nuestros Presidentes, y Oidores de las nuestras Audiencias de Valladolid, y Granada, que quando alguno viniere ante ellos, quexándose que no se le otorga la apelación que justamente interpone, de algún juez Eclesiástico, den nuestras cartas en la forma acostumbrada en nuestro Consejo, para que se otorgue la apelación ... [así] alçando la fuerça' (Recop. II.5.36). The third law in the series prohibits bringing an ecclesiastical case to the High Courts when it is by means of 'interlocutory force, except in those cases when there might be definitive force' (Recop. II.5.37). The fourth allows hearing cases brought by 'vía de fuerza' when 'they should be heard on the order of a rehearing,' the fifth regularizes the geographical limits of each High Court for such cases, and the sixth and last prohibits that the High Courts hear by 'vía de fuerza' ecclesiastical business dealing with 'visitations and correction of the religious

persons, made by their superiors' because it could be 'inconvenient … due to the secret matters' dealt with in such cases (Recop. II.5.40).

102 See CORDE: prior to 1500 and up until 1575, the uses of *tuerto* are common in legal documents and volumes. In the Repertorio universal de todas las leyes destos reinos de Castilla, published between 1540 and 1553, 'tuerto' is 'agravio' (harm) (CORDE). From 1580 to 1600, the percentage of legal usages is almost nil.

103 'mi señora sea vengada del tuerto que ha rescibido' (*Palmerín de Oliva* 1996).

104 'usado como substantivo, vale agravio, sinrazón, o injuria, que se le hace a alguno'; 'Se dice también de los Jueces, que se inclinan a las partes, que tienen menos justicia' (*Autoridades*).

105 'El juez que juzga tuerto por ruego o por ignorancia' (Fuero Juzgo II.1.19).

106 'Deste término tuerto usan mucho las escrituras castellanas antiguas, y particularmente las leyes de Partida' (Covarrubias, 'tuerto').

107 'la persona o animal a quien le falta un ojo o lo tiene falta de vista' (Moliner 1997).

108 'Sedme testigos que el señor juez me es sospechoso y temo que me sentenciará tuerto, pues me mira de mal ojo' (Santa Cruz de Dueñas 1997).

109 The full quote reads: 'No sé cómo pueda ser eso de enderezar tuertos … pues a mí de derecho me habéis vuelto tuerto, dejándome una pierna quebrada, la cual no se verá derecha en todos los días de su vida; y el agravio que en mí habéis deshecho ha sido dejarme agraviado de manera que me quedaré agraviado para siempre' (DQ I.19).

110 'el torcido juicio del juez' (DQ I.22).

111 'Hermana mía, si el mismo aliento y valor que habéis mostrado para defender esta bolsa le mostrárades, y aun la mitad menos, para defender vuestro cuerpo, las *fuerzas* de Hércules no os *hicieran fuerza*' (DQ II.45, emphasis added).

112 'En lo forense significa el agravio que el Juez hace a la parte en conocer de su causa, o no otorgarle la apelación. Es voz mui usada en las causas que penden en los Tribunales Eclesiásticos, de donde se recurre al Consejo o Chancillerías por via de fuerza, y allí se declara si el Eclesiástico hace o no hace fuerza en conocer y proceder, o en no otorgar' (*Autoridades*).

113 'Do fuerza hay derecho se pierde'; 'A estas fuerzas se opone la justicia y el poder de los reyes, a cuya cuenta está el defendernos y ampararnos. Otras fuerzas hay que los mismos jueces suelen hacer a los litigantes, no les queriendo admitir las apelaciones para el juez superior y llevan las causas por vía de fuerza, adonde se declare si hacen fuerza o no' (Covarrubias).

114 'el agravio que el juez eclesiástico hace a la parte, cuando conoce de causa que no le compete, cuando no observa las reglas prescritas por las leyes y cánones, y cuando niega injustamente la apelación'; '*Alzar o quitar la fuerza* es quitar, anular o reformar los tribunales reales los efectos de la violencia que hacen los jueces eclesiásticos' (Escriche 1852).

115 The most complete description of 'public sin' lists 'blasphemy, concubinage, usury, fortunetelling and soothsaying, and other similar things' and then adds 'offering false testimony' (Recop.III.6.36). The nepharious sin (sodomy) is described as 'that against nature' and that 'not worthy of name' (Recop. VIII.21).

116 'me parece duro caso hacer esclavos a los que Dios y naturaleza hizo libres' (DQ I.22).

117 'podría ser que el poco ánimo que aquél tuvo en el tormento, la falta de dineros déste, el poco favor del otro, y, finalmente, el torcido juicio del juez, hubiese sido causa de vuestra perdición y de no haber salido con la justicia que de vuestra parte teníades'; 'allá se lo haya cada uno con su pecado: Dios hay en el cielo' (DQ I.22). Thompson (1976) describes municipal recruiting improprieties and abuses that imposed militia duty or granted exemption at the whim of a particular official, with men jailed for refusing to be illegally conscripted, which can be read as further support for Don Quixote's insistence on questioning the galley slaves one by one as to their crimes.

118 'muy gentil latino'; 'diablo'; 'Si vuestra merced, señor caballero, lleva alguna cosa con que socorrer a estos pobretes, Dios se lo pagará en el cielo, y nosotros tendremos en la tierra cuidado de rogar a Dios en nuestras oraciones por la vida y salud de vuestra merced' (DQ I.22).

119 'uno de los pecados que más a Dios ofende es la ingratitud'; 'alguna cantidad de avemarías y credos'; 'las ollas de Egipto' (DQ I.22, and n. 38).

120 'somos informados de algunos inconvenientes, que resultan de dar libertad a los forzados, que en estos nuestros Reynos han sido condenados a galeras por diferentes delitos, y causas … muchas vezes sucede, que algunos son embiados a galeras con la primer[a] sentencia, sin esperar la de revista. Mandamos que ninguno pueda ser embiado a las dichas galeras, ni a las cárceles, donde para este efecto se suelen mudar, y conduzir, hasta que en revista esté condenado, y rematado a ellas' (Recop. VIII.24.11).

121 'E la justicia, que la fagan derechamente' (Partidas II.21.4).

122 'le habían de dejar por loco' (DQ I.46).

123 Fuero de Zorita de los Canes, from the year 1218 to c. 1250: 'Ley [?] 191. Del fijo perverso. Si el padre ola madre fijo loco o auiesso ovieren, et temieren las calonnas que el fiziere, tengan lo preso o atado, fasta que se amase o recobre sanidat, que si loco fuere non faga ningún daño. Ca por el danno que fiziere qual quiere que sea, anlos padres de responder por él'; Fuero de Plasencia, c. 1300: para. 464, Ley IIa. 'Si el padre o la madre fijo traviesso ovieren e temieren que él fiziere, ténganlo preso fasta que sea manso o reciba sanidade si fuere loco. Caten que non faga danno, que por quanto danno fiziere los parientes an de responder.' Both are cited from CORDE. The wording is the same in the Fuero de Teruel, year 1300.

124 'hidalgo'; 'rematado su juicio'; 'que jamás se dio loco en el mundo' (DQ I.1).

125 'por loco se libraría' (DQ I.3); 'le tuvieron por loco' (DQ I.13).

126 'Si algún loco desmemoriado fiziere pleyto, mientre dura la locura en él non vala tal pleyto como éste. Mas si en algún tiempo cobra su sanidat et su sentido, el pleyto que fiziere en tal tiempo vala, maguer que después torne en la locura' (Fuero Real VI).

127 'Cum ergo furor excuset furiosum a poena merita propter crimen, multo magis, a poena, & servitio debito: ob non solutam pecuniam' (Baeza 1570, 9.6, fol. 75v).

128 'Furiosus sententia iudicis absolutus: an sit reddeat ad sanam mentem possit a creditoribus peti ad servitium' (Baeza 1570, 9.summa 9, fols 74v–5r).

129 'loco de atar' (DQ II.10); 'no es loco ... sino atrevido' (DQ II.17); 'fuera de juicio y loco de todo punto' (DQ II.23).

130 'un cuerdo loco y un loco que tiraba a cuerdo ... ya le tenía por cuerdo y ya por loco' (DQ II.17). Gaos notes that no one who had received the honour in jest, nor could a madman, or a poor man, be knighted (Cervantes 1987, I.3, n. 3b).

131 'quiero que vuestra merced advierta que no soy tan loco ni tan menguado como debo de haberle parecido' (DQ II.17).

132 'Hasta ahora ... no os podré yo juzgar por loco'; 'él es loco bizarro'; 'es un entreverado loco, lleno de lúcidos intervalos' (DQ II.18).

133 It is noteworthy that, in the Fuero Real, the category is broadened to include Jews and Moors, neither of whom is allowed to serve as a 'vocero' (advocate) for a Christian: '[IV] Mandamos que ningún hereje, nin iudio, nin moro non sea vozero por christiano contra christiano, nin siervo, nin ciego, nin descomulgado, nin sordo, nin loco, nin omne que non aya edat complida' (year 1251–5), nor can they be a 'cabezal' (group representative), a word also used for the executor of a will: '[VII] Mandamos que ningún siervo, nin religioso, nin mugier, nin omne que non sea de edat, nin loco, nin erege, nin moro, nin iudío, nin mudo, nin sordo, nin ome que sea dado por alevoso o por traydor, nin omne que sea iudgado a muerte, nin omne que sea echado de tierra, que non puedan seer cabezales en ninguna manda.' This last is the same in the Fuero de Soria, which dates to approximately 1196: 'ningún siervo, nin religioso, nin omne nin mugier que non sea de edat, ni loco, ni erege, ni iudío, ni moro, ni mudo, ni sordo por natura, ni ome que ssea dado por alevoso o por traydor, ni omne que ssea yudgado a muerte, ni omne que sea echado de tierra, non puedan seer cabezales en ninguna manda.' I cite both of these last from CORDE. The category of infant, insane, etc., seems to have been employed as a flexible and useful catch-all for political exclusionary manoeuvrings.

134 'discurre con bonísimas razones ... un entendimiento claro y apacible en todo ... como no le toquen en sus caballerías' (DQ I.30); 'De tal manera y por tan buenos términos iba prosiguiendo en su plática don Quijote que obligó a que, por entonces, ninguno de los que escuchándole estaban le tuviese por loco' (DQ

I.37); 'en cuanto hablaba y respondía mostraba tener bonísimo entendimiento' (DQ I.49).

135 'ninguno de los que escuchándole estaban le tuviese por loco' (DQ I.37).

136 'tornará loco cualquier hombre cuerdo' (Covarrubias).

137 'Toto omne qui mesare vel firiere con puño aut cozes a vecino aut filio de vecino in taberna vel in azoche aut in carera aut in quali loco' (Fuero de Madrid, IV, p. 44); 'Qui mesare vel firiere aut omne mudo aut sordo aut loco & exido de suo sensum, non pectet nullo coto' (Fuero de Madrid, XLVII, p. 55).

138 'y assí mismo el furioso o loco, por el delito que confessó mientras le dura la locura, no puede ser castigado, si no es que huviesse delinquido en el intervallo que está en su juizio' (Villadiego Vascuñana y Montoya 1612, fol. 57v). The jurist is most commonly referred to, and will be in what follows, as Villadiego.

139 'el vulgo tiene a vuestra merced por grandísimo loco, y a mí por no menos mentecato'; 'En lo que toca ... a la valentía, cortesía, hazañas y asumpto de vuestra merced ... unos dicen: «loco, pero gracioso»; otros, «valiente, pero desgraciado»' (DQ II.2).

140 'Por cierto, señor Sansón Carrasco, que tenemos nuestro merecido ... Don Quijote loco, nosotros cuerdos: él se va sano y riendo, vuesa merced queda molido y triste. Sepamos, pues, ahora, cuál es más loco: ¿el que lo es por no poder menos, o el que lo es por su voluntad?' (DQ II.15).

141 'fuera de juicio' (DQ I.29); 'quebrantado y fuera de juicio' (DQ I.32).

142 'el que ha perdido el juicio, carece de razón, y hace y dice disparates'; 'el sujeto de poco juicio y assiento, disparatado e imprudente' (*Autoridades*).

143 'Rursus quaero an furor excuset a dispositione huius legis ... Primo, negari non potest furorem infirmitatem esse, non solum corporis, verum etiam animi: unde furiosos malesanos & insanos appelamus, & quod furiosus censeatur esse' (Baeza 1570, 9.1, fol. 75r).

144 'el furioso, estando físicamente presente a un acto, es igual que si estuviera ausente, porque no hay voluntad jurídicamente relevante' (Paulus, cited by García Sánchez y García Fueyo 2007, 79, and notes 161–2). From Paulus: '«*furiosus nullum negotium contrahere potest*»,' Pomponius: '«*furiosi, vel eius, cui bonis interdictum est, nulla voluntas est*»,' and Paulus again, in the Digest: 'el furioso, estando físicamente presente a un acto, es igual que si estuviera ausente, porque no hay voluntad jurídicamente relevante' (all citations from García Sánchez y García Fueyo 2007, 79, and notes 161 and 162, emphasis in original).

145 'Tú, que imitaste la llorosa vida / que tuve ausente y desdeñado sobre / el gran ribazo de la Peña Pobre, / de alegre a penitencia reducida, / tú, a quien los ojos dieron la bebida / de abundante licor, aunque salobre, / y alzándote la plata, estaño y cobre / te dio la tierra en tierra la comida' (DQ I, p. 18, vv. 1–8).

146 See Egido 2004, Javier García 1997, Thiher 1999, Castilla del Pino 2005, Goodey 1994, Klibansky et al. 1964, Shuger 2008, and Dols 1992. Also of interest for the sixteenth-century approach to madness, albeit for Germany instead of Spain, is the work by Midelfort 1999.
147 'No puedo ser tu igual; que este decoro / se debe a tus proezas y a tu fama, / puesto que, como yo, perdiste el seso' (DQ I, p. 22, vv. 9–11). The phrase 'puesto que,' in this context, should be read as 'aunque' (although), as I have translated it here.
148 'quiero imitar a Amadís, haciendo aquí del desesperado, del sandio y del furioso, por imitar juntamente al valiente don Roldán' (DQ I.25).
149 'sin hacer locuras de daño, sino de lloros y sentimientos' (DQ I.25).
150 'Roldán en las locuras desaforadas que hizo, o Amadís en las malencónicas' (DQ I.26).
151 'agravio manifiesto'; 'loco de aquel género de locura de Roldán el furioso' (DQ I.26).
152 'Etiam si propria culpa quis in furorem incidat (puta medicamina accipiendo) non addicitur suo creditori. Etiam si debitum descendat ex delicto' (Baeza 1570, 9. summa. 7, fol. 74v).
153 'los caballeros que lo tal ficieron fueron provocados y tuvieron causa para hacer esas necedades y penitencias; pero vuestra merced, ¿qué causa tiene para volverse loco?'; 'Ahí está el punto ... y ésa es la fineza de mi negocio; que volverse loco un caballero andante con causa, ni grado ni gracias; el toque está desatinar sin ocasión ... en seco' (DQ I.25).
154 'Loco soy, loco he de ser hasta tanto'; 'acabarse ha mi sandez'; 'si fuere al contrario seré loco de veras' (DQ I.25).
155 'como si estuviera sin juicio' (DQ I.25).
156 'Committens delictum, dum est sane mentis. Si postea in furorem incidat parcitur ei' (Baeza 1570, 9.summa 6, fol. 74v).
157 'Si furor superueniat debitori postquam est addictus creditori eximitur a manibus creditoris sicuti ratione senectutis' (Baeza 1570, 9.summa 8, fol. 74v).
158 'en su entero juicio, libre de aquel furioso accidente' (DQ I.27).
159 'Venereus affectus vehementissimus est' (Baeza 1570, 9.13, fol. 77v).
160 'Scribit Aristoteles Politi. lib.2 cap.19. Pithacum Mithilenenssem unum e septem Graeciae sapientibus legem edidisse vt ebrius damnum dan grauius puniatur quam si sobrius illud dedisset quoniam in sua potestate fuit non inebriari' (Baeza 1570, 9.13, fol. 77v).
161 'Ex his apparet insanum omnino esse dubitare' (Baeza 1570, 9.13, fol. 77v).
162 'a costa de sus acostumbrados fiadores ... sus espaldas' (DQ I.17).
163 'dum brevissimum tempus statuit quo serviendo satisfaciat debito. Tenetur enim quiuis Christianus misericordiam exhibere fratri suo, & eleemosynam elargiri' (Baeza 1570, 9.11, fol. 77r).

164 'yo fui loco, y ya soy cuerdo'; 'Yo tengo juicio ya, libre y claro, sin las sombras caliginosas de la ignorancia' (DQ II.74).

165 'Quare cum hic deficiat res quam lex affectam voluit: deficit eius mens & ex consequenti deficit eius dispositio' (Baeza 1570, 9.1, fol. 75r).

166 'si cobrare el seso después que lo perdió & la demandare' (Partidas I.4.71).

167 'Yo soy enemigo de Amadís de Gaula y de toda la infinita caterva de su linaje; ya me son odiosas todas las historias profanas del andante caballería ... las abomino' (DQ II.74).

168 'haber puesto las manos en cosa sagrada' (DQ I.19).

169 'después de recibidos todos los sacramentos y después de haber abominado con muchas y eficaces razones de los libros de caballerías' (DQ II.74).

170 'aquel que fuese loco de tal locura, que non sabe lo que se face' (Partidas I.1.21); 'todo cuanto yo he hecho, hago e hiciere, va muy puesto en razón' (DQ I.25). Most of Spain's *fueros* did not prosecute in the case of a 'loco,' much as the ventero tells the harrieros: 'The innkeeper yelled that they should let him go, as he had already told them he was mad and as a madman he would be let go, even if he were to kill them all' (El ventero daba voces que le dejasen, porque ya les había dicho como era loco, y que por loco se libraría, aunque los matase a todos) (DQ I.3). Just how crazy Don Quijote is is a running commentary in the text, and has been frequently commented upon: see, for example, Johnson 1983, and Gaos on the voluntary nature of Alonso Quijano's madness and its ramifications (Cervantes 1987, vol. 3, Appendix 'La locura de don Quijote,' 162–88).

5. Laws Broken, Glossed, and Made: Sancho Panza et al.

1 For a review of critical takes on Sancho, see the Centro Virtual Cervantes website, and also Eduardo Urbina, who offers a list of studies of Sancho (1982, 93, 94).

2 'sé que la Santa Hermandad tiene que ver con los que pelean en el campo' (DQ I.10).

3 'y además C azotes públicamente y, para eterna infamia, sea decalvado deformemente' (Fuero Juzgo VI.4.5).

4 Cejador y Frauca notes that the form 'omecillo' is used in the *Fuero Juzgo* for 'homicidio' but, like modern editors of Cervantes' masterpiece, thinks that Sancho has misunderstood: 'No sé de odios ni los he visto en mi vida: así parece entenderlo Sancho' (1906, 793).

5 'Omezillo es cosa que fazen los omes a las vegadas con tuerto, a las vegadas con derecho'; 'Homicidium en latín tanto quiere decir en romance como matamiento de ome. E deste nome fue tomado omezillo según lenguaje de España' (Partidas VII.8.1).

6 'Valdés: Demás me stava; si me detuviesse en cada cosilla déstas, nunca acabaríamos. También vamos dexando *omezillo* por *enemistad;* yo todavía me atrevería

a usarlo alguna vez, pero quando quadrasse muy bien, y no de otra manera. / Marcio: ¿Tenéislo por arávigo o por latino? / Valdés: Pienso sea corrompido; de *homicidio, omezillo*' (Valdés 1999, fol. 70).

7 'Yo no sé nada de omecillos ... ni en mi vida caté a ninguno' (DQ I.10).

8 'Advierta vuestra merced, señor Don Quijote, que si el caballero cumplió lo que se le dejó ordenado de irse a presentar ante mi señora Dulcinea del Toboso, ya habrá cumplido con lo que debía, y no merece otra pena si no comete nuevo delito' (DQ I.10).

9 'Decíale, entre otras cosas ... que se dispusiese a ir con él de buena gana porque tal vez le podía suceder aventura que ganase, en quítame allá esas pajas, alguna ínsula, y le dejase a él por gobernador della' (DQ I.7). The translation of 'ínsula' as island, as it would be from the Latin, is made difficult by Cervantes' use of it in the novel. Sancho does not seem to go off to an island but, rather, a region that he reaches by foot. In further references, it will be left as *ínsula.*

10 'Iba Sancho Panza sobre su jumento como un patriarca ... con mucho deseo de verse ya gobernador de la ínsula que su amo le había prometido'; 'Mire vuestra merced, señor caballero andante, que no se le olvide lo que de la ínsula me tiene prometido, que yo sabré gobernar, por grande que sea' (DQ I.7).

11 'Diéronle a entender que se llamaba «la ínsula Barataria», o ya porque el lugar se llamaba «Baratario» o ya por el barato con que se le había dado el gobierno' (DQ II.45).

12 'Y el ir en Romance este libro, tiene en sí particular gracia y utilidad, para que los que no saben Latín, no sean privados de estas materias, y cosas tan comunes, que les conviene saber; sin que por esto parezca que se apoca, ni profana esta ciencia, pues que entre todas las lenguas vulgares, esta [la castellana] es la más abundante, viril, y sonora, y más común a diversas naciones del mundo. Mayormente, que las leyes Reales, por donde se ha de juzgar y abogar, y sustanciar los pleitos y causas, primero que por las del derecho común, están, como vemos, en nuestra lengua vulgar de romance, como es justo: y assí lo parece ser también, que la prá[c]tica que en ellas mismas principalmente va fundada, vaya en la misma lengua Castellana' (Villadiego 1612, Prologue, no page numbers).

13 'No puede recibir cosa alguna el juez, por hazer, o dexar de hazer justicia, porque es barateria, y tiene la misma pena, aunque por la tal sentencia no se aya hecho agravio, ni perjuizio a nadie, porque hazer vendible lo que es gracioso, es corruptela, y barateria' (Villadiego 1612, fol. 117r). Riveros Subizar notes that in Cervantes' day: 'Arbitrariness corrupted justice and bribes were commonplace' (La arbitrariedad corrompía la justicia y el soborno era corriente) (1951, 157).

14 'De la obligación, que tienen los padres de enseñar a sus hijos, la sciencia a que más se inclinan'; 'que desde pequeños les encamina por el estrecho camino de la virtud' (1992 [1612], 6, 8).

15 'desde pequeños por los pasos de la virtud … sería yo de parecer que le dejen seguir aquella ciencia a que más le vieren inclinado' (DQ II.16).
16 'sino es en caso que no llevasse salario público' (Villadiego 1612, fols 117r–18v).
17 'Que los oficiales de contadores, ni los tesoreros, y recaudadores no baraten. Ordenamos, que no sean osados nuestros recaudadores, ni tesoreros, ni oficiales de los nuestros contadores, ni otras personas algunas de qualquier estado, o condición, proeminencia, o dignidad que sean, de baratar, ni comprar tierras, ni mercedes, raciones, ni quitaciones, ni juro de eredad, ni dádivas, ni otros qualesquier maravedís que qualesquier personas han, o ovieren de aver de Nos en qualquier manera, ni hazer otro pacto, ni conveniencia, o contrato alguno en tal caso: porque las personas que de Nos lo han, o ovieren de aver, no pierdan cosa alguna de lo que de Nos han, o ovieren de aver' (Recop. IX.16.17).
18 'Otrosí, que haga executar las sentencias que dieren contra los Corregidores y sus oficiales, conforme a lo en esta ley contenido: y las otras depositar los condenados. Otrosí, que haga executar las sentencias que diere contra el Assistente, o Governador, o Corregidor, y sus oficiales, que restituyan y paguen qualquier quantía, seyendo la condenación de tres mil maravedís, o dende ayuso, aunque la condenación no sea de cohecho, ni baraterías, aunque el condenado apele' (Recop. III.7.17).
19 'que no lo baraten, ni se dexen cohechar por persona alguna antes de la paga, salvo que esperen a aver la paga' (Recop. VI.5.5).
20 'Baratadores & engañadores ay algunos omes de manera que quieren fazer muestra a los omes que han algo, & tocan saccos, & bolsas, o arcas cerradas, & llenas de arena, o de piedras, o de otra cosa ssemejante, & ponen de ssuso para fazer muestra dineros de oro, o de plata, o de otra moneda, & encomiendan los, o danlos en guarda en la ssacristania de alguna eglesia, o en casa de algund ome bueno faziéndoles entender que es thesoro aquello que les dan en condesijo, & con este engaño toman dineros prestados, & ssacan otras malas baratas' (Partidas VII.16.9).
21 'Engaño o fraude en compras, ventas, trueques' (*Autoridades*).
22 'cualidades de juicio expeditivo y recto'; 'llana, sencilla y certera administración de justicia' (Alcalá-Zamora y Torres 2001, 106).
23 'fui a gobernar vuestra ínsula Barataria, en la cual entré desnudo, y desnudo me hallo, ni pierdo ni gano' (DQ II.55).
24 In subsequent references and in bibliography, Quaderno 1610.
25 Book III, Title 16 of the Recopilación has eight laws, and the monarch adds this ninth: 'Ley ix. *De nueva orden en el examen de los Médicos, y Cirujanos, y boticarios, demás de lo que hasta aquí está proveydo.* Por la premática que últimamente mandamos hazer, y se publicó el año passado de ochenta y ocho, acerca de la orden que el Protomédico, y Examinadores han de tener en el examen de los Médicos, Cirujanos, y Boticarios y visitas de boticas, y administración [fol. 50v ends] de

justicia en lo a ellos tocante no está bastantemente proveydo, y ay nueva necesidad de remedio en algunas cosas ... hasta que yo otra cosa mande proveer, no aya un solo protomédico, sino que aya más personas que hagan este oficio, para que mejor, y con más cuydado se haga lo que conviene en el ministerio del ... en lugar del Protomédico que hasta ahora ha habido, aya tres protomédicos, que por nos serán nombrados' (Quaderno 1610, Recop. III.16.9).

26 'Remedios para el bien de la salud del cuerpo de la República.' Pérez de Herrera was a *protomédico,* and also what was called, in the Spain of his day, an *arbitrista.* They offered (usually) unsolicited advice to the monarchs, recommending political solutions for everything from overconsumption of food to moderation in dress codes, care for the poor, etc. The *arbitristas* were reformers who proposed various remedies for society's ills. Evaristo Correa Calderón has published a catalogue of their writings, and José María Sánchez Molledo offers a *Diccionario de arbitristas aragoneses.*

27 'Otrosí dezimos que como es notorio los excessos y desordenes que passan en las comidas y banquetes y gastos ordinarios y extraordinarios ... resulta dello mucho deservicio de Dios porque de allí nascen los vicios, y otros peccados de la república' (Quaderno 1563, fol. 35). This is a different collection of notes from the Cortes, referred to here and subsequently as Quaderno 1563.

28 'que en ninguna mesa de qualquier calidad, que fuesse no pudiesse aver más de dos frutas de principio, y dos de fin, y quatro platos cada uno de su manjar y que de allí no se excediesse' (Quaderno 1563, fol. 35).

29 'que mandaremos platicar sobre esto para que se ponga el mejor orden y remedio que convenga' (Quaderno 1563, fol. 35).

30 'se ponga orden en la mucha desorden que ay en los platos y comidas, que son causa de tantas enfermedades y necesidad ... [de] almas y cuerpos, y grandes necesidades y menoscabos de hazienda, como lo murmuran Plutarco, Plinio y Séneca diziendo: Coacervatio saporum pestifera, & condimenta perniciosiora [marginal note identifies the source as Plutarc. conv.li.4], Que la diversidad de manjares en el estómago, es muy dañosa, y peor la variedad de los condimentos con que se guisan. Pues bastaría por premática (que todos obedecerán de muy buena gana) quatro o seis platos a lo más, con otros tanto principios y postres, como la ay en Portugal' (Pérez de Herrera 1610, fol. 15).

31 'Que la diversidad de manjares en el estómago, es muy dañosa, y peor la variedad de los condimentos con que se guisan'; 'a quitarle lo que imagino que le ha de hacer daño y ser nocivo al estómago'; 'demasiadamente caliente y tener muchas especies'; 'aquella ternera, si no fuera asada y en adobo' (DQ II.47).

32 'en la lista de los muchos advertimientos impertinentes que se suelen dar a los príncipes' (DQ II.1). Pérez de Herrera acknowledges complaints have been made about his writings: 'que no queriendo ser de provecho a la república, por tratar sólo de su negocio, y no tener talento para ello, no llevan bien, que otros tengan esta

inclinación' (fol. 3r), and repeats in his epilogue: 'no merecen estos mis pensamientos nombre de arbitrios (que el vulgo llama)' (1598, fol. 30r).

33 'No hagas muchas pragmáticas; y si las hicieres, procura que sea buenas y, sobre todo, que se guarden y cumplan; que las pragmáticas que no se guardan lo mismo es que si no lo fuesen; antes dan a entender que el príncipe que tuvo discreción y autoridad para hacerlas no tuvo valor para hacer que se guardasen' (DQ II.51).

34 'y aunque pensaba hacer algunas ordenanzas provechosas, no hice ninguna, temeroso que no se habían de guardar, que es lo mesmo hacerlas que no hacerlas' (DQ II.55).

35 'regulaban el ordinario vivir de las gentes. No sólo las acciones y obligaciones de las personas, sino también el uso de las cosas'; 'los escritores satíricos las tomasen a chacota'; 'fácil es relacionar la pragmática de los romeros con el viaje de Ricote, que en un capítulo del *Quijote* se descubre al que fue su convecino, Sancho' (Gil Ayuso 1935, 9).

36 'porque bien vi, y vieron todos nuestros ancianos, que aquellos pregones no eran sólo amenazas, como algunos decían, sino verdaderas leyes, que se habían de poner en ejecución a su determinado tiempo' (DQ II.54).

37 'aquella tarde la pasó Sancho en hacer algunas ordenanzas' (DQ II.51); 'ordenamos ... que el vino de Aragón, y de Navarra, y de Portugal, y de otros qualesquier Reynos, que no trayan, ni vendan a los nuestros Reynos' (Ordenanzas VI.9.37); 'Defendemos que ninguno sea osado de meter vino en las Ciudades de Segovia, Zamora, Salamanca: Córdova, ni Cuenca, ni en los otros lugares que tienen privilegios de nos y de los Reyes donde venimos' (Ordenanzas VI.9.45).

38 *Las constituciones del gran gobernador Sancho Panza;* 'ordenó cosas tan buenas, que hasta hoy se guardan en aquel lugar' (DQ II.51).

39 'no para que los persiguiese, sino para que los examinase si lo eran: porque a la sombra de la manquedad fingida y de la llaga falsa andan los brazos ladrones y la salud borracha' (DQ II.51). For those who feigned poverty so as to seek alms in the era, see Redondo 1979 and Martz 1983.

40 The Hispanic Society of America copy of the treatise consists of two folios unbound with any other work; those folios bear hand-written numbers 21 and 22, which are unidentified. The full text reads:

'Lo que parece que es conveniente proveer, para el amparo de los pobres mendigantes, y reformación de los que no lo son, es lo siguiente. Que se haga visita general de todos los que piden limosna mendigando, y si pareciere que lo hazen con necessidad, o causa bastante, se le dé licencia por escrito, poniendo en ella nombre propio, y apelativo, naturaleza, edad, y señas corporales, y si es soltero, o casado, y qué hijos tiene, con las edades, y señas dellos, y que esta licencia sea limitada por un año, que comience desde Pascua de Resurrección, hasta el siguiente.

A los que no vinieren a este examen, o que en el parezca que no tiene causa legítima de mendigar, se mandará que no lo hagan, so pena que passados veynte, o treynta días, serán condenados por la primera vez, a que sirvan en las fábricas de los mismos albergues, y en otros servicios dentro dellos, y por la segunda vez serán castigados en la pena de vagamundos.

Que a los que se diere la dicha licencia, para que puedan usar della, ayan de traer un Rosario hecho en una cadenilla de hierro fuerte, donde corran las cuentas, y al cabo della trayran [traigan] una insignia con la Imagen de Nuestra Señora de una parte, y de la otra las armas de la Ciudad, o villa donde el pobre hubiere sido examinado: y esta seña del Rosario parece ser más conveniente, por ser honrosa, y devota, y de ninguna nota.

Que para estos pobres aya una Casa y Albergue de patio y sitio espacioso con piezas largas, y portales alrededor, y en ellas lámparas encendidas toda la noche, y camas, que solamente tengan xergones con paja, o heno, y una manta grossera, pues han de servir para que los que ahora duermen por las calles y portales, se recojan allí.

Que los que tuvieren otra Casa o Albergue conocido, donde los recojan, no será necessario que vayan al Albergue general, sino los Domingos, y fiestas de guardar, para que los unos, y los otros, estos días oyan allí Missa, y los Domingos la doctrina Christiana, y esto hecho, saldrán a pedir limosna como en los otros días de la semana, hasta la noche, o puesto el Sol, que se han de recoger.

En esta casa habrá un Rector sacerdote de confianza, que los dichos días les diga Missa, y enseñe la doctrina Christiana, con tres, o quatro hombres de servicio, que serán bien menester para tener cuenta con las luzes que se les han de dar, y con las dichas camas, y agua, y de invierno fuego.

Con intervención del dicho Rector han de hazer las justicias ordinarias el examen de los que han de quedar por pobres verdaderos, y ambos firmar las dichas licencias, que como está dicho han de valer por un año, y éste acabado, las han de revalidar los mesmos, constándoles que el pobre que la tiene, se ha confessado y comulgado en el tiempo que manda la Iglesia, y no de otra manera.

Que el dicho juez ordinario haga que el escrivano del Cabildo tenga libro donde se pongan los exámenes, y el Rector lista de los nombres: y ninguno destos pobres se pueda ausentar sin licencia de la justicia, y Rector, la qual se les dará por escrito con qualquiera justa causa, borrando de los libros al que se le diere.

Aunque sean ciegos, coxos, o mancos, o tullidos, han de traer el Rosario, y efigie de Nuestra Señora, como dicho es.

Los del mal de San Lázaro, y Santo Antón, y de otros que inficionan, se han de curar en sus casas, y no se ha de consentir que salgan fuera a mendigar.

Esta orden no ha de comprehender a los peregrinos, yendo o viniendo recta vía, y ha se de guardar con ellos lo proveydo por leyes, y premáticas. Tampoco ha de comprehender a los estudiantes pobres que suelen acudir a pedir limosna, como tengan licencia para pedir, la qual se les ha de dar por tiempo limitado.

Con los pobres vergonzantes, que por serlo, no mendigan por las casas, y con esta orden estarán más precisamente necessitados, se tenga particular cuenta con que sean socorridos, tomando este cargo el Cura de sus perrochias, ayudándose para ello de algunos de los Regidores, que serán nombrados cada año, y de personas virtuosas de las mesmas perrochias.

Entiéndese que, en este Albergue, han de estar apartados hombres de mugeres, aunque sean casados, y podrán el padre, o la madre tener y acostar consigo a sus hijos, que se presupone han de ser niños, y que en siendo algo crecidos, se los han de quitar, y que sirvan, o se ocupen en algún ministerio. En Madrid a diez y seys de Enero, de mil y quinientos y noventa y siete años.' ('Lo que es conveniente,' Hispanic Society ms. HC 398–1642).

41 'Bando muy raro e interesante' ('Lo que es conveniente,' Hispanic Society ms. HC 398–1642).

42 'que no la alcancen sino con llamarla "señoría"' (Cervantes 1998b, II.5).

43 According to Rico, the 1637 Madrid edition reads 'señora' instead of señoría, as does that of Schevill y Bonilla (Cervantes 1998b, II.5, notes).

44 'Tusón, Maesses de Campo, Generales o Gobernadores de ejércitos, y a los Vizcondes, y a las Ciudades cabezas de Reyno, y a las otras, y villas que tienen voto en Cortes, y a los Cabildos y Iglesias metropolitanas, donde hubiere costumbre de llamársela' (Recop.VI.12.1).

45 'de hasta edad de catorce a quince años'; 'no pasaban de diez y siete' (Cervantes 1995 1:191).

46 González Echevarría notes the literal possibility for the name, 'one foot' (2005, 199).

47 'qualquier de los nuestros reynos los puedan tomar por su autoridad, y servirse dellos un mes sin soldada, salvo que les den de comer y de beber' (Recop. VIII.11.1).

48 'los ladrones, rufianes, vagamundos, y Egypcianos' (Recop. VIII.11, title epigraph); 'ligas, monipodios, y cofradías' (Recop. VIII.14, title epigraph).

49 'so color de bien' (Recop. VIII.14.1); 'advocación y apellido de algún Santo o Santa' (Recop. VIII.14.3); 'estatutos honestos para mostrar en público' (Recop. VIII.14.3); 'buena intención' (Recop. VIII.14.1).

50 'Infantes, Duques, Condes, Maestres, Priores, Marqueses, Ricos-hombres, Caballeros y Escuderos'; 'y personas singulares de cualquier estado o condición que sean' (Recop. VIII.14.1).

51 'ayuntamiento ni ligas con juramento … en que se obliguen de guardarse los unos a los otros contra otros cualesquier'; 'los perlados … arzobispos y obispos, y otras personas eclesiásticas' (Recop. VIII.14.1). On a related lexical point, it is interesting to note that in the Siete Partidas, 'liga' is used in the sense of marriages forbidden between certain relatives (Partidas IV.2.16).

52 'los obispos y abades, u otras cualesquiera personas eclesiásticas no sean osados de aquí adelante de escandalizar las ciudades, y villas y lugares de los nuestros reinos,

ni se muestren de bando ni parcialidad, ni hagan ligas ni monipodios, ni para lo tal den consejo, favor ni ayuda' (Novísima Recopilación XII.12.3). This 1473 law is not found in the 1640 edition of the Recopilación, but surfaces again in the 1775 Novísima Recopilación.

53 'Aristocratia, que es la gobernación de los sabios, y poderosos en libertad, como hoy día es la República de Venecia: y esta manera de gobierno (por la mala inclinación de los hombres) vemos, que con facilidad se buelve en monipodio, ambición, y pretensión, que los Griegos llamaron Oligarchia' (Castillo de Bobadilla 1775 [1597], 1.1.13, 1:9).

54 'pienso que habemos de ser, déste hasta el último día de nuestra vida, verdaderos amigos'; 'y pues nuestra amistad ... ha de ser perpetua, comencémosla con santas y loables ceremonias' (Cervantes 1995, 1:194, 198).

55 '[el] alguacil de los vagabundos ... es amigo' (Cervantes 1995, 1:217).

56 'Nunca los amigos han de dar enojo a los amigos ni hacer burla de los amigos, y más cuando se enojan los amigos' (Cervantes 1995, 1:230).

57 'No hay aquí amigo ... que quiera enojar ni hacer burla de otro amigo; y pues todos somos amigos, dense las manos los amigos'; 'Todos voacedes han hablado como buenos amigos, y como tales amigos se den las manos de amigos' (Cervantes 1995, 1:230).

58 'no se meta en puntillos con sus servidores y amigos' (Cervantes 1995, 1:234).

59 'pero por esto no entendemos defender las buenas amistades, porque todos sean amigos, y vivan en paz' (Recop. VIII.14.2).

60 'las nuestras Justicias'; 'los presos que se llevan a las cárceles' (Novísima Recopilación XII.12.6). Some of these laws are found in the 1640 edition of the Recopilación, and others are not, which is emblematic of the era's juridical confusion. Those cited here from the Novísima Recopilación are those not contained in the earlier edition.

61 'defraudar nuestras Rentas ... haciendo liga y monipolio de no vender ni contratar aquellas cosas que son de su trato' (Recop. IX.8.5). The 1640 edition separates the economically oriented laws on leagues and monopolies into a specific section on royal income (Book IX, Title 8).

62 Sabor de Cortazar and Lerner note that there are other pragmatics of Phillip II and Phillip III that specifically prohibit groups of Catalán bandits such as Cervantes' character Roque Guinart's group (DQ II.60, notes 5 and 10).

63 'solamente para causas pías y espirituales' (Recop. XII.12.12).

64 'padre, maestro y amparo'; 'tan santa y buena ... rezamos nuestro rosario ... muchos no hurtamos el día del viernes, ni tenemos conversación con mujer que se llame María el día del sábado' (Cervantes 1995, 1:208).

65 'candelicas a Nuestra Señora de las Aguas y al Santo Crucifijo de Santo Agustín' (Cervantes 1995, 1:219).

66 'traer en los cuellos, ni en puños, guarnición alguna' (*Premática en que se manda guardar*).

67 'de los que llaman valones' (Cervantes 1995, 1:192).

68 In his edition of the exemplary novel, Rodríguez Marín (1920) notes further illegal details, such as the prohibited arms carried by some characters.

69 'En la villa de Madrid ... delante de Palacio y casa Real de su Magestad, y en la puerta de Guadalajara de la dicha villa, donde es el trato y comercio de los mercaderes y oficiales ... Por pregoneros públicos con trompetas y atabales, se publicó y pregonó, a altas e inteligibles boces' (*Premática en que se manda guardar*).

70 'Porque somos informados, que muchas leyes y premáticas que hemos hecho para el buen govierno destos Reynos, no se han guardado; ni guardan: lo qual ha procedido assí del poco cuydado que de su execución, y de las penas por ellas impuestas, han tenido las nuestras justicias, como de averse usado de diversos medios e invenciones para defraudar lo por ellas proveydo: Mandamos que de aquí adelante las dichas leyes y premáticas se guarden y cumplan inviolablemente; so las penas en ellas contenidas' (Recop. VIII.26.21).

71 'Mandamos, que ninguna muger de qualquier estado, calidad, y condición que sea en todos estos nuestros Reynos, pueda yr, andar, ni ande tapado el rostro en manera alguna, sino llevándole descubierto' (Recop. V.3.11).

72 *Velos antiguos y modernos en los rostros de las mujeres, sus conveniencias y daños. Ilustración de la Real Premática de las Tapadas.*

73 'si esto fuere por sólo liviandad, será pecado venial. Si por algún fin o circunstancia, que de suyo sea culpa mortal, lo será la mudanza del traje así en el hombre como en la mujer. Y si fuere por necesidad, no habrá culpa alguna: según doctrina de S. Tomás' (León Pinelo 1641, II.304).

74 Sabor de Cortazar and Lerner note that the transport of a corpse is common in the books of chivalry, and that the episode might also contain an allusion to the transfer of San Juan de la Cruz's corpse from Úbeda to Segovia in 1593 (DQ I.19, n. 1).

75 Ordenanzas Reales, Tit. III, law 15: 'que los clérigos religiosos, o sacristanes, que anduvieren de noche sin hábitos de clérigos, sean presos' (orig. year 1401), included in the Recopilación at I.3.9.

76 The prohibition is found in the constitutions of the Synod of Carvajal, Catedral de Plasencia, as cited by Pérez-Coca Sánchez-Matas 1994, constitution 33.

77 'En quanto toca a los entierros, obsequias, y cabos de año, mandamos que por ninguna persona de qualquier calidad, condición, o preeminencia, aunque sea persona de título, o de dignidad, no se pueda llevar en su entierro, ni poner en su sepultura al tiempo de las obsequias, o cabo de año, más de doze hachas o cirios' (Recop. V.5.1).

78 'pero esto no se entienda en quanto a las candelas, o velas que le dan a los clérigos, o frayles, y niños de doctrina que van a los dichos entierros, ni en la cera que llevan las Cofradías que acompañan los cuerpos de los difuntos, ni en la cera que se da, y manda dar por los difuntos, o testamentarios, y herederos para el servicio de la

Iglesia, y altares, y lumbre: que en aquesto todo, ni en el vestir de los pobres, ni en otras limosnas, no entendemos hazer novedad' (Recop. V.5.1).

79 'Iten, que ninguna persona fuera de los grandes, se pueda alumbrar con más de dos hachas, y que los grandes puedan traer quatro, y no más, so pena de cien ducados por cada vez que lo contrario hizieren' (Ordenanzas fols 86v–7r).

80 'los que fiziessen encantamiento, o otras cosas con entención buena, assí como sacar demonios de los cuerpos de los omnes; o para desligar a los que fuessen marido, e muger, que non pudiessen convenir; o para desatar nube, que echasse granizo, o niebla, porque non corompiesse los frutos; o para matar langosta, o pulgón, que daña el pan, o las viñas; o por alguna otra razón provechosa semejante destas, non deve haber pena; ante dezimos, que deve recebir gualardón por ello' (Partidas VII.23.3).

81 'el oficio de alcahuete … es oficio de discretos y necesarísimo en la república bien ordenada' (DQ I.22).

82 'ricos corales … anillos de oro, y muy de oro … cada una debe de valer un ojo de la cara' (DQ II.21); 'todas ascua de oro, todas mazorcas de perlas, todas son diamantes, todas rubíes, todas telas de brocado de más de diez altos' (DQ II.10); 'sillón de plata' (DQ II.30); 'telas riquísimas de oro y de brocado' (DQ II.31); 'mil velos de tela de plata, brillando por todos ellos infinitas hojas de argentería de oro' (DQ II.35); 'medias de seda encarnada, con ligas de tafetán blanco y rapacejos de oro y aljófar; los gregüescos eran verdes, de tela de oro, y una saltaembarca o ropilla de lo mesmo … un jubón de tela finísima de oro y blanco' (DQ II.49).

83 'Defendemos, y mandamos, que agora, ni de aquí adelante ninguna persona de nuestros Reynos, y señoríos, ni fuera de ellos, de qualquier condición, calidad, preeminencia, o dignidad que sean, excepto nuestras personas Reales, y nuestros hijos, sean osados de traer, ni vestir brocado, ni tela de oro, ni plata tirada, ni de hilo de oro, ni plata, ni seda alguna que lleve oro, ni plata, ni cordón, ni pespunte, ni passamano, ni otra cosa alguna de ello, ni bordado, ni recamado, ni escarchado de oro, o plata, fino, o falso, o de perlas, o aljófar, o piedras, ni guarnición alguna de abalorio, de seda, ni cosa hecha en vastidor' (Recop. VII.12.1).

84 'más perlas pendían de su hermosísimo cuello, orejas y cabellos que cabellos tenía en la cabeza … dos carcajes … de purísimo oro, con tantos diamantes engastados, que ella me dijo después que su padre los estimaba en diez mil doblas, y las que traía en las muñecas valían otro tanto' (DQ I.41).

85 'Ley lxxix. Que los veyntiquatrenos, y dende arriba puedan ser tintos en paño para verde escuros, y azules, y ferretes, llevando de azul los verde escuros dos celestres … y el que quisiere hazer los dichos paños verde escuros en más perfección tintos en lana, que lo pueda hazer: con tanto que después en paños, si fueren verde escuros se lo cumplan a dos celestres del dicho azul: y sino los quisieren tanto escuros, que los puedan dar el azul, conforme a la color del verde que quisieren,

con tanto que sean primero sellados del azul ... enjabonándolos con alumbre, y rasuras, y dándoles un verdor con gualda: y que puedan echar en el enverdir cendra, o ceniza, si quisieren: y que no puedan enverdir con otro verdor alguno, ni ningún paño se pueda hazer verde, sin que primero lleve el azul que le convenga, so pena que el tintorero que de otra manera lo hiziere, pierda el dicho paño, y lo pague al dueño cuyo fuere' (Recop. VII.13.79).

86 'capuz, o capellar verde sobre sus ropas, y vestidos; o a lo menos luneta' (Ordenanzas 8.3.27).

87 Cátedra (2007) speaks to other social messages in the use of the colour green by knights.

88 José Luis Bermejo Cabrero notes that the early sixteenth-century *Ordenanzas de Carmona* did prohibit such diluting of wine with water (1980, 145–7), although Sancho's death penalty does seem to go a bit further.

89 'La segunda manera de adevinanza, es la de los agoreros, e de los sorteros, e de los fechizeros, que catan agueros de aves, o de estornudos, o de palabras (a que llaman Proverbio) o echan suertes, o catan en agua, o en cristal, o en espejo, o en espada, o en otra cosa luciente; o fazen fechuras de metal, o de otra cosa cualquier; o adevinanza en cabeza de ome muerto, o de bestia, e todos los más de niño, o de muger virgen. E estos truhanes, e todos los otros semejantes dellos, porque son omnes dañosos e engañadores, e nascen de sus fechos muy grandes males a la tierra, defendemos que ninguno de ellos non more en nuestro Señorío, nin use ý destas cosas' (Partidas VII.23.1).

90 're-escritura antagonista'; 'continuar y cambiar la Primera parte y, por ello, el género'; 'reflexión sobre el texto mismo [que] se aleja del género y se concentra, especularmente, sobre la Primera parte' (Lerner 1990, 821).

91 'que los mercaderes y hombres de negocios estén presos hasta que los pleitos se acaben' (Pérez Pastor 1970, 176, no. 343).

92 'significa la absolutización del principio inquisitivo, y la eliminación de todas o de casi todas las defensas del procesado'; 'verdadero absolutismo judicial' (Tomás y Valiente 1975, 230, 231).

93 Moncada complains to Phillip III of abuses committed by unruly *cuantiosos* who, according to reports, steal wine from workers, beef and oil from widows and orphans, etc.: 'El Servicio de Millones es muy dañoso a España. La experiencia, y la común voz, dice los Lugares que ha perdido, y despoblado este Servicio, y lastimosos daños que causa: quebrará las piadosas, y Reales entrañas de V. Mag. ver quitar de la boca al pobre jornalero el trago de vino, y a la pobre viuda, y huérfanos la corta ración de vaca, y aceite, que desea para trasnochar, y ganar un pan, y a los executores de ellos echar de las pobres pajas a los miserables, y todo sin tener en que ganar para pagarlos, como solían cuando los pagaban, porque ganaban para todo. Y no mande v. Mag. que le refiera el mal nombre que a este Servicio se ha

puesto, pues le llaman Sifa, ni los inconvenientes que algunos hallan en mudar las medidas legales, ni otros muchos: y porque sería gran bien escusar estos daños, y lástimas, si se pudiesse sin daño de las rentas Reales. Digo, que España puede socorrer de nuevo a v. Mag. sin el Servicio de Millones' (1746 [1619], Discurso II).

94 Speaking of the relationship between the 1605 and 1615 *Quixotes,* Lerner suggests that one of the strongest appeals of Cervantes' novel for a modern writer is the component of admiration incorporated into its self-parody: 'Me atrevo a sugerir que uno de los más intensos atractivos del *Quijote* para el escritor moderno es precisamente esta componente de admiración que incluye la parodia cervantina' (2005, 364). This is also Cervantes' approach to the law.

95 Kagan does note specific differences in the lawyer's need to meet a 'burden of proof' and convince a judge, pointing out that 'the verdict of history is far more uncertain, much harder to shape than the result in a court of law' (2009, 7).

6. History and Historiography in the *Quixote*

1 'La conjunción de ambas tendencias, clásica y medieval, constituye en el Renacimiento un género histórico nuevo, floreciente y genial' (Montero Díaz 1948, 14).

2 'dispero en diversos escritos'; 'el primero en articular un pensamiento sistemático ... sobre los problemas fundamentales de la Historia'; 'unidad profunda ... [en] la permanente identidad del hombre a través de las edades y los pueblos' (Montero Díaz 1948, 22, 17).

3 Kagan (2009) offers details on the various types of histories, partisans of each, and chronological developments in the field.

4 'dar a conocer los hechos narrados sin buscar, por lo general, las relaciones causa-efecto' (Orcástegui and Sarasa 1991, 17). Orcástegui and Sarasa do point to medieval uses of history as example-setter, and note that there were exceptions to the no cause-effect trend, using the eleventh-century's Guillermo de Poitiers who, in a work on Guillermo of Normandy, 'was not content with simple narration of events, but tried to also justify them, thinking that history should demonstrate, instruct and advise, as would any other discipline' (no se había contentado simplemente con narrar los hechos, sino que intentó justificarlos pensando que la Historia debía demostrar, instruir y advertir como cualquier otra disciplina) (1991, 17).

5 'se libera'; 'la filosofía, pues ambas buscan lo verdadero, no lo dudoso o mentiroso como la oratoria, ni lo fabuloso y fingido como la poesía' (Cortijo Ocaña 2000, 16).

6 'non è più un «metodo» per leggere o per scrivere la storia, bensì ... un vero e proprio discorso filosofico sulla storia' (Cotroneo 1971, 15–16).

7 'explicar la génesis de los sucesos'; 'buscar la causalidad y motivaciones de los hechos' (Montero Díaz 1948, 23).

8 'Escribir historia, decía un poeta, es caminar sobre las brasas escondidas debaxo de una blanca ceniza, que nos engaña' (Páez de Castro 1892, 28).
9 The *libros plúmbeos* of Sacromonte, 'discovered' in a cave in Granada in 1588, purported to be lost documents that supported Morisco land claims. For Cervantes' use of the 'found document' trope, see Johnson 2007.
10 Howard Mancing prefers 'to read this passage as another reference to the public narrator Cervantes and his playful, metafictional search for sources' (2003, 130). I agree with that proposal, but not with the subsequent conclusion that Cervantes is 'careless, or, at least, inconsistent' in referring to himself as 'father, stepfather, author, second author, and so forth' (2003, 132). Multiple voices are a key part of historical volumes of the era, in the debates between those who favoured archival sources versus those who preferred to interview multiple eyewitnesses. Mancing's conclusion that we should read all the narrators in *Don Quixote* as merely the voice of Cervantes himself, by appreciating 'the ease with which he transforms himself from a historical person into a narrator of fiction' (2003, 135), seems to deny the very narrative achievement of Cervantes that Mancing purports to praise.
11 See Gaylord (1998) on the multiplicity of narrators and (non)reliability of a narrator in regards to the episode of the Cueva de Montesinos in DQ II.23.
12 See Díaz-Más 1996, especially on historical, frontier, and novel-like romances. José Rodríguez Molina notes that Sevillian historian Argote de Molina uses 'literary sources as historical sources,' and points out that this does not surprise us given that, at the time Argote de Molina was writing in the second half of the sixteenth century, Spanish historiography had already taken material from the *cantares de gesta* (1985, 363).
13 A connection between Antonio de Herrera y Tordesillas and the apocryphal Second Part of the *Quixote* supposedly written by Avellaneda, who identifies himself as from Tordesillas, remains to be determined. In his prologue to the 1615 *Quixote,* Cervantes criticizes the author of the apocryphal Second Part as having used a false name and misidentified his origin, 'as if he might have committed some traitorous act of *lese magestad*' ('como si hubiera hecho alguna traición de lesa megestad') (DQ II, Prologue), and the last paragraph of the work includes a warning that Don Quixote belongs only to the pen of Cide Hamete, despite any 'false and Tordesillas-like writer' who might think otherwise (DQ II.74). Herrera y Tordesillas had a number of legal problems that led to his being arrested, humiliated, and exiled from the court in 1609 (Kagan 2009, 185). Kagan has a monograph in process on the royal chronicler and his legal troubles. See also Mayer 1994, 98–9.
14 'La vivacidad, el realismo e inaudita inventiva de los historiadores de Indias, dotados de prodigiosa flexibilidad para hacer frente a situaciones inéditas y a inesperados problemas'; 'superan constantemente los moldes ijados por los retóricos' (Montero Díaz 1948, 16).

15 'Quita el fastidio la breuedad y variedad y yr el libro en prosa y verso' (Baeza 1568, 'Dedicatoria'). In order to 'complete' Giovio's 'interrupted' histories, Baeza takes details from the semi-apocryphal *Elogios*. See below.
16 'a juyzio de los hombres graues, el más excelente y prudente libro que de hystoria en nuestro tiempo se [h]a escripto' (Baeza, 1568, 'Dedicatoria,' *Elogios*).
17 'es excelencia de la historia que qualquiera cosa que en ella se escriba puede pasar, al sabor de la verdad que trae consigo' (Cervantes 2003, III, 10, 527).
18 Riley points out that 'the nature of truth and fiction indeed became in the seventeenth century the primary object of philosophical inquiry' (1962, 222). The seeds of that inquiry are earlier in the texts cited here, and Cervantes' commentaries should also be seen in the light of those earlier works.
19 'Radica en el hombre un appetitus immortalitatis que está impuesto por la Naturaleza misma (*qui est omnibus a natura insitus*), y en el que hallan su raíz el sentimiento y la actividad históricos' (Montero Díaz 1948, 29–30).
20 Flores (1975) studies differences in the printed versus manuscript versions of the work and notes that, in the latter, Cide is not active in I.9 but only mentioned as 'Cide Mahamate Benengeli,' to then enter fully only later, in I.16. According to Flores, after writing I.27, Cervantes divided the work into parts, wrote four new passages with Cide references and interpolated them. My analysis here is based on the printed text.
21 'Cide Hamete, *historiador* árabe'; 'desta *historia*'; 'tan sabrosa *historia*'; 'tan gallarda *historia*'; 'su *historia* debía de ser moderna'; 'desta agradable *historia*'; 'esta *historia* referida' (DQ I.9). For earlier studies of the figure of Cide Hamete, see Godoy Alcántara (1868), Stagg (1956), Riley (1962), Haley (1965), El Saffar (1968), Márquez Villanueva (1973), Hahn (1992), López Navia (1996), and Weiger (1996).
22 'la *historia* cuenta'; 'la *historia*'; 'verdadera relación de la *historia*'; 'los *historiadores* puntuales, verdaderos y no nada apasionados'; 'la verdad, cuya madre es la *historia*' (DQ I.9).
23 Part I, chapter 1 (3 uses), chapter 2 (2 uses), chapter 3 (2 uses), etc. The chapters in which the word is used frequently include: Prologue (10 uses), chapter 13 (6 uses), chapter 20 (8 uses), and chapters 24 and 27 (7 uses each).
24 'muy docto en las disciplinas y Philosophia, según la doctrina de Auerrois' (Giovio 1568, fol. 203r); 'filósofo mahomético' (DQ II.53).
25 Klinger points out that Giovio planned for woodcuts in the second work, the *Elogia virorum bellica* … and suggests that for this volume 'Giovio took into account the intended presence of illustrations when he composed the eulogies … with the incorporation of descriptions of the subject's physical appearance and references made to the painting itself. Such passages occur infrequently in' the first volume (*Elogia veris clarorum virorum imaginibus apposita quae in Musaeo comi*

spectantur, published in Venice in 1546) and 'when they do, they are not very explicit' (1991, 208).

26 'Esta larga ropa de lienço, trae el Xarife, y cúbrese la cabeça con un lienço senzillo, cuya vltima parte (saliendo por la oreja derecha) le baxa por los ombros y le llega a los talones. Deste hábito vsaban antiguamente los sacerdotes Aegypcios, y dellos creo, que se tomó la alua de que nuestros sacerdotes vsan, quando dizen missa. Tiene Muley Hamet, por sobrenombre Xarife, porque deciende del linage del falso propheta Mahoma, y Cyrif (que así se a de pronunciar) quiere dezir en Aráuigo varón sancto, dado a contemplación de los mysterios' (Giovio 1568, fol. 217r).

27 'La manera conque este hombre (con gran milagro de nuestro tiempo) siendo vn maestro de estudio, vino a ser señor de tantos poderosos reynos, contaré lo mas breue que pudiere, paraque se entienda que los pronósticos delos Astrólogos, no son siempre vanos' (Giovio 1568, fol. 217r).

28 'leones coronados, de condición generosa, que no hazen mal a hombres' (Giovio 1568, fol. 217v).

29 'pardos ... también muy recios, y crueles, y no hacen mal a los hombres, si no es cuando les hacen mal a ellos' (Mármol Carvajal 1573, I.18, fol. 26v).

30 'que le diese de palos y le irritase' (DQ II.17).

31 'en tiempo de los Romanos, es *verissímil* que fue del rey Bogudis' (Giovio 1568, fol. 217v, emphasis added).

32 'Quieren decir que tenía el sobrenombre de Quijada, o Quesada, que en esto hay alguna diferencia en los autores que deste caso escriben; aunque por conjeturas verosímiles se deja entender que se llamaba Quejana' (DQ I.1).

33 'no me consta que nadie haya aducido obras del género con vacilaciones análogas' (Rico 2005, 449–50).

34 'como si hubiese cosa más sabida en la guerra que los sacos'; 'Como si fuera algún gran mal, en un saco de un pueblo, tomado por fuerza de las armas (en este propósito de la guerra habla), tomar todo el provecho que se les biniese a las manos. Pues por eso se llama saco' (1952, 220).

35 'así como Don Quijote quiere reformar heroicamente el mundo ... así quiere Quesada restituir la verdad originaria de la historia' (Frankl in Jiménez de Quesada 1952, 679).

36 'dátiles y otras cosas'; 'era tenido por hombre muy prudente, y auisado ... principalmente, era gran Astrólogo' (Giovio 1568, fol. 217r).

37 'siendo doctos en letras Aráuigas, abrieron estudio, y enseñauan moços'; 'ganauan largo, y tenían fama en la comarca' (Giovio 1568, fol. 217r).

38 'para ver mundo, y conocer costumbres, de naciones estrangeras, fuessen en romería a Arabia, a adorar el sepulcro de Mahoma, en Meca, y en Talnabi' (Giovio 1568, fol. 217r–v).

39 'ciertos señores árabes'; 'ejercitar las armas'; 'con los vagabundos Alárabes, que en África (sin tener morada cierta) andan de vna parte a otra, dende el Nilo, hasta el mar de Canaria, y hazen que los reyes les paguen tributo, y a los que no quieren su venal amistad, házenles guerra, como a este tiempo passaua, en que con grandes fuerças, hazían guerra a Bucentufo rey de Marruecos' (Giovio 1568, fol. 217v).

40 'cudicia insaciable, puso los ojos en el reyno de Fez y vsando de sus engaños, y dichosas armas, venció al rey Muley Hamet y echólo del reyno' (Giovio 1568, fol. 218r).

41 'aunque lo tenía vencido, y poco antes era su enemigo' (Giovio 1568, fol. 218r).

42 'todos los parientes de Mahoma ... son conocidos, por una toca verde, que traen en la cabeza, y son de todos llamados Xarifes' (Haedo 1612, 33). A recent edition and study of this work published under the name of Diego de Haedo proposes that it was actually written by Antonio de Sosa, who had also been held captive in Algiers. After his escape and return, Sosa was charged with 'being an ordained Augustinian friar, who had fled from his Order by taking the habit of a lay priest' and living with a woman he passed off as his sister. Phillip II was unforgiving, and María Antonia Garcés suggests that the work was published under Haedo's name as it would have been prohibited under that of Sosa (Garcés 2011, 67–8, 73–8).

43 'herido, y ciego del ojo derecho'; 'pedir socorro al Emperador' (Giovio 1568, fol. 218v).

44 'con tiempo no passe a España, a conquistar el Reyno de Granada'; 'si el Xarife quisiesse passar a España, a hazer guerra por estender su ley, se juntaría con él multitud infinita de Moros, y Alárabes'; 'en fin él es ya viejo de ochenta años, y aunque está rezio, y fresco, y vsa mucho leche de camellos, su hado lo consumirá, o Dios no permitirá que passe a España, y si passare salir le an al encuentro los Españoles (soldados verdaderos) vsados a vencer valerosamente en toda la redondez de la tierra, los quales lo matarán, o lo prenderán' (Giovio 1568, fol. 218v).

45 Thompson's sources for this information are the Archivo General de Simancas and the 8 July 2003 Consulta of the Council of War.

46 'Villanueva de los Infantes y las demás [villas] de su partido, Sigura de la Sierra y las demás del suyo, & la villa de Torrenueva' (Thompson, personal communication).

47 'su hado lo consumirá' (Giovio 1568, fol. 218v).

48 'aunque en este libro se dize hado y fortuna son palabras que se usan, sin que el que las dize dexe de entender que no ay fortuna ni hado, sino que todo se govierna por la infinita providencia y voluntad de Dios nuestro señor' (Baeza 1568, Al lector).

49 'El cielo aún hasta ahora no ha querido que yo ame por destino' (DQ I.14); 'quiero que sepáis que mi destino o, por mejor decir, mi elección, me trujo a enamorar de la sin par Casildea de Vandalia' (DQ II.14).

50 'la causa sospechosa d'estar algunos libros del Jobio tan abrebiados' (Jiménez de Quesada 1952, 80); one of the 'otras naciones que aborrecen y están mal con el ynperio de los españoles es la nación ytaliana' (Jiménez de Quesada 1952, 27).

51 'autor arábigo, siendo muy propio de los de aquella nación ser mentirosos; aunque, por ser tan nuestros enemigos, antes se puede entender haber quedado falto en ella que demasiado' (DQ I.9).

52 Close explains: 'Around 1600, *moriscos* were despised ... So, in a kind of merry variant of the traditional paradox, Cervantes claims his story to be a scrupulously true history written by a member of a race of liars' (2000, 151).

53 'Y agora se dará de los yerros del Jobio acerca de lo que quenta del mismo Harradín'; 'perseguido de vn Cara Haçén, su capitán (y no Hamete como nuestro autor lo llama), ni alárave tanpoco, porque no lo hera' (Jiménez de Quesada 1952, 332).

54 'el qual Mahomedín, saliendo después buen moço, y estando en edad para ello, se bino a bibir a Meteleno y hizo su asiento en la çiudad de Bonaba, y allí se casó con vna biuda christiana, avnqu'él hera turco, que avía sido muger de un saçerdote griego llamado Alejandro, y avn tenía hijos d'este saçerdote, que el Jobio haçe padre y yo padrastro' (Jiménez de Quesada 1952, 316).

55 Like Giovio, Haedo gets his information from former captives and soldiers although, as stated above, for the *Elogios,* Giovio does not limit himself to such sources.

56 'señor más principal que todos los señores Alárabes' (Giovio 1566, 23.1). Mármol Carvajal, like Giovio in receiving his information from captives and like Cervantes in having been one, agrees with Giovio's details: in his volume, Xeque Ben el Cadi was 'rey del Cuco ... hombre noble ... a quien Horux Barbarroja mató' (King of Cuco ... a noble man ... killed by Horux Red Beard) (1573, 1.5). The New York Public Library copy is a 3-volume set of the work; the first two volumes contain the six books of the 1573 *Primera parte* and the third volume, published in 1599, has five of the six books promised in the First as a *Segunda parte.*

57 'nunca vistas hazañas' (DQ I.9); 'otras algunas menudencias había que advertir, pero todas son de poca importancia y no hacen al caso a la verdadera relación de la historia' (DQ I.9); 'le tiene por apócrifo ... pero que no quiso dejar de traducirlo por cumplir con lo que a su oficio debía' (DQ II.15).

58 'la madre de las artes'; 'la primera ley de la historia'; 'que unas cosas son apropósito para gente docta, y otras para la vulgar' (Mariana 1617 [1601], Prologue, no page numbers).

59 'breve plática o narración con alabanza'; 'tiene dificultad en hacerse bien'; 'solamente a los capitanes generales y personas gravísimas' (Cabrera de Córdoba 1948 [1611], 108).

60 The friend who painted the portrait was supposedly Juan de Jáuregui, although Sieber refers the reader to studies by Rodríguez Marín and Lafuente Ferrari that call into doubt the real existence of such a portrait (Cervantes 1995, 1:50, n. 9). Díaz de Benjumea believes that the prologue is a defence against criticism by Cervantes' rivals, who might have prevented him from benefitting from the conde de Lemos (1878, 284–7).

61 'solamente professa Paulo Iouio escriuir de aquellos caualleros cuyos retratos tenía al biuo pintados en su Museo. De tal manera que ningún gran rey, ni famoso caualllero de ninguna nación se puede quexar de no estar aquí, si su retrato no estaua enel Museo ... Y assi aunque demás de tantos príncipes y caualleros Españoles como aquí ay, merecían generosíssimo y exagerado Elogio los antiguos reyes de Castilla, por su admirable valor y virtud, y infinitas victorias (ganadas con belicosa mano y ánimo sin pauor, contra infinita multitud de Bárbaros) no están aquí los reyes del tiempo antiguo, porque no creo que ay enel mundo quien tenga sus retratos' (Baeza 1568, Al lector).

62 'Éste que véis aquí, de rostro aguileño, de cabello castaño, frente lisa y desembarazada'; 'porque pensar que dicen puntualmente la verdad los tales elogios, es disparate, por no tener punto preciso ni determinado las alabanzas ni los vituperios' (Cervantes 1995, 1:51).

63 'Ésta que veis de rostro amondongado, / alta de pechos y ademán brioso' (DQ I, p. 451, vv.1–2); 'Sancho Panza es aquéste, en cuerpo chico / pero grande en valor, ¡milagro estraño!' (DQ I, p. 453, vv. 1–2).

64 'por ser muy gordo, era muy pacífico' (DQ I.2); 'Era ... aunque se llamaba Sansón, no muy grande de cuerpo'; 'carirredondo, de nariz chata y de boca grande'; 'señales todas de ser de condición maliciosa y amigo de donaires y de burlas, como lo mostró en viendo' (DQ II.3).

65 'La historia, la poesía y la pintura simbolizan entre sí y se parecen tanto que, cuando escribes historia, pintas y, cuando pintas, compones' (Cervantes 2003, III, 12, 570).

66 In 1634 Alonso Gerónimo de Salas Barbadillo writes *El curioso y sabio Alejandro, fiscal y juez de vidas ajenas.* His protagonist Alejandro is a 'wealthy gentleman' (caballero rico), 'resident in the court' (residente en la corte de España), who wanted posterity to benefit from his observations, and so painted portraits and then wrote 'short sketches of the lives' (breve epítomes de las vidas) of the subjects. His first painting and sketch are of 'the lucky Panza' (Panza dichosa), obviously a satirical take on Cervantes' Sancho Panza, described as 'a barbarian who worshiped his gut' (un bárbaro idólatra de su vientre) (1847, 2:3). Salas Barbadillo's work is a baroque reworking of Giovio's *Elogios* that incorporates Cervantes' character Sancho as subject of a fictional web of portraits.

67 'Juntóse a mi buena suerte / Haber el Jovio entendido / En sublimar mi partido / Su pluma me hizo fuerte / Contra el río del olvido / Contra el poder de la muerte / Bien podemos conferir / Y aun podemos preferir / Los dos a los dos sin par / Yo a Cesar en el obrar / Jovio a Homero en escribir' (Giovio 1568, fol. 209v, vv. 73–83).

68 'Para mí sola nació don Quijote, y yo para él; él supo obrar, y yo escribir' (DQ II.74).

69 Both de Armas (2006) and Laguna (2009) argue convincingly for further associations between Cervantes' character Don Quixote and the real Charles V.

70 'contra todos los fueros de la muerte' (DQ II.74).

71 In recommending to law students that they read constantly, 'porque con la continua lición se halla la preciosa Margarita de la sabiduría,' Bermúdez de Pedraza allows that, when tired of the legal volumes, they may read histories, divine or human, and the jurist notes that Ulpian made use of the orators Cicero and Demosthenes, of poets Virgil and Homer, of philosophers Plato and Aristotle, and of the medical works of Hippocrates. After history, Bermúdez de Pedraza recommends the verse of Virgil for its gravity, that of Ovid for its ease, Martial's for its charm, and the concepts of Seneca and Lucan. For Italians, he recommends Ari[o]sto and Tasso, for Spaniards Garcilaso, Ercilla, Silvestre, Diego [Hurtado] de Mendoza, and Francisco de Aldana. He further advises only four more works in the vernacular: Celestina, Lazarillo de Tormes, the First Part of the Diana, and the 'floresta Española' (1992 [1612], 42–3).

72 'de la fuerza tan virtuosa deste animal, yo no affirmo más de lo que la pública fama persuade a los que lo creen. Porque ninguno de los antiguos (que yo aya leydo) haze mención desta admirable virtud del Unicornio, si no es Heliano griego' (Giovio 1566, 18.8).

73 'Como escribir Historia no sea cosa de invención ni de solo ingenio, sino también de trabajo y fatiga para juntar las cosas que se han de escribir, es necesario buscarlas ... Ir tomando relaciones de personas antiguas y diligentes, leer las memorias de piedras públicas y letreros de sepulturas, desenvolver registros antiguos de notarías donde se hallen pleitos de Estado, testamentos de reyes y grandes hombres y otras muchas cosas que hacen a la Historia; revolver librerías de colegios y monasterios y abadías; ver los archivos de muchas ciudades para saber sus privilegios y dotaciones y propios, y sus fueros y ordenanzas' (Páez de Castro 1892, 35).

74 'Tendrán otros por ocupación muy humilde, traduzir, para mí no ay nada que no sea demasiado. Traduxo Cicerón un libro de Platón. Traduxo muchas cosas S. Hierónymo, y en aquel tiempo la lengua Griega era más vulgar en Roma, que oy lo es la Castellana en Valencia. Traduxeron Erasmo, Ángelo Policiano, Theodoro Gaza, y otros muchos varones de summa erudición y nombre eterno' (Baeza 1566, 'Dedicatoria,' *Histories*).

75 'su historia debía de ser moderna'; 'caballeros antiguos y modernos'; 'sin quitarles ni añadirles nada' (DQ I.9).

76 'otras algunas menudencias había que advertir, pero todas son de poca importancia y [que] no hacen al caso a la verdadera relación de la historia' (DQ I.9).

77 'arrojó los libros como presa inútil'; 'que no era nada necio'; 'siendo hecho pedazos' (Baeza 1566, Summa, Book V).

78 In Baeza's introduction to the second edition of the translated *Histories,* published in 1566, four years after the first edition, we read: 'no ay una sola palabra, que no sea a la letra sacado [*sic*] de Paulo Jovio' (Baeza 1566, Introduction, *Histories*).

79 'a juicio de los hombres graves, [it is] el más excelente y prudente libro que de historia en nuestro tiempo se ha escrito' (Baeza 1568, 'Dedicatoria').
80 'En la villa de La Mancha a nueve días del mes de noviembre de mill y quinientos y noventa y nueve años'; 'dijo que no la sabe'; 'dijo que sabe y es verdad' ('En la villa de La Mancha ... ' 1598, Real Chancillería de Granada, sign. 2576.009).
81 'En un lugar de la Mancha, de cuyo nombre no quiero acordarme' (DQ I.1). I use the legal case to exemplify the language appropriation by Cervantes, not to conflate a specific place called La Mancha with the region identified in Cervantes' novel. See also González Echevarría (1990, 59), who relates Cervantes' use of the phrase to formulaic legal usage.
82 'cuentos disparatados'; 'tierras del Preste Juan de las Indias' (DQ I.47).
83 From Sabor de Cortazar and Lerner: '*Trapisonda o Trebisonda:* capital y nombre de una de las partes del imperio bizantino, situada en la costa sur del Mar Negro; es la antigua Trapezus, fundada por los griegos hacia el siglo VIII a. C. Conoció el esplendor bajo el emperador Adriano y fue saqueada por los godos. De su mención abundante en las novelas de caballerías y el *Quijote* procede la acepción vulgar de *trapisonda: bulla, riña con voces, embrollo* y sus derivados (*trapisondista,* etc.)' (DQ I, Prologue, n. 10).
84 From Rico's edition: 'Personajes legendarios con presencia frecuente en la literatura caballeresca' (Cervantes 1998b, I, Prologue, n. 49). Rico notes that fictional character Reinaldos de Montalbán was crowned with the empire of Trapisonda (Cervantes 1998b, I.1, n. 44). Avalle-Arce tells the reader: 'El Emperador de Trapisonda es otro personaje fabuloso, mencionadísimo en los libros de caballerías. Trapisonda, Constantinopla, Tesalónica y Nicea fueron las cuatro partes en que se dividió el imperio griego hasta su caída'; 'El Preste Juan de las Indias es un personaje fabuloso de inmensa popularidad en la Edad Media y cuyo origen la crítica ha identificado con la personalidad del emperador de Etiopía' (Cervantes 1979, I, Prologue, notes 8 and 9).
85 'libró su coraçón de vano miedo' (Giovio 1566, 13.5).
86 'el qual después se llamó Cusselbas (que quiere dezir Cabeça roja)' (Giovio 1566, 13.5).
87 'Pero el Turco Mahometo confiando en tiros que llevava de artillería (que eran nuevos y por esso terribles a los Persianos) rompió al rey Usuncasano en los campos de las Anseres cabo Tabenda (llamada oy Tocata) y con ellos destruyó después fácilmente a Caloyanes rey de Trapisonda, y reduziendo en forma de provincia su imperio de Trapisonda, y de todo el mar mayor, hasta la isla de los Mengrelos, truxo lo a Constantinopla, y mató lo en la prisión' (Giovio 1566, 13.5).
88 'Pues en verdad que en sólo manifestar mis pensamientos, mis sospiros, mis lágrimas, mis buenos deseos y mis acometimientos pudiera hacer un volumen mayor' (DQ II.3).

89 'Pues [h]avemos llegado aquí paréceme que será conveniente contar en pocas palabras lo que he sabido del reyno de Túnez, y de las costumbres de los Moros. Porque como escribo historia, he sabido con la victoria del Emperador muchas cosas que mucho tiempo han sido sólo sabidas de mercaderes' (Giovio 1566, 33.6); 'Fueron grandes y memorables las hazañas que los Españoles y Gonzalo Hernández hizieron en la guerra de Granada quando don Fernando rey cathólico ganó aquel poderoso reyno, las quales no será molesto a los lectores que contemos brevemente para bolver luego al curso de la historia' (Giovio 1566, 5.2).

90 'gozamos ahora en esta nuestra edad, necesitada de alegres entretenimientos, no sólo de la dulzura de su verdadera historia, sino de los cuentos y episodios della, que en parte no son menos agradables y artificiosos y verdaderos que la misma historia' (DQ I.28).

91 'no tiene que ver con la historia de su m. del señor don Quijote' (DQ II.3).

92 'hasta los confines de los reynos de David potentísimo rey de Ethiopía, a quien los nuestros llaman el Preste Juan' (Giovio 1566, 18.5).

93 'Pues [h]emos venido a hazer mención del Preste Juan, no me parece que será molesto a los lectores que (después de tantas sangrientas batallas y successos tristes de casi todas las cosas) haga aquí una digressión de materia más agradable para que descansen los cansados de leer. Será esta digressión grata, porque conterná la descripción de Ethiopía, para que las cosas que a muchos parece fábula sean tenidas por verdaderas y se escriban en verdadera historia' (Giovio 1566, 18.6).

94 'es excelencia de la historia que cualquiera cosa que en ella se escriba puede pasar, al sabor de la verdad que trae consigo' (Cervantes 2003, III, 10, 527).

95 'osadía grande'; 'rebate las ondas de otro mar'; 'parece otro differente Océano' (Giovio 1566, 18.6); 'debaxo del Polo Antártico a veynte y dos grados' (Giovio 1566, 18.7).

96 'Pero porque quiero dezir brevemente algunas cosas de la nobleza del Preste Juan, y de su grandeza, y de las costumbres de su corte, y de sus exércitos, y de su aparato de guerra, y hazañas, y del nacimiento del Nilo y lagunas de la Luna, y de varios géneros de fieras, paréceme que será bien dezir de quién lo supe, porque los ignorantes no tengan por fábula lo que por testimonio de muchos es tenido por cierto y notorio. Pero yo quiero que todo el crédito desto se dé a los que (haziéndoles yo largas y curiosas preguntas) me las contaron. Entre los quales fueron Pedro Álvarez Portugués, el qual fue con don Rodrigo de Lima por embaxador al Preste Juan' (Giovio 1566, 18.7).

97 'dexó escritos unos comentarios, en que por días cuenta todo su camino y sucessos' (Giovio 1566, 18.7).

98 'Después de Pedro Álvarez, Pedro Abissino hombre de gentil y prudente ingenio, que ha estado largo tiempo en la corte del Preste Juan me contó con gran humanidad y verdad las cosas notables de los Abissinos' (Giovio 1566, 18.7).

99 'impressos en Roma con letras Chaldeas'; 'algunos curiosos' (Giovio 1566, 18.7).

100 'Este gran rey de Ethiopía, y de los Abissinos, a quien los nuestros corrupto el vocablo llaman Preste Juan, es llamado de los suyos Belulgian, sobre nombre antiguo de los Reyes sus passados, que quiere dezir perla de precio immenso y de excelencia incomparable. El que oy reyna se llama David, y por sobrenombre Atanadidinghel, que quiere dezir encienso de la virgen' (Giovio 1566, 18.7).

101 'la incorrupta nobleza de su real sangre se prueva con testimonio de historias. Porque entre ellos la memoria de los successos y la decendencia y succesión del linage real se pone por ley, fielmente por escrito' (Giovio 1566, 18.7). In his dedication of his own translation of Giovio's *Histories* to Charles V, translator Villafranca extols the importance of histories honouring heroes to all civilizations, and says that 'among the kings of Ethiopia, commonly although erroneously called Preste Juan, there is a law that obliges all to read, for one hour each day, the histories and deeds of their ancestors' (Villafranca 1562, image 2), and mentions that even the Indians of the New World do so in their Areitos '(assí nombran ellos sus fiestas) (as they call their parties).' I cite from the online edition of the Biblioteca de la Universidad de Valencia, with its numbered page images.

102 'nacen las piedras de los Obeliscos' (Giovio 1566 18.9); 'Queriendo publicar esta obra, supe que el Preste Juan David era muerto. Reynó después de salir de la tutela de su madre veyente [*sic*] y siete años, vivió quarenta y ocho. Fue hombre muy virtuoso, y de ingenio hábil para todo negocio de paz y guerra, y muy docto en letras, tanto que sabía Astrología. Tenía cuerpo mediano. La cara redonda de color de un membrillo tostado debaxo la ceniza. Los ojos vivos. Unos cabellos no motosos, como los Negros (según se puede ver de su retrato que yo tengo al vivo)' (Giovio 1566, 18.9).

103 'con las palabras ordinarias y cerimonia militar conviene a saber hiriéndole ligeramente el ombro siniestro con una espada desnuda' (Giovio 1566, 15.12).

104 'para con la novedad de tan terrible espectáculo entretener los ojos de su señor cuando passase por allí y representarle la victoria que avían ganado' (Giovio 1566, 17.8); 'llenos de pies y de piernas humanas' (DQ II.60).

105 'que tuvo sus ciertos puntos de borracho' (DQ II.2).

106 Rodríguez Marín (1947–9) links the mention to the historical person Tomunbeyo, captain of Alexandria who died in 1517, according to the history of Díaz Tanco.

107 'Porque mató traydoramente veynte y dos hermanos, o (lo que es más duro que la muerte) los cegó, quemándoles los ojos' (Giovio 1566, 33.4).

108 'recuperar los sentidos que debería haber tenido el *Quijote* para sus primeros lectores' (Lerner 1996, 64).

109 Aurelio González (2009) has said the same of Cervantes as a dramatist.

7. Cervantes' mos hispanicus: Considerations and Conclusions

1 I am grateful to my colleague Paulo Moreira for this succint statement of fact.

2 I am grateful to my colleague Heather Klemann for bibliographical information on this text.

3 'buenas letras y doctrina'; 'buenas letras e disciplinas'; 'las buenas letras e la filosofía'; 'la doctrina y erudición de buenas letras, cuya ocupación y exercicio' (CORDE). These examples resulted from a search for the phrase 'buenas letras,' restricted to the years 1500–1600.

4 'Demás desto el arte y exercicio de los escritores de buena letra, y maestros de leer y escriuir, que por otro nombre se llaman Gramatistas, ludimagistros, antiquarios, amanuenses, exceptores, y literatos, logógrafos, cuya professión se dize también literatura, la excluye Vlpiano Iurisconsulto de las liberales. Pero con todo ora, porque es fundamento de la Gramática, ora porque imita a las liberales, es a saber en las letras, pudo la costumbre tanto que (según el mismo Vlpiano) se conocía delos salarios delos maestros de escuela extraordinariamente, de la misma manera que si fueran professores de artes liberales: y después con la sucessión del tiempo de vna edad en otra vino a tanta estimación, que por vna constitución Imperial se metió en el número de las liberales, en la qual se dizen estas palabras: que el arte de leer y escriuir bien es vna de las mayores virtudes que ay entre todos los estudios y artes liberales, &c. Ha venido el día de oy a subir tanto esta arte, que es ya más fácil y cierto el hazerse vn hombre noble por la pluma que por la lança' (Gutiérrez de los Ríos 1600, 92–3).

5 Of Sancho's decisions, Álvarez Vigaray notes that the character's first High Court hears three cases, two civil and one penal, and that in two of them Sancho reaches Solomon-like decisions while in the other he punishes the 'bad faith' of both parties (1987, 128–32). Alcalá-Zamora y Castillo notes of the old man with the cane in which he has hidden the coins so as to be able to hand it off and then swear he does not have the money, that Cervantes 'contraposes, perfectly differentiated, two methods of proofs' (1961, 97). According to Filippo Ermini, 'gli ordinamenti del buon governatore Sancho Panza mostrano una virtù innovatrice, che parrebbe audacia' (the ordinances of the fine governor Sancho Panza teach an innovative and almost audacious virtue) (1906, 9).

6 'la natura y astucia de los hombres de cada día inventa cosas nuevas y exquisitas malicias' (Pramáticas, fol. 36, law 42, dated Madrid 4 dic. 1502).

Bibliography

Adorno, Rolena. 2007. *The Polemics of Possession in Spanish American Narrative.* New Haven: Yale University Press.

Aguilera Barchet, Bruno, ed. 2006. *El Derecho en la época del Quijote.* International Seminar, organized by the Instituto de Estudios Jurídicos Internacionales Conde de Aranda, 15–17 March 2005. Navarra: Thomson, Aranzadi.

Alcalá-Zamora y Castillo, Niceto. 1961. *Estampas procesales de la literatura española.* Buenos Aires: Ediciones Jurídicas Europa-América.

Alcalá-Zamora y Torres, Niceto. 2001 [1947]. *El pensamiento de 'El Quijote' visto por un abogado.* Priego de Córdoba: Patronato Niceto Alcalá-Zamora y Torres.

Alonso, Amado. 1948. 'Prevaricaciones idiomáticas de Sancho.' *Nueva Revista de Filología Hispánica* 11.2:1–20.

Álvar Ezquerra, Alfredo. 2004. *Cervantes, genio y libertad.* Madrid: Temas de Hoy.

Álvarez Vigaray, Rafael. 1987. *El Derecho civil en las obras de Cervantes.* Intro. Rafael Gibert Sánchez de la Vega. Granada: Comares.

Anderson, Ellen M. 1994. 'His Pen's Christian Profession: Cide Hamete Writes the End of *Don Quixote.*' *Romance Languages Annual* 6:406–12.

Antonio, Nicolás. 1999 [1788]. *Bibliotheca hispana nueva.* 2 vols. Madrid: Fundación Universitaria Española. [Madrid: Joachimum de Ibarra].

Armstrong-Roche, Michael. 2009. *Cervantes' Epic Novel: Empire, Religion, and the Dream Life of Heroes in Persiles.* Toronto: University of Toronto Press.

Astrana Marín, Luis. 1948. *Vida ejemplar y heroica de Miguel de Cervantes Saavedra.* 7 vols. Madrid: Reus.

Aubrun, Charles. 1986. 'The Reason of Don Quijote's Unreason.' In *Critical Essays on Cervantes,* edited by Ruth El Saffar, 60–6. Boston: G.K. Hall & Co.

Avalle-Arce, Juan Bautista. 1976. *Don Quijote como forma de vida.* Fundación Juan March. Madrid: Castalia.

– 1988. 'La Galatea: The Novelistic Crucible.' In *A Celebration of Cervantes on the Fourth Centenary of La Galatea, 1585–1985*, edited by John J. Allen, Elias Rivers, and Harry Sieber, 7–15. Special issue of *Cervantes: Bulletin of the Cervantes Society of America.*

Backus, Irena. 2008. *Life Writing in Reformation Europe. Lives of Reformers by Friends, Disciples and Foes.* Aldershot, England: Ashgate.

Baeza, Gaspar de [Gasparem Baetivm]. 1566. 'Dedicatoria' and 'Summa del libro V.' In [*Historias*] *Paolo Giovio añadido con doze libros qve hasta agora faltavan de todas las cosas svccedidas enel mundo enestos cincuenta años de nuestro tiempo: en que se escriuen las victorias del inuictissimo Emperador Don Carlos, dende que començó a reynar en España, hasta que prendió al Duque de Saxonia. Escrita en lengua Latina por el doctíssimo Pavlo Iovio Obispo de Nochera, traduzido de Latin en Castellano por el Licenciado Gaspar de Baeça.* 2 vols. Vol. 1, Granada: Hugo de Mena. Vol. 2, Granada: Antonio de Librixa.

– 1568. 'Al lector' and 'Dedicatoria.' In [*Elogios*] *Elogios o vidas breues de los Caualleros antiguos y modernos, Illustres en valor de guerra, que están al biuo pintados en el Museo de Paulo Iouio. Es autor el mismo Pavlo Iovio. Y tradúxolo de Latin en Castellano, el Licenciado Gaspar de Baeça.* Granada: Hugo de Mena.

– 1570. *Tractatus de Inope debitore ex Castellana consuetudine creditoribus addicendo.* Granada: Hugo de Mena. http://www.juntadeandalucia.es/cultura/bibliotecavirtualandalucia.

– 1592. 'De non meliorandis ratione dotis filiabus.' In *Opera omnia Gasparis Beatiae: Baetiensis, et in Senatus Granatensi aduocati,* fols 1r–118v. Madrid: Ludovicum Sanctium.

– undated. Handwritten gloss on last folio of *Ordenamientos reales.* Real Biblioteca de El Escorial, ms.Z.I.10.

Báig Baños, Aurelio. 1916. *Al margen de una obra interesantísima: Rodríguez Marín, documentador Cervantino.* Madrid: Bailly-Bailliere.

Bañón Hernández, Antonio Miguel. 2001. 'Apuntes para el estudio del tratamiento apelativo en el Siglo de Oro español.' *Revista electrónica de estudios filológicos* 1 (March 2001). http://www.um.es/tonosdigital/znum1/principal/m2.htm.

Basave Fernández del Valle, Agustín. 1968 [1959]. *Filosofía del* Quijote (*Un estudio del antropología axiológica*). Mexico: Espasa-Calpe mexicana.

Batiza, Rodolfo. 1964. *Don Quijote y el Derecho.* Mexico: Porrúa.

Baudouin, Françoise. 1561. *De institutione historiae vniuersae, et eivs cvm ivrisprvdentia coniunctione.* Paris: Andream Wechelum.

Baztán, Carlos, and Beatriz Mariño, directors. 2001. *20 documentos sobre Cerbantes en el Archivo Histórico de Protocolos de Madrid.* Madrid: Comunidad de Madrid, Consejería de las Artes.

Bell, Aubrey F.G. 1947. *Cervantes.* Norman, OK: University of Oklahoma Press.

Benardete, Mercedes José. 1965. 'Los galeotes: el criminal y la sociedad.' *Revista hispánica moderna* 31.1–4:57–70.

Bermejo Cabrero, José Luis. 1980. *Derecho y pensamiento político en la literatura española.* Madrid: G. Feijoo.

Bermúdez de Pedraza, Francisco. 1612. *Arte legal para estudiar la jurisprudencia.* Salamanca: Emprenta de Antonia Ramírez. Facsimile, Navarra: Editorial Civitas, 1992.

Black's. 2004 [1891]. *Black's Law Dictionary.* 9th ed. Edited by Bryan A. Garner. St Paul, MN: West.

Blasco Pascual, Francisco Javier. 2006. *Cervantes, un hombre que escribe.* Valladolid: Difácil Editores.

Bloch, Howard. 1977. *Medieval French Literature and Law.* Berkeley: University of California Press.

Bouza, Fernando, and Francisco Rico. 2009. 'Digo que yo he compuesto un libro intitulado *El ingenioso hidalgo de la mancha.*' *Cervantes: Bulletin of the Cervantes Society of America* 29.1:13–30.

Braun, Harald E. 2007. *Juan de Mariana and Early Modern Spanish Political Thought.* Aldershot, England: Ashgate.

Brooks, Peter, and Paul Gewirtz, eds. 1996. *Law's Stories: Narrative and Rhetoric in the Law.* New Haven: Yale University Press.

Brundage, James. 2008. *The Medieval Origins of the Legal Profession: Canonists, Civilians, and Courts.* Chicago: University of Chicago Press.

Byrne, Susan. 2002. '¿Por qué una "niña de nuef años"? la edad de razón y la razón del poeta del CMC.' *La corónica* 31.1:5–17.

– 2007. 'Cervantes' *Don Quijote* as Legal Commentary.' *Cervantes: Bulletin of the Cervantes Society of America* 27.2:81–104.

– 2009. 'Cervantes and the *Histories* of Paolo Giovio: Translators and Truths.' *Cervantes: Bulletin of the Cervantes Society of America* 29.2:185–201.

– 2010. 'Miguel de Cervantes y Paolo Jovio: los caballeros antiguos y modernos y el de la Mancha.' In *Actas del XVI Congreso de la Asociación Internacional de Hispanistas: Nuevos caminos del hispanismo* [Paris, 9–13 July 2007], edited by Pierre Civil and Françoise Crémoux, 3:72–82. Literatura aúrea. Madrid: Iberoamericana.

– 2011. 'Aspectos histórico-jurídicos en las obras de Miguel de Cervantes.' In *Actas del VIII Congreso de la Asociación Internacional Siglo de Oro: Compostella Aurea* [Santiago de Compostella 7–11 July 2008], edited by Antonio Azaustre Galiana and Santiago Fernández Mosquera, 501–8. Santiago: Servizo de Publicacións.

Cabanellas, Guillermo. 1976. *Diccionario de Derecho usual.* 4 vols. 9th ed. Buenos Aires: Heliasta.

Cabrera de Córdoba, Luis. 1948 [1611]. *De historia para entenderla y escribirla.* Edited by Santiago Montero Díaz. Madrid: Instituto de Estudios Políticos.

– 1857. *Relaciones de las cosas sucedidas en la Corte de España, desde 1599 hasta 1614.* Madrid: J. Martín Alegría.

Cáceres y Espinosa, Pedro de. 1592. Introduction to *Gregorio Silvestre: Las obras del famoso poeta Gregorio Sylvestre.* Recopied and corrected by his heirs, and by Pedro de Cáceres y Espinosa. Lisbon: Manuel de Lyra.

Calderón de la Barca, Pedro. 2011. *La dama duende.* Ed. Jesús Pérez Magallón. Madrid: Cátedra.

Canavaggio, Jean. 1979–80. 'Burlas y veras en la aventura de los galeotes: nueva reflexión sobre un episodio del "Quijote".' *Anales cervantinos* 18:1–9.

– 1998. 'Resumen cronológico de la vida de Cervantes.' Miguel de Cervantes. *Don Quijote de la Mancha.* Edition directed by Francisco Rico. Barcelona: Crítica. http://cvc.cervantes.es/obref/quijote/introduccion/resumen/default.htm.

Caporossi, Olivier. 2004. 'La Babilonia del crimen o la nueva Roma de la policía cristiana.' In *La declinación de la monarquía hispánica en el siglo XVII: Fundación Española de Historia Moderna. Reunión científica 7, Ciudad Real, 2002.* Coordinated by Francisco José Aranda Pérez, 844–62. Cuenca: Ediciones de la Universidad de Castilla-La Mancha.

Cárdenas Bunsen, José A. 2010. *El derecho canónico en los escritos mayores de Bartolomé de las Casas.* Madrid: Vervuert-Iberoamericana.

Carrión, María M. 2010. *Subject Stages: Marriage, Theatre, and the Law in Early Modern Spain.* Toronto: University of Toronto Press.

Cassirer, Ernst, et al., eds. 1948. *The Renaissance Philosophy of Man.* Chicago: University of Chicago Press.

Castilla del Pino, Carlos. 2005. *Cordura y locura en Cervantes.* Barcelona: Ediciones Península.

Castillo de Bobadilla, Jerónimo. 1775 [1597]. *Política para corregidores, y señores de vasallos, en tiempo de paz, y de guerra, y para prelados en lo espiritual, y temporal entre legos, Jueces de Comisión, Regidores, Abogados, y otros Oficiales Públicos: y de las Jurisdicciones, Preeminencias, Residencias, y salarios de ellos: y de lo tocante a las Órdenes, y Caballeros de ellas.* Madrid: Imprenta Real de la Gazeta.

Castro, Américo. 1972 [1925]. *El pensamiento de Cervantes.* Barcelona: Noguer.

Castro Dassen, Horacio N. 1953. *El derecho en* Don Quijote. Buenos Aires: Araijú.

Catalán, Diego. 2000. *La épica española: nueva documentación y nueva evaluación.* Madrid: Fundación Ramón Menéndez Pidal.

Cátedra, Pedro. 1989. *La historiografía en verso en la época de los Reyes Católicos: Juan Barba y su* Consolatoria de Castilla. Salamanca: Ediciones Universidad de Salamanca.

– 2007. *El sueño caballeresco. De la caballería de papel al sueño real de don Quijote.* Madrid: Abada.

Cejador y Frauca, Julio. 1906. *La lengua de Cervantes: Gramática y diccionario de la lengua castellana en El ingenioso hidalgo Don Quijote de la Mancha*. Madrid: Jaime Ratés.

Cervantes Saavedra, Miguel de. 1910–13. *El ingenioso hidalgo Don Quijote de la Mancha*. 4 vols. Edited by Diego Clemencín. Paris: Sociedad de Ediciones Literarias y Artísticas.

– 1920. *Rinconete y Cortadillo, novela de Miguel de Cervantes Saavedra*. Edited by Francisco Rodríguez Marín. Madrid: Revista de Archivos, Bibliotecas y Museos.

– 1947–9. *El ingenioso hidalgo Don Quijote de la Mancha*. Edited by Francisco Rodríguez Marín. 10 vols. Madrid: Atlas.

– 1970. *Entremeses*. 4th ed. Edited by Augenio Asensio. Madrid: Castalia.

– 1979. *Don Quijote de la Mancha*. 2 vols. Edited by Juan Bautista Avalle-Arce. Madrid: Alhambra.

– 1981. *Poesías completas*. 2 vols. Edited by Vicente Gaos. Madrid: Castalia.

– 1984. *Viaje del Parnaso: Poesías completas, I*. Edited and intro. by Vicente Gaos. Madrid: Castalia.

– 1987. *El ingenioso hidalgo Don Quijote de la Mancha*. 3 vols. Edited by Vicente Gaos. Madrid: Gredos.

– 1995. *Novelas ejemplares*. 2 vols. Edited by Harry Sieber. Madrid: Cátedra.

– 1997. *El gallardo español*. Edited by Florencio Sevilla Arroyo and Antonio Rey Hazas. Madrid: Alianza Editorial. http://digital.library.wisc.edu/1711.dl/IbrAmerTxt.Spa0039.

– 1998a. *Don Quijote de la Mancha*. Edited by Florencio Sevilla Arroyo. Madrid: Castalia.

– 1998b. *Don Quijote de la Mancha*. Directed by Francisco Rico. Barcelona: Crítica.

– 1999. *La Galatea*. Edited by Francisco López Estrada and María Teresa López García-Berdoy. Madrid: Cátedra.

– 2003. *Los trabajos de Persiles y Sigismunda*. Edited by Carlos Romero Muñoz. Madrid: Cátedra.

– 2005 [1969]. [DQ] *El ingenioso hidalgo Don Quijote de la Mancha*. 2 vols. Edited by Celina Sabor de Cortazar and Isaías Lerner. Prologue by Marcos Morínigo. Buenos Aires: Eudeba.

– 2006 [1781]. *Historia del famoso cavallero, Don Quixote de la Mancha*. Edited by John Bowle. Preface by Eduardo Urbina. Intro. by Daniel Eisenberg. Newark, DE: Juan de la Cuesta.

Céspedes, Baltasar de. 1965. *De la historia: El maestro Baltasar de Céspedes, humanista salmantino y su Discurso de las letras humanas*. Edited by Gregorio de Andrés. San Lorenzo de El Escorial: Biblioteca 'La ciudad de Dios,' Real Monasterio de El Escorial.

Close, Anthony. 1994. 'Cervantes's Aesthetics of Comic Fiction and His Concept of "La Verdad de la Historia."' *The Modern Language Review* 89.1:88–106.

- 2000. *Cervantes and the Comic Mind of His Age.* Oxford: Oxford University Press.

Colahan, Clark, and Alfred Rodríguez. 1990. 'Parodic Alteration of the Picaresque in Cervantes' Ginés de Pasamonte / Ginesillo de Parapilla.' *Modern Language Review* 85.3:609–11.

CORDE. Real Academia Española. *Corpus Diacrónico del Español.* http://corpus.rae.es/cordenet.html.

Corominas, Joan. 1980. *Diccionario crítico etimológico castellano e hispánico.* Madrid: Gredos.

Coronas González, Santos Manuel. 2005. 'El derecho en la España de Cervantes.' In *El Quijote: 1605–2005, IV centenario.* Coordinated by Jesús Menéndez Peláez, 59–65. Oviedo: Fundación Municipal de Cultura, Educación y Universidad Popular del Ayuntamiento de Gijón.

Correa Calderón, Evaristo. 1981. *Registro de arbitristas, economistas y reformadores españoles, 1500–1936: catálogo de impresos y manuscritos.* Madrid: Fundación Universitaria Española.

Cortés, Narciso Alonso. 1916. *Casos cervantinos que tocan a Valladolid.* Madrid: Centro de Estudios Históricos.

Cortijo Orcaña, Antonio. 2000. *Teoría de la historia y teoría política en Sebastián Fox Morcillo: De Historiae Institutione Dialogus; Diálogo de la enseñanza de la historia.* Alcalá: Universidad de Alcalá.

Cotroneo, Girolamo. 1971. *I trattatisti dell' 'Ars Historica.'* Naples: Giannini.

Covarrubias Orozco, Sebastián de. 1994. *Tesoro de la lengua castellana o española.* Madrid: Castalia.

Crónica mozárabe de 754. 1991 (1980). Edited and translated by José Eduardo López Pereira. Zaragoza: Textos Medievales.

Crónica sarracina de 1430. 1958. *Floresta de leyendas heroicas españolas: Rodrigo, el último godo.* 3 vols. Edited by Ramón Menéndez Pidal. Madrid: Espasa-Calpe.

de Armas, Frederick. 1974. 'Classical Tragedy and Cervantes' *La Numancia.*' *Neophilologus* 58:34–40.

- 2006. *Quixotic Frescoes: Cervantes and Italian Renaissance Art.* Toronto: University of Toronto Press.

Díaz de Benjumea, Nicolás. 1878. *La verdad sobre el Quijote: Novísima historia crítica de la vida de Cervantes.* Madrid: Gaspar.

Díaz de Valdepeñas, Hernando. 1544. *Summa de notas copiosas muy sustanciales y compendiosas.* Toledo: Hernando Díaz y Juan de Medina.

Díaz-Más, Paloma, ed. 1996. *Romancero.* Directed by Francisco Rico. Preliminary Study. Samuel G. Armistead. Barcelona: Crítica.

*Diccionario de Autoridades.*1964. Real Academia Español. Madrid: Gredos.

Dios, Salustiano de. 2001. 'Tendencias doctrinales en la época de la jurisprudencia clásica salmantina.' *Salamanca, Revista de Estudios* 47:285–311.

Dols, Michael W. 1992. *Majnūn: The Madman in Medieval Islamic Society.* Edited by Diana E. Immisch. Oxford: Clarendon Press.

Egido, Aurora. 2004. 'Don Quijote, enfermo de amores.' In *Los rostros de Don Quijote: IV Centenario de la publicación de su primera parte,* 73–95. Coordinated by Aurora Egido. Zaragoza: IberCaja, Obra Social y Cultural.

Eisenberg, Daniel. 2002. *La biblioteca de Cervantes, una reconstrucción.* (Versión preliminar). http://bigfoot.com/ ~daniel.eisenberg.

– 2006 [1781]. Introducción to *Historia del famoso cavallero, Don Quixote de la Mancha.* Edited by John Bowle. Preface by Eduardo Urbina. Newark, DE: Juan de la Cuesta.

El Saffar, Ruth Snodgrass. 1968. 'The Function of the Fictional Narrator in Don Quijote.' *MLN* 83.2:164–77.

'En la villa de La Mancha ...' 1598. Pleito. Gutiérrez. Real Chancillería de Granada, signatura 2576. 009.

Ermini, Filippo. 1906. *Il Pensiero Etico e Giuridico nel Quijote del Cervantes.* Rome: Unione Tip. Cooperativa.

Escriche, Joaquín. 1852. *Diccionario razonado de legislación y jurisprudencia.* New ed. Paris: Librería de Rosa, Bouret y cia.

Etienvre, Jean-Pierre. 1987. 'Paciencia y barajar: Cervantes, los naipes y la burla.' In *Actas del coloquio cervantino, Würzburg 1983,* edited by Theodor Berchem and Hugo Laitenberger, 48–68. Münster Westfalen: Aschendorffsche Verlagsbuchhandlung.

Ettinghausen, Henry. 1996. 'De edad de oro a edad de hierro: cabreros, caballeros, cautivos y cortesanos en el Quijote.' *Edad de Oro* 15:25–39.

Fernández Álvarez, Manuel. 2005. *Cervantes visto por un historiador.* Madrid: Espasa.

Fernández de Navarrete, Martín. 2005 [1819]. *Vida de Miguel de Cervantes Saavedra.* Alicante: Biblioteca Virtual Miguel de Cervantes. Digital ed. [Madrid, Imprenta Real]. http://www.cervantesvirtual.com/servlet/SirveObras/72392516192387941060891/p0000009.htm.

Fernández Llera, Víctor. 1929. *Grámatica y vocabulario del Fuero Juzgo.* Madrid: Imprenta Clásica Española.

Fernández Mosquera, Santiago. 1986. 'Los autores ficticios del *Quijote.*' *Anales Cervantinos* 24:47–66.

Fernández-Morera, Darío. 1993. 'Chivalry, Symbolism, and Psychology in Cervantes.' *Hispanic Review* 61:531–46.

Finello, Dominick L. 1994. *Pastoral Themes and Forms in Cervantes' Fiction.* Lewisburg: Bucknell University Press.

– 2008. *Evolution of the Pastoral Novel in Early Modern Spain.* Tempe, AZ: Arizona Center for Medieval and Renaissance Studies.

Flores, R.M. 1975. *The Compositors of the First and Second Madrid Editions of Don Quixote, Part I.* London: The Modern Humanities Research Association.

– 1982. 'The Rôle of Cide Hamete in *Don Quixote.*' *Bulletin of Hispanic Studies* 59.1:3–14.

– 1997. '¿Qué hay en los apellidos Quijada, Quesada y Quijana? Fuentes históricas, teoría narratológica y bibliografía analítica en la crítica literaria.' *Bulletin Hispanique* 99.2:409–22.

Folena, Gianfranco. 1985. 'L'espressionismo epistolare di Paolo Giovio.' In *Atti dei Convegni Lincei 71: L'espressivismo linguistico nella letteratura italiana (Roma, 16–18 gennaio 1984),* edited by Vittore Branca, 121–59. Rome: Academia Nazionale dei Lincei.

Forcione, Alban K. 1970a. 'Cervantes and the Freedom of the Artist.' *Romanic Review* 61.4:243–55.

– 1970b. *Cervantes, Aristotle and the Persiles.* Princeton: Princeton University Press.

Forster, E.M. 1927. *Aspects of the Novel.* New York: Harcourt Brace and Co.

Frankl, Victor. 1963. *El «Antijovio» de Gonzalo Jiménez de Quesada, y las concepciones de realidad y verdad en la época de la Contrarreforma y del Manierismo.* Prologue by José Antonio Maravall. Madrid: Ediciones Cultura Hispánica.

Frenk, Margit. 2010. 'Don Quijote: ¿muere cuerdo?' Conference presentation. Asociación Internacional de Hispanistas. Rome, Italy (18–24 July 2010).

Friedman, Edward H. 1977. '*La Numancia* within Structural Patterns of Sixteenth-Century Spanish Tragedy.' *Neophilologus* 61:74–89.

– 1980. 'Cervantes' *Rinconete y Cortadillo* and the Imposition of Form: Part of the Story.' *Rocky Mountain Review of Language and Literature* 34.4:205–13.

– 1994. 'Executing the Will: The End of the Road in Don Quixote.' *Indiana Journal of Hispanic Literatures* 5:105–25.

– 2000. 'Insincere Flattery: Imitation and the Growth of the Novel.' *Cervantes: Bulletin of the Cervantes Society of America* 20.1:99–114.

– 2006. *Cervantes in the Middle: Realism and Reality in the Spanish Novel from Lazarillo de Tormes to Niebla.* Newark, DE: Juan de la Cuesta.

Fuero Juzgo. 1815. *Fuero Juzgo en latín y castellano, cotejado con los más antiguos y preciosos códices por la Real Academia Española. Discurso.* Don Manuel de Lardizabal y Uribe, del Consejo y Cámara de S.M. Edited by Don Manuel de Lardizabal, Don Antonio Tavira, Don Antonio Mateos Murillo, Don Gaspar de Jovellanos, and Don José Miguel de Flores, et al. Madrid: RAE, Ibarra.

Fuero de Madrid. 1963. *El fuero de Madrid y los derechos locales castellanos.* Edited by Galo Sánchez. Transcription by Agustín Millares Carlo. Translation by Agustín Gómez Iglesias. Madrid: Raycar.

Fuero de Plasencia. 1984. Edited by María Josefa Postigo. Madrid: Revista de Filología Románica II y III. Real Academia Española: Banco de datos (CORDE). Web. *Corpus diacrónico del español.* http://www.rae.es (1 April 2009).

Fuero de Soria. 1919. Edited by Galo Sánchez. Madrid: Centro de Estudios Históricos. Real Academia Española: Banco de datos (CORDE). Web. *Corpus diacrónico del español.* http://www.rae.es (1 April 2009).

Fuero de Zorita de los Canes. 1911. Edited by Rafael de Ureña y Smenjaud. Madrid: Fontanet. Real Academia Española: Banco de datos (CORDE). Web. *Corpus diacrónico del español.* http://www.rae.es (1 April 2009).

Fuero Real. 1991. Edited by Azuzena Palacios Alcaíne. Barcelona: Promociones y Publicaciones Universitarias.

Fuero Viejo. 1847. *Fuero viejo de Castilla.* Edited by Joaquín Francisco Pacheco. Vol. 1, *Los códigos españoles concordados y anotados.* 12 vols. Madrid: Rivadeneyra.

Galbis, Ignacio R.M. 1981. 'Aspectos forenses de la obra cervantina: *El Quijote* a la luz del derecho natural.' In *Cervantes: Su obra y su mundo.* Director, Manuel Criado de Val, 699–705. Madrid: EDI-6.

Garcés, María Antonia, ed. 2011. *An Early Modern Dialogue with Islam: Antonio de Sosa's* Topography of Algiers *(1612).* Translated by Diana de Armas Wilson. Notre Dame, IN: University of Notre Dame Press.

García, Javier. 1997. *Cervantes y la melancolía.* Valencia: Alfons el Magnánim.

García Gallo, Alfonso. 1967. *Manual de historia del derecho español.* 2 vols. Madrid: Artes Gráficas y Ediciones.

García Sánchez, Justo, and Beatriz García Fueyo. 2007. 'Anotaciones a la vida y obra de Juan de Orozco, legista salmantino del siglo XVI.' *Revista española de derecho canónico* 64:9–130.

Gaylord, Mary Malcolm. 1998. 'Pulling Strings with Master Peter's Puppets: Fiction and History in *Don Quixote.*' *Cervantes: Bulletin of the Cervantes Society of America* 18.2:117–47.

Gil Ayuso, Faustino. 1935. *Textos y disposiciones legales de los reinos de Castilla impresos en los siglos XVI y XVII.* Madrid: S. Aguirre (Biblioteca Nacional).

Gil Fernández, Luis. 2003. *Formas y tendencias del humanismo valenciano quinientista.* Prologue by Antonio Mestre Sanchis. Madrid: Alcañiz.

Giovio, Paolo. 1558. *Le Inscrittioni poste sotto le vere imagini de gli huomini famosi in lettere. Di Mons. Paolo Giovio Vescovo de Nocera. Tradotte di latino in Volgare da Hippolito Orio Ferrarese.* Venice: Giouanni de Rossi.

– 1566. *Histories,* chapters 1–24. *Paolo Iovio añadido con doze libros qve hasta agora faltavan de todas las cosas svccedidas enel mundo enestos cincuenta años de nuestro tiempo: en que se escriuen las victorias del invictissimo Emperador Don Carlos, dende que començó a reynar en España, hasta que prendió al Duque de Saxonia. Escrita en lengua Latina por el doctissimo Pavlo Iovio Obispo de Nochera,*

traduzido de Latin en Castellano por el Licenciado Gaspar de Baeça. Granada: Hugo de Mena.
- 1566. *Histories*, chapters 25–45. *Segunda parte de la Historia general de todas las cosas succedidas en el mundo en estos cinquenta años de nuestro tiempo*. Granada: Antonio de Librixa.
- 1568. *Elogios o vidas breues de los Caualleros antiguos y modernos, Illustres en valor de guerra, que están al biuo pintados en el Museo de Paulo Iouio. Es autor el mismo Pavlo Iovio. Y tradúxolo de Latin en Castellano, el Licenciado Gaspar de Baeça*. Granada: Hugo de Mena.
- 1984. *Dialogus de viris et foeminis aetate nostra florentibus. Paolo Giovio. Opera*. Vol. 9. *Dialogii et descriptiones*. Edited by Ernesto Travi and Mariagrazia Penco. Rome: Istituto Poligrafico e Zecca dello Stato.
- 1999. *Ritratti degli uomini illustri*. Edited by Carlo Caruso. Palermo: Sellerio.

Godoy Alcántara, José. 1868. *Historia crítica de los falsos cronicones*. Madrid: Rivadeneyra.

González, Aurelio. 'Construcción y funciones del espacio dramático en el teatro de Cervantes.' Plenary Conference, 1 October 2009. Moderator José Manuel Lucía Megías. VII Congreso Internacional de la Asociación Internacional de Cervantistas, 30 de septiembre al 4 de octubre de 2009, Münster, Germany.

González Echevarría, Roberto. 1990. *Myth and Archive: A Theory of Latin American Narrative*. Cambridge: Cambridge University Press.
- 2005. *Love and the Law in Cervantes*. New Haven & London: Yale University Press.

Goodey, C.F. 1994. 'John Locke's Idiots in the Natural History of Mind.' *History of Psychiatry* 5:215–50.

Grafton, Anthony. 2007. *What Was History? The Art of History in Early Modern Europe*. Cambridge: Cambridge University Press.

Guillén, Claudio. 1971. *Literature as System: Essays toward the Theory of Literary History*. Princeton: Princeton University Press.

Gutiérrez de los Ríos, Gaspar. 1600. *Noticia general para la estimación de las artes, y de la manera en qve Se conocen las liberales de las que son Mecánicas y seruiles, con vna exortación a la honra de la virtud y del trabajo contra los ociosos, y otras particulares para las personas de todos estados*. Madrid: Pedro Madrigal.

Guzmán Brito, Alejandro. 1978. 'Mos Italicus y Mos Gallicus.' *Revista de Derecho de la Universidad Católica de Valparaiso* 2:11–40.

Haedo, Diego de. 1612. *Topographia e historia general de Argel, repartida en cinco tratados*. Valladolid: Diego Fernández de Córdoba y Oviedo.

Hahn, Juergen. 1992. *Miracles, Duels, and Cide Hamete's Moorish Dissent*. Potomac, MD: Scripta Humanistica.

Haley, George. 1965. 'The Narrator in Don Quixote: Maese Pedro's Puppet Show.' *Modern Language Notes* 80.2:145–65.

Hanafin, Patrick, et al., eds. 2004. *Law and Literature*, special issue of *Journal of Law and Society* 31.1. Oxford: Blackwell Press.

Herrera, Fernando de. 1972. *Garcilaso de la Vega y sus comentaristas*. Edited by Antonio Gallego Morell. 2nd ed. Madrid: Gredos.

Herrera [y Tordesillas], Antonio. 1606. *Primera parte de la historia general del Mundo, de XVII. años del tiempo del señor Rey don Felipe II. el Prudente, desde el año de M.D.LIIII. hasta el de M.D.LXX.* 2 vols. Valladolid: Juan Godíne de Millis.

- 1615. *Historia general de los hechos de los castellanos en las islas y tierra firme del mar Océano escrita por Antonio de Herrera, Coronista de Castilla y Mayor de las Indias*. Madrid: Juan de la Cuesta.

Herrero García, Miguel. 1948. *Vida de Cervantes*. Madrid: Editora Nacional.

Hinojosa, Eduardo de. 1904. 'Las relaciones entre la poesía y el derecho.' *Discurso leído ante S.M. El Rey Don Alfonso XIII*, 7–41. Madrid: RAE.

Ife, B.W. 1985. *Reading and Fiction in Golden-Age Spain: A Platonist Critique and Some Picaresque Replies*. Cambridge: Cambridge University Press.

Jiménez de Quesada, Gonzalo. 1952. *El antijovio*. Edited by Rafael Torres Quintero. Preliminary study by Manuel Ballesteros Gaibrois. Bogota: Caro y Cuervo.

Johnson, Carroll. 1983. *Madness and Lust: A Psychoanalytical Approach to Don Quijote*. Berkeley: University of California Press.

- 2007 [2008]. 'Phantom Pretexts and Fictional Authors: Sidi Hamid Benengeli, Don Quijote and the Metafictional Conventions of Chivalric Romances.' *Cervantes: Bulletin of the Cervantes Society of America* 27.1:179–99.

Joost-Gaugier, Christiane L. 1982. 'The Early Beginnings of the Notion of "Uomini Famosi" and the "De Viris Illustribus" in Greco-Roman Literary Tradition.' *Artibus et Historiae* 6:97–115.

Kagan, Richard L. 1974. *Students and Society in Early Modern Spain*. Baltimore, MD: Johns Hopkins University Press.

- 1981. *Lawsuits and Litigants in Castile 1500–1700*. Chapel Hill, NC: University of North Carolina Press.

- 2009. *Clio and the Crown: The Politics of History in Medieval and Early Modern Spain*. Baltimore, MD: Johns Hopkins University Press.

Kahn, Aaron M. 2007. 'Representation and Interpretation of Historical Characters in Cervantes' *La Numancia:* Jugurtha and Viriatus.' *Bulletin of Hispanic Studies* 84.5:573–87.

Kelley, Donald R. 1970. *Foundations of Modern Historical Scholarship: Language, Law and History in the French Renaissance*. New York: Columbia University Press.

Klibansky, Raymond, Erwin Panofsky, and Fritz Saxl. 1964. *Saturn and Melancholy: Studies in the History of Natural Philosophy, Religion, and Art*. New York: Basic Books.

Klinger, Linda Susan. 1991. 'The Portrait Collection of Paolo Giovio' (volumes 1 and 2). PhD diss, Princeton University.

Laguna, Ana. 2009. *Cervantes and the Pictorial Imagination*. Lewisberg: Bucknell University Press.

Langer, Ullrich. 1999. 'The Renaissance Novella as Justice.' *Renaissance Quarterly* 52:311–41.

Lázaro Carreter, Fernando. 1998. 'Estudio preliminar: Las voces del *Quijote*.' *Don Quijote de la Mancha*. CVC. Directed by Francisco Rico. Barcelona: Crítica. http://cvc.cervantes.es/obref/quijote/introduccion/estudio/default.htm.

León, Luis de. 1891–5. *Opera*. Mag. Luysii Legionensis Augustiniani divinorum librorum primi apud Salmanticenses interpretis. 7 volumes. Salamanca: Episcopali Calatravae Collegio.

León Pinelo, Antonio de. 1966 [1641]. *Velos antiguos y modernos en los rostros de las mujeres, sus conveniencias y daños. Ilustración de la Real Premática*. Santiago de Chile: Centro de Investigaciones de Historia Americana [Madrid: Juan Sánchez].

Lerner, Isaías. 1990. '*Quijote*, Segunda Parte: Parodia e invención.' *Nueva Revista de Filología Hispánica* 38.2:817–36.

– 1991. 'América y la poesía épica áurea: la versión de Ercilla.' *Edad de Oro* 10:125–40.

– 1996. 'El *Quijote* palabra por palabra.' *Edad de Oro* 15:63–74.

– 1998. 'Entre Cervantes y Ercilla: *Quijote*, I, 8–9.' In *El comentario de textos*, edited by Inés Carrasco and Guadalupe Fernández Ariza, 207–20. *Analecta Malacitana*, Anejo XVII. Málaga: Universidad de Málaga.

– 2005. *Lecturas de Cervantes*. Málaga: Universidad de Málaga.

Léxico hispánico primitivo (siglos VIII al XII): Versión primera del primitivo léxico iberorrománico. 2004. Directed by Ramón Menéndez Pidal. Edited by Manuel Seco. Edited by Rafael Lapesa and Constantino García. Madrid: RAE, Espasa-Calpe.

Leyes de Toro. In Pramáticas. 1528. *Las pramáticas del Reyno. Recopilación de algunas bulas del summo pontífice: concedidas en favor de la jurisdicción Real: con todas las pramáticas: y algunas Leyes del reyno: hechas para la buena governación y guarda de la justicia: y muchas Pramáticas y Leyes añadidas que hasta aquí no fueron Impressas: en especial están añadidas las leyes de Madrid y de los Aranzeles y de los paños y lanas y capítulos de corregidores y leyes de toro y leyes de la hermandad: y tabla de todo lo contenido en este libro nuevamente Impressa vista y corregida y por orden de Leyes puesta*. Alcalá de Henares: Miguel de Eguya.

Llamas y Molina, Sancho. 1853. *Comentario crítico, jurídico, literal, a las ochenta y tres Leyes de Toro*. 2 vols. Madrid: Gaspar y Roig.

'Lo que es conveniente ...' Broadsheet. 1597. *Cortes de Madrid. Año de Lxiii. Quaderno de las leyes y pregmáticas que su Magestad mandó hazer en las cortes que tuvo y celebró en la villa de Madrid el año de D.Lxiii. con las decisiones de los capítulos de las cortes passadas desde el año de d.xxiii. a que no estaba respondido. E con la pregmática nuevamente hecha sobre los trajes*. Alcalá: Andrés de Angulo. [Hispanic Society of America, NY, ms. HC 398/1642. fol. 1r–v.]

Lope de Vega, F. 1968–1971. *Obras sueltas*. 4 vols. Cieza: A. Pérez Gómez.

López Navia, Santiago Alfonso. 1996. *La ficción autorial en el Quijote y en sus continuaciones e imitaciones*. Madrid: Universidad Europea de Madrid-CEES Ediciones.

López Pinciano, Alonso. 1953 [1596]. *Philosophía antigua poética*. 3 vols. Edited by Alfredo Carballo Picazo. Madrid: Centro Superior de Investigaciones Científicas, Instituto Miguel de Cervantes.

Madden, Marie Regina. 1930. *Political Theory and Law in Medieval Spain*. New York: Fordham University Press.

Mancing, Howard. 2003. 'Cervantes as Narrator of *Don Quijote*.' *Cervantes: Bulletin of the Cervantes Society of America* 23.1:117–40.

Maravall, José Antonio. 1972. *Estado moderno y mentalidad social (Siglos XV a XVII)*. 2 vols. Madrid: Revista de Occidente.

– 1976. *Utopía y contrautopía en el Quijote*. Santiago de Compostela: Pico Sacro.

Mariana, Juan de. 1617 [1601]. *Historia general de España: Compuesto primero en Latín, después buelta en Castellano por el padre Iuan de Mariana, de la Compañía de Iesus. De nueuo corregida, y muy aumentada por el mismo*. Madrid: Alonso Martín.

Marín Pina, Marí Carmen. 1998. 'Primera Parte. Nota '+', capítulo III.' *Lecturas: Don Quijote de la Mancha*. Directed by Francisco Rico. Barcelona: Crítica, 1998. http://cvc.cervantes.es/obref/quijote/edicion/parte1/parte01/cap03/default.htm.

Mármol Carvajal, Luis del. 1573. *Primera [-Segunda] parte de la descripción general de África, con todos los successos de guerras que a auido entre los infieles, y el pueblo Christiano, y entre ellos mesmos desde que Mahoma inuentó su secta, hasta el año del señor mil y quinientos y setenta y vno*. Granada: René Rabut.

Márquez Villanueva, Francisco. 1973. *Fuentes literarias cervantinas*. Madrid: Gredos.

Martínez Bonati, Félix. 1992. *Don Quixote and the Poetics of the Novel*. Ithaca: Cornell University Press.

Martínez Marina, Francisco. 1808. *Ensayo histórico-crítico sobre la antigua legislación y principales cuerpos legales de los reynos de León y Castilla, especialmente sobre el código de d. Alonso el Sabio, conocido con el nombre De las siete partidas*. Madrid: Ibarra.

Martínez Olmedilla, Augusto. 1905. 'Referencias legales y jurídicos del Quijote.' *La España Moderna* 197:18–31.

Martínez Torrón, Diego. 1998. 'La locura de don Quijote: Ideología y literatura.' *Anales cervantinos* 34:23–36.

Martz, Linda. 1983. *Poverty and Welfare in Habsburg Spain*. Cambridge: Cambridge University Press.

Mayer, María E. 1994. 'El detalle de una "historia verdadera": Don Quixote y Bernal Díaz.' *Cervantes: Bulletin of the Cervantes Society of America* 14.2:93–118.

Menéndez y Pelayo, Marcelino. 2008. *Orígenes de la novela*. 2 vols. Madrid: Gredos.

Mercado, Fray Tomás de. 1571. *Summa de tratos y contratos.* Seville: Hernando Díaz.

Mexía, Pedro. 2003. *Silva de varia lección.* Edited by Isaías Lerner. Madrid: Castalia.

Midelfort, H.C. Erik. 1999. *A History of Madness in Sixteenth-Century Germany.* Stanford: Stanford University Press.

Moliner, María. 1997. *Diccionario de uso del español.* Madrid: Gredos.

Moncada, don Sancho de. 1746 [1619]. *Censura de las causas a que se carga el daño general de España: Discurso séptimo.* In *Restauración política de España, y deseos públicos, que escrivió en ocho discursos el Doctor Sancho de Moncada, Catedrático de Sagrada Escritura en la Universidad de Toledo,* edited by Francisco Manuel de Mena. Madrid: Juan de Zúñiga.

Montells y Nadal, don Francisco de P. 1870. *Historia del origen y fundación de la Universidad de Granada.* Granada: Imprenta de D. Indalecio Ventura.

Montero Díaz, Santiago, ed. 1948 [1611]. *De historia para entenderla y escribirla,* by Luis Cabrera de Córdoba. Madrid: Instituto de Estudios Políticos.

Morgan, J. 1970 [1731]. *A Complete History of Algiers.* New York: Negro Universities Press. [London: J. Bettenham].

Motooka, Wendy Michiko. 1992. 'The Age of Reasons: Quixotism and Sentiment in Eighteenth-Century Britain.' PhD diss, University of Michigan. Dissertations & Theses: Full Text, Proquest. Web. 4 Feb. 2010.

Nebrija, Antonio de. 1973 [1516]. *Vocabulario de romance en latín. Transcripción crítica de la edición revisada por el autor (Sevilla, 1516).* Introduction and transcription by Gerald J. MacDonald. Madrid: Castalia.

Novísima recopilación de las leyes de España. 1805–29. *Dividida en XII. libros, en que se reforma la recopilación publicada por el Señor Don Felipe II. en el año de 1567, reimpresa últimamente en el de 1775.* 6 vols. Madrid.

Nuevo tesoro lexicográfico del español: (S. XIV–1726). 2007. 11 vols. Edited by Lidio Nieto Jiménez and Manuel Alvar Ezquerra. Madrid: Arco Libros.

Olmeda, Mauro. 1973. *El ingenio de Cervantes y la locura de don Quijote.* 2nd ed. Madrid: Ayuso.

Orcástegui, Carmen, and Esteban Sarasa. 1991. *La Historia en le Edad Media: Historiografía e historiadores en Europa Occidental: siglos V–XIII.* Madrid: Cátedra.

Ordenanzas Reales de Castilla. 1849. Vol. 6 of *Los códigos españoles, concordados y anotados.* 12 vols. Madrid: Rivadeneyra.

Ossorio Morales, Juan. 1949. *Derecho y literatura.* Granada: Universidad de Granada.

The Oxford English Dictionary. 1989. 2nd ed. Prepared by J.A. Simpson and E.S.C. Weiner. 20 vols. Oxford: Clarendon Press.

Páez de Castro, Juan. 1892. 'Método para escribir la historia.' Edited by Eustasio Esteban. *Ciudad de Dios* 28:601–10, and 29:27–37.

Palacín, Gregorio B. 1971. 'Sobre el acto de armar caballero a Don Quijote.' *Hispanófila* 42 (May):1–6.

Palencia, Alfonso de. 1967. *Universal vocabulario en latín y en romance.* Facsimile ed. 2 vols. Madrid: Comisión Permanente de la Asociación de Academias de la Lengua Española.

Palmerín de Oliva. 1966. Edited by Giuseppe di Stefano. Pisa: Università di Pisa. Real Academia Española: Banco de datos (CORDE). Web. *Corpus diacrónico del español.* http://www.rae.es (1 April 2009).

Parr, James. 1988. *Don Quixote: An Anatomy of Subversive Discourse.* Newark, DE: Juan de la Cuesta.

– 2005. *Don Quixote: A Touchstone for Literary Criticism.* Kassel: Reichenberger.

Partidas. See [Siete] Partidas.

Pemán, José M. 1948. 'La "armazón de caballería" de Don Quijote.' *Boletín de la RAE* 27 (April):7–19.

Pérez-Coca Sánchez-Matas, Carmen. 1994. *Derecho, vida y costumbres de Plasencia y su diócesis en los siglos XV y XVI (Documentación sinodal de la segunda mitad del siglo XVI).* 2 vols. Cáceres: Universidad de Extremadura.

Pérez de Herrera, Cristóbal. 1598. *Discursos del amparo de los legítimos pobres, y reducción de los fingidos: y de la fundación y principio de los albergues destos reynos, y amparo de la milicia dellos.* Madrid: Luis Sánchez.

– 1610. 'Remedios para el bien de la salud del cuerpo de la República.' In *En razón de muchas cosas tocantes al bien, prosperidad, riqueza y fertilidad destos Reynos y restauración de la gente que se ha echado dellos.* Madrid. Gale Modern Economy Series. http://gdc.gale.com/products/the-making-of-the-modern-world-the-goldsmiths-kress-library-of-economic-literature-1450–1850/.

Pérez y López, Antonio Xavier. 1791. *Teatro de la legislación universal de España e Indias, por orden cronológico de sus cuerpos, y decisiones no recopiladas: y alfabético de sus títulos y principales materias.* Vol. 1. Madrid: Manual González.

Pérez Pastor, D. Cristóbal. 1897. *Documentos cervantinos hasta ahora inéditos.* 2 vols. Madrid: Fortanet.

– 1970 [1891]. *Bibliografía madrileña de los siglos XVI y XVII.* 3 vols. Amsterdam: Gérard Th. Van Heusden.

Pradilla Barnvero, Francisco de la. 1613. *Tratado y summa de todas las leyes.* Seville: Luys Estupinan.

Pramáticas. 1528. *Las pramáticas del Reyno. Recopilación de algunas bulas del summo pontífice: concedidas en favor de la jurisdicción Real: con todas las pramáticas: y algunas Leyes del reyno: hechas para la buena governación y guarda de la justicia: y muchas Pramáticas y Leyes añadidas que hasta aquí no fueron Impressas: en especial están añadidas las leyes de Madrid y de los Aranzeles y de los paños y lanas y capítulos de corregidores y leyes de toro y leyes de la hermandad: y tabla de todo lo contenido en este libro nuevamente Impressa vista y corregida y por orden de Leyes puesta.* Alcalá de Henares: Miguel de Eguya.

Prat Westerlindh, Carlos. 2006. *La justicia en 'El Quijote.'* Madrid: Dykinson.

Predmore, Richard L. 1973. *Cervantes.* New York: Dodd Mead.

Premática en que se manda guardar ... 1594. *Premática en que se manda guardar lo proveído por un capítulo de las Cortes, del año de ochenta y seis: en que se prohibió que los hombres no puedan traer en los cuellos, ni en puños, guarnición alguna, ni almidón, ni gomas, ni filetes: sino sola la lechuguilla de olanda, o lienzo, con una, o dos vaynillas, y se declara que sean de un dozavo de vara de medir, y que las vaynillas y filetes no sean de color sino blancas: y se acrecientan las penas contra los que excedieren.* Madrid: Pedro Madrigal.

Prester, Juan. 1533. 1603. Legatio. [Letter, in Ethiopian; Lat. tr. by Paolo Giovio.] Legati David Aethiopiae Regis, ad Sanctissimum D.N.Clementem Papam VII. una cum obedientia, eidem sanctis. D.N. Praestita. Antuerpiae apud Guilelmum Vorstermannum. In *Hispaniae Illustratae,* 2:1285–7. Edited by Andreas Schottus, et al. Frankfurt, Marnius & Aubrius.

Quaderno 1563. *Quaderno de las leyes y pregmáticas que su Magestad mandó hazer en las cortes que tuvo y celebró en la villa de Madrid el año de d.Lxiii. con las decisiones de los capítulos de las cortes passadas desde el año de. d.xxiii. a que no estaba respondido. E con la pregmática nuevamente hecha sobre los trajes.* Alcalá: Andrés de Angulo.

Quaderno 1610. *Quaderno de las leyes añadidas a la nueva Recopilación de leyes destos Reynos, hecha por mandado de la Magestad Católica del Rey don Felipe II. nuestro Señor: donde se contenían las leyes hechas hasta el año de mil y quinientos y noventa y ocho, excepto las leyes de Partida, y de Fuero, y del Estilo, en que también fueron las visitas de las Audiencias: la qual Recopilación se imprimió en Alcalá de Henares, año de mil y quinientos y noventa y ocho. Y añadense en este Quaderno las leyes que se han hecho desde el dicho año de mil y quinientos y noventa y ocho, hasta el de mil y seiscientos y diez. Y otras de algunos años atrás, que no estaban puestas en la dicha nueva Recopilación. El qual Quaderno se mandó hazer, y imprimir por mandado de los señores Presidente, y los del Consejo del Rey nuestro Señor.* Madrid: Juan de la Cuesta.

Quint, David. 1997. 'Narrative Interlace and Narrative Genres in *Don Quijote* and the *Orlando Furioso.' Modern Language Quarterly* 58.3:241–68.

Rabell, Carmen. R. 2003. *Rewriting the Italian Novella in Counter-Reformation Spain.* Woodbridge: Tamesis.

Recopilación. 1982 [1640]. *Recopilación de las leyes destos reynos, hecha por mandado de la Magestad Católica del Rey don Felipe Segundo nuestro señor; que se ha mandado imprimir, con las leyes que después de la vltima impressión se han publicado, por la Magestad Católica del Rey don Felipe Quarto el Grande nuestro señor.* 5 vols. Facsimile ed. Valladolid: Lex Nova.

Redondo, Augustin. 1979. 'Pauperismo y mendicidad en Toledo, en época del *Lazarillo*.' In *Hommage des Hispanistes français à Noël Salomon*, 703–24. Barcelona: Laía.

– 1991. 'Don Quijote "caballero" e "hijo" de ventero y rameras: Algunas calas en la parodia cervantina.' *Ínsula* 538 (October):30–4.

– 2006. 'Algunos aspectos religiosos del *Quijote*. Entre burlas y veras.' *Edad de Oro* 25:457–72.

Reed, Helen H. 1987. 'Theatricality in the Picaresque of Cervantes.' *Cervantes: Bulletin of the Cervantes Society of America* 7.2:71–84.

Ricapito, Joseph V. 1996. *Cervantes's Novelas ejemplares: Between History and Creativity*. West Lafayette, IN: Purdue University Press.

Rico, Francisco. 1993. *El sueño del humanismo*. Madrid: Alianza.

– , ed. 2002. *Lazarillo de Tormes*. Madrid: Cátedra.

– 2005. *El texto del 'Quijote.' Preliminares a una ecdótica del Siglo de Oro*. Valladolid: Universidad de Valladolid, Centro para la Edición de los Clásicos Españoles.

Riley, E.C. 1962. *Cervantes's Theory of the Novel*. Oxford: Clarendon Press.

Riquer, Martín de. 1967. *Aproximación al Quijote*. Barcelona: Teide.

Riveros Subizar, María Irene. 1951. 'La justicia de Don Quijote.' *Boletín del Instituto de Investigaciones Literarias* 6:123–77.

Rivers, Elias L. 1982. 'Narrators, Readers, and Other Characters in Don Quixote.' *Cervantes: Bulletin of the Cervantes Society of America* 2.1:96–8.

Rodríguez Marín, Francisco, ed. 1920. *Rinconete y Cortadillo, novela de Miguel de Cervantes Saavedra*. Madrid: Revista de Archivos, Bibliotecas y Museos.

– 1947. *Estudios cervantinos*. Prologue by Agustín González de Amezúa. Madrid: Atlas.

– 1947–9. *El ingenioso hidalgo Don Quijote de la Mancha*. 10 vols. Madrid: Atlas.

Rodríguez Molina, José, coordinator. 1985. *Historia de Baeza: Historia, Literatura, Arte*. Baeza: Ayuntamiento de Baeza.

Rodríguez Pequeño, Javier. 2006. '*Don Quijote de la Mancha* o el arte nuevo de hacer novelas.' *Edad de Oro* 25:503–18.

Rodríguez Pequeño, Mercedes. 2008. 'Cervantes ante la teoría literaria de la historia.' *Anuario de Estudios Cervantinos* 4:265–79.

Rosenblat, Ángel. 1971. *La lengua del 'Quijote.'* Madrid: Gredos.

Sabor de Cortazar, Celina. 1979. 'La sociedad española del 1600 y la literatura.' *Revista Universitaria de Letras* 1.1 (April–May):41–59.

Salas Barbadillo, Alonso Gerónimo de. 1847. *El curioso y sabio Alejandro, fiscal y juez de vidas agenas*. In *Tesoro de novelistas españoles antiguos y modernos*. Vol. 2. Introduction and notes by Eugenio de Ochoa. Paris: Baudry.

Sánchez de la Vega, Rafael Gibert. 1987. Introduction to Rafael Álvarez Vigaray, *El Derecho civil en las obras de Cervantes*, 9–21. Granada: Comares.

Sánchez Molledo, José María. 2005. *Diccionario de arbitristas aragoneses de los siglos XVI y XVII*. Zaragoza: Institución Fernando el Católico (CSIC.).

Sancho Izquierdo, Miguel, intro. and ed. 1916. *El fuero de Molina de Aragón*. Madrid: Victoriano Suárez.

Santa Cruz de Dueñas, Melchor de. 1997. *Floresta española*. Edited by Maxime Chevalier. Barcelona: Crítica. Real Academia Española: Banco de datos (CORDE). Web. *Corpus diacrónico del español*. http://www.rae.es (1 April 2009).

Schevill, Rudolph. 1919. *Cervantes*. New York: Duffield.

Scholes, Robert, James Phelan, and James Kellogg. 2006. *The Nature of Narrative*. 40th Anniversary Edition. Oxford: Oxford University Press.

Schottus, Andreas, Johann Pistorius, and Franciscus Schottus. 1603–8. *Hispaniae illvstratae*. 4 vols. Frankfurt: Marnius & Aubrius.

Shuger, Dale. 2008. *A Thousand and One Quijotes: Madness in Life and Literature in Early Modern Spain*. PhD diss, New York University.

[Siete] Partidas. 1576. *Las Siete Partidas del sabio Rey don Alonso el Nono, nuevamente Glosadas, por el Licenciado Gregorio López, del Consejo Real de Indias de su Magestad. Con su Repertorio muy copioso, assi del Testo como de la Glosa*. En Salamanca, En casa de Domingo de Portonarijs Ursino, Impressor de la Sacra Real Magestad, Con privilegio Imperial.

Simon and Schuster's International Dictionary. English/Spanish, Spanish/English. 1973. Edited by Tana de Gámez. New York: Simon and Schuster.

Sliwa, Krzysztof. 2005. *Documentos de Miguel de Cervantes Saavedra y de sus familiares*. Texas: Texas A & M University.

– 2006. *Vida de Miguel de Cervantes Saavedra: en conmemoración del IV centenario de El ingenioso hidalgo don Quijote de la Mancha, Madrid, Juan de la Cuesta, 1605 con su continuación, diez años más tarde, de la Segunda parte del ingenioso caballero don Quijote de la Mancha, Madrid, Juan de la Cuesta, 1615*. Fayetteville: Fayetteville State University; Barcelona: Edition Reichenberger.

– , and Daniel Eisenberg. 1997. 'El licenciado Juan de Cervantes, abuelo de Miguel de Cervantes Saavedra.' *Cervantes: Bulletin of the Cervantes Society of America* 17.2:106–14.

Spitzer, Leo. 1948. *Linguistics and Literary History*. Princeton: Princeton University Press.

Stagg, Geoffrey. 1956. 'El sabio Cide Hamete Venengeli.' *Bulletin of Hispanic Studies* 33:218–25.

Thiher, Allen. 1999. *Revels in Madness: Insanity in Medicine and Literature*. Ann Arbor: University of Michigan Press.

Thompson, I.A.A. 1976. *War and Government in Habsburg Spain 1560–1620*. London: Athlone Press.

Tomás y Valiente, Francisco. 1969. *El Derecho penal de la Monarquía absoluta, siglos XVI–XVII–XVIII*. Madrid: Editorial Tecnos.

– 1975. 'Castillo de Bobadilla (c. 1547–c. 1605). Semblanza personal y profesional de un juez del antiguo régimen.' *Anuario de Historia del Derecho Español* 45:159–238.

Turchetti, Mario. 1984. *Concordia o Tolleranza? François Bauduin (1520–1573) é i 'Moyenneurs.'* Geneva: Librairie Droz.

Urbina, Eduardo. 1982. 'Sancho Panza a nueva luz: ¿tipo folklórico o personaje literario?' *Anales cervantinos* 20:93–102.

Usatges. 1544. *Antiquiores Barchinonensium leges, quas vulgus Usaticos appellat, cum comentariis Supremorum Iurisconsultorum Iacobi a monte Iudaico Iacobi et Guielermi a Vallesicca & Iacobi Calicii cum Índice copiosísimo non antea excussae.* Edited by Juan Quintana. Barcelona: Carlos Amorós.

Valdés, Juan de. 1999. *Diálogo de la lengua.* Edited by Antonio Quilis. Madrid: Clásicos.

Vega Carney, Carmen. 1994. 'Righting Wrongs: Don Quixote and the Rhetoric of Justice.' *Indiana Journal of Hispanic Literatures* 5. *Magical Parts: Approaches to Don Quixote*: 37–55.

Villadiego Vascuñana y Montoya, Alonso de. 1612. *Instrucción política, y práctica iudicial, conforme al estilo de los Consejos, Audiencias, y Tribunales de Corte, y otros ordinarios del Reyno. Utilíssima para los Governadores y Corregidores, y otros juezes ordinarios, y de commissión: y para los Abogados, escrivanos, procuradores, y litigantes.*Madrid: Luis Sánchez.

Villafranca, Antonio Ioan. 1562. *Libro de las historias y cosas acontescidas en Alemaña, España, Francia, Italia, Flandres, Inglaterra, Reyno de Artois, Dacia, Grecia, Sclauonia, Egypto, Polonia, Turquia, India, y mundo nueuo, y en otros reynos y señoríos: comenzando del tiempo del Papa León, y de la venida de la Magestad del Emperador y rey nuestro señor Carlos quinto en España, hasta su muerte. Compuesto por Paulo Iouio Obispo de Nuchera [sic] en Latín, y traduzido en romance Castellano por Antonio Ioan Villafranca médico Valenciano: y por el mismo añadido lo que faltaua en Iouio hasta la muerte del inuictíssimo Em[pe]radorCarlos quinto nuestro rey y señor.* Valencia: Ioan Mey. http://biblioteca.uv.es/index_sp.php.

Wardropper, Bruce W. 1965 [2005]. '*Don Quixote:* Story or History?' *Modern Philology* 63.1 (August):1–11. Reprinted in *Cervantes' Don Quixote: A Casebook,* edited Roberto González Echevarría, 141–62. NY: Oxford University Press.

Weiger, John G. 1996. 'On the "Autores" of Don Quijote.' *Bulletin of Hispanic Studies* 73.3:263–9.

West's Encyclopedia of American Law. 2005. 2nd ed. Edited by Jeffrey Lehman and Shirelle Phelps. Detroit: Thompson/Gale.

White, Hayden. 1987. *The Content of the Form: Narrative Discourse and Historical Representation.* Baltimore, MD: Johns Hopkins University Press.

Williams, Robert Haden. 1946. *Boccalini in Spain: A Study of His Influence on Prose Fiction of the Seventeenth Century.* Menasha, WI: George Banta.

Wiltrout, Ann E. 1978. 'Ginés de Pasamonte: The "pícaro" and His Art.' *Anales cervantinos* 17:11–17.

Wolf, John B. 1979. *The Barbary Coast: Algiers under the Turks 1500 to 1830.* New York: Norton.

Ynduráin, Domingo. 2006. 'Historia y ficción en el siglo XV.' In *Estudios sobre Renacimiento y Barroco,* edited by Consolación Baranda et al., 285–335. Madrid: Cátedra.

Zapata, Luis. 1984. *Carlo famoso: el primer poema que trata del descubrimiento y conquista del Nuevo Mundo.* Edited by José Toribio Medina and Winston A. Reynolds. Madrid: José Porrús Turanzas.

Zimmerman, T. Price. 1972. 'The Publication of Paolo Giovio's Histories: Charles V and the Revision of Book XXXIV.' *La bibliofilia* 74.1:49–90.

– 1995. *Paolo Giovio: The Historian and the Crisis of Sixteenth Century Italy.* Princeton: Princeton University Press.

Index